Applied Macroeconomics

Christian A. Conrad

Applied Macroeconomics

A Practical Introduction

 Springer

Christian A. Conrad
htw Business School, University of Applied
Science, Hochschule für Technik und
Wirtschaft des Saarlandes
Saarbrücken, Germany

ISBN 978-3-658-39314-4   ISBN 978-3-658-39315-1   (eBook)
https://doi.org/10.1007/978-3-658-39315-1

Responsible Editor: Nora Valussi
This Springer imprint is published by the registered company Springer Fachmedien Wiesbaden GmbH, part of Springer Nature.
The registered company address is: Abraham-Lincoln-Str. 46, 65189 Wiesbaden, Germany

Preface

This book is the result of my work as a scientific employee at the Eberhard Karls University of Tübingen and of more than twelve years of professional experience in a large German bank, which repeatedly brought me into contact with the management of many German companies as a corporate customer consultant. The period of my professional experience also included the stock market boom and crash at the beginning of the new millennium and the financial crisis. These practical experiences influenced the events Macroeconomics at the Applied University of Applied Sciences (HTW) in Saarbrücken. This teaching experience also flowed into this book, as did an extensive literature study. In addition, numerous new findings fromexperimental studies were taken into account.

Finally, I would like to thank Professor Hartherz and the asset manager Mr. Dr. Markus Stahl for their support of this book. I would like to thank Mr. Dr. Markus Stahl in particular for many stimulating discussions.

Saarbrücken   Christian A. Conrad
in September 2022

Introduction

The following textbook has the goal of explaining the overarching connections of an economy in a way that they are immediately understood. Complicated connections are to be made understandable through examples and exercises. Particular value is placed here on an application-oriented approach and a detailed explanation, so that even non-economists can understand the connections. The topics were chosen so that they correspond to the international standard of the Macroeconomics course. The target group of the book are students of business administration at German universities. Towards this end, the economic material was deliberately chosen so that it supplements business administration studies in a meaningful way. The goal is that the reader is imparted economic knowledge that they can apply in business practice. It is explained how different factors influence the macroeconomic conditions of a company, what specifically determines aggregate demand, how unemployment arises, what causes inflation, how growth can be promoted, how the money, capital and goods markets function, how economic crises can occur and what the state can do about it, among other things.

In this sense, the reader should be able to, after reading the book,

1. understand and explain macroeconomic variables such as "inflation".
2. make individual economic decisions taking into account the macroeconomic background.
3. be able to think in macroeconomic terms in order to adapt creatively to new situations.

The chapters build on each other. After we have discussed the basics in Chap. 1 of how macroeconomics fits into the field of economics, we want to deal with its concepts and measurement concepts in Chap. 2 within the framework of what is known as national accounting. This is the basis from which we will, in Chaps. 3 to 7, work out general theoretical explanations of the economic relationships.

In the context of the long-term perspective of the neoclassical model, we explain in Chap. 3 the functions of macroeconomic markets and derive a model for the entire economy. From the neoclassical general model, we will then derive specific implications for economic policy. How does wage and monetary policy affect employment? Can an expansionary fiscal policy financed by credit increase employment? How does technical progress affect employment?

In Chaps. 4 and 5 we then deal more closely with monetary policy. In Chap. 4 the causes and effects of inflation are presented in order to be able to understand the ECB's primary objective of ensuring price stability. Chap. 5 is dedicated to the euro. How did the single currency come about and what are the advantages and disadvantages? An introduction to the ECB's monetary policy rounds off the chapter.

The neoclassical perspective is supply-oriented and thus corresponds to the normal state of the economy and the prevailing opinion until the world economic crisis of 1929. This crisis showed that under certain circumstances there can be persistent unemployment situations. The neoclassics could not explain this and a new theory was needed. The depression of the world economic crisis can be explained using Keynes by examining short-term disturbances of the long-term equilibrium. Keynes brought the demand-oriented perspective into the economy. Since then, the demand-oriented and supply-oriented perspectives have repeatedly competed in science and public discussion for the right economic explanations and the appropriate means. This book tries to bring this apparent competition to a synthesis. Rather, it differentiates between the supply-oriented neoclassics for the normal economic situation and the Keynesian theory for the depression as an economic exceptional situation.

In Chap. 6 The neoclassical synthesis is extended here to the Keynesian view as a macroeconomic theory of depression within the framework of the neoclassical synthesis. The essential theories of the business cycle are presented and critically questioned in Chap. 7. Here, the new findings of behavioral economics are also included. In view of the financial crisis, which almost caused a depression like 1929, the book ends with its own chapter on financial markets.

Contents

List of Abbreviations

TFEU	Treaty on the Functioning of the European Union
UE	unemployment
B	Bonds (nominal value of securities)
GDP	Gross domestic product
C	Consumption
c	consumption ratio
c'	marginal consumption ratio
CDO	Collateral Debt Obligations
CDS	Credit Default Swap
CP	Commercial Paper
D	Deficit (state budget deficit) or Demand (demand)
EMU	European Monetary Union
Ex	Exports
F	leisure
F.A.Z.	Frankfurter Allgemeine Zeitung
G	Government Spending
HH	household
I	Investment demand
i	nominal or real interest rate
i*	Equilibrium interest rate
Im	Imports
K	Capital stock
k	Cash holding coefficient
L	Liquidity (liquidity demand)
M	nominal money supply
MA	Macoeconomic Accounting
N	Number (of hoursworked)

p, P   prices
p*   Equilibrium price
QE   Quantitative Easing
R   Marginal efficiency of the capital
S   Savings o. Supply
T   Taxes
v   Velocity of money
MA   Macoeconomic Accounting
w   wages (general wage level)
WP   securities
Y   Yield (income or gross domestic product)
π   Pi, Profit (profit)

Basics

Learning Objectives of Chap. 1. Basics

After the overview of the lecture, the following introduction should enable you to place the lecture Macroeconomics in your previous economic knowledge. For this purpose, some basic concepts will be explained and you will be given a taste of working with economic variables based on a case study.

Example

Case Study: What do business economists need macroeconomics for?

Question: Imagine you were the manager of a company? How would you position your company in mid-2011 and in the second quarter of 2013? For your information: Price-adjusted means that price influences have been taken out (see Fig. 1.1). ◄

Answer

Mid-2011: The decline in gross domestic product is a reversal of trend. It signals an economic downturn. You will be able to realize less sales in the next few years and thus also less revenue and profit. As an entrepreneur you should now avoid new fixed costs. Investments to expand capacity would no longer amortize. You should not hire employees that you can not employ in a underutilization. It would make sense to get your bank to extend the credit lines in writing.

In the second quarter of 2013 Again, a change of trend is emerging. The upturn is coming. Now you should use the time to stock up on prepayments and staff. After the downturn, prices and interest rates are low, making it also sensible to take out loans with long-term interest rate fixation. The labor market is still full of good job-seeking employees. Here you will find good employees for the upturn. Conclusion: By taking into account the overall economic development, not only can expenditure be saved, but in the medium term this is crucial for the success of your business. Making fewer mistakes than

C. Conrad, *Applied Macroeconomics*, https://doi.org/10.1007/978-3-658-39315-1_1

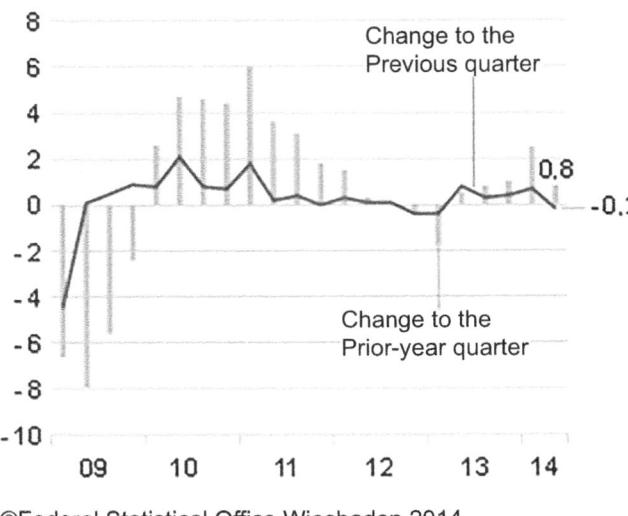

Fig. 1.1 Development of gross domestic product. (Source: Federal statistical office, https://www. destatis.de/DE/ZahlenFakten/GesamtwirtschaftUmwelt/VGR/VolkswirtschaftlicheGesamtrechnungen.html)

the competition is a key success factor. But for that a manager also has to be willing to form his own economic opinion and to defend and implement it against the trend. Entrepreneurial behavior requires a certain degree of self-responsibility and risk-taking.

Difference between microeconomic and macroeconomic analysis:

▶ The **microeconomics** examines the decision-making **of individual economic** decision-makers (companies and households) and their interactions in the goods and factor markets.

▶ The **macroeconomy** analyzes on the basis of microeconomic findings **aggregate economic** problems of real and monetary nature. The macroeconomy is indeed behaviorally single-economically, that is, microeconomically based, but in the interaction of the many economic subjects over the markets other results arise than single-economically (e.g. in the financial crisis). The plans of the many market participants must be aggregated and brought into agreement via the price mechanism of the markets. Therefore, aggregate economic markets are also the main object of observation of macroeconomics. The macroeconomy thus considers, for example, the aggregated sum of all households and researches how their behavior affects the markets of an economy.

The science of economics is **not an exact natural science,** but a social science. It deals with the behavior of people in large groups.

This behavior is different depending on culture and situation, which is why there are also many different economic models and concepts.

Worldwide, all existing **economic systems** are **division of labor** today organized systems in which the actors (economic subjects) carry out the required **exchange transactions** predominantly with the help of **money.**

▶ **Economic subjects** are all organizational units that have the disposal over the execution of economic activities.

▶ **Economic activities** are all activities that serve the **satisfaction of needs** directly or indirectly, such as production, consumption, asset formation or credit granting. The **objects** of these activities are, for example, goods (e.g. raw materials), production services of the companies and services of the production factors (labor, capital and land), services as well as claims (liabilities).

▶ Economics uses so-called models to explain economic relationships. **Models** show simplified relationships between economic variables (definition). Only by simplifying and using **assumptions** can the relationships be isolated and made clear. The model explains **endogenous** variables while **exogenous** are determined outside the model. However, every model should be checked for its relevance to reality. Models with unrealistic assumptions have no explanatory value for the real economy.

In an economy, it is about maximizing prosperity with limited resources, that is, being efficient.

▶ **Definition of efficient (economic)**
a) achieve a given goal with the minimum effort *or*
b) realize a maximum goal with given effort.

(effective: effective in relation to the resources used)

Example: A candle can be extinguished with water and with champagne (both effective). But extinguishing the candle is only efficient with water.

Any method that leads to the goal at all is effective; but one acts efficiently only when one achieves a given goal with the minimum effort or achieves a maximum goal with given effort.

▶ **Definition**
Definition of a market: The place of meeting of supply and demand.

Functions of the market: Price formation and exchange.

Definition of competition: Competition always exists when at least two economic subjects compete on one market side for a business transaction.

Summary

Macroeconomics deals with macroeconomic issues. It therefore considers, for example, unlike microeconomics, the aggregate sum of all households and researches how their behavior affects the markets of an economy. ◀

Comprehension Questions

1. What is the difference between micro- and macroeconomics?
2. What is a market?
3. Give an example of a market. Which actors appear on which market side?

Macoeconomic Accounting

2

What Follows Why

After we have discussed in the introduction how macroeconomics is to be classified in economics, we want to deal with its concepts and measurement concepts in Chap. 2. This is the basis from which we will work out general explanations of economic relationships in Chaps. 3 to 7.

Learning objectives

After this chapter you should be able to

1. explain the key concepts of Macoeconomic Accounting and
2. explain the most important economic relationships between the major aggregates (sectors) of state, household and enterprise as well as
3. be able to explain and apply the different methods of calculation of gross domestic product.

▶ In 1999, the Federal Statistical Office introduced the revised European System of National and Regional Accounts in Germany (ESA 95). Since 01.09.2014 the ESA 2010 applies.

▶ The SNA is the result of the synthesis of two research areas: input-output analysis and national income statistics. The **national income statistics** wanted to capture the economic performance of a country (no longer exists), while the **input-output analysis** aimed at the capture of economic interdependencies.

© The Author(s), under exclusive license to Springer Fachmedien Wiesbaden GmbH, part of Springer Nature 2022

C. Conrad, *Applied Macroeconomics*, https://doi.org/10.1007/978-3-558-39315-1_2

2.1   Circuits in the Macoeconomic Accounting

In the following circulation analysis, we want to examine how the actors in the economy carry out which transactions. How does everything fit together?

This circulation idea was first used by **Francois Quesnay** (1694–1774) in his "Tableau économique", then by **Karl Marx** and later by **John Maynard Keynes** and developed further for their respective macroeconomic theories.

Macroeconomics regards the economic web of relationships as an **economic cycle,** in which economic subjects grouped into various **sectors** interact with each other by means of various **transactions**. Sectors and transactions together form an economic cycle.

In a cycle

1. at least one stream flows from and to each pole (i.e. at least 2 streams per pole).
2. all poles are directly or indirectly connected to each other.
3. there are no stocks.
4. what flows in also flows out again (in terms of value).

▶ In economics, two types of quantity are distinguished: stream quantities and stock quantities. **Streams** are related to a certain **period of time** and have a certain direction and a certain strength. While **stream quantities** are period-related quantities, **stock quantities** are time-related quantities, i.e. snapshot quantities. The connection between the two quantities is that stock quantities can be **written forward** using stream quantities.

Example

The sand on the ground of a sundial is a stock size, because it is a quantity size that is measured at a certain time. The amount of sand that flows to the ground is a stream size. The stream allows, based on the period, the measurement of the elapsed time (see Fig. 2.1).

Stock sizes, for example, are in the balance sheet of the Federal Statistical Office. The German capital stock (fixed assets) amounted, for example, to the end of 2015 17.2 billion euros. ◀

Question

Give examples of stock and stream sizes.

Taxes: stream size (there is a river)
Equity: stock size
Revenue: stream size

Fig. 2.1 Current and stock
sizes

Current size: Sandblast

Stock size: Sand piles

Examples of Stock and Flow Variables

Wealth: Stock variable, *Income:* Flow variable

   Investment: Flow variable, *Capital stock:* Stock variable

   In a circuit, the value of all outgoing flows is always equal to the value of all incoming flows. Circuits can be **open** or **closed**. A **closed circuit** exists if for each node of the circuit it holds (see Fig. 2.2), that the value of the flows leaving it is equal to the value of all flows entering it within the circuit **(definition, circuit axiom).** ◄

Explanation

This is a representation of flows (without stocks): If something goes into a node, it must also come out again, because there are no stocks. If this is not the case, there must be at least one node from which something leaves the circuit. This is, for example, the case in the open economy with the flows going abroad (see Fig. 2.3).

Fig. 2.2 Example of a closed
circuit

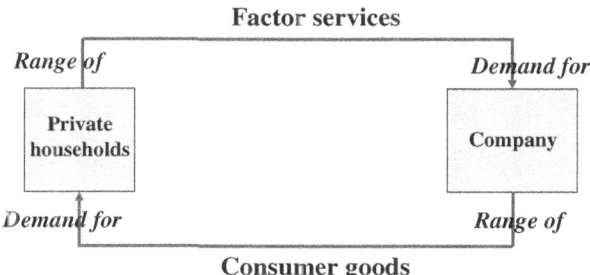

Fig. 2.3   Example of an open circuit

As an example, take a circuit as a real exchange, consumer goods for factor services (labor) between the business sector and the private household sector (Fig. 2.2). ◀

Definition Expenditures for all goods and services produced domestically **or** all incomes that have arisen domestically. GDP measures the respective money flows of an economy in one year.

GDP is a measure of the economic performance and prosperity of a country (Fig. 2.4). ◀

Why can gross domestic product be captured from two sides?

Explanation
Objects pass through **transactions** from one economic subject to another. Each transaction has two sides. One buys and the other sells something. If, for example, the household sells its labor, it will generate income and the company will have expenses. GDP can therefore also be calculated from two sides: on the one hand by the sum of all economic incomes from factor services including entrepreneur profits, and on the other hand by the expenditure for the produced goods.

Fig. 2.4   Calculation of GDP
from two sides

Example

If Karl paints Hans's house for 500 €, Hans has expenses for the painting of 500 € and Karl has income of 500 € and the GDP has increased by 500 € through this transaction. ◄

Transactions are either carried out through the market (**market transactions**) or not carried out through a market (**imputed transactions**).

Note

In the end, the economy is always about goods and services and their benefits for people. For monetary flows, their **valuation** takes place in Macroeconomic Accounting

1. at market prices (for market transactions) or
2. at market prices of similar transactions or
3. at production costs (for imputed transactions).

Example

An economy produces 10 cars and 20 bicycles. A car is sold for 50,000 € and a bicycle for 1,000.00 €. Then the gross domestic product is 10 × 50,000 € plus 20 × 1,000.00 €, or 520,000.00 €. ◄

If no valuation is possible, the transaction cannot be recorded as a monetary flow.

Question

Two mothers want to acquire a pension entitlement and decide to hire each other as childminders. What are the consequences for GDP?

Answer

GDP increases by the salary of both childminders.

Question

Is GDP measured the same in every country?

No, this is not the case because different countries can have different price levels, there are different self-sufficient countries and in some countries many economic transactions are not even recorded. A comparison of the wealth of countries based on GDP per

**Total
production**

Market transactions			imputed	Transactions
Informal not	*Sector covered*	Formal sector (market prices)	Production costs or market prices of analogue Transactions	*not covered*
"Moonlight-ing"	*Criminal Economy* <u>*Exception:*</u> *Drugs, Prostitution and Cigarette smuggling*	Production of the companies	1. Government performance 2. Private withdrawals by entrepreneurs	1. *Homework* 2. *Subsistence farming (self-sufficiency orgung)*

Fig. 2.5 Total production

capita is therefore also problematic. Countries with a lot of black work or non-officially recorded transactions, such as sales on private markets, have a much lower GDP than other countries (see Fig. 2.5).

2.2   Case Study: New GDP Calculation

Task

Discuss the following article in groups. In your opinion, are the new approaches to GDP calculation useful?

Overview
Handelsblatt online from 14.08.2014, Politics/Economics/News,[1]

New GDP Calculation
Good morning, we are richer!
By Jan Mallien

---

[1] By Jan Mallien, Handelsblatt from 14.08.2014, http://www.handelsblatt.com/politik/konjunktur/ nachrichten/neue-bip-berechnung-guten-morgen-wir-sind-reicher/10329916.html. Translated from German.

Despite the shrunken economic performance: Germany has become 80 billion euros richer overnight. Because gross domestic product is now measured without moral glasses—with noticeable consequences.

Early to bed, early to rise makes one healthy, wealthy, and wise. Whoever doubts proverbs will be taught better today: Germany has become many billions richer overnight—at least if statistics are to be believed. However, this miracle is unique. The reason for the increase in income is a change in statistics.

This Thursday, the Federal Statistical Office presented figures for gross domestic product (GDP) in the second quarter for the first time according to a new calculation method. This implements the rules of the "European System of National and Regional Accounts" (ESA) from 2010. All GDP figures from 1991 were revised upwards. The statistical effect is about 80 billion euros or about three percent of total economic output.

At the same time, however, GDP fell by 0.2% compared to the previous quarter. The decline is due to the fact that all GDP figures from 1991 were revised upwards and switched to the new calculation method.

The new rules are mandatory throughout Europe from 1 September. Germany is one of the pioneers. In March, the Netherlands and France took the lead. In total, more services are included in gross domestic product. For example, prostitution, drug trafficking and cigarette smuggling. This increases the overall economic performance.

"Basically, gross domestic product should cover the entire economic performance, regardless of a moral assessment," says Norbert Räth, head of the domestic product group at the Federal Statistical Office. "For the recording of special cases, such as the illegal tobacco and drug trade, we did not have a statistical approach in Germany so far. This is now being standardized at European level through the switch."

For example, a waste study by the German Cigarette Association is used to estimate cigarette smuggling. At least 12,000 cigarette boxes are analyzed for their tax stamps at around 22 representative locations. The influence that the informal economy can have on gross domestic product (GDP) is shown by the example of Italy. When it was first included in the calculation in 1987, GDP rose overnight by 18%.

The effect is not as drastic this time. The Ifo Institute in Munich estimates that the German economy will be raised by two to three percent as a result of the recalculation. On average, GDP in the EU countries would increase by 2.4% according to this estimate. The leaders would be Finland and Sweden with an increase in level of four to five percent—less would benefit, among others, Poland, Lithuania and Latvia with less than one percent.

The recalculation also affects the calculation of the debt limits under the European Stability Pact. According to this, the annual budget deficit must be less than three percent of GDP and total government debt must be less than 60% of GDP. If GDP increases for statistical reasons, this gives the Euro countries more room for higher deficits.

The inclusion of cigarette smuggling and drug trafficking are the most prominent examples of changes in GDP calculation. However, something else is economically more important. "The most important point in the switch is the inclusion of research and development expenditure as investment," says statistician Norbert Räth.

Expenditures for research and development are no longer treated as a pre-delivery, but as an investment. The same applies to military goods. So far, only civilian-usable military facilities such as airports, barracks or hospitals were considered as investments—military weapon systems such as tanks were not. The reclassification increases GDP.

On paper, every German and even every EU citizen is now a little richer per head. However, nothing has changed in real wealth (Table 2.1).

Table 2.1 The recalculation of GDP lets the debt ratio sink (estimation of the state debt ratio 2013). (Source: Société Générale, European commission; numbers quoted according to handelsblatt from 14.08.2014, http://www.handelsblatt.com/politik/konjunktur/nachrichten/neue-bip-berechnungguten-morgen-wir-sind-reicher/10329916.html)

Euro states (selection)	Increase of GDP level in %	Debt ratio (debt in % of GDP)	
		Old	New
Finland	4–5	58.9	56.1–56.7
Netherlands	3–4	75.2	72.3–73.0
Austria	3–4	75.2	72.3–73.0
Germany	2–3	79.7	77.4–78.2
France	2–3	93.8	91.1–92.0
Italy	1–2	133.6	131.0–132.3
Spain	1–2	94.6	92.8–93.7
Portugal	1–2	129.2	126.7–127.9
Ireland	1–2	126.9	124.5–125.7
Euro area	2.4	96.3	94.0

Interpretation

One can argue about what should be included in GDP and consider it a disadvantage that not all economic transactions are included. However, if goods cannot be recorded and are therefore estimated, this brings with it the risk of misestimates. Gross domestic product also serves as an indicator of a country's debt servicing capacity. If drug consumption and prostitution are now included, these are transactions that the state has no access to in taxation. The debt servicing capacity is thus distorted. This is even more true for the 18% undeclared work that Italy has included.

We have defined investments as production that will be used in future periods for production. For research expenditure, this only applies to a limited extent. It is not certain whether a research result will emerge that can be used. Military expenditure can not be used in future periods for production. Therefore, no higher debt serviceability arises here either.

In Fig. 2.6 we have additionally depicted the markets in the circulation.

Consider Fig. 2.7. Monetary flows are always opposite to the real flows: companies produce consumer goods (real flow) and receive money for it (monetary flow).

The entrepreneurs offer their labor as households and receive the entrepreneur's wage. They thus also achieve labor income.

In Fig. 2.8 only monetary flows are again recorded. **Transfers** are benefits that the household receives from the state without consideration. These include child benefits and social assistance. If companies receive benefits from the state without consideration, this is called **subsidies**.

How is the output used here?

For consumption, investment and government expenditure (expenditure).

Why must I = S apply?

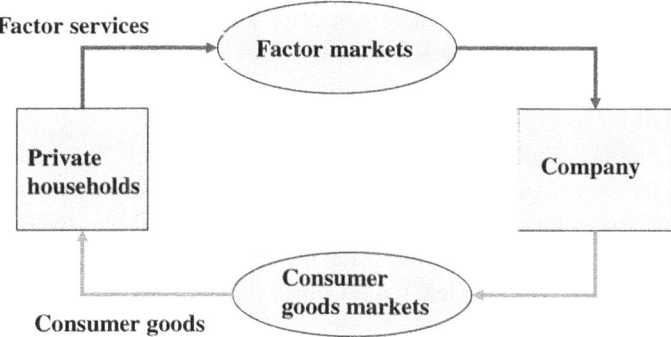

Fig. 2.6   Markets in the real economic cycle

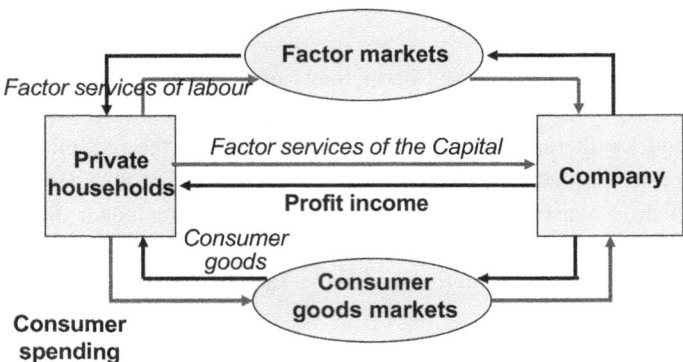

Fig. 2.7 Markets in the real and monetary economy

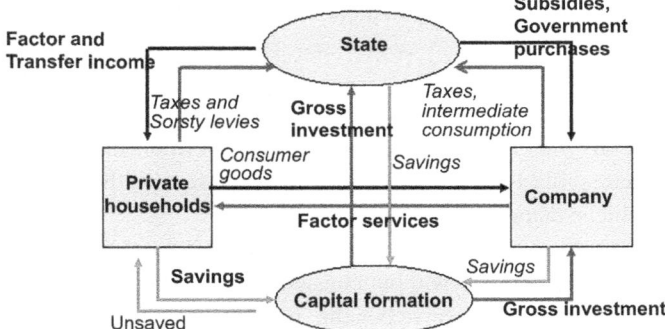

Fig. 2.8 Cash flows in the monetary economy

Companies can also save if they build up reserves. The economy is in equilibrium if savings and net investment are equal. Income can be consumed or saved.

Although each individual household can also dissolve its savings or even become indebted, in a closed economy the net flow of all households must be positive, because otherwise all goods would go into consumption and there would be no value added (GDP share) left for investment.

The goods produced in the year are available to the economy. In production, incomes are created to the same extent, because, as we have seen, each transaction has two sides, the income and expenditure side. The companies produce and pay for their production factors. The employees working in the company receive an income. All inputs are also goods that have to be produced. Here too, incomes are generated for the employees. Both together are referred to as production costs, and what remains is the profit. The profit, as we have seen, is also an income of households. Entrepreneurs or owners of companies receive it as so-called residual income. This also means that the profit can only be consumed or saved, which either creates demand or eliminates demand. All savings together then represent a waiver of shares in the annual production to which the workers or capital providers would have been entitled from their participation in production. This production is then available for the additional demand from entrepreneurs for investments. Without savings, none of the production would be left, as all value added would be used for consumption. If, on the other hand, savings are made, parts of the production can be used in the so-called investment goods industry to produce goods such as machines, without which there would be no productivity gains and thus no growth (see Fig. 2.8).

Exercise

Determine the income and expenditure of the business sector in Fig. 2.9.
   Business sector income:

1. Sales of consumer goods
2. Gross investment financed by the financial sector (savings)
3. Subsidies and government purchases

Expenditures:

1. Wages for factor services
2. Savings
3. Taxes, fees, and advance payments

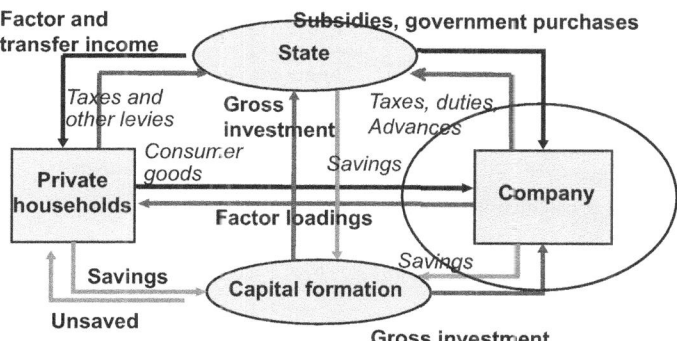

Fig. 2.9 Cash flows in the monetary economy

Summary

The Macoeconomic Accounting's circuit analysis depicts economic relationships in the form of sectors and monetary flows. The sectors represent the aggregated economic sectors and the flows represent the goods and money transactions. The flows are based on transactions that are valued on markets. ◄

Questions for Understanding

1. What is the difference between current and stock variables?
2. Name examples of transactions that are not captured in the Macoeconomic Accounting.
3. Explain why GDP can be captured from two sides.
4. What is meant by a closed circuit?
5. In country A, more transactions are settled through official markets than in country B. Where is GDP higher?

Exercise

Calculate GDP (Billion €) in this simplified monetary and real circuit using both the income and expenditure streams (Fig. 2.10).

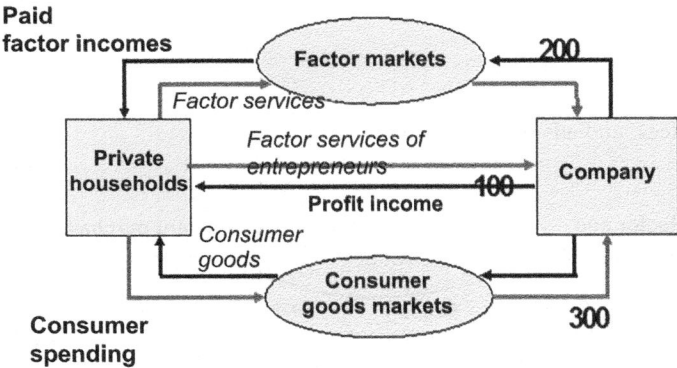

Fig. 2.10 Double GDP calculation

2.3   Terms of the Macoeconomic Accounting

What Follows Why
After we have analyzed the interdependencies of economic actors and activities using cycles, we now turn to parts of the national product. With special definitions of terms, the Macoeconomic Accounting wants to work out statements about the different components of the national product.

Learning objectives
The goal is that you can explain the terms in your own words.

Terms

▶ **Definition**
The goods produced are consumed in the current period in the broadest sense or are still available at the end of the period in the economy (expenditure account).

In the first case, it is either intermediate consumption [VL] or consumption (consumption) [C] or it is lost to the economy as exports [Ex].

▶ Intermediate consumption are services of domestic companies for other domestic companies or the state and are consumed completely in the same period in which they are delivered. Do you know examples? All goods that are further processed count: materials, steel sheets, milk.
To the extent that the goods produced are still available at the end of the period in the economy, they enter as gross investments either in the productive capital of companies or the state **(gross—investment)** or they go into stock and thus influence the extent of changes in inventories (inventory investment).

▶ **Gross investments** $=$ Gross fixed investment $+$ Inventory investment

▶ **Definition of Investments**
Goods that are produced in this period and used in future periods for production.

Investments increase the capital stock. They are the opposite of **consumption,** that is, the goods that are produced and consumed in this period. Inventory investment, that is, produced but unsold goods, increase GDP. If it is sold at the same price next year, GDP does not change. Otherwise, if the price is higher, then GDP grows by the profit margin. The same is true for trade in goods produced in previous periods.

▶ **Depreciation**
Measures the wear and tear of the capital factor caused by the use of capital in production during a period.

▶ **Definition**
Net investment is calculated as the difference between gross investment and depreciation in a given period.

Example: Real estate company A buys two office buildings from real estate company B. The first was built in 2000 and the second this year. Are these investments?

Answer: The purchase of the apartment building with a construction year of 2000 is not an economic investment in contrast to the construction of a new apartment building, because only the new house was produced this year and therefore also included in this year's GDP.

▶ **Replacement Investments**
The part of gross investment that serves the maintenance of the production apparatus. In the event of positive net investment, the value of replacement investment corresponds to the depreciation because then the gross investment is greater than the depreciation.

▶ **Net Positive Investments**
They indicate by how much the factor capital (capital stock) has grown through investment activity.

Net positive investments are divided between expansion investments and rationalization investments. Positive net investments increase the capital stock.

▶ **Rationalization Investments**
The part of positive net investments that changes production technology in such a way that the increased capital expenditure is offset by a lower use of the factor labor and/or land. Human labor is replaced by machines. The factor input ratio (K/N) changes in favor of capital.

Rationalization investments usually destroy existing jobs where they are made. The increased production costs due to the higher capital expenditure are offset or more than offset by savings in labor or land costs. Rationalization investments can also be justified by technical progress. There is labor-saving and capital-saving technical progress (process innovations).

We further distinguish between process innovations and product innovations. In process innovation, a process is developed anew (assembly line production). Where, in product innovation, a new product is created (iPhone, iPad).

> **Question**

Give examples of rationalization investments from your environment. Is labor-saving technical progress negative?

Work-saving technical progress in the form of process innovations is not generally to be evaluated negatively. The negative aspect is that employees lose their jobs and with them the income to generate demand. They then have to be supported by the state, which burdens public finances. On the other hand, we have had work-saving technical progress for millennia. Approx. 90% of the population used to be employed in agriculture. There were no tractors and no artificial fertilizers back then. Nowadays, less than 10% of employees are employed in agriculture. So we should have an unemployment rate of approx. 80%. What do all these people do? Thanks to product innovations, we have much greater prosperity today than in the past. The goods, such as cars and TVs, also have to be produced. If productivity in agriculture had not increased due to process innovations and had released workers, we would not be able to produce these products. We would first have to produce our food. The increase in productivity due to work-saving technical progress was so high that we can afford to invest time in education today. Without technical progress, we would all have to work on the fields. However, the time delays of process and product innovations are problematic. Not every time process innovations release workers, there are also new products to catch the resulting unemployment. In addition, employees need to be retrained so that they can produce the new products. They may also have to move if the new products are not produced where they live. That is why so-called structural unemployment arises.

▶ **Expansion Investments**

serve to expand the production apparatus without changing the existing factor input ratio. They therefore create new jobs where they are made. The rising production costs are to be covered by the revenues generated by the sale of the increased production volume.

> **Question**

Are these investments?

Mr. Müller buys an older house and a new car. The company Hydac builds a new production hall and buys an old truck. The University of Applied Sciences (HTW) buys a new truck.

Answer

Mr. Müller is a private household and, from an economic point of view, private households cannot make investments. Households can only consume or save. If a private household buys a car, this is consumption. The company Hydac, as a company, makes investments again when it builds a production hall. Since the truck is old and was not built in this period, it is not an investment from an economic point of view. If the HTW buys a new truck, it is an investment made by the state and referred to as public investment.

The State
The services produced by the state actually represent uncharged services for domestic companies or uncharged consumption by domestic households or uncharged exports.

Since a fair sectoral allocation of state services is not possible statistically, they are exclusively attributed to the state (and therefore also to GDP) in the amount of state expenditure as **state consumption [C_{St}]**.

An economy with a high state share can therefore have a lower GDP than other states because the state benefits are only offset by their costs (expenditures).

▶ **Net and Gross Products**
Gross products—depreciation = net products

Net products are what is available for new investment or consumption from value creation (without the reinvestment necessary to maintain the capital stock).

In order to capture the economic value creation and the causes of value creation as well as the influences on this, there are different measurement concepts. If one speaks of production as value creation, the term products is used. If one emphasizes the incomes that have arisen from this production in the same amount by way of reflection, one speaks of income.

Domestic and National Products
GDP is supposed to serve as an indicator for the prosperity of a country. The higher the GDP, the more needs can be met, the greater the benefit for the population. There are two concepts of recording here, the domestic concept and the concept of residents.

▶ **Domestic Product**
Where was the product produced or the income generated? Within the respective state borders in cooperation with the foreign companies and foreign workers producing there (domestic concept). This concept corresponds to gross domestic product.

▶ **National Product**
Who produced the product or generated income? The income of all residents outside the state borders, for example also including the profit of a German company in France or German employees in France with residence in Germany (concept of residents). This concept corresponds to gross national product.

If the national product is greater than the domestic product, the residents have earned more abroad than foreigners in the country.

1. Example: A Frenchman owns an apartment in Germany. With the domestic concept, the rental income is included, with the resident concept not. The same applies to profits of a German company to the Frenchman.
2. Example: Bosch subsidiary in India makes a profit (revenue—wages and inputs) and transfers it to the parent company in Germany. According to the domestic concept, the entire production or income is attributed to India. According to the resident concept, the profit is attributed to Germany, but the wages and input purchases to India.

The difference between domestic and national product is called the **balance of primary incomes with the rest of the world** (labor and property income between in- and out-land). This includes, for example, dividends and interest on foreign securities, wages of cross-border workers.

Exercise

Calculate the balance of primary incomes of Germany with France based on the following money flows:

The French have rental income from Germany of 500 million euros.
The Germans have rental income from France of 200 million euros.
The French have interest income from Germany of 400 million euros.
The Germans have interest income from France of 300 million euros.
The French get profits from Germany of 500 million euros.
The Germans get profits from France of 1 billion euros.
Is the German gross national product greater than the GDP?

There are two other measurement concepts: output at market prices and factor costs. With this distinction, one wants to calculate the influence of the state on prices.

▶ The so-called **output at factor costs** is the sum of the costs incurred in the private sector, that is, the prices without state intervention.

▶ **Definition**
Under **output at market prices** one understands the sum of the goods *market* prices (that is, with state price interventions). Output at factor costs and market prices differ by the production and import duties (goods taxes such as value added tax, insurance tax, mineral oil tax, tobacco tax, etc.), import duties (mainly tariffs) and production taxes (such as property taxes) as well as subsidies for goods (subsidies for public transport, subsidies for agricultural and animal products, coal subsidies, etc.).

Output at market prices and output at factor costs can be calculated by deducting or adding the state influences:

Output at factor costs

\+   Production and import duties (mainly **goods taxes**)
\−   **Subsidies for goods**

\=   **Output at market prices**
Or, more concretely:

Factor costs	Market price
Production costs—goods subsidies =	Company price + VAT
+ →	–

▶ **Real GDP**
In the Macoeconomic Accounting, one wants to determine economic performance. Effective performance is distorted by price influences. Therefore, one distinguishes between nominal products, which include the price influences, and real products, both of which have the price influence subtracted. The value added of the overall economic products can be broken down into an increase in quantity and an increase in price:
Real GDP = current quantities x prices of the previous year.

▶ **Deflator**
The deflator answers the question of what I need to divide the nominal values of a year by to get the real values. It is calculated by dividing the nominal gross domestic product by the real one.
$$\text{Deflator} = Y_{\text{nom.}}/Y_{\text{real}}$$

▶ **Definition**
The **net national product** (or **-income**) **at factor costs** is called national income because it is a suitable measure for the goods provision **(welfare)** of the population.

National income includes, and only includes, the income earned by the residents which is available to them, which is why depreciation and production and import taxes are deducted.

▶ Depreciation is deducted because it is not available as income, but represents economic wear and tear. Also deducted are consumption taxes such as value added tax, insurance tax, tobacco tax, etc., import duties (especially tariffs) and production taxes such as land taxes.

Goods subsidies: subsidies for public transport, subsidies for agricultural and animal products, coal subsidies, etc.

Production and import taxes (e g. VAT) are not available as income to households (−), but goods subsidies are (+).

▶ National income is divided into wages (proportionate to the wage share) and corporate and property income (proportionate to the profit share). This is based on the sources of income and not on the recipients, which is why a worker can also receive income from profits in the form of dividends (see GDP in the distribution calculation). The so-called disposable income is obtained by adjusting household income for transfers and taxes.

From GDP to National Income
Gross domestic product
(Domestic concept: everything that was produced in the country)
± Balance of primary incomes with the rest of the world (earnings and property incomes between in- and outland)*
= Gross national income (domestic concept: everything that was produced or earned by residents, i.e. for example Germans)
− Depreciation**
= Net national income at market prices
− Production and import duties (incl. goods taxes + goods subsidies***)
= Net national income at factor costs****
(National income)
*e.g. dividends and interest from foreign securities, wages of cross-border workers etc. Example: A Frenchman owns an apartment in Germany According to the domestic concept, the rental income is included, but according to the resident concept, it is not. The same applies to dividends paid by a German company to the Frenchman.
**economic wear and tear of plant and equipment as well as immediate write-offs.
***Goods taxes such as value added tax, insurance tax, tobacco tax etc., import duties (incl. customs duties) and production taxes, such as property taxes.
Goods subsidies: subsidies for public transport, subsidies for agricultural and animal products, coal subsidies, etc.
****National income includes wages received by residents as well as enterprise and property incomes (enterprise profits—including an allowance for entrepreneurial wages—and property income received and paid by the state on net basis by private households).

From GDP to national income in 2018		
	Gross domestic product (domestic concept)	3,386.0 €
±	Balance of primary incomes with the rest of the world	+72.5 €
=	Gross national income (residents' concept)	3,458.5 €
−	Depreciation	−600.0 €

=	Net national income at market prices	2,858.5 €
−	Production and import duties (incl. goods taxes) 314.0 € + goods subsidies 25.5 €	−326.5 €
=	Net national income at factor costs National income	2,532.0 €

Summary

The various terms made it clear how complex economic production is. The main investment terms, government production, net and gross products, domestic and national products, and products at factor costs or market prices were discussed. ◀

Comprehension Questions

1. Explain net investments and expansion investments.
2. Why can an economy with a high state share have a lower GDP than others?
3. How do domestic and national products differ?
4. What is the consequence if maintenance investments are smaller than the write-offs or the net investments are negative?

Exercise Questions

1. In an economy, only cell phones and RVs are produced.
   a) Using the data in the table with 2000 as the base year, calculate the nominal and real GDP for both years. What was the real growth rate, what do you estimate?
   b) Calculate the deflator for 2020.

Year	2010	2020
RV price	60,000 €	70,000 €
Cell phone price	10 €	15 €
Number of RVs	1100	1200
Number of cell phones	900,000	300,000

2. Siemens AG sells a phone to 1) the University of Technology and Economics (HTW), 2) Daimler AG, 3) Mr. Muller, 4) the French company ALSTOM AG and 5) builds a telephone system in addition to sell it next year. 6) In addition, Siemens buys a new delivery truck from the French company Renault. Assign these transactions to the expenditure components of private consumption, government consumption, private investment, government investment, exports and imports.
3. Calculate the Gross National Income (GNI) from the GDP for 2010 based on the following information: Gross Domestic Product 3364.2 €, balance of primary incomes with the rest of the world +51.4 €, depreciation 431.6 €, balance of taxes on goods and services and subsidies on goods 411.2 €.

2.4   Output, expenditures and distribution approach

What Follows Why
After we have analyzed the interdependencies of economic actors and activities using the circuits and explained numerous terms, we now want to finally turn to the three methods of calculation of the GDP.

Learning objectives
After the third part of the chapter on the GDP, you should be able to completely explain the relationships of the actors and actions that generate the GDP and to critically question the content of economic terms such as the GDP.

There are three concepts for the official calculation of gross domestic product:

A. **The Output approach of GDP**
It determines the extent of production from the available data of the individual economic sectors (**overall economic supply**).
B. **The expenditures approach of GDP**
It summarizes the individual demand components in the form of expenditure on **overall economic demand**.
C. **The distribution approach of national income**
It calculates the value of **national income** over the incomes generated in production. From this, in turn, GDP can be calculated.

2.4.1   The Output (or Value Added) approach

The calculation of GDP at market prices in the Output approach takes place on the supply side. In official statistics, the output approach is differentiated according to economic sectors. This makes it possible, inter alia, to map the economic structural change over time. Only final products flow into GDP. Therefore, the value of intermediate products is deducted in the production calculation. Otherwise, the intermediate products would be double-counted: once separately as intermediate products and once in the final products.

The value added of a company corresponds to the value of production minus the value of the intermediate products used, which the company has bought from other companies. Consequently, the sum of the value added of all sectors must correspond to GDP (adjusted for taxes on goods and subsidies), as the value added of an economy.

A winegrower grows grapes and sells them for 1.50 € per kg to a winery. This presses the grapes, ferments them and sells the wine for 3.50 € per bottle to a supermarket chain. The supermarket chain sells the wine to an architect for 7 €. The architect drinks the wine.

What is the value added that each person creates? How big is the total contribution to GDP? ◄

Income Statement
1. Sales of goods and services of an economic sector (without goods taxes)
2. ± Inventory changes in semi-finished and finished goods
3. + Value of self-made facilities
4. = Production value
5. − Inputs from domestic companies to domestic companies and imports = gross value added
6. Sum of the gross value added of all sectors
7. + Goods taxes − goods subsidies = GDP

2.4.2   Expenditures Approach

The calculation of gross domestic product takes place on the demand side:

1. Private household consumption expenditure (incl. private sector withdrawals) and expenditure of private non-profit organizations (e.g. churches)
2. + State consumption expenditure (value of services produced by the state),
3. + Private and public gross investment
4. (Gross fixed investment ± changes in inventories of semi-finished and finished goods)
5. + Exports of all goods and services produced domestically
5. − Imports of all goods and services produced abroad

In the production account, imports must be deducted because they are not produced domestically and therefore do not belong to the domestic product.

The calculation of gross domestic product on the demand side (**expenditure account**) is:

$$\mathbf{GDP_M = C + I^b + G + (Ex - Im)}$$

C = Consumption
I^b = Gross investment
G = Government spending
Ex − Im = Contribution to the balance of trade

The external trade difference "exports minus imports" is called external contribution.

Gross domestic product 2018 in bn. €		
	private consumption expenditure	1,775.9
+	government consumption expenditure	661.2
+	Gross investment	719.7
(Gross fixed capital formation +703.4 ± Inventories and stock changes + 16.3)		
+	Exports	1,590.2
−	Imports	−1,316.0
		3,386.0

2.4.3   The Distribution Approach of National Income

Due to unsolvable recording problems, the official
   Statistics the gross national income in only two income types:

1. *Wages* (gross) as well as
2. *Corporate and property income* (gross).

Distribution of gross national income in 2018 (billion €)	
Wages (gross)	1,746.1
+ Corporate and	
property income (gross)	785.9
= Gross national income	2,532.0
(Wage share: 68.94%, Profit share: 31.04%)	

Calculation of disposable income and savings rate

Detailed Distribution of Gross National Income
1. **Employee compensation (gross)**
   - **−Employer social security contributions**
   - **= Gross wages and salaries**
   - −Income tax
   - **Employee social security contributions**
   - = Net wages and salaries
2. **Corporate and capital income (gross)**
   - −Direct taxes
   - **=Corporate and capital income (net)**

If we add together the net wages and salaries and the corporate and capital income (net) accruing to domestic private households and add the monetary social benefits, we get the disposable income (2018: 1,929.8 billion euros) of private households.

The disposable income is used for private consumption (2018: 1,731.03 billion euros) and for savings (2019: 198.8 billion euros).

The national savings rate (savings as a percentage of disposable income) was 10.3% in 2018 after 9.9% in 2017.

Figures 2.11 and 2.12 give an overview of the different ways to calculate GDP.

Is GDP a suitable growth or prosperity indicator?

1. Not all services are captured, as only the services that are valued on markets are counted. For example, black work, housework, charitable services, hobby services, etc. are not captured.
2. GDP is a purely quantitative measure, as quality improvements or deteriorations are not measured unless they are reflected in prices.
3. GDP does not make a statement about the distribution of GDP.
4. The value of goods for society is eliminated because there is only one valuation by the market. No statements can be made about how the goods produced affect the quality of life of people (e.g. no consideration of the consumer good "leisure time").
5. External effects[2], such as environmental damage, are not taken into account in GDP.
6. GDP at market prices is misleading because prices can also be artificially increased, for example by an increase in demand, without changing the amount of goods produced. $\rightarrow$ Inflation (see also Siebe & Wenke, 2014; Blanchard, 2014; Blanchard & Illing, 2006; Wagner & Böhne, 2003; Felderer & Homburg, 2005; Drost et al., 2003; Mankiw, 2013; John, 2004; Mussel, 2009 as well as Federal Statistical Office, 2015).
7. A BIP comparability between countries is difficult due to different recording accuracy.

Quote by Senator Robert Kennedy about the GDP as he ran for president of the United States in 1968.

Yet the gross national product does not allow for the health of our children, the quality of their education, or the joy of their play. It does not include the beauty of our poetry or the strength of our marriages; the intelligence of our public debate or the integrity of our public officials. It measures neither our wit nor our courage; neither our wisdom nor our learning; neither our compassion nor our devotion to our country; it measures everything, in short, except that which makes life worthwhile. And it tells us everything about America except why we are proud that we are Americans.[3]

---

[2] Definition: An external effect is the effect of economic action on the welfare of an uninvolved third party (externalities).

[3] See http://www.theguardian.com/news/datablog/2012/may/24/robert-kennedy-gdp (11.11.2015).

Output Approach
Sales
± Inventory change
+ s.e. plants
- Intermediate consumption and imports
(+Taxes on goods,-Goods sub.)
Expenditure Approach:
Private consumption
± Government consumption
± Gross investment
± Net exports
Gross domestic product
± Balance of primary income
- Depreciation
± (Taxes on products - Subsidies on products)
Distribution Approach:
National income

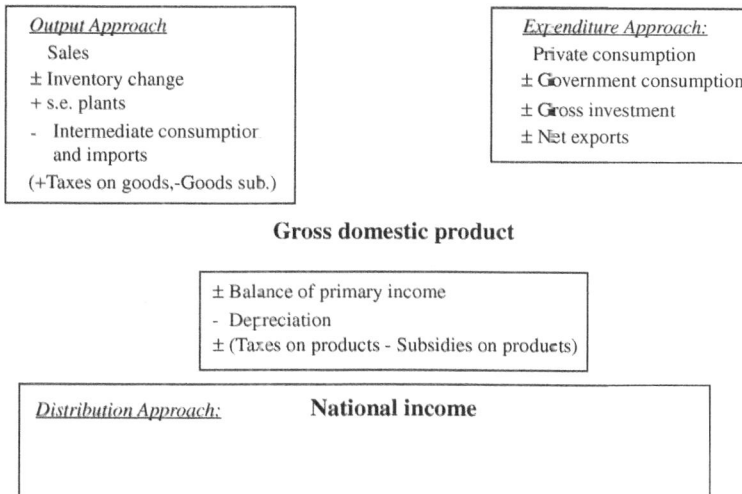

Fig. 2.11 Different calculation methods for GDP

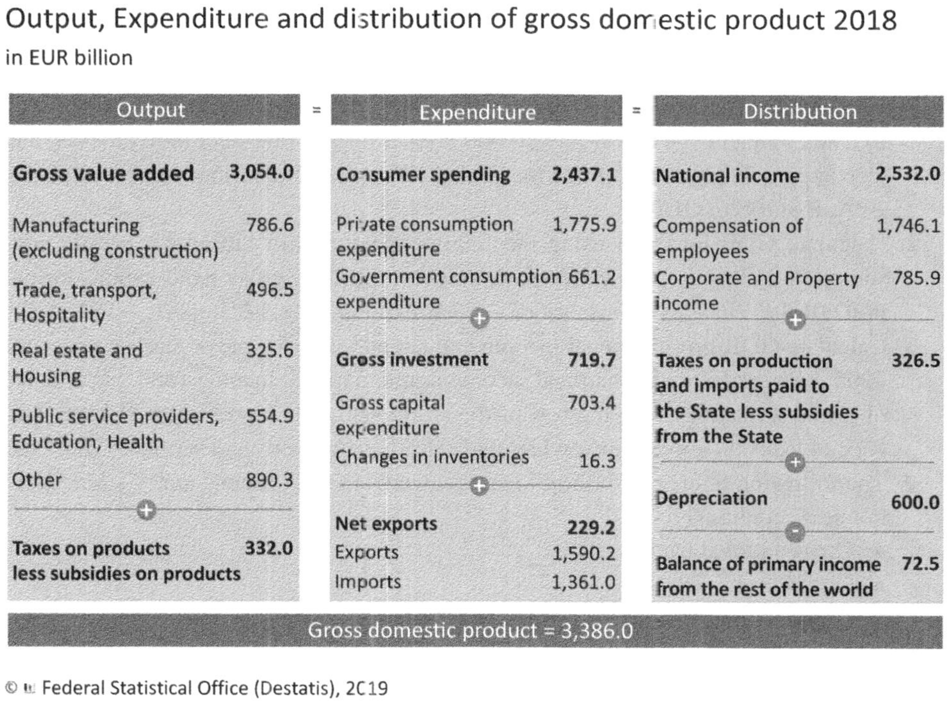

Output, Expenditure and distribution of gross domestic product 2018
in EUR billion
Output
=
Expenditure
=
Distribution
Gross value added 3,054.0
Manufacturing (excluding construction) 786.6
Trade, transport, Hospitality 496.5
Real estate and Housing 325.6
Public service providers, Education, Health 554.9
Other 890.3
Taxes on products less subsidies on products 332.0
Consumer spending 2,437.1
Private consumption expenditure 1,775.9
Government consumption expenditure 661.2
Gross investment 719.7
Gross capital expenditure 703.4
Changes in inventories 16.3
Net exports 229.2
Exports 1,590.2
Imports 1,361.0
National income 2,532.0
Compensation of employees 1,746.1
Corporate and Property income 785.9
Taxes on production and imports paid to the State less subsidies from the State 326.5
Depreciation 600.0
Balance of primary income from the rest of the world 72.5
Gross domestic product = 3,386.0
© Federal Statistical Office (Destatis), 2019

Fig. 2.12 Creation, use and distribution of gross domestic product. (Source: Federal statistical office, https://www.destatis.de/DE/ZahlenFakten/GesamtwirtschaftUmwelt/VGR/VolkswirtschaftlicheGesamtrechnungen.html)

Summary

In the economy, everything is connected. We have seen that income and expenditure are mutually dependent or the two sides of the BIP. Who has produced in the period also has expenses that are income and revenue for employees and other companies. Who produces is also asking. The BIP captures all transactions that are valued on markets. ◄

Comprehension Questions

1. Explain in your own words the accounting equation of the GDP.
2. Give two examples of value added or external effects that are not captured in the GDP.
3. Why are wage and profit margin not suitable for distributional discussions? ◄

Exercise Tasks

1. A car is sold by Daimler for 90,000 €. For the production of the car, Daimler receives various steel parts from company (U) A for 40,000 €, steel sheets from company B for 15,000 €, plastic parts from company C for 15,000 € and seats from company D for 5000 €.
   a) Calculate Daimler's value added contribution to the gross value added of the manufacturing sector.
   b) The companies A and B pay 10,000 € each for the raw steel they process, and company C pays 8000 € for the plastic. What is the contribution of companies A, B and C to GDP?
2. Calculate GDP for 2008 using the following figures (in billion €): private consumption 2138.4 €, government consumption 536.1 €, gross fixed capital formation 601.3 €, changes in inventories −2.7 €, exports 1948.5 €, imports −1547.8 €.
3. Calculate GDP, gross national income and net national income at market prices for 2008 from the following national income figure: national income 1880.2 €, balance of primary incomes with the rest of the world +40.4 €, depreciation 363.9 €, balance of taxes on goods and services and subsidies on goods and services (285.7 €).
4. The following figures (in billion €) are known from the Utopia country's Macoeconomic Accounting:
   - Gross national income: 935
   - Goods taxes: 199
   - Gross national product at factor costs: 1004
   - Goods subsidies: 15
   Calculate
   a) the amount of depreciation

    b) the net national product at market prices

    c) the gross national product at market prices

5. The following information is given (in bn. €):

Private consumption expenditure: 5.0

Gross fixed capital formation: 2.9

Government expenditure: 1 9

Decrease in inventories: 0.3

Exports: 4.1

Imports: 3.2

Depreciation: 3

Balance of primary incomes with the rest of the world: 0.5

Subsidies: 0.6

Wages and salaries: 4.2

Enterprise and property incomes: 2.1

Determine:

    a) GDP and Gross National Income.

    b) NNI at market prices and National Income.

    c) Goods taxes and the profit ratio.

6. Calculate GDP according to the distribution approach for 2016 using the following information: Wages and salaries 1,600.3, enterprise and property incomes 737.7, balance of primary incomes with the rest of the world 53.1 €, depreciation 552.3 €, production and import taxes (incl. goods taxes) 334.7 €. goods subsidies 27.8 €

7. Calculate the gross national income, the net national income, the disposable income of employees for 2016 from the GDP using the following information: Gross domestic product 3,144.1 €, balance of primary income with the rest of the world 53.1 €, depreciation 552.3 €, production and import duties (incl. goods taxes) 334.7 €, goods subsidies 27.8 €, corporate and property income 737.7, social security contributions of employers 288.9, deductions of employees 444.2; monetary social benefits 943.9

8. Calculate the GDP for 2016 using the following information: Gross value added by sector: agriculture and forestry 17.4, manufacturing industry excluding construction 728.6, construction 134.9, service sector 1,951.0; goods taxes 319.3; goods subsidies 7.2 ◄

2.5   Case Study: European Wealth and GDP

Task

Read the following article and try to answer the question of the title: Where has the money of the Germans gone? How can it be that Germany is one of the richest countries in Europe, but the poor southern European countries have more wealth per head?

Little Wealth

Where has the money of the Germans gone?

FAZ from 21.04.2013[4]: The Germans have little wealth, that's true. But to appreciate the wealth of a country, it is better to look at the disposable income.

By Lisa Nienhaus (http://www.faz.net/redaktion/lisa-nienhaus-11104401.html)

The title sounds as exciting as a visit to the local Ordnungsamt (office of public order): "The Eurosystem Household Finance and Consumption Survey. Results from the first wave". But the study should come with a big red warning sign: Danger, explosive! Rarely has a study scared Germans as much as this one from the European Central Bank. Because the researchers, through an extensive survey, have determined: Germans are the poorest people in the Eurozone. The average German has a fortune of €51,400, while the average Italian has €174,000, the Spaniard €182,700 and the Cypriot even €266,900.

This is a scandal. Because even though the Germans struggle with their role as Euro-rescuers, they had gotten used to the fact that it is them who make sure that Greece, Ireland, Portugal and now also Cyprus don't go bankrupt. And now the robust rescuers of Europe are supposed to have the poorest population? Poorer than the population of the countries that had to go under the rescue umbrella? Can this be true?

This is what the country is asking itself. And rightfully so. After all, every tourist has the impression that Greece and Portugal can't possibly be wealthier than Germany. Now even Chancellor Angela Merkel has joined the debate. In the "Bild" newspaper she announced on Friday that the numbers from the ECB researchers are "distorted" and that Germans are actually richer than surveyed.

The researchers measure wealth—not prosperity

It is certain: The study is scientifically quite correct. But it is also certain what the president of the Institute for the World Economy, Dennis Snower, very nicely formulated: "I can reassure you. Germans are doing better than the ECB study suggests."

This is because the researchers—admittedly—do not measure the prosperity of European countries, but the wealth of private households. And that is the wrong measure to use to judge how wealthy a country is. Because: "For the prosperity of a country, the income of its citizens is more relevant than their wealth", says Snower.

This is partly because assets are often tied up: for example, farmers often have a lot of assets in the form of house, farm and machinery, but they are not at all liquid. This makes them appear richer in statistics than, say, a young lawyer earning €100,000 a year, but who has saved very little. But are they really?

In addition, the value of assets often fluctuates sharply. This affects not only shares, but also investments that many people consider to be rock-solid. Gold, for example, or the favourite investment class of Europeans: houses that they live in themselves. If there is a property boom in a country, then the value of one's own house suddenly

---

[4]Translated from German.

rises sharply. "But this rarely results in people having a higher income than before," says Snower, "or a correspondingly higher standard of living." At least, not as long as they don't sell or mortgage their house. So if Spain has a property boom and Germany doesn't, this leads to distortions that have little to do with prosperity.

The German welfare state has more to offer than Cyprus or Portugal

If only private assets are taken into account, another important factor is also missing: the state. Someone who goes to school or studies for free, who does not use up their assets for their health, but instead takes out state insurance, enjoys a standard of living that cannot be measured by their private assets. This also applies to state pensions. A future state pension increases prosperity, but it is not included in assets. Of course, it is uncertain whether it will actually be paid out as promised today. But since the financial crisis, one also has to say: No one knows for sure whether private savings for retirement will be worth what is assumed today in twenty years' time.

For Germans, the welfare state factor is likely to be particularly relevant in the prosperity comparison with other European countries. Because Germany has more to offer in this respect than, for example, Cyprus or Portugal.

This is how Ulf von Kalckreuth of the Deutsche Bundesbank, who was significantly involved in the study in Germany, says: "Assets are certainly important, but from the comprehensive concept of welfare it only provides one part aspect."

By far the better way to capture the wealth of a country is still through gross domestic product per capita. This roughly corresponds to the sum of all incomes (from work, assets and businesses) that are generated in a country in one year, divided by the number of inhabitants. If you use this as a measure for a ranking of the Euro countries, then the world falls back into place (see chart). Because Germany is not a top performer there with 32,000 € GDP per capita, but at least in sixth place among the 15 countries examined by the ECB. All crisis countries from Greece to Cyprus are well behind.

So: Breathe a sigh of relief! We're not that poor.

However, one must recognize: The study is to be taken seriously in terms of private wealth—and shows several things that are surprising.

So there is apparently a lot of private wealth in some crisis countries despite the poor state. That Cyprus appears just behind Luxembourg at the top of the wealth scale provokes—and is also surprising for all researchers who have dealt with wealth so far. For example, for the author of the Credit Suisse Wealth Report, Michael O'Sullivan. "We have Cyprus much further back in the wealth scale than the ECB report, behind Germany," he says and believes in errors in the ECB study. In his report, the average Cypriot has only about 66,000 € in assets, the German about 110,000.

If the ECB and not the Credit Suisse is right, a question arises, finds Dennis Snower: "If there are large assets in the Euro crisis countries, why are they not taxed to pay off the state's debts?"

The second puzzle relates to Germany. Because—even if we know that private wealth is not everything—it is still surprising how low the wealth of the Germans is. After all, we had a high GDP and a high savings rate for decades. Where is the money of the Germans if it does not show up in assets?

There are numerous explanations for this. They range from an effect of reunification with the Eastern Bloc to the lack of a real estate boom in Germany. But so far, none of them have been completely satisfactory. Even the ECB researchers admit: The low private assets of the Germans is a mystery that urgently needs to be solved (Fig. 2.13).

Interpretation

As the article also rightly notes, one reason for the higher assets of the southern European countries may be the real estate bubble that formed after these countries joined the euro. It is cited as a reason for the lower assets that Germans on average own fewer own properties than other Europeans. However, the German houses, as they are not state-owned, must belong to households. Here, indirect ownership of real estate funds, real estate companies or life insurance can be assumed. In addition, Germany has a high GDP compared to the southern European countries. Since the purchasing power for the purchase of real estate can be derived from the GDP, the prices for real estate in Germany would also have to be high.

It is also noteworthy that in Germany the median of the distribution of assets (i.e. the assets of households which are in the middle of all households listed in series) is lower than in the other countries. This initially points to a much more unequal distribution of assets. Furthermore, one can say that this half of households, which are to the left of this

Median Wealth		Average Wealth		GDP	
rank	in thousands of euros per household	rank	in thousands of euros per household	rank	In 2012, thousands of euros per inhabitant
1. Luxembourg	398	1. Luxembourg	710	1. Luxembourg	83
2. Cyprus	267	2. Cyprus	671	2. Austria	37
3. Malta	216	3. Malta	366	3. Netherlands	36
4. Belgium	206	4. Belgium	339	4. Finland	36
5. Spain	183	5. Spain	291	5. Belgium	34
6. Italy	174	6. Italy	275	6. Germany	32
7. France	116	7. Austria	265	7. France	32
8. Netherlands	104	8. France	233	8. Italy	26
9. Greece	102	9. Germany	195	9. Spain	23
10. Slovenia	101	10. Netherlands	170	10. Cyprus	21
11. Finland	86	11. Finland	162	11. Slovenia	17
12. Austria	76	12. Portugal	153	12. Greece	17
13. Portugal	75	13. Slovenia	149	13. Malta	16
14. Slovakia	61	14. Greece	148	14. Portugal	16
15. Germany	51	15. Slovakia	80	15. Slovakia	13

Fig. 2.13 Assets and income in Germany. (Source: F.A.Z. http://www.faz.net/aktuell/wirtschaft/wenig-vermoegen-wo-ist-das-geld-der-deutschen-hin-12156406.html. accessed 18.05.2016)

value, are poorer than the left half of the other European countries. There is therefore also much poverty in Germany by European standards. This assessment is confirmed by a recent study of assets by Allianz SE. For 2018, it came to a German median assets of 16,891 €.[5] The article refers to Germany's higher GDP and the welfare state including social assistance and pension rights. However, we have learned that GDP represents the value added within the country before taxes and social security contributions. All the benefits of the German welfare state are financed by taxes, even pensions are subsidized by tax money and pension contributions are also deducted from GDP (better GNP). There are no state reserves for pensions or social assistance, so the welfare benefits of the state cannot be cited as consolation for the Germans.

Ultimately, therefore, only the high GDP can be cited here as a compensatory effect for the unequal distribution of assets. In order to make inferences about income, one would actually have to know the national income, since GDP does not relate to Germans as residents. However, this can indirectly lead to inferences about income, but only before taxes. In order to say whether Germans are doing better than other Europeans, a comparison on the basis of disposable income is required. In the case of the asset comparison, the state debt per capita would also have to be taken into account.

However, the fundamental question remains open as to how it can be that in countries with a lower GDP and thus indirectly income, a large fortune can arise? Apart from possible measurement errors and the real estate boom, this could also be due to higher tax evasion on average. Despite all these inaccuracies, there is a bad feeling as this is also expressed in the article. At least it is plausible that if there are high private assets in the indebted countries, these will also be used for debt service.

References

Blanchard, O. (2014). *Makroökonomie*. Pearson Studium.

Blanchard, O., & Illing, G. (2006). *Übungen zur Makroökonomie*. Pearson Studium.

Drost, A., Linnemann, L., & Schabert, A. (2003). *Übungsbuch zu Felderer/Homburg*. Springer Gabler.

Felderer, B., & Homburg, S. (2005). *Makroökonomik und neue Makroökonomik* (9. Aufl.). Springer.

John, K. D. (2004). *Arbeitsbuch Makroökonomik* (12. Aufl.). Schäffer-Poeschel.

Mankiw, G. N. (2013). *Makroökonomik* (7. Aufl.). Schäffer-Poeschel.

Mussel, G. (2009). *Einführung in die Makroökonomik* (10. Aufl.). Vahlen.

Siebe, T., & Wenke, M. (2014). *Makroökonomie*. UTB.

Statistisches Bundesamt. (2015). Deutsche Wirtschaft, Wiesbaden https://www.destatis.de/DE/Publikationen/Thematisch/VolkswirtschaftlicheGesamtrechnungen/DeutscheWirtschaftQuartal.pdf?__blob=publicationFile. Zugegriffen: 8. Aug. 2016.

Wagner, H., & Böhne, A. (2003). *Übungsbuch Makroökonomie*. Vahlen.

---

[5] Allianz SE (2019): Allianz Global Wealth Report 2019, https://www.allianz.com/de/economic_research/publikationen/spezialthemen-fmo/GWR2019_18092019.html.

Further Reading

Forster, J., Klüh, U., & Sauer, S. (2014). *Makroökonomie – Das Übungsbuch*. Pearson Studium.

Frenkel, M., John, K. D., & Fendel, R. (2016). *Volkswirtschaftliche Gesamtrechnung* (8. Aufl.). Vahlen.

Miles, D., Scott, A., & Breedon, F. (2014). *Makroökonomie. Globale Wirtschaftszusammenhänge verstehen*. Wiley.

Olney, M. L. (2015). *Wiley Schnellkurs Makroökonomie*. Wiley.

Schröder, H. (2016). *Makroökonomie transparent vermittelt, VWL Grundlagen für Managementscheidungen*. Schröder Consulting.

Neoclassical Macroeconomic Model

> **What Follows Why?**
> After we have captured and explained the essential overall economic market trans-
> actions in the first chapter on the Macoeconomic Accounting, we now want to take
> a closer look at the markets on which these transactions take place. We will try to
> explain the essential economic relationships using the neoclassical overall model.
> This is an offer-oriented, long-term view, because in neoclassicism the markets are
> always in equilibrium. This corresponds to the normal case if the markets work.
>
> **Learning objectives**
> You should be able to
>
> - explain and apply the quantities and price mechanisms of the neoclassical mar-
>   kets.
> - explain why there is no demand problem in neoclassicism.
> - explain the relationships between money supply, price and real national product.

3.1   Marshall's Supply and Demand Cross

The Human Image

The predecessors of neoclassicism are classical:

With Adam Smith (1723–1790), an individualistic world view that emphasizes individual
freedom and responsibility also prevails in economic affairs, which allows the individual
to pursue his own interests. Division of labor increases productivity, a strict competition
prevents monopoly power. That the self-interest is realized in the context of competition
in the general economic interest (invisible hand) is the connecting idea of the classical
school (Fig. 3.1).

© The Author(s), under exclusive license to Springer Fachmedien Wiesbaden GmbH,
part of Springer Nature 2022
C. Conrad, *Applied Macroeconomics*. https://doi.org/10.1007/978-3-658-39315-1_3

Fig. 3.1 Law of increasing
marginal costs

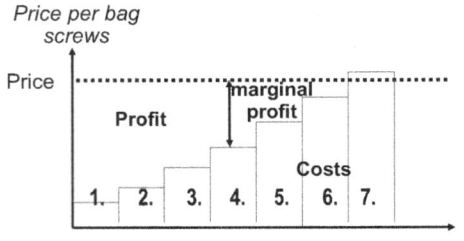

$$\text{Marginal cost} = \frac{\Delta \text{ Costs}}{\Delta \text{ Bags}} \quad (1. \text{ to } 7.)$$

▶ Marginal costs are the costs that arise from the production of an additional unit of a product.

The soils or machines or workers have different productivity. The producer will first use the production factor with a high productivity and then the next productive. Furthermore, the wear increases with a higher load or amount of production, so that the overall yield decreases with an increasing use of production factors.

How do entrepreneurs behave as market providers? Neo-classicism is based on micro-economics. What applies to a company also applies to all companies together. How the individual supply curves are aggregated into a total supply curve is shown in Fig. 3.3. The price is set by the market for the companies. They are quantity adjusters. The supply graph in the figure shows that companies increase their supply if the price is increased. They produce until the costs of the last additional unit of goods produced (increasing marginal costs, see Fig. 3.2) match the additional revenue for this good, i.e. the price. So the supply graph has a course from lower left to upper right (corresponds to the marginal cost curve), i.e. the opposite of the demand graph.

Company A produces more cheaply than B.

Fig. 3.2 Production behavior
of companies depending on
costs

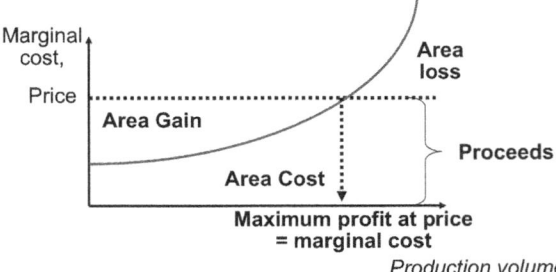

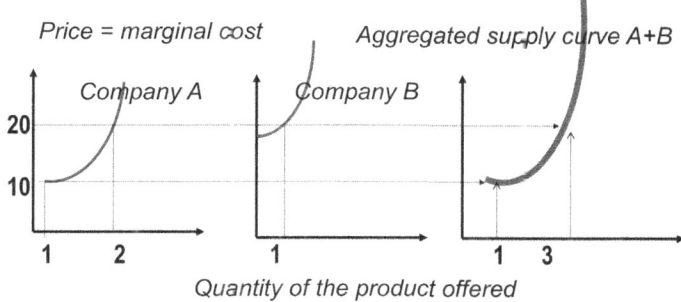

Fig. 3.3 Cost structure and aggregation of all companies (suppliers)

According to the marginal costs, the aggregate supply curve can be determined. The companies are lined up according to their production costs for an additional unit of goods and thus form the supply graph (see Fig. 3.3). Company A can produce one more unit of the product more cheaply than company B, i.e. company A has lower marginal costs. Company A produces more efficiently, i.e. cheaper than B, which is why A already offers a product at a price of 10. The companies are asked how many goods they offer at what price. At a price of 10 only A can produce without loss and only offers one product. Only at a price of 20 does company B also offer a good, because it produces here at a profit. A can produce two goods at a profit, so that a total of 3 goods are obtained.

Neoclassicism complements the cost-based or supply-oriented view with the utility-based or demand-oriented view with the law of diminishing marginal utility by Hermann Heinrich Gossen (1810–1858) (subjective or marginalist value theory):

$$\text{Marginal utility} = \frac{\Delta \text{ Benefit}}{\Delta \text{ Glasses}}$$

Neoclassicism: The Marginal Utility of the Buyer

The law of diminishing marginal utility states that the consumption of a good with increasing quantity always provides a smaller additional utility (marginal utility). The marginal utility of the buyer decreases (Fig. 3.4).

Example

The willingness to pay of a man dying of thirst in the desert for an additional glass of water decreases the more water he has drunk. The price is the opportunity cost, i.e. the opportunity utility, from another product that he could buy for the price in money units, which the customer has to forego if he spends the money for a glass of water. ◄

Fig. 3.4 Utility of an
additional glass of water

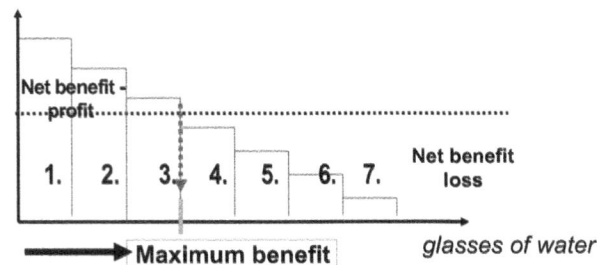

In this case, the price is given to the consumer. The consumer compares the loss of util-ity, which he has by giving away the money at the price in the form of non-consump-tion of other, purchasable goods (opportunity utility), with the utility gain by purchasing the good (water). As long as the additional utility from another glass (marginal utility) is higher than the loss of utility, he buys it. With the consumption, the marginal utility decreases until at point G* utility gain and opportunity cost are equal. This is an equilib-rium point: If the consumer consumed more, he would deteriorate because his net utility would be negative (Fig. 3.5).

The demand curve corresponds to the marginal utility curve (left top to right bottom).

In equilibrium G* it applies: The marginal utility from the last demanded unit is equal to the utility loss from the non-consumption of the alternative good, which the demander can now no longer buy (opportunity cost).

The demanders are lined up according to their additional utility when consuming another unit of goods, which corresponds to their willingness to pay in money units. As can be seen in Fig. 3.6, for example, person A values the good higher than person B, which can be seen in that he is willing to pay a higher price for the good. At a price of 20, A already demands a good, B only at a much lower price of 10. The lower the price, the more demanders have a marginal utility that is higher than the opportunity cost of consuming another alternative good, and consequently there are always more households that demand goods. The aggregate demand curve therefore runs from left to right bottom.

Fig. 3.5 Household demand
depending on price and utility

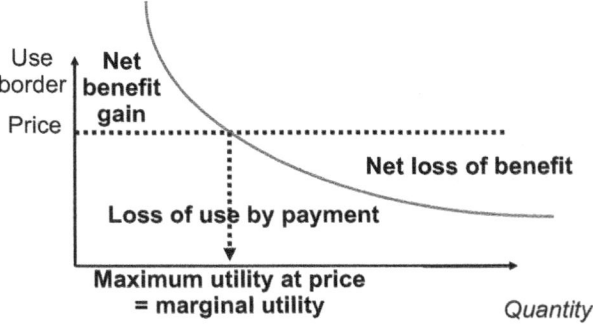

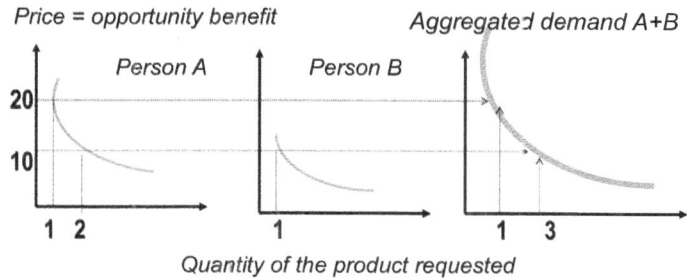

Fig. 3.6 Demand structure and aggregation to total demand

Normally, households only demand products until the marginal utility from this equals the price as a measure of the opportunity cost of other goods. However, in the neoclassical model there is only one good, so the opportunity cost from the price, i.e. the consumption, equals the utility from future consumption plus the interest as compensation for the waiting cost.

The model can be used as a general market model by aggregating the different production costs of the companies and the willingness to pay of the demanders. The approach of combining the aggregate marginal utility curve and the marginal cost curve to the supply and demand cross is due to Alfred Marshall (* 26 July 1842 in Bermondsey near London; † 13 July 1924 in Cambridge).

In the case of p* the following applies: Marginal utility, marginal payment willingness of the demander = price in monetary units = production marginal costs (Fig. 3.7).

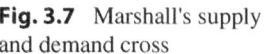 **Producer Surplus**
Difference between the price the seller of a good would like to achieve at least on the basis of his marginal costs and the actually received, higher market price.

▶ **Consumer Surplus**
Difference between the price the buyer of a good would be willing to pay at most on the basis of his marginal utility and the actually paid lower price in the market equilibrium.

Fig. 3.7 Marshall's supply and demand cross

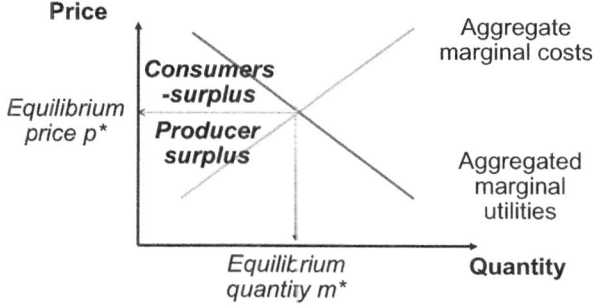

As long as there is no equilibrium price on the market, there is an imbalance either in the form of an excess supply or a demand deficit or in the form of a demand surplus or a supply deficit.

However, imbalances trigger processes again that lead back to equilibrium:

⇨Supply > Demand ⇨ Individual suppliers incur losses due to storage costs or lower revenues ⇨ Supplier reduces production ⇨ falling marginal costs ⇨ can offer cheaper ⇨ Market price and quantity offered fall, but at the same time the demand increases ⇨ Movement to market equilibrium.

Supply < Demand ⇨ Demanders compete for the scarce quantity, which causes prices to rise ⇨ This in turn attracts new suppliers and motivates all suppliers to produce more ⇨ offered quantity increases ⇨ at the same time some demanders withdraw due to rising prices ⇨ Movement to equilibrium.

The price mechanism ensures that the market is cleared.

Plans of suppliers and demanders are brought into correspondence by p by rationing the longer market side through the shorter (Fig. 3.8):

Plans of suppliers and demanders are brought into correspondence by p, p is also a signal for the new plans:

Due to the production cost differences of the companies as providers and the marginal utility differences of the consumers, there is always an equilibrium price at which the offered quantity exactly corresponds to the demanded quantity.

a) If the price were higher than the equilibrium price, there would be companies (see supply graph) that would offer at a lower price because their costs per additional unit offered would be lower (marginal costs). They could not sell their goods, so they would be rationed. They would then try to lure the consumers of the other companies with a lower offer price (competition) and thus lower the market price (see Fig. 3.9).

b) If the price were below the equilibrium price, there would be consumers with a higher marginal utility and thus a higher willingness to pay who would not get any goods (see demand graph). They would compete for the goods with the other consumers by bidding them. The price rises. This happens until the last consumer with a higher

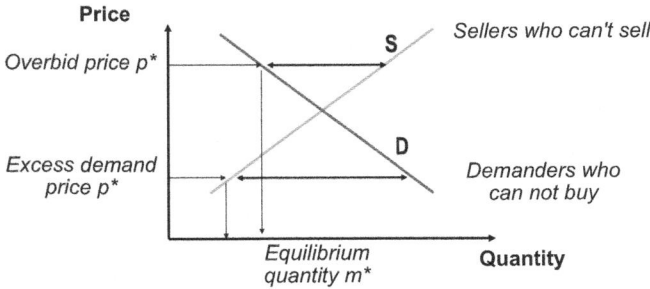

Fig. 3.8 Rationing of the market sides

Fig. 3.9 Stable market
clearing at the equilibrium
price

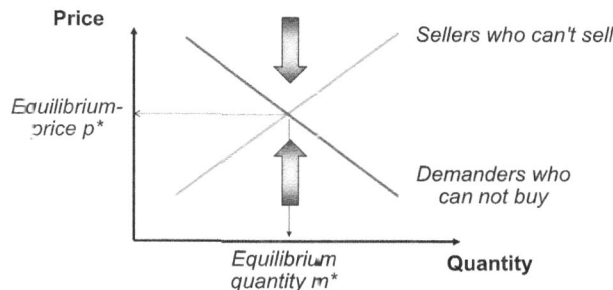

willingness to pay was satisfied. To satisfy the consumers, the production quantity
would have to be extended, thus simultaneously increasing the costs of the last additional unit produced. At the equilibrium price, the costs of the last unit produced then
correspond exactly to the willingness to pay of the last satisfied consumer. It applies:
The marginal utility corresponds to the price as an opportunity cost, which is equal to
the marginal costs. There is neither oversupply nor overdemand, the market is cleared.

Since the supply of goods is constant in the short term, the price is determined in the
short term by the demand, that is, the marginal utility, and in the long term by the costs
of the last used, least efficient production factors (enterprises, workers, machines, etc.).

3.2   The Companies

3.2.1   The Production Function

The assumptions of our model correspond to our simple circular flow model of the VGR.
    The **households** that appear as demanders on the **consumer goods market** are there-
fore striving to **maximize their utility** when realizing their consumption plans, while the
companies (U) offering consumer goods are striving for **profit maximization**.

▶ The **profits** (π) are determined as the **difference** between the **revenues** that can be
realized on the **consumer goods market** and the **costs** influenced by the conditions on
the **factor markets**.

The Production Function
In perfect competition (polypol), companies are quantity adjusters, the price is given to
them. Thus they expand production until marginal costs match the price. Y is the production of one year, which corresponds to the GDP, which becomes a corresponding income
(Fig. 3.10).

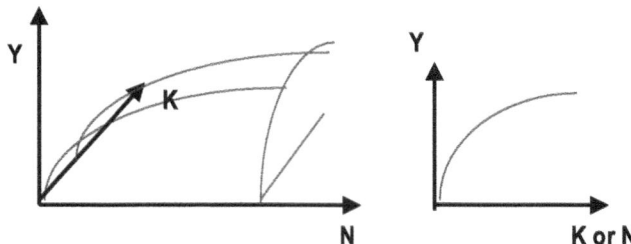

Fig. 3.10 The production function

<u>Cobb-Douglas production function $Y=aN^{\alpha}K^{1-\alpha}$</u>
(scale elasticities: α and $1-\alpha<1$ bzw. $\alpha+1-\alpha=1$)
Production factors:

1. Labor (N) as the sum of working hours
2. Capital (K): machines, buildings
3. Land (external, i.e. also exogenous=constant)

The Production Function
N and K can be used in any ratio (substitutability). 1) N and K are interdependent, but if one factor is kept constant, the additional return of the other factor decreases with its increase. Output increases, but disproportionately (law of diminishing marginal returns with partial factor variation). 2) And vice versa: if one factor is increased, this increases the marginal return of the other. Because the production factors N and K are interdependent. 3) If N and K are increased evenly, Y increases proportionally (constant scale returns).

The workers in Fig. 3.11 are manufacturing fans on an assembly line. Work and capital are mutually dependent. If we now keep the factor of capital constant and only increase the workers on the assembly line, the overall production will increase, but the additional income per additional worker will decrease, as the workers at one assembly line will increasingly hinder each other. There is less and less space for each worker and the assembly line cannot always run faster. This is the law of diminishing marginal productivity (marginal productivity) at constant other production factor. If we now ask, after we have increased the workers from 10 to 20, whether it is now worth it to buy a second assembly line to be able to use the 20 workers better, this will certainly be the case more than with the 10 workers as everyone still had enough space and could work optimally. This means that the marginal productivity of the second factor of capital has increased after the first factor, work, was increased (Fig. 3.12).

Everywhere positive, but decreasing slope, i.e.
declining first derivative and
negative second derivative

Fig. 3.11 Chinese assembly line workers

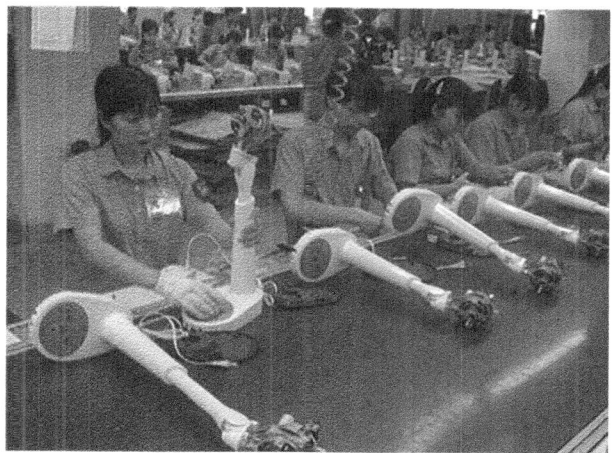

Fig. 3.12 Partial factor variation

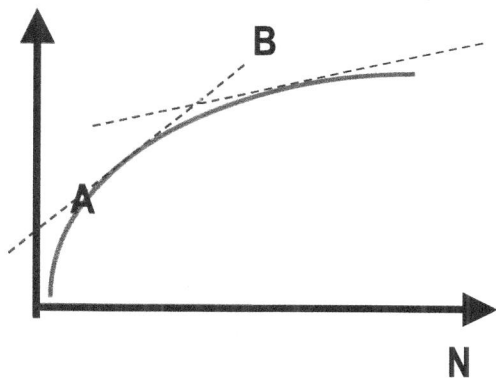

decreasing marginal productivity Y':

$$\frac{d\,Y}{d\,N} > 0 (1.\ Abl.)$$

Negative second derivative Y":

$$\frac{d^2\,Y}{d\,N^2} < 0 (2.\ Abl.)$$

In neoclassicism there are three submarkets, the capital market, the labor market and the goods market. The companies ask on the capital and labor market and offer on the goods market. In perfect competition, the companies are quantity adjusters, the price is given to them (Fig. 3.13).

Fig. 3.13 The marginal
product

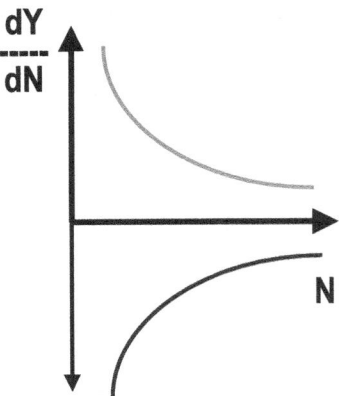

In the neoclassical model, the capital stock is short-term constant (one period): K =
const.

Expansions of capacity through investments only take effect after 1 year (= 1 period)
accordingly on the capital stock. This is a realistic assumption because the companies
first have to borrow the capital on the capital market. Then they have to buy the machines
and then also integrate them into the production process.

The companies want to maximize their profit π. Given the price and the use of the
two production factors labor N and capital K (I = investments, i = interest rate), we get
the following profit function:

The profit function thus results from the following consideration. How much work
(N) and capital (K) do the companies need to maximize their profit at a given price.

Profit = p • Y (revenues) – w • N (labor costs) – i • p • K (capital costs)

For the Profit π We Therefore Have:

$$\pi = p \cdot Y - w \cdot N - i \cdot p \cdot K$$
$$= p \cdot Y(N, K) - w \cdot N^D - i \cdot p \cdot K$$

with $I = K - K_0$; w = general nominal wage level, K = real capital expenditure in the
form of machines (corresponds to the capital stock of VGR).

Companies maximize their profits. We now want to analyze at which work input and
then at which capital input the profit function of the companies has its maximum. This
allows us to determine the labor demand and the capital demand of the companies. From
mathematics we know that the necessary condition for a maximum is that the first derivative is zero.[1]

---

[1] The second derivative is here smaller than zero, with which also the second, sufficient condition
for a maximum is fulfilled.

Partial derivative of π with respect to N:

$$\frac{d\pi}{dN} = p \cdot \frac{dY}{dN} - w \quad \overset{\text{necessary condition!}}{=} 0$$

This means that the condition for the profit-maximizing work input is:

Marginal product = real wage

$$\frac{dY}{dN} = \frac{w}{p}$$

Marginal product = real wage

$$p \cdot \frac{dY}{dN} \cdot (dN) = w \cdot (dN)$$

Marginal revenue = marginal cost

At which capital input does the profit function have its maximum?
   Partial derivative of π with respect to K

$$\frac{d\pi}{dK} = p \cdot \frac{dY}{dK} - i \cdot p = \overset{\text{necessary condition!}}{0}$$

This means that the condition for the profit-maximizing capital input is:

$$\frac{dY}{dK} = i$$

Marginal product = real interest rate

$$p \cdot \frac{dY}{dK} \cdot (dK) = i \cdot (dK) \cdot p$$

Marginal revenue = marginal cost

Companies maximize their profit by increasing their demand for labor until the additional output, valued at the market price (marginal revenue), equals the additional cost. Due to the diminishing marginal productivity of the factor labor, the additional output decreases. The additional costs (nominal wage w) remain the same. The same applies to the use of capital. Companies maximize their profit by increasing their demand for capital until the additional output, valued at the market price (marginal productivity), equals the additional cost. Due to the diminishing marginal product of the factor capital, the additional output decreases. The additional costs (nominal interest i · p, i is the real interest rate here) remain the same (Fig. 3.14).

   Companies keep asking for labor and capital until the real price of the production factor N and K (w/p, i) equals their additional real contribution, the marginal product.

   As a result, we have derived the demand of the companies for labor and capital. If we know the price of the production factor on the Y-axis, we can derive the corresponding demand of the companies that they make to come to their maximum profit. If, for example, the real wage falls at a given productivity of the factor labor, the companies

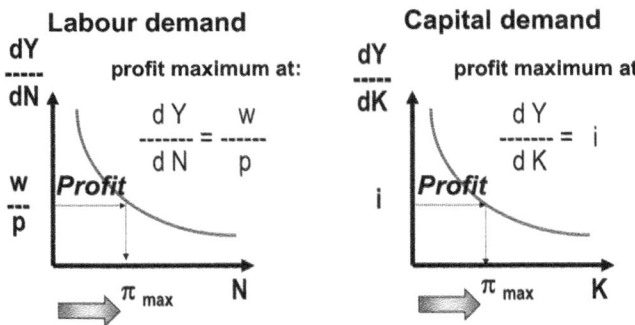

Fig. 3.14 The profit maximum

will extend the demand for labor until the condition of maximum profit is met again: marginal product of labor equals real wage (vice versa). Real is that the maximum profit is achieved when the marginal product of labor corresponds to the real wage w/p and the marginal product of capital corresponds to the real interest rate i. This means that as long as this condition is not yet met, the company can increase its profit by hiring more labor (capital). If the company hired more labor (capital) beyond this maximum condition, the marginal product would fall below the real wage (interest) and the company would make a loss.

1. Example:
   A bakery produces bread
   The price of a bread is 2 €
   A worker gets 20 € per hour wage (w = 20 €)
   The real wage w/p is then 10 breads per hour in breads.
   • Real the employer must give the employee 10 breads so that he works for the company.
   • As a result, the bakery owner would hire workers until the productivity of the worker has fallen to 10 breads per hour.
   • The employer sets the workforce as long as the general wage rule applies: real wage = marginal product.

When the employee begins his work at 8:00 a.m., he is rested and therefore productive. He produces 20 loaves of bread per hour. The more he works, the more tired he gets, which is why he produces 2 fewer loaves of bread in each subsequent hour. This reflects the law of diminishing marginal returns. As long as the marginal return is greater than the marginal cost in the form of the real wage, the bakery owner will continue to employ the employee. At 1:00 p.m., the employee's contribution to the bakery is just as high as what the employer has to pay him. Now the profit-maximizing condition marginal return equals real wage has been reached. If the employer were to continue to employ the

Time	dY/dN Breads (€)	w/p	dπ/dN	Production Y	Total wages	Total profit
8.00	20 (40€)	10 (20€)	10 (20€)	20	10 (20€)	10 (20€)
9.00	18 (36€)	10 (20€)	8 (16€)	38	20 (40€)	18 (36€)
10.00	16 (32€)	10 (20€)	6 (12€)	54	30 (60€)	24 (48€)
11.00	14 (28€)	10 (20€)	4 (8€)	68	40 (80€)	28 (56€)
12.00	12 (24€)	10 (20€)	2 (4€)	80	50(100€)	30 (60€)
13.00	10 (20€)	10 (20€)	0			
14.00	8 (16€)	10 (20€)	-2 (-4€)			
15.00	6 (12€)	10 (20€)	-4 (-8€)			

Fig. 3.15 Labor demand in a bakery

employee, he would realize a loss because he would have to pay the worker more than he earns from the employment (Fig. 3.15). For this reason, there can only be a "right to work" in socialism, because a private owner cannot be expected to engage in work at a loss, which is ultimately a waste of resources from a societal perspective.

It can be seen that the company has reached its maximum profit at 1:00 p.m. If the employer were to continue to employ the employee, he would make a loss with him. Therefore, a company cannot be forced to offer jobs. The owners would be expected to produce at a loss. If you want to create jobs, you have to try to make the work profitable. If it is worth it, the company will voluntarily demand work.

3.2.2   Case Study: Supply-Oriented Employment Policy

How can one achieve that the employee is employed for a longer period of time?

From the employer's point of view, there are only two reasons why he would employ the employee in his bakery for a longer period of time. Either the employee him per hour more or it costs him per hour less. Only then would he employ him longer than 1:00 p.m. In neoclassicism, employment depends only on two factors, the real wage and productivity (Fig. 3.16).

1. Real wage reduction

   If, for example, given the productivity of the factor of labor, the real wage decreases, the companies will expand the demand for labor until the profit maximization condition applies again: the marginal product of labor is equal to the real wage (vice versa) (Fig. 3.17).

   If the worker only demands 15 €, that is, 8 loaves of bread per hour, the employer will employ him for one hour longer, that is, until 2:00 p.m. However, the real wage reduction does not bring the worker higher earnings. On the contrary, the wage sum

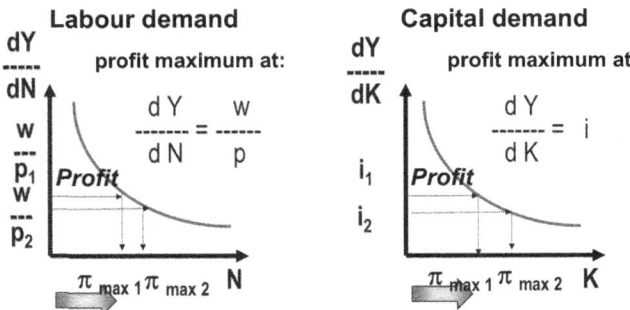

Fig. 3.16 Labor and capital demand

Time	dY/dN Breads (€)	w/p	dπ/dN	Produc- tion Y	Total wages	Total profit
8.00	20 (40€)	8 (16€)	12 (24€)	20	8 (16€)	12 (22€)
9.00	18 (36€)	8 (16€)	10 (20€)	38	16 (32€)	22 (44€)
10.00	16 (32€)	8 (16€)	8 (16€)	54	24 (48€)	30 (60€)
11.00	14 (28€)	8 (16€)	6 (12€)	68	32 (64€)	36 (72€)
12.00	12 (24€)	8 (16€)	4 (8€)	80	40 (80€)	40 (80€)
13.00	10 (20€)	8 (16€)	2 (4€)	90	48 (88€)	42 (84€)
14.00	8 (16€)	8 (16€)	0			
15.00	6 (12€)	8 (16€)	-2 (-4€)			

Fig. 3.17 Labor demand with falling real wages

decreases from 100 € to 88 €. This is because productivity falls so sharply that he is only employed for one hour longer, even though he has waived 10% of his wage.

2. Increased productivity

An increase in marginal revenue from 20 to 24 loaves of bread allows employment until 3:00 p.m. at the same real wage, with both the wage sum and the profit increasing.

Alternatively, the wage could increase to 24 €, that is, 12 loaves of bread. Then the productivity growth would match the wage increase, so no unemployment would result. This results in the wage increase rule for collective bargaining: wage increases should match productivity growth plus an inflation adjustment. If this rule is followed, wage increases cannot cause unemployment because labor does not become more expensive for the employer in real terms.

3.2.3   Case Study: Productivity in Germany

Interpretation

We have learned that the company always strives for the maximum profit and therefore the wage-setting rule marginal product equals real wage. For wage increases, there is therefore the "golden rule" that they should not be higher than the productivity plus an inflation adjustment. In Fig. 3.18 the unit labor costs, productivity and wages, ie w, are shown. If wages and productivity develop equally, unit labor costs do not change. If unit labor costs do not change, the competitiveness of products remains the same. What can be observed in Fig. 3.18? From 1991, wages rise more strongly than productivity, so that unit labor costs also rise. As a result, the competitiveness of Germany has deteriorated. How can this be explained?

At the beginning of the 1990s, there was a reunification boom in Germany. The state borrowed money to adjust the living conditions in East Germany to those in West Germany. As a result, there was a strong demand for goods and services and high wage increases, as companies were able to pass on the increased costs to consumers in the form of higher prices. When the reunification boom subsided, Germany was more

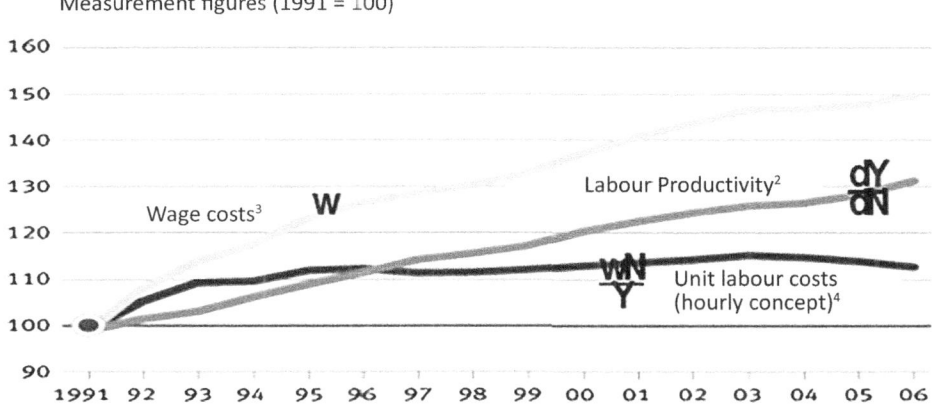

Domestic labour productivity, labour costs and unit labour costs[1]

Measurement figures (1991 = 100)

[1] Source for hours worked: Institute for Labour Market and Occupational.
     Research (IAB) of the Federal Employment Agency (BA). Nuremberg.
[2] Gross domestic product (price-adjusted) per hour worked.
[3] Compensation of employees per hour worked.
[4] Wage costs in relation to labour productivity

©Federal Statistical Office Germany 2007

Fig. 3.18 Productivity and wage costs in Germany. (Source: Federal statistical office, https://www.destatis.de/DE/ZahlenFakten/GesamtwirtschaftUmwelt/VGR/VolkswirtschaftlicheGesamtrechnungen.html)

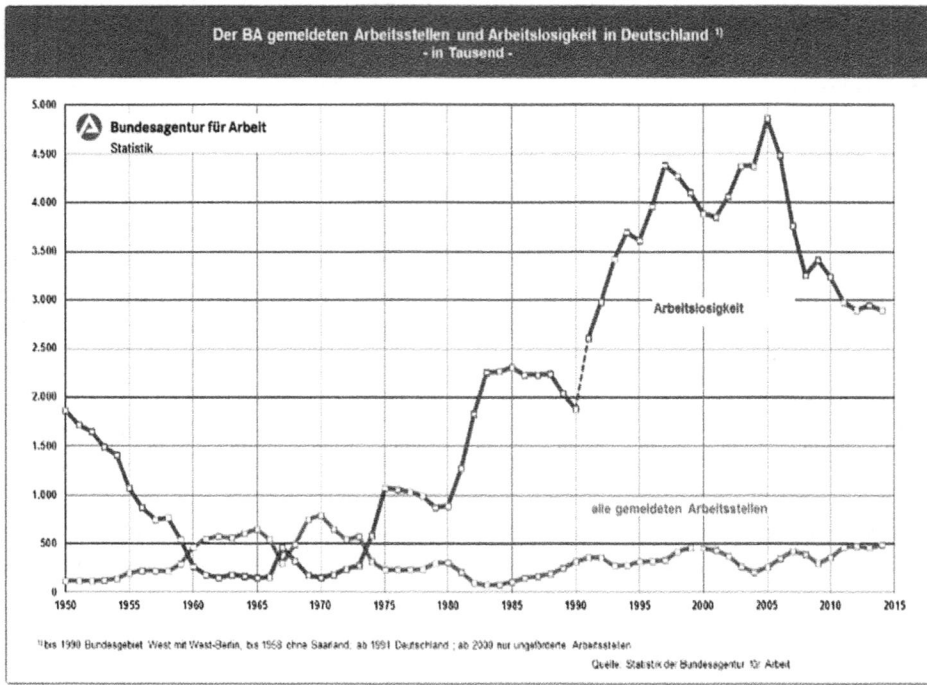

Fig. 3.19 Development of unemployment in Germany. (Source: Federal employment agency, https://statistik.arbeitsagentur.de/Navigation/Statistik/Statistische-Analysen/Analyse-in-Grafiken/Jaehrliche-Zeitreihen/Jaehrliche-Zeitreihen-Nav.html)

indebted and less competitive, which led to increased unemployment (see Fig. 3.19) and public finances ran into deficit. The then red-green government was forced to implement reforms. Only the Agenda 2010 at the beginning of the new millennium, coupled with restraint on the part of the trade unions in wage increases, levelled out the competitive disadvantage again. This led to falling real wages.

3.2.4 Case Study: Development of Real Wages

How can the development of real wages shown in Fig. 3.20 be explained?

Answer
The strong increase in real wages since 1800 can be explained by the increase in labor productivity caused by the industrial revolution. In combination with machines, work could produce more and more. The unions set higher wages in parallel to the increase in productivity, so that overall wealth and purchasing power increased. Later, the pro-

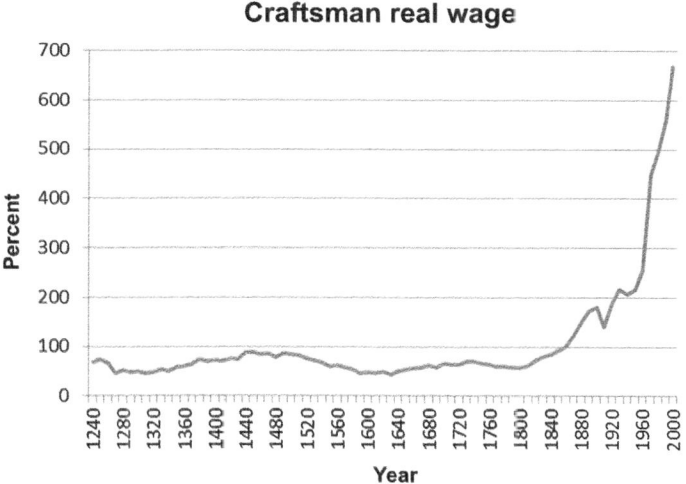

Fig. 3.20 Development of the real wage. (Numbers taken from Clark, Gregory, 2005)

ductivity of work increased as a result of better training. The released work could be used to produce product innovations, such as cars, so that the overall standard of living increased.

3.2.5 Case Study: The Plague and Factor Prices

The effects of different factor proportions can be seen well by the example of the effects of the plague in the Middle Ages.

Task

Explain the effects of the plague on income distribution using the properties of the Cobb-Douglas production function and the above-derived condition for a profit maximum.

In Europe, about one third of the population died from the effects of the plague, which broke out in 1348. At that time there was no machine production, but the second production factor next to labor were the agricultural soils. As a result of the lower amount of labor available, real wages increased significantly. According to estimates, it doubled. Inversely, rents for the land decreased by an estimated half. This means that the plague changed the income distribution between workers and landowners to the advantage of the agricultural workers.[2]

---

[2] See Mankiw, Gregory N. (2013, p. 70).

Answer

The plague has made agricultural workers much fewer. The factor of labor has fallen by a third. But the factor of land has remained the same. Therefore, the marginal product of labor increased. Each additional worker brought a much higher contribution to production than before, when more workers were on each field. This increased the demand for labor, so that real wages rose until it was again the case that the higher marginal product was equal to the increased real wages.

The marginal product is inversely related to the rents, because the production factor of labor has declined. If the fields can only be cultivated with fewer workers, they do not yield as much. The demand for land falls. The landlord would make a loss at the old rent, because the rent is higher than the marginal product that has fallen. Therefore, the rent falls until it is again the case: rent equals marginal product.

3.3   The Households

Households (HH) have three functions in the model:

1. They consume, i.e. they ask for goods on the goods market.
2. They offer their work on the labor market.
3. They save, i.e. they forego current consumption in order to offer capital on the capital market.

Households aim to maximize their utility. Their decision how much to consume, save and work depends solely on their preferences in relation to the opportunities (alternatives), i.e. the value as price, real wage and interest rate. Their decisions (plans) are coordinated across markets in the period as shown below.

Job Offer

Why does the household offer work? He has to make a living and would like to buy goods or earn interest by investing part of his income. Work is not fun for him, but it is a sacrifice for him. On the one hand, work is strenuous, on the other hand he has to forego leisure time to work. If he works 10 h a day, the rest of the leisure time becomes more valuable. The marginal utility of leisure increases. The utility of the real wage compensates the household for the marginal suffering of work or the alternative utility of leisure. With increasing real wages, the household's labor supply increases less than proportionally. The longer the household works, the harder it is for him. The marginal suffering of work increases when the work is extended. With increasing work effort, the marginal utility of leisure increases parallel to the marginal suffering of work.

As long as the marginal utility from the real wage is higher than the marginal suffering from work, the household increases its labor supply and thus maximizes its net utility. The households offer work until the marginal utility from the real wage just compensates the marginal suffering from work or is equal to the marginal utility from the alternative leisure. If the marginal suffering (or the marginal utility as the alternative leisure) increases to the marginal utility from the real wage, he is in the utility maximum. If he worked longer, he would deteriorate in utility (Fig. 3.21).

With increasing real wages, the household's labor supply increases:

Individual Maximum Benefit at

$$\frac{w}{p} = \frac{\text{marginal suffering of labor}}{d\,N} \quad \uparrow$$

There are many reasons to save, such as saving for retirement, or to prepare for future financial burdens or expenses like a home. Neoclassicism only recognizes one motive to save, interest. People save to have more resources in the future (interest). Otherwise, it would make more sense to spend income today, because then the benefit would be earlier. Today to forego the benefit of income in the form of purchasing goods, is a loss of benefit, the sacrifice of consumption. A precautionary or fear of saving, as we will later see with Keynes, does not exist in neoclassicism (Fig. 3.22).

Therefore, households only expand their supply of capital when interest rates rise, because the opportunity cost of future consumption increases. The interest compensates for the opportunity cost of an additional unit of consumption as a supply of capital. If they expand their supply of capital, the opportunity cost of current consumption rises disproportionately. This is the marginal benefit of current consumption, which the household has to forego as an opportunity cost. If someone saves 10% of an income of 2000 €, there is still enough for a good standard of living. If someone saves 30%, it becomes more difficult.

The more someone saves, the greater the marginal cost of consumption, because in this model only consumption provides a benefit. The opportunity cost of future consumption increases, which is why interest rates must rise if the supply of capital is to increase.

Fig. 3.21 The labor supply

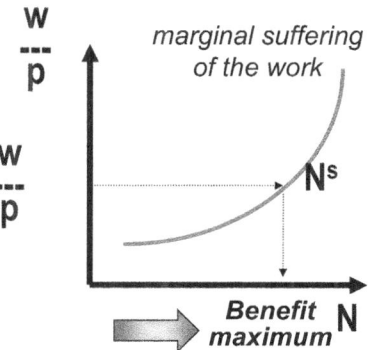

Fig. 3.22 Capital supply

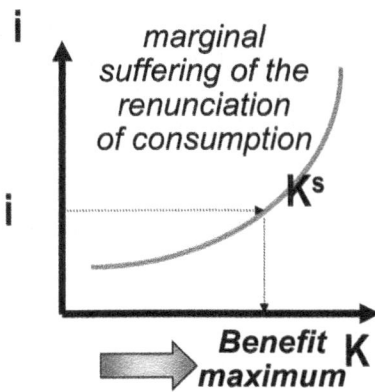

Households offer capital until the marginal benefit of interest is equal to the increasing opportunity cost of future consumption (or equal to the marginal benefit of the alternative of current consumption). Then they are at the maximum benefit:

Individual Maximum Benefit at

$$i = \frac{\text{marginal suffering of consumption renuciation}}{d\,K} \uparrow$$

The Budget Planning of Households
Households maximize their utility by adjusting their labor supply, consumption and saving to the market real wage and the real interest rate. The basis are their subjective preferences. They weigh the benefits of compensation and interest with the loss of temporary consumption and the border pain of work. The household plans consumption and saving (capital supply) in relation to interest and its labor supply in relation to the real wage.

With consumption and saving, the household plans the use of income. The higher the interest rate, the more is saved and the less is consumed. In parallel, he must consider where he gets the income from, that is, plan the income generation. Possible here are the income types work (wages), interest as capital income and the profit from a business involvement. We speak of a budget restriction, because he can only use the income he has previously generated ($\mathbf{B^0}$ (Bonds) = securities at time 0, (+) = positively dependent on):

$$\mathbf{P \cdot C(i) + P \cdot S(i) = w \cdot N^s(w/p) + i \cdot \left(B^0 + P \cdot S(i)\right) + p}$$
$$(-) \qquad (+) \qquad\qquad (+) \qquad\qquad\qquad (+)$$

Income usage = Income creation

The household wants to generate an income of 100 €. At an interest rate of 5%, he wants to save an additional 10 €, which increases the income accordingly. He wants to consume 90 €. He has 190 € as assets (securities), which, together with the saved 10 €, add up to a capital of 200 € and at an interest rate of 5% lead to an interest income of 10 €. At the given real wage, he would have to work 80 € and he would get 10 € in profit income. This results in the following budget restriction:

$$90 \text{ €} + 10 \text{ €} = 80 \text{ €} + 5 \text{ \%} \cdot (190 \text{ €} + 10 \text{ €}) + 10 \text{ €} \blacktriangleleft$$

3.4   Capital and Labor Market

After we have derived labor supply and demand as well as capital supply and demand, we now want to focus on the markets.

Labor Market

How does the equilibrium process come about? The markets bring the plans of households and the labor demand and capital demand plans of businesses into alignment through the price mechanism. The plans of suppliers and demanders are brought into alignment by the price of labor (w/p).

a) If the real wage is higher than the equilibrium real wage, there are households (see supply graph) that offer at a lower real wage because their benefit from the real wage per additional work unit offered would be higher than the marginal disutility of work or vice versa the leisure foregone. At the high real wage they cannot sell their work, they will therefore be rationed. They will then try to undercut other workers with a lower real wage (competition) and thus lower the real wage (see Fig. 3.23).

b) If the real wage is below the equilibrium real wage, there are companies as demanders with a higher marginal productivity and thus also a higher willingness to pay, which have not received any workers (see demand graph). They will compete for the

Fig. 3.23 Equilibrium mechanism on the labor market

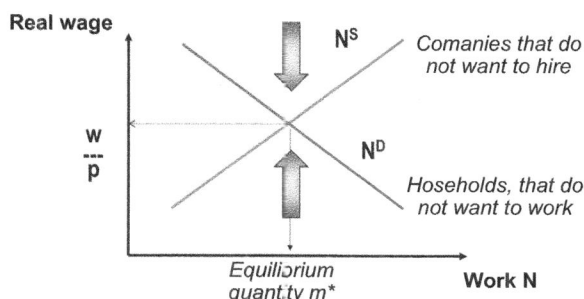

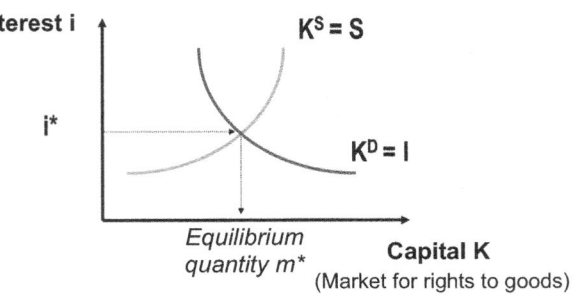

Fig. 3.24 The capital market

workers with the other demanders by outbidding them. The real wage rises. This happens until the last company with a higher willingness to pay has been served. The amount of work increases, with the marginal product (the productivity) of the last worker hired falling at the same time. At the equilibrium real wage, the marginal product of the last worker hired then corresponds to the equilibrium real wage, with the companies being in the profit maximum. The equilibrium real wage corresponds exactly to the benefit that is necessary as compensation for the disutility of work or the leisure foregone so that the last worker hired is willing to work. There is neither oversupply nor overdemand, the labor market is cleared.

Due to the different preferences of households as providers and the marginal producer orientation of companies as demanders, a labour market equilibrium price always arises, at which the quantity offered corresponds exactly to the quantity demanded.

Capital Market
Households forego spending part of their income. They save and offer this money to companies on the capital market. Companies ask for capital for their investments (Fig. 3.24).

The market price mechanism also applies to the capital market. If the interest rate is too high, there are companies that do not want to borrow this capital because the marginal product of capital is lower. On the other hand, there is an oversupply of capital because many households have a higher utility from the high interest rate than the utility loss from later consumption. Since they cannot lend their capital due to the oversupply, they lower the interest rate until they no longer have any additional utility from lending to companies. The marginal pain of foregone consumption then corresponds to the marginal utility from the interest rate as compensation for the waiting cost of later consumption (Fig. 3.25).

In the following, we want to bring the markets together into the neoclassical overall model. So far, we have derived the labour market and the capital market. The goods market results as a third market, as a residual variable.

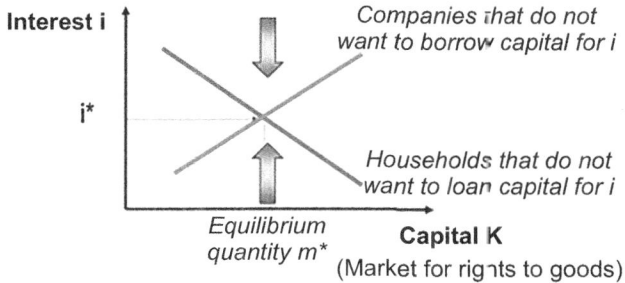

Fig. 3.25 Market price mechanism on the capital market

3.5   The Real Sector

Except for the nominal wage w, all real variables are quantities of goods. The nominal wage is divided by the price level and thus becomes the real wage, which is why we speak of the real sector. If the markets are in equilibrium, all plans are implemented and the planned supply meets the planned demand:

$$Y^S(N^*) = I(i^*) + C(i^*) = Y^D$$

Goods market: In order to maximize their profits, companies expand their production and demand for labor until the factor costs, i.e. the real wage, are equal to the marginal product. The same applies to the capital market, where they demand capital until the interest rate is equal to the marginal product of capital. The decision of households on how much they consume, save and work depends solely on their preferences in relation to the opportunities (alternatives), i.e. the utility from real wage and real interest rate. Real wages and interest rates are therefore formed according to the preferences of households and the marginal products of labor and capital. At the beginning of the period, the household sets its plans for the period for consumption and saving (the supply of capital) depending on the interest rate and its labor supply depending on the real wage. The decisions (plans) of households are implemented or limited at the end of the period, i.e. coordinated. The same applies to the plans and decisions of companies. While they base their profit maximization on the productivity (marginal products) of the production factors labor and capital, the price is set for them by the market, i.e. also by the supply of households.

Households only offer as much work as they also want to consume and save. The equilibrium in the capital market is also formed by the price mechanism, so that just as much capital is demanded for investments by entrepreneurs as households save, i.e. forego consumption. Simultaneous equilibrium is established (Fig. 3.26).

If all markets are cleared, there is a simultaneous equilibrium. In our case, this means that if the labor market and the capital market are in equilibrium, the goods market is

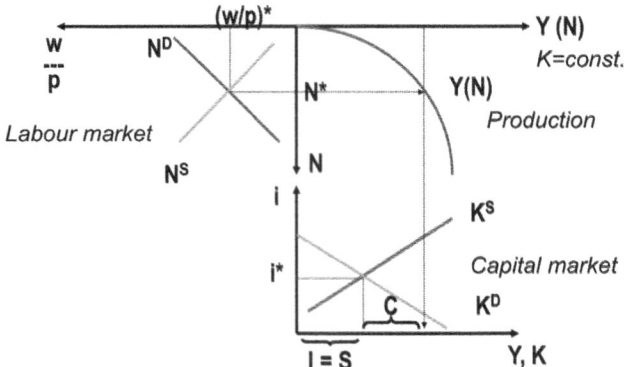

Fig. 3.26 The real sector

also in equilibrium. Savings create a demand shortfall because households no longer demand their entire income. Since income is equal to the same high production, savings create part of the un-demanded. At the equilibrium interest rate i*, households save exactly as much as companies want to invest and therefore consume the rest of their income, which they can achieve in the planned amount through their labor supply in the equilibrium real wage w/p*. Since by the capital market equilibrium as much is saved, that is, demand falls as is invested, thus additional demand arises, the demand shortfall is offset. By the same high additional demand of companies for capital and thus also for investments, as much demand arises as there is supply. The goods market is cleared (see Fig. 3.27). The capital market ensures the balance of demand and supply in the goods market. If the capital market is in equilibrium, the goods market is also in equilibrium. And in neoclassicism, due to the functioning market mechanism, always an equilibrium arises.

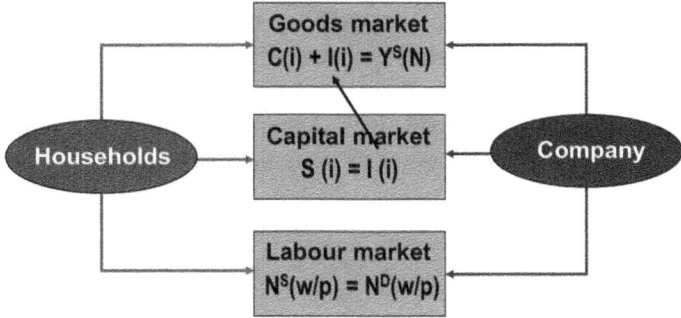

Fig. 3.27 Markets and actors of the neoclassical total model

Excursus

How is it in practice? If you as a household invest your saved money in a bank and want interest for it, the bank will lend it on. Otherwise ro interest can be earned. The bank lends the money to the companies that use this money to finance their investments, i.e. they order machines. You can also invest your money directly in the stock market and buy a corporate bond.

The goods produced during the year are available to the economy. In the process of production, incomes arise to the same extent, because—as we have seen—each transaction has two sides, income and expenditure side. The companies produce and pay for their production factors. The employees working in the company receive an income. All inputs are also goods that have to be produced. Here too, incomes arise for the employees. Both together are referred to as production costs, what remains is the profit. The profit, as we have seen, is also an income of households. Entrepreneurs or owners of companies receive it as so-called residual income (residual income). This also means that the profit can only be consumed or saved, which either creates demand or eliminates demand. All savings together then represent a waiver of shares in the annual production to which the employees or capital providers would have been entitled from their participation in the production. This production is then available for the additional demand from the entrepreneurs for investments. Without savings, none of the production would be left, as all value added would be used for consumption. If, on the other hand, savings are made, parts of the production can be used in the so-called investment goods industry to produce goods such as machines, without which there would be no productivity gains and thus no growth.

Figure 3.27 shows this relationship graphically. The drop in demand for consumption is equal to the savings of households, since households can either save or consume their income. In the capital market, the interest rate always creates a balance between savings, i.e. the supply of capital, and the demand for capital, i.e. investments, as part of the market mechanism. Thus, investments are equal to savings. In addition, investments by companies represent demand that exactly offsets the drop in demand for savings due to the market balance in the capital market.

Alternatively, one can also use the law of supply and demand: If two of three markets are in equilibrium, the third market is also in equilibrium. This means that all markets are cleared.

Exercise

We now want to calculate the theoretically derived profit maximization condition in an application example. We want to determine the demand for labor and the demand for capital of the company. The companies ask for profit maximization. The question is: at which labor input and which capital input is the profit maximum reached? The production function of our company is:

$$Y(N, K) = N^{3/4} + K^{1/2}.$$

Furthermore, let $p = 8$, $w = 2$ and $i = 10\%$.

Calculate the demand for labor, the demand for investment and the supply of goods assuming that the initial stock $K_0 = 9$.

3.6   The Saysche Theorem

The Saysche Theorem states:

Every supply creates its own demand!

Reason

We recall the accounting equation of GDP in the Macroeconomic Accounting. Anyone who wants to offer must produce and thus ask for inputs, that is, goods and services. This creates demand. The services generate income. What remains is the profit that is distributed to the entrepreneurs, that is, also available as income. Income can be consumed or saved. Consumption is also demand. Nobody offers work if he cannot pursue goals with the income. Either he wants to buy goods or earn interest through savings. What is saved is indeed a demand shortfall, but it is invested on the capital market due to the interest. There the companies get into debt and take the capital for their investment demand. The demand for machines is again demand, so that the offer creates its own demand to 100%.

Restriction

However, this only applies if money, that is, purchasing power, is not hoarded. This makes no sense in neoclassicism, because then one would have to forego the interest on the capital investment.

We come to the decisive question of macroeconomics, which always concerns people: What is more important, demand or supply? Every business economist will instinctively answer that demand is more important because he cannot sell anything without demand. But he assumes that the buyers can also pay the demand. For this purpose, supply is required. So that we can finally say that the supply is more important and neoclassicism is the general theory. Or, in other words, neoclassicism is to be applied as a theoretical basis when the economy is in the normal situation.

We have to explain this in a little more detail. Let's imagine a one-man economy. Robinson has to provide for himself, to satisfy his own needs. In other words, he produces a supply to meet his own demand. To do this, he hunts game and catches fish. Now Friday comes along and the first division of labor is created. Now Friday catches fish while Robinson specializes in hunting. In the evening they exchange their food. Both offer their products and ask for those of the other. Both have the basic needs for food, but only if they produce their own offer can they also pay for their own needs, their own demand. If Friday did not catch any fish, he would have nothing to trade for Robinson's game.

Then it has to be asked whether Robinson and Friday are contentedly happy on the island. One could philosophize about this for a long time. Objectively, however, they still lack a lot to lead a life in modern luxury. The standard of living has continuously increased in the Western industrial nations and yet the people are not contentedly happy and will probably never be, because their needs grow with their fulfillment. If we have bought something we have been longing for a long time, our feeling of happiness does not last long and we soon think about what we want to buy next. We hold on to this:

Human needs are infinitely great, the question is whether one can afford one's own demand, that is, pay for it. So there was no demand problem in the Greek crisis either. Greece was simply unable to pay for its demand due to the lack of competitive supply. Wages and prices rose so sharply after the introduction of the euro that, for example, many vacationers who used to go to Greece switched to Turkey. Greeks became unemployed and could no longer satisfy their needs due to lack of income. Demand was there, but not affordable. There is, as with Friday without fish, the offer to trade.

3.7   The Money Market

Classical Functions of Money

Money plays a central role in a market economy. We know that the functions of the market are price formation and exchange. They would not be possible without money. In the 18th century, money consisted of precious metal coins. There was no fiduciary money yet. There are a total of three classical functions.

1. Unit of account and <u>means of payment</u>
   Without money there would be no prices. The average price level is the ratio between the money supply and the amount of goods. It applies:
   $P = M/Y$, where M is the money supply (Money) and Y is the gross domestic product. Unless there is gold coverage, the value of money is also determined solely by the purchasing power of domestic products, that is, the value one gets for money in goods.
   Without a single currency, one could not express the exchange relations of goods with each other. If, for example, there were no money in an economy with 10^6 (1 million) goods, one would have to know about 500 billion relative prices, that is, exchange relations of goods. The relative prices express the exchange relation:

$$\frac{P_1}{P_2} = \frac{10\,€}{20\,€} = {}^1\!/_2 \text{ also 2 zu 1 (exchange relation)}$$

As a result, prices enable a universal exchange relation between goods.

Prices, as a scarcity indicator, are the basis for resource allocation, that is, the production control. They show entrepreneurs profit and loss potentials. The prices are also the prerequisite for competition. Without them, the consumer would not be able to compare the goods.

2. Payment and exchange media

Money enables the skipping of exchange levels. Without money, one would always have to offer a good that the trading partner needs themselves for a trade. For example, if a farmer wanted to trade potatoes for clothing and the tailor didn't want potatoes, but needed shoes, no trade would take place. With money, however, the tailor could buy the shoes (transaction motive).

Furthermore, money enables a reduction in transport costs. It can be transported more cheaply than the goods one would have to trade in return.

For example, if one wanted to buy tea in China, it would be cheaper to do so with gold coins than with the cows that the Chinese want to buy with the money. The transport costs for the cows were much higher than for the gold coins.

3. Value storage means (-function)

The value storage function is a very important function. Without it, every economic system collapses. What would you be willing to trade for worthless money? What would economic actors do with their income if they knew that it would only be worth half as much next year as money. They would spend it, so they wouldn't save. Saving (and financing investments through the capital market) is only possible if money does not lose value. Money does not spoil like many goods. You can lend it and get the same value back later, possibly even in the last stage of life as a private pension.

In the neoclassical model, P is the price of good Y as gross domestic product, i.e. the average price of all goods, i.e. their exchange ratio to money. Simply put: $P = M/Y$ At the so-called money market, money supply and demand meet ($\neq$ bank money market). In neoclassicism, money is only a veil and does not influence the real economy, because economic actors only orient themselves to real quantities.

Money is a veil[3].
Arthur Cecil Pigou

Case Study: Money Functions in a Prisoner of War Camp[4]

In the prisoner of war camps of the Second World War, the prisoners had no money to exchange goods. They wanted to exchange, for example, chocolate for shirts, soap or a comb. They used cigarettes to trade. The same could be observed on the black markets in civilian life. The German money had become worthless. All products

---

[3] Pigou, Arthur Cecil (1949), The Veil of Money, London 1949.
[4] See Mankiw, N. Gregory (2000, p. 180).

that could be purchased could be paid for with dollars but also with cigarettes. So the goods had a price in cigarettes. Cigarettes thus took over the functions of storing value, accounting and exchange.

Question: Why were cigarettes used as a means of payment in addition to the dollar? Would cigarettes assume these functions again in a similar situation today? What is your assessment?

The Money Market

The offer is given by M. The central bank controls the money supply. We need money to buy goods, i.e. for our transactions. What determines the demand for money? For the demand for money for transaction cash L we have:

$$L = k \cdot p \cdot Y \text{(Cambridge Equation)}$$

People want to use money to buy goods, which is why we also refer to the demand for money as the demand for money for transactions, i.e. the demand for transaction cash. What influences this demand?

To the extent that money is needed for exchange purposes (L_T) (liquidity), the need, i.e. the demand, depends on the value of the production volume to be exchanged (Y) and the cash holding coefficient (-duration) k based on the payment habits of the public.

If there are more goods, the demand for money also increases, because otherwise people would not be able to buy or pay for the goods. The same applies if the price level rises, because then more money is needed to implement the planned real purchases of goods. This is therefore a behavioural explanation.

The cash holding duration k increases the more people assess the probability of getting money again or the more expensive money is to obtain. k is the cash holding coefficient, i.e. the average cash holding duration in years, i.e. how long economic subjects hold their money, e.g. ¼ year, i.e. 3 months ($k = ¼$). The more they hold in cash for transactions (purchases), the higher the demand for money. If, for example, they want all the money for the expenses of one year in their pocket, $L = 1 \cdot P \cdot Y$, also $L = Y_{nominal}$ applies.

Example

If Y is the per capita annual production or income in units of money, 3600, one would need to have 3600 units of money in one's pocket in order to be able to pay for expenses. In that case, k would be equal to 1 and the money demand would be 3600. The money would be held in one's pocket for one year. However, if there is an ATM around the corner from which one can withdraw money every day without much effort, then $k = 1/360$. That is, the money would only be held in one's pocket for one day. ◀

Quantity Equation or the Fisher Equation

Conversely, the so-called quantity equation (or Fisher equation) explains the quantitative relationship between the money supply, its velocity of circulation, and the price level and domestic product:

$$\mathbf{M \cdot v = Y \cdot p}$$

▶

M	Money supply

▶

M/p	Real cash. It measures the purchasing power of the existing volume of money

---

Example

If the money supply is 10 € and a loaf of bread costs 0.5 €, then the real cash is 20 loaves of bread, because 20 loaves of bread can be bought with the money supply. ◀

▶

v	Velocity of money circulation speed of money: how often in the year the economic subjects spend their money, or how often a € is spent in a year (reciprocal value or inverse of k). To spend a year's income, you need the same amount of money. I.e. if households want to keep less money in their pockets for their expenses because they get new money all the time, less money is needed
	For example, during the financial crisis, the circulation speed of money decreased because people spent less money and fewer loans were granted

---

Example

Transaction cash holding at $v = 4$

$$\mathbf{M \cdot v = Y \cdot p}$$

i.e. if $Y = 100$, $P = $ const. (1) and $v = 4$ ($k = 1/4$), this results in a money supply of 25. $M = 25$, $Y = 100$, cash holding duration, $12/4 = 3$ months on average ($v = 4$) ◀

According to the quantity theory, nominal GDP is therefore proportional to the money supply. If the quantity equation is formulated as percentage changes, the following results (Fig. 3.28):

M %+v %=p %+Y % (percentage changes).

If the other variables remain constant, this thus determines the growth rate of the money supply, and hence the monetary policy of the central bank, also determines the inflation rate (sustained rise in the price level).

Fig. 3.28 Transaction cash holding at v = 4

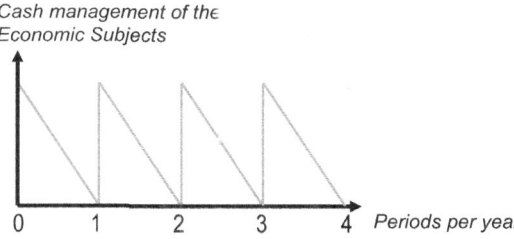

Fig. 3.29 Ten-Year Historical Average Money Supply Growth and Inflation in the U.S.A. (Friedman/Schwartz, chart based on Mankiw, N. Gregory, Makroökonomie, Stuttgart 2000, p. 189)

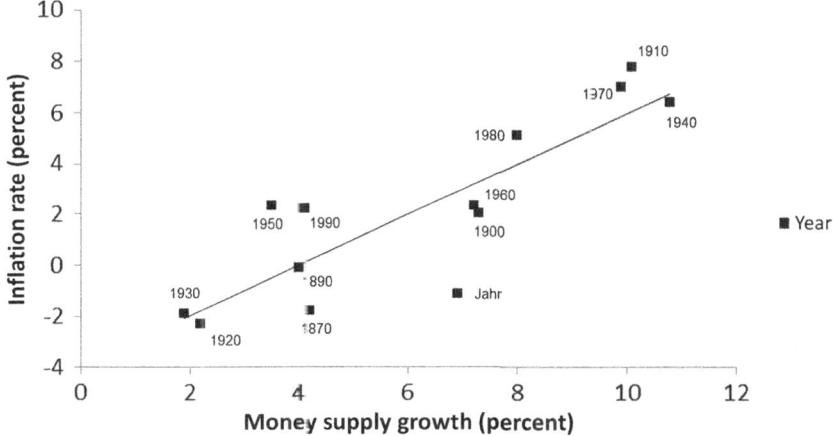

Inflation is always and everywhere a monetary phenomenon.
Milton Friedman[5]

The value of money—unless there is a gold standard—is determined only by its purchasing power, that is, the amount of goods in the GDP opposed to the money (Fig. 3.29).

You can see the connection between money supply growth and inflation with the naked eye. It is basically significant. Money supply growth leads to inflation. The demanders compete for the scarce goods. If they have more money available for the same amount of products, they will offer more to get the product. Since everyone has more money, they offer each other high until the higher price level restores the old money-goods ratio in the quantity equation: $M\%\uparrow + v\% = P\%\uparrow + Y\%$, where $v\%$ and $Y\%$ are zero.

---

[5] "Inflation is always and everywhere a monetary phenomenon." Quoted from Mishkin, Frederic S. (1984).

Fig. 3.30 The monetary
sector

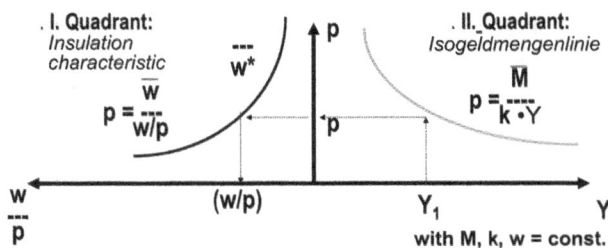

with M, k, w = const.

We can now add the monetary sector to our overall model. In the I. Quadrant is the isoline as a line that indicates what real wage results from the respective price level (and vice versa).

The money market is in the II. Quadrant. Here money supply and money demand meet. The money supply is given by M by the central bank. The money demand results from the Cambridge equation L = k p Y. The iso-money supply line indicates with the Cambridge equation at which price the respective gross domestic product results M = p k Y. The price level is always in equilibrium between money supply and money demand (Fig. 3.30).

We can now summarize the so-called neoclassical overall model.

3.8   The Neoclassical Overall Model

It is a simultaneous equilibrium on all markets, that is, all plans of households and firms are fulfilled after they have been adjusted via the price mechanism. On all markets, the following applies: Supply = demand (Fig. 3.31).

I.   Quadrant: Isolohnlinie, $p = w/(w/p)$
II.   Quadrant: Isogeldmengenlinie, Geldmarkt: $M = pkY$ bzw.

$$p = M/(k \cdot Y)$$

III. Quadrant: Arbeitsmarkt, $N^S(w/p) = N^D(w/p) \Rightarrow N^*(w/p^*)$
IV. Quadrant: Produktion, $Y^S = Y^S[N(w/p)^*]$
V.   Quadrant: Kapitalmarkt, $S(i^*) = I(i^*)$

There is the so-called **dichotomy.** This means that the real sector is independent of the monetary sector (Fig. 3.32) (see also Siebe & Wenke, 2014; Blanchard, 2014; Blanchard & Illing, 2006; Wagner & Böhne, 2003; Felderer & Homburg, 2005; Drost et al., 2003; Mankiw, 2013; John, 2004 as well as Mussel, 2009).

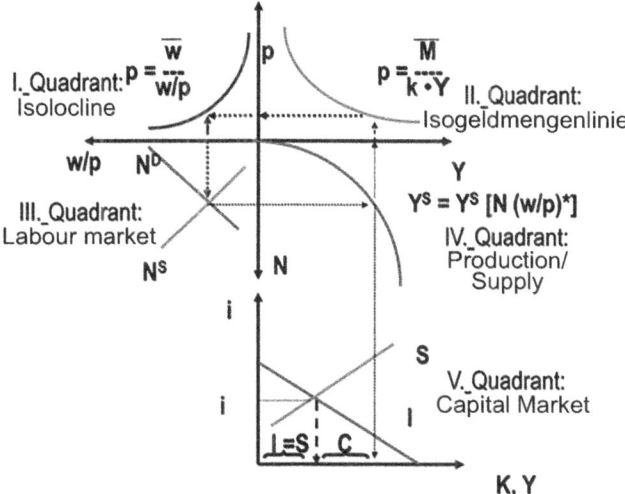

Fig. 3.31   The overall model

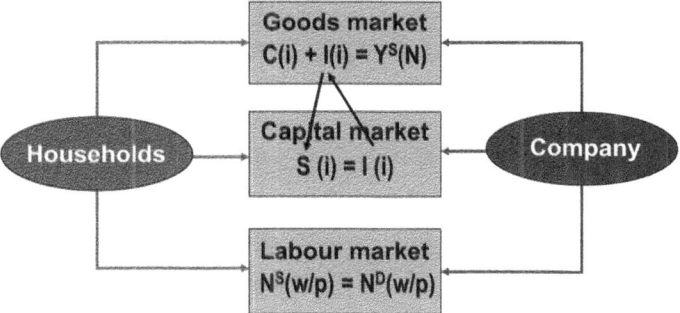

Fig. 3.32   The simultaneous equilibrium

Summary

1. In order to maximize profits, companies expand their production until factor costs, which are real wages and interest, are equal to the marginal product. Real wages and interest are formed according to the preferences of households and the marginal productivity of capital and labor.
2. Say's theorem states that supply creates its own demand. Whoever wants to offer has to produce and thus demand inputs. Income is generated. What remains is the profit, which is invested or consumed just like income.

3. In neoclassicism, the price mechanism provides simultaneous equilibrium in all markets.
4. Money serves as a value storage, a unit of account and a means of exchange.
5. According to the quantity theory, nominal GDP ($p \cdot Y$) is proportional to the money supply. Consequently, the growth rate of the money supply also determines the inflation rate.
6. In neoclassicism, money has no influence on the real sector (dichotomy). ◄

Questions for Understanding

1. How do real wages and interest rates as well as the marginal product of labor and capital change if
   a) Given a fixed capital investment, an immigration wave increases the number of employed persons?
   b) Given a fixed capital investment, the plague decreases the number of employed persons?
2. How do real wages and interest rates as well as the optimal amount of capital and labor employed by firms change if a war (e.g. World War in Germany) destroys part of the capital stock?
3. How does the installation of ATMs affect the velocity of money?
4. Which of these three functions of money are fulfilled by the following objects and which are not?
   a) A house
   b) An old rare stamp
   c) Gold coins

Exercise Questions

1. Draw the neoclassical overall model and explain why it must be in simultaneous equilibrium.
2. The central bank increases the money supply by 15%, much more than the real growth of 7%. If you know that the velocity of money remains constant, you can calculate the inflation rate. What is the real interest rate if the nominal interest rate is 13%?

3.9   Economic Policy in the Neoclassical Model

What Follows Why?
After we have analyzed the functioning of the neoclassical model, we now want to draw specific conclusions for the economic policy of a government from this.

Learning objectives
You should be able to explain the possibilities of the state to influence the economic development in the neoclassical model with their effects.

There are four forms of state intervention:

1. Monetary policy: Change in the money supply by the central bank
2. Technology policy by government research funding
3. Fiscal policy: taxes and government spending
4. Wage policy: Change in wages by the state (or the unions)

1. Monetary Policy
Dichotomy:

$$1.\ M \uparrow = k \cdot p \uparrow \cdot Y\,(\text{or } M \uparrow \cdot v = Y \cdot p \uparrow),$$

$$\text{mit } k, v = \text{konst.}, \quad \Rightarrow\ w/p \text{ and } M/p = \text{konst.}$$

Let's assume the central bank increases the money supply (see Fig. 3.33). An increase in the money supply leads to inflation, which actually means that the real wage decreases in Quadrant I. If the money supply is changed, the price level adjusts according to the quan-

Fig. 3.33 Monetary policy

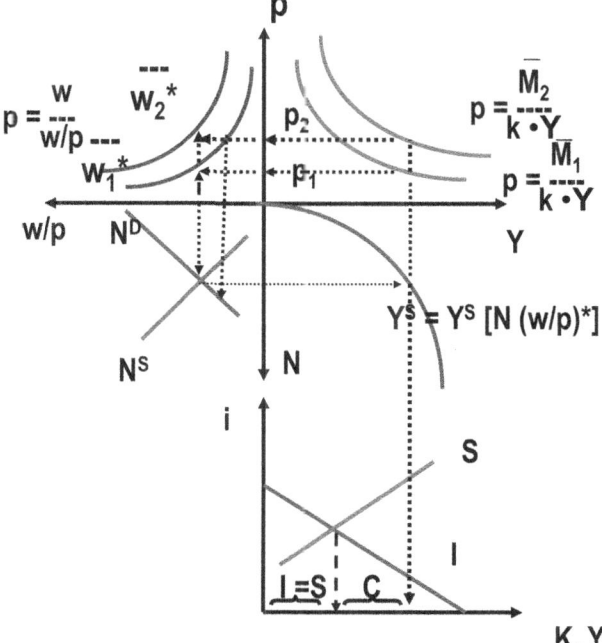

tity equation in Quadrant II. The price of bread, for example, doubles from 2 € to 4 €. In our standard example, the nominal wage is 20 € per hour. Before, the worker could buy 10 loaves of bread for his hourly wage, but now only 5. The workers notice this. They are not subject to money illusion in neoclassicism. They are not willing to work for half the wage. The compensation for the disutility of work is only half as large. On the other hand, the firms demand much more work. In our example, they would ask the worker in the bakery to work until 3:30 p.m. There is a short-term over-demand for labor on the labor market. Since the employers cannot cover their demand for labor at the nominal wage, they increase it until the old real wage of 10 loaves of bread is reached again. The nominal wage will therefore increase to 40 €. Then the old real wage of 10 loaves of bread is reached again.

If, on the other hand, the money supply decreases, this means deflation and falling wages, since firms adjust according to the real wage. The workers are then willing to work for a lower nominal wage. Consequently, no effects flow from the monetary sector to the real sector. The dichotomy applies.

On the contrary, economic actors have to adjust to new prices and wages. First, the real wage decreases and less is produced because the labor supply decreases. Then the nominal wage increases again until the old equilibrium real wage is reached. This creates adjustment costs and irritation.

2. Technical Progress at Work (Technology Policy Through State Research Funding)

How can the state promote growth? By, for example, financing basic research at universities and research institutes. In the medium term, companies can develop innovations from research results that work saving in production, i.e. the same output can be produced with less work or alternatively the same amount of work can produce more. How does technical progress now work out in neoclassicism?

1. Work productivity increases
2. Labor demand increases
3. Production increases, prices fall
4. Income increases
5. Consumption and saving increase
    1. First, the demand for labor increases. Since labor productivity has increased and the real wage is unchanged, firms demand more labor.[6] We had already discussed the example that the employer lets the employee work in the bakery until 3:00 p.m. instead of 1:00 p.m., if he produces 12 instead of 10 breads per hour in the morning. This results in a shift of the labor demand curve, since more labor is demanded at the same real wage. The real wage increases, otherwise households would not be willing to work more (Figs. 3.34 and 3.35).

---

[6]The second effect, that higher labor input leads to higher capital productivity, is not considered here, ($N\uparrow \Rightarrow dY/dK\uparrow$).

Fig. 3.34 Technical progress

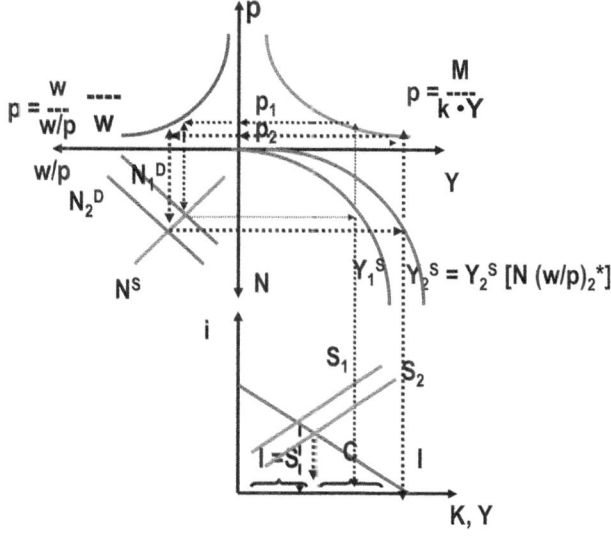

Fig. 3.35 Profit maximization
and labor demand in technical
progress

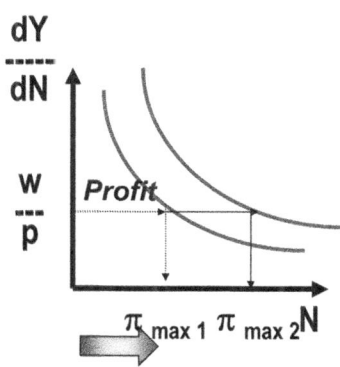

Profit max at:

$$\frac{dY}{dN} = \frac{w}{p}$$

Firms will continue to demand labor and capital until the real price of the production factor N (w/p) equals its marginal real contribution, the marginal product (or marginal productivity dY/dN).

2. Work productivity increases with labor-saving technical progress, i.e. the same output can be produced with less work or alternatively with the same amount of work more can be produced. In neoclassicism, workers only offer their labor power if they want to consume and save (securities offer) the planned income, which is why there is no demand problem and thus no work-reducing progress. Since more

can now be produced with the same amount of work, the production curve must shift (since technical progress is exogenous, i.e. not included as a variable in the model).

3. The work demanded more by employers is used. This is in addition to the technical progress, which is why production increases.
4. With the higher production, income also increases.
5. Consumption and savings increase according to the higher income as the workers had planned. The saving curve shifts because with the same interest rate more is saved now due to the higher income.

Conclusion

Everything has risen: real wages, employment, production and thus income. With the income, consumption and savings have also increased. The increase in savings caused a decrease in the interest rate and the lower interest rates more investments. Higher investments reinforce the growth effect, as they increase the capital stock in the next period, which in turn leads to more employment and a higher real wage. Technical progress or technology policy leads to welfare gains. ◄

3. Fiscal Policy: Taxes and Government Spending

Government spending can be financed through tax revenue or borrowing.

According to the English terms, one can write:

$$G (\text{Government Expenditures}) = T (\text{Taxes}) + D (\text{Deficit})$$

In addition to private demand, there is now also public demand: $Y^D = C + I + G$. Since production depends on the productivity of labor and the real wage given the capital stock, and these do not change, production also remains constant. Therefore, the additional public demand must displace private demand, which is called total crowding out.

A. *Tax financing (without illustration)*

Households' disposable income is reduced, leading to a corresponding decrease in consumption and savings. In other words, only the saving function shifts to the left, causing interest rates to rise and investment to decrease. Government purchases of goods are thus possible here by displacing private investment and consumption.

B. *Credit financing*

The state is insensitive to interest rates, but private investment I (i −), private saving S (i +), and indirectly private consumption C (i −) are not. The state borrows from the capital market, interest rates rise, and investment decreases I (i −) and saving increases S (i +), and indirectly consumption decreases C (i −). The decrease in investment and consumption makes the goods of constant production available to the state (see decrease $-\Delta I$ and $+\Delta S = -\Delta C$ in the capital market diagram).

Fig. 3.36 Fiscal policy

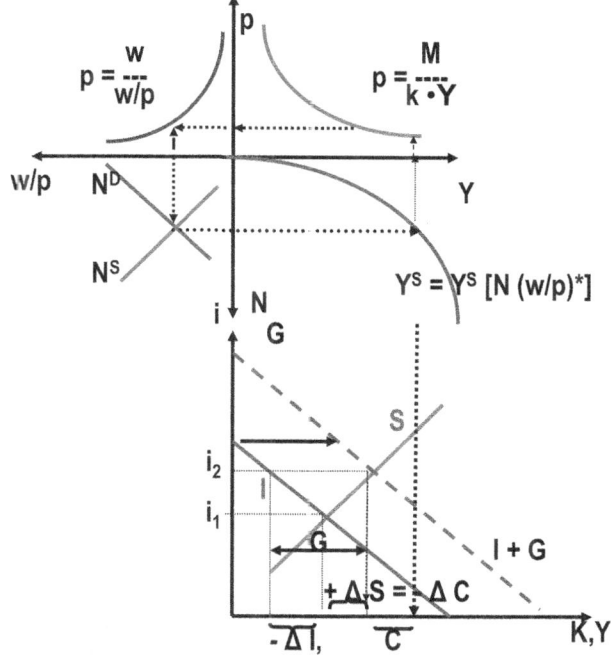

Conclusion

The state's crowding out of private investment leads to a relative decrease in the capital stock. The state intervention thus also leads to less growth through the displacement of investments. However, a tax financing of state expenditure is less growth-damaging than a financing through debt because of the predominant taxation of consumption. A credit financing of tax expenditure can therefore only be justified if the state also invests, e.g. in infrastructure. It is therefore not surprising that the German Constitution states that the new indebtedness of the state may not exceed state investment (Fig. 3.36). ◄

4. Wage Policy

What happens in neoclassicism if the government (or the unions) sets too high wages, i.e. wages above the equilibrium wage? Let's assume that in our bakery example, wages are increased from 20 to 30 €. The price level remains unchanged, so that the real wage rises from 10 to 15 loaves of bread. The result will be that the worker will want to work much longer because the compensation for his marginal disutility of work has increased greatly. In turn, the entrepreneurs will reduce the demand for labor because the marginal product, i.e. productivity, has remained the same. In our example, the bakery owner would send the employee home at 10.30 a.m., while the employee wants to work until evening. There is an excess supply of labor. The worker will find that he cannot realize his plans in the mar-

Fig. 3.37 Wage policy

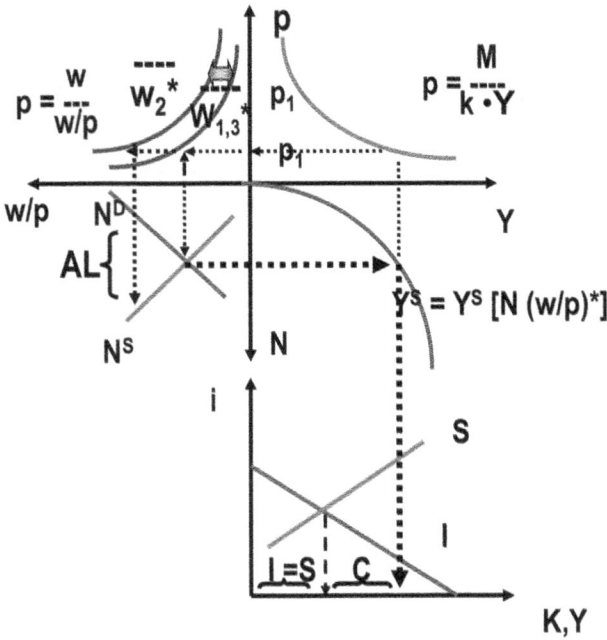

ket. According to his preferences, he is willing to work for less real wages, because then his marginal disutility of work per hour is also lower. Consequently, he lowers his wage demands until the original equilibrium at 1 p.m. is reached. Here, the marginal disutility of work per hour is equal to the real wage, which is equal to the marginal product. Higher wages arise in neoclassicism only if productivity increases (Fig. 3.37).

Case Study Reunification

In East Germany, people demanded "equal pay for equal work", but without taking into account that productivity was only 60% of the western level. Since the East German companies were not yet privatized, they were represented by the state-owned Treuhand and the East German workers were represented by the western unions, which wanted to gain new members in the east. The high expectations of the East German workers were not restrained by politics. The then Chancellor Helmut Kohl promised on 1 July 1990 in his television address to the economic and monetary union "flourishing landscapes". The significantly higher than productivity wages led to high unemployment in the following years, which made high transfers from West to East Germany (as of 2010 2.1 billion €) necessary.[7] In the end, the East German workers had little to show for their high wages due to unemployment. In our model, the East German workers would have lowered their wages until they matched their productivity (marginal product) and they would have been hired by the firms. However, this was not possible due to the binding tariff.

---

[7] See http://www.handelsblatt.com/politik/deutschland/teure-wiedervereinigung-das-billionen-projekt-bluehende-landschaften/3552370.html (14.12.2012).

Supply-Oriented Economic Policy

Supply-oriented economic policy was derived from neoclassicism. Growth and employment can only be achieved in neoclassicism at a given wage level through productivity increases. If one leaves aside technical progress, this can only be achieved through investments, i.e. through a larger capital stock. The companies decide on the basis of their profit or return expectations on investments and thus also on the creation of jobs. The focus is therefore on the supply-oriented economic policy the improvement of investment conditions and earnings expectations:

1. Less state and more market and competition:
   a) Reduction of bureaucracy and deregulation
      Fewer regulations and reduced administrative processes reduce transaction costs and increase the speed of implementation of investments.
   b) Privatization of public companies
      The approach behind this is to increase the productivity of public companies through competition. For private companies and their employees, there is no state takeover of losses. They have to go bankrupt and the employees lose their jobs if they do not offer market-conform services.
   c) Reduction of subsidies
      As a result of the incentives to perform in competition presented above, companies should also not be financed by the state. There should only be subsidies where markets and competition do not produce socially desired results.
   d) Reduction of public debt
      Since a credit-financed fiscal policy only leads to the displacement of private investment and thus to less growth and employment.
2. Reduction of payroll taxes
   This serves to increase the demand for labor neoclassically given the marginal product.
3. Reductions in social benefits to a minimum
   This measure is also supply-oriented. With lower social benefits, the incentive to offer work is increased. In some cases, the difference between an income from work and an unemployed social income was only a few hundred euros.
4. Simple tax system with low rates
   It must be transparent to companies how high the post-tax return on their investments is. The income tax also affects the investments of private capital providers, such as corporate owners. The lower the taxes, the more worthwhile the performance and investment.
5. Price stability: orientation of the money supply to GDP
   The case study of monetary policy has shown that an increase in the money supply does not generate positive economic effects. Rather, prices and wages have to adjust. This creates costs and irritation until prices and wages again reflect the real exchange relationships. A rule-based monetary policy that is oriented towards the growth of the goods supply, i.e. GDP, avoids this uncertainty.

As political applications (at least partially) the so-called Reaganomics in the USA, the Thatcherism in GB and the reforms of Chancellor Schröder in the Agenda 2010 can be mentioned in Germany.

Conclusion and Summary of Neoclassicism

In neoclassicism, the market mechanism works. Everyone can work and save as much as they want at the respective market equilibrium price. The companies produce as long as they can earn a marginal profit at the given real wage and labor productivity, and invest depending on the market interest rate and capital productivity as long as they can still earn a marginal profit. Everyone is satisfied and all markets are cleared. This is only true in the long term! (see also Siebe & Wenke, 2014; Blanchard, 2014; Blanchard & Illing, 2006; Wagner & Böhne, 2003; Felderer & Homburg, 2005; Drost et al., 2003; Mankiw, 2013; John, 2004 as well as Mussel, 2009).

John Maynard Keynes says, however:

In the long run, we are all dead.[8] ◄

Comprehension Questions

1. The state increases taxes by 1 billion € and spends the money. What are the short-term effects on employment in the neoclassical model?
2. Why is domestic product in the neoclassical model independent of the money supply?
3. As a neoclassicist, would you recommend a minimum wage?
4. What would you as a neoclassicist think of the stimulus programs that were adopted as a result of the financial crisis by the German government?
5. In the last hundred years, the productivity of farmers has increased significantly, but not that of hairdressers. What effect should this have on the wages of both professions? Why has it turned out differently? And who benefits from it?

Exercise Questions

1. Show the effects of a credit-financed expansive fiscal policy in the neoclassical overall model and explain them briefly.
2. In a neoclassical economy, the following applies:

1. Production function:	$Y = 8N^{1/2}$
2. Labor supply function:	$N^S = 2w/p$
3. Investment function:	$I = 10 - 100i$

---

[8] See Keynes, John Maynard (1923, p. 80).

4. Savings function:	$S = 100i$
5. Money supply:	$M = 100$
6. Cash holding coefficient:	$k = 1/8$

Calculate the equilibrium values for the **equilibrium interest rate,** the **real wage,** the **equilibrium employment level** in the labor market, the **GDP** as real output, the **price level,** the **nominal wage** and **consumption.**

7. Case Study Population Change: Try something new in the neoclassical model. Show graphically in the neoclassical overall model the effects of a population increase and explain them briefly.

References

Blanchard, O. (2014). *Makroökonomie*. Pearson Studium.

Blanchard, O., & Illing, G. (2006). *Übungen zur Makroökonomie*. Pearson Studium.

Clark, G. (2005). The condition of the working-class in England, 1209–2004. *Journal of Political Economy, 113*(6), 1307–1340.

Drost, A., Linnemann, L., & Schabert, A. (2003). *Übungsbuch zu Felderer/Homburg*. Springer Gabler.

Felderer, B., & Homburg, S. (2005). *Makroökonomik und neue Makroökonomik* (9. Aufl., S. 119). Springer.

John, K. D. (2004). *Arbeitsbuch Makroökonomik* (12. Aufl.). Schäffer-Poeschel.

Keynes, J. M. (1923). *A tract on monetary reform*. Macmillan and Co.

Mankiw, G. N. (2000). *Makroökonomik* (4. Aufl.). Schäffer-Poeschel.

Mankiw, G. N. (2013). *Makroökonomik* (7. Aufl.). Schäffer-Poeschel.

Mishkin, F. S. (1984). The causes of inflation (NBER Working Paper No. 1453, issued in September 1984). http://www.nber.org/papers/w1453.

Mussel, G. (2009). *Einführung in die Makroökonomik* (10. Aufl.). Vahlen.

Siebe, T., & Wenke, M. (2014). *Makroökonomie*. UTB Lucius.

Wagner, H., & Böhne, A. (2003). *Übungsbuch Makroökonomie*. Vahlen.

Further Reading

Eller, R., et al. (Hrsg.). (2005). *Handbuch Derivativer Instrumente*. Schäffer-Poeschel.

Forster, J., Klüh, U., & Sauer, S. (2014). *Makroökonomie – Das Übungsbuch*. Pearson Studium.

Grögens, E., Ruckriegel, K., & Seitz, F. (2013). *Europäische Geldpolitik, Theorie – Empirie – Praxis* (6. Aufl.). UTB.

Miles, D., Scott, A., & Breedon, F. (2014). *Makroökonomie. Globale Wirtschaftszusammenhänge verstehen*. Wiley.

Olney, M. L. (2015). *Wiley Schnellkurs Makroökonomie*. Wiley-VCH.

Schröder, H. (2016). *Makroökonomie transparent vermittelt: VWL Grundlagen für Managementabtscheidungen*. Mastering-ConceptConsult.

Inflation

4

What Follows Why?
Inflation is one of the great macroeconomic problems,
   which is why we now want to deal with it in a short excursion.

Learning objectives
You should be able to

- explain in your own words how inflation is calculated and
- describe the economic effects.

4.1   What is Inflation?

▶ Inflation (Deflation) sustained increase (decrease) in the general price level.

It is important to note here that the definition of the general price level and a sustained increase is meant. This means that an average of many prices must increase and that this increase is of lasting nature, that is, it does not go back again. This is intended to exclude the constant fluctuations of individual prices.

One speaks of **perceived inflation** when households perceive inflation more strongly than it is indicated and attribute this to their distorted perception. If the prices of goods of daily use rise more strongly than the prices of goods that are bought less often, more inflation can be "felt" than is actually present on average.

Lenin is said to have declared that the best way to destroy the Capitalist System was to debauch the currency. By a continuing process of inflation, governments can confiscate, secretly and unobserved, an important part of the wealth of their citizens (John Maynard Keynes).

What does Lenin mean by this and why is he quoted by Keynes?

On the one hand, he says that inflation is a means of destroying the capitalist system. This points to the harmfulness of inflation or, conversely, to the importance of price stability for the market economy system. In addition, it shows us the central effect of inflation on the distribution of assets and incomes. For example, it has often happened that the currency of the enemy was reprinted and distributed during wars in order to damage the enemy's economic system.[1] The second part of the quote describes the possibility that the state finances its expenditure through money printing. The new money displaces the old one in the bidding process for the same quantity of goods. Prices rise. Due to the higher prices as a result of the increased money supply, the citizens can no longer buy the same quantity of goods as before.

Inflation Measurement
In order to calculate the ongoing changes in the general price level, a representative basket of goods is needed. The German consumer price index is supposed to reflect the consumption structure of an average German household. It is a Laspeyres price index with a fixed base year, i.e. the index values refer to the consumption structures of the year (quantities 2015: 5 chocolate bars and 2 chewing gums), which is fixed as the base year.

$$Lp(x, y)_{0,1} = \frac{px_1 \cdot qx_0 + py_1 \cdot qy_0}{px_0 \cdot qx_0 + py_0 \cdot qy_0}$$

(p: prices, q: quantities, with the periods 0 and 1)

Example

Normally, the re-weighting of the basket of goods or the weighing scheme is carried out at five-year intervals. The current base year is currently 2015 (Fig. 4.1).

$$\text{Price index } (Laspeyres) = \frac{(5 \times \text{ current candy bar price}) + (2 \times \text{ current chewing gum price})}{\left(5 \times \text{ candy bar price}_{2015}\right) + \left(2 \times \text{ chewing gum price}_{2015}\right)}$$

What Does the Stated Inflation Rate Tell Us?
When looking at the weighting scheme, one should ask oneself whether one buys the same goods in this structure in the year. Only if this is the case, the stated inflation applies to oneself. For example, not all people will spend approx. 3.8% of their expendi-

---

[1] See Handelsblatt of 17.02.2012, http://www.handelsblatt.com/panorama/aus-aller-welt/zweiter-weltkrieg-nazis-wollten-mit-gefaelschten-pfundscheinen-den-briten-schaden/6225748.html.

Weighting in the consumer price index
Weighing scheme for the base year 2015 in %

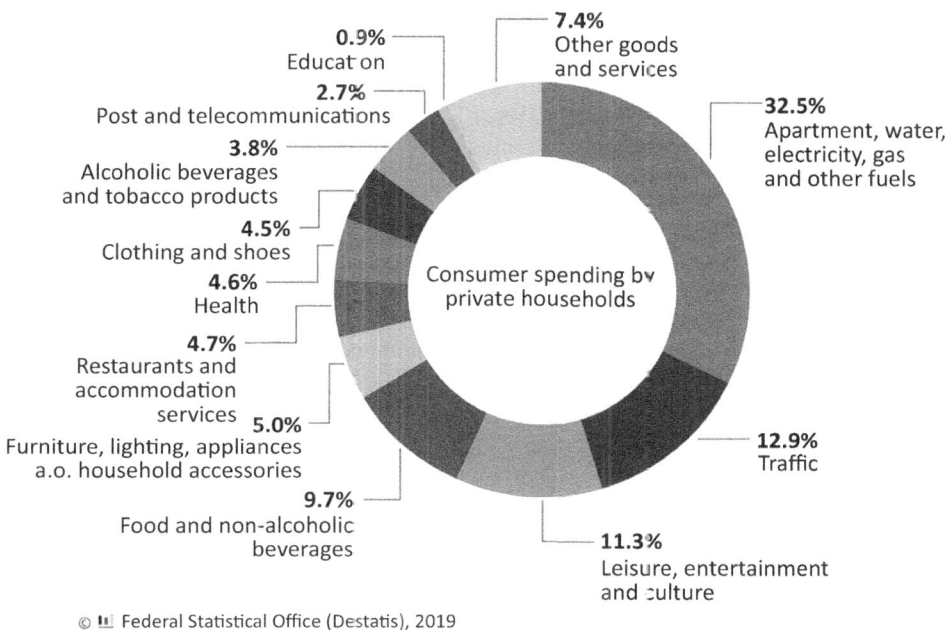

7.4%
Other goods
and services

0.9%
Education

2.7%
Post and telecommunications

3.8%
Alcoholic beverages
and tobacco products

4.5%
Clothing and shoes

4.6%
Health

4.7%
Restaurants and
accommodation
services

5.0%
Furniture, lighting, appliances
a.o. household accessories

9.7%
Food and non-alcoholic
beverages

32.5%
Apartment, water,
electricity, gas
and other fuels

Consumer spending by
private households

12.9%
Traffic

11.3%
Leisure, entertainment
and culture

© Ⅲ Federal Statistical Office (Destatis), 2019

Fig. 4.1 Weighting in the consumer price index. (Source: Federal Statistical Office, https://www. destatis.de/DE/ZahlenFakten/GesamtwirtschaftUmwelt/VGR/VolkswirtschaftlicheGesamtrechnungen.html)

ture on alcohol and tobacco. Those who wish can calculate their personal inflation rate on the Internet with the personal inflation calculator of the Federal Statistical Office.

Often one sees overviews of the historical development of the inflation rate. However, one must take into account that the inflation rates are hardly comparable, as there were substantial changes in the recording in 2002 and 2004.

As of 2002, quality improvements are being deducted from prices (but not quality deteriorations), and as of 2004, the hedonic price index is being used, from which capacity improvements are deducted. If a computer is twice as fast, it is only included in the shopping basket with half the price. It is unfortunately not possible to assess what effect this has on price development. The Federal Statistical Office also unfortunately does not provide any statistics according to the old calculation.[2] But if one imagines that since

---

[2] See Federal Statistical Office, Quality Adjustment in Consumer Price Statistics, July 2006/ Themenkasten der Preisstatistik No. 35 as well as https://www.destatis.de/DE/ZahlenFakten/GesamtwirtschaftUmwelt/Preise/HedonischeMethodenUebersicht.html.

then everything that represents a quality improvement has been tried to be captured, then the influence becomes tangible. For example, the standard equipment improvements on cars are deducted from the price.

The question of the advantage of such a method from the perspective of consumers can be raised in general terms. Statistically, it may be correct if the office tries to make the products comparable in order to capture the price effect. But the consumer is not aware of this. And even if he were aware of it, the influence on his spending could not be estimated. The consumer rather assumes that the quality improvements benefit him unconditionally with his income. He will therefore not be able to explain that he cannot buy the same goods as in the previous years with a stated inflation rate of zero and constant income. He will not come to the conclusion that this is due to quality improvements. It is also questionable whether the consumer would still see a Commodore 64 as a PC today. But the inflation rate refers to this product. Today he can only buy a Commodore 64 at that time's price if it is available at all. If he wants a faster computer, he has to spend a lot more money.

The structure of the basket of goods also affects the inflation rate. Thus, the change in the basket of goods has reduced the inflation rates from 2010 to 2012 and from 2010 to 2015 (see Figs. 4.2 and 4.3). Figure 4.4 shows the development of the inflation rate over time taking into account all changes in the calculation method.

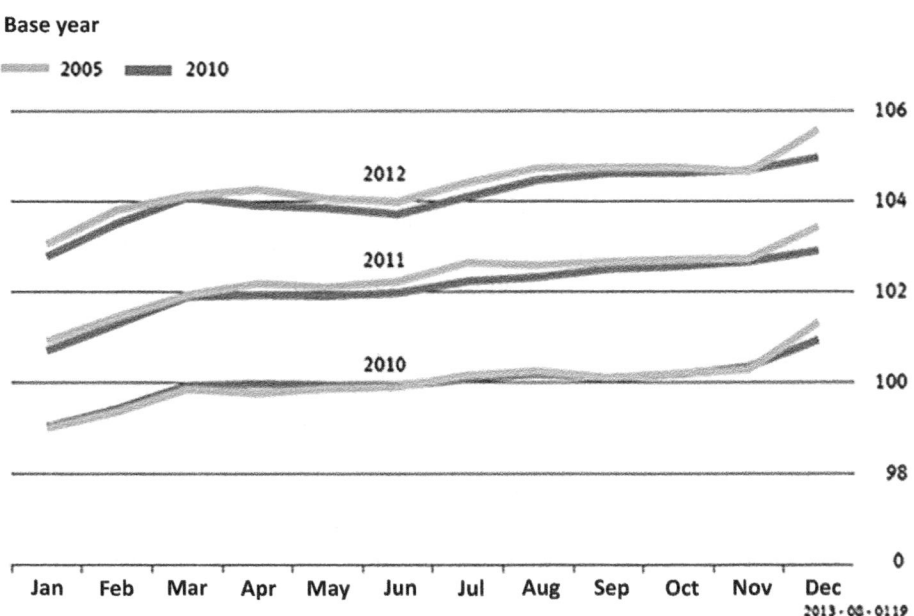

Chart 8 Comparison of consumer price index results on old and new basis

Fig. 4.2 Consumer price index after change in basket of goods 2010. (Source: Federal Statistical Office, https://www.destatis.de/DE/Publikationen/Thematisch/Preise/Verbraucherpreise/VerbrauchpreisindexUmstellung5611106139004.pdf?__blob=publicationFile)

Consumer Price Index for Germany
Change compared to previous year in %

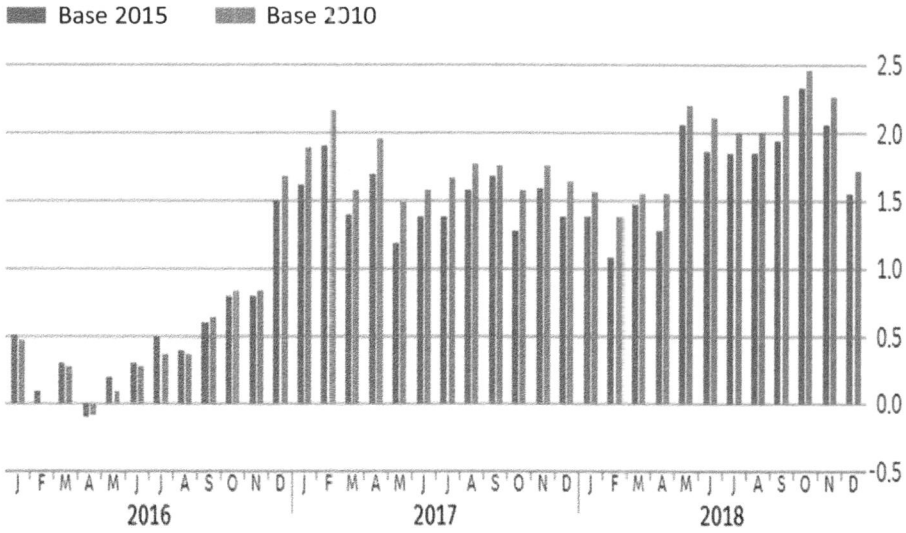

Fig. 4.3 Consumer price index after change in the basket of goods 2015. (Source: Federal Statistical Office, Background paper on the revision of the consumer price index for Germany 2019, Wiesbaden, 21 February 2019, p. 4. https://www.destatis.de/DE/Presse/Pressekonferenzen/2019/HGG_VPI/Statement_HGG_VPI_PDF.pdf?__blob=publicationFile)

The website Shadowstats calculated an annual inflation rate for the USA at the beginning of 2019 of approx. 5.4% on the basis of the 1990 method compared to an officially declared rate of approx. 2% (see Fig. 4.5).[3]

4.2 Disadvantages of Inflation

1. **The price relations are distorted**
   Inflation is a displaced process of price increases. Not all companies increase prices at the same time. This has the consequence that some prices rise while others remain the same. Relative price increases can be lost in the high absolute. If all prices rise,

---

[3] On the basis of the calculation method of 1980, Shadowstats ever comes to over 9%. See http://www.shadowstats.com/alternate_data/inflation-charts (query of 01.12.2019).

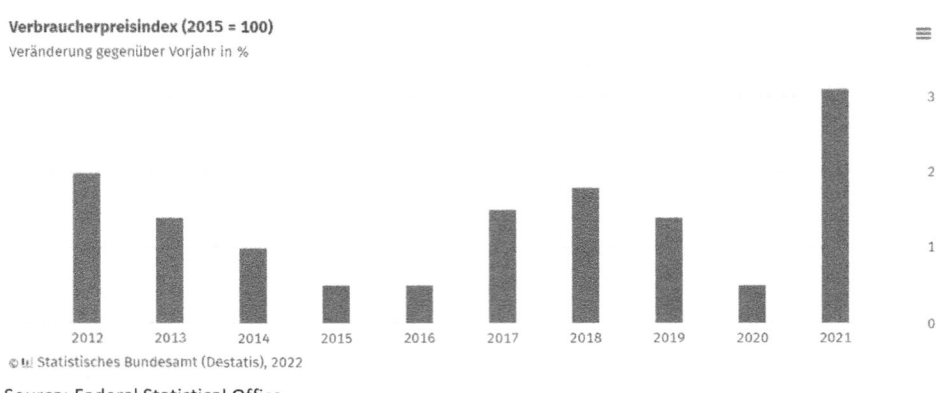

Verbraucherpreisindex (2015 = 100)
Veränderung gegenüber Vorjahr in %

© lu Statistisches Bundesamt (Destatis), 2022

Source: Federal Statistical Office

Fig. 4.4   Inflation rate. (Source: Federal Statistical Office)

the price increases due to higher demand or higher costs are no longer distinguisha-
ble from inflationary increases. An allocation of production in the more cost-effective
or desired direction by demand becomes difficult. In addition, there may be misallocations. For example, if the price of plastic rises faster than that of steel, companies
could switch production of technical equipment to higher steel content. This is associated with costs. If the price of steel finally rises, the restructuring of production turns
out to be a misallocation.

2. **The function of money as a value storage medium is lost**
   The loss of value of money will lead investors to seek out more stable money or invest
   their money in assets. There is capital flight.

3. **Loss of assets**
   If money loses its value, this corresponds to a expropriation of property owners
   with far-reaching consequences. People who have worked hard their whole lives are
   cheated out of the fruits of their labor. Seen in this light, it was a mistake to save, that
   is, to work more than one needs to live, thus losing the most important incentive of
   the market economy, property.
   Assuming an inflation rate of 2.5% (ECB target: below, but close to 2%), the purchasing power of capital would be halved after 30 years. If in the same time a fortune
   grows from 50,000 € to 100,000 €, this increase would just cover the loss of purchasing power due to inflation.[4] Taxation would reduce the purchasing power of capital.
   A flat deduction of the inflation rate in the assessment basis or at least higher allow-

---

[4] See Manager Magazin from 27.06.2007 http://www.manager-magazin.de/finanzen/geldan-
lage/0,2828,490041,00.html and http://www.0711-aktienclub.de/download_gratis_Inflation.htm
(retrieval on 03.05.2011).

Fig. 4.5 Consumer Inflation. (Source: http://www.shadowstats.com/alternate_data/inflation-charts (01.12.2019)

ances would be urgently needed here, because only the real interest rates represent an increase in productivity. In addition, the taxation of nominal interest favors investment forms without capital consumption through inflation, such as rentable real estate, thus distorting the allocation of capital.

4. **Redistributions**

Even a small, gradual inflation has lasting redistributions as a result. All persons who have claims to fixed payments are disadvantaged, while the debtors or, better, the obligors benefit.

Creditor-debtor hypothesis: Debtors have to pay back less in purchasing power than they borrowed. The decisive factor here is whether the interest rate sufficiently compensates for the loss in value.

Fiscal hypothesis: The state is usually the largest debtor. It benefits because its tax revenues increase with inflation. Value-added tax rises proportionally and income tax is delayed. Here the state benefits from the cold progression, that is, the increase in tax rates due to inflation-related increases in income. Finally, the state benefits from the taxation of nominal interest. The inflation compensation contained in the interest is also taxed.

Companies also benefit from inflation because they can buy their inputs earlier and at a lower price than they sell the produced goods.

Pensioners and recipients of fixed incomes are disadvantaged because their benefits are only delayed—if at all—to inflation (pensioner hypothesis, wage-lag hypothesis). With the currently historically low interest rate, which is below the inflation rate in the short term, many investors may have to accept a negative real interest rate even after deduction of the withholding tax. The principle of capacity is grossly violated here.

5. **Risk premium on interest rates**

   In the short term, households are subject to a so-called money illusion. They are sur-prised by inflation. The real interest rate falls because they do not demand a timely inflation adjustment. The investor bears the risk of rising interest rates. In this case, a later investment would have been more advantageous for him. Of course, he could also improve, but he wants to pay a risk premium for the uncertainty. In addition, there is the inflation risk. In the long term, however, savers not only demand an infla-tion adjustment, but also a risk premium on the interest rate because of the uncertainty about how inflation will develop. This means that the real interest rate rises, which reduces economic growth.

6. **Employment effects**

   Real wages also fall because workers do not demand an inflation adjustment in time due to the money illusion. Since real wages fall, employment rises, which is why the Phillips curve is valid in the short term (see Fig. 4.6). In the long run, however, expec-tations adjust, which can lead to a wage-price spiral. Like savers, workers demand a risk premium on wages to hedge against inflation. Real wages rise, causing unem-ployment. As a result, there is no long-term reduction in unemployment through infla-tion (see Fig. 4.7).

Here is a quote from Abraham Lincoln:

> You can fool some of the people all of the time, and you can fool all of the people some of the time, but you can not fool all of the people all of the time.

Disadvantages of Deflation

Deflation is the opposite of inflation. The central problem is that companies earn less than they spend on prerequisites because they buy their prerequisites earlier and thus more expensive than they sell the produced goods. This results in losses, which can lead to bankruptcy. If prices fall sharply, there may also be a shift in purchases because one hopes for an even cheaper purchase. However, substantial price cuts would be required for this. With discount actions, it can be observed that prices have to be reduced by 30% or more to create an incentive to buy.

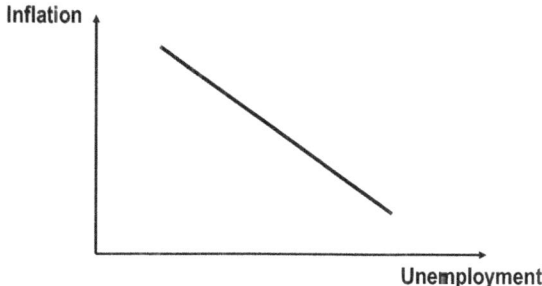

Fig. 4.6 Short-term Phillips curve. (The original Phillips curve from 1958 based on data from GB from 1861 to 1957 showed the relationship between average nominal wage increases and the unemployment rate.). (See the modified Philips curve by Samuelscn, Paul A. & Solow, Robert M., 1960)

Fig. 4.7 Long-term Phillips curve. (See Friedman, M. 1968 & Phelps, E. S., 1968)

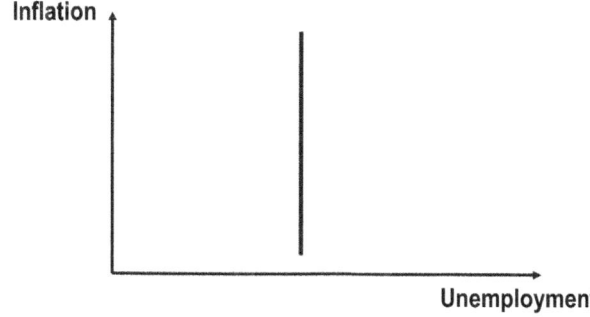

This has a negative effect on the companies' sales. However, as we will see later, the cause of deflation, the massive drop in demand, is the actual problem. Deflation then occurs together with the depression.

▶ An **hyperinflation** is said to exist when the monthly inflation rate is more than 50% (definition). This implies a more than hundredfold price increase in one year (13,000%).

Hyperinflations arise when the state finances large budget deficits through the printing press. The state's profits, which accrue to it through the monopoly of money production, are called seigniorage. The rapid destruction and change in value leads to the money losing its function as a value storage medium, unit of account and means of exchange. The money is then rejected by people as a means of payment (see also Siebe & Wenke, 2014; Blanchard, 2014; Blanchard & Illing, 2006; Wagner & Böhne, 2003; Felderer &

Homburg, 2005; Drost et al., 2003; Mankiw, 2013; John, 2004; as well as Mussel, 2009). The money functions are then taken over by unofficial currencies, such as US dollars or cigarettes, as the following article on the German hyperinflation of 1923 shows.

4.3   Case Study: Hyperinflation Germany

Task

Discuss the effects of hyperinflation based on the following article.

Overview

Spiegel Online from 31 July 2009,[5]

Hyperinflation 1923

When the Mark was destroyed

Two coffees for 14,000 marks, a theatre ticket for one billion: during hyperinflation in 1923, people carried wheelbarrows of banknotes to the shops to buy groceries. The value of money fell faster than it could be reprinted. The event still shapes German monetary policy today. By Alexander JungSpiegel Online 23.07.2009, http://www.spiegel.de/einestages/hyperinflation-1923-a-948427.html.

What happened to journalist Eugeni Xammar can probably be called good luck for a reporter. In autumn 1922, Barcelona's newspaper "La Veu de Catalunya" sent him to Berlin at a historic moment: the German financial system was collapsing and the Mark was beginning to dissolve into thin air. In the following months, there was no other place in the world more exciting to report from.

"Every week, the prices for tram and beef, theatre and school, newspaper and hairdressers, sugar and bacon rise," Xammar wrote in February 1923. "This has the consequence that nobody knows how long the money they have in their hands will last, and people live in constant unrest, that nobody thinks about anything other than food and drink, buying and selling, and that the only topic of conversation in all of Berlin is: the dollar, the mark, the prices … Did you see that? Just stop! I've just bought sausage, ham and cheese for the next month and a half."

Almost every day, the Catalan sent new stories of hyperinflation to his homeland—stories of everyday madness in a country whose currency was playing havoc. At the beginning of the war in 1914, one dollar was still worth 4.20 marks. After that, the German currency steadily lost value, from autumn 1922 it plummeted into the abyss. In November 1923, one dollar was worth 4.2 billion marks. Soon after, the spell was broken, a dollar was worth 4.20 marks again—but now it was Rentenmark.

---

[5] Translated from German

Hardly anyone understood what had happened. Much of it sounds incredible even today, three generations later.

For example, a family sells its house and wants to emigrate to America, but at the Hamburg harbor they have to realize that their money is no longer enough for the crossing, not even for the ticket back home. Another example: A café visitor drinks two cups of coffee for 5000 marks each, but receives a bill for 14,000 marks with the explanation that he should have ordered both cups at the same time, and in the meantime the price had gone up. Yet another example: Theatergoers come to the box office with a few hundred million marks, but the bundles of money are not enough: The ticket now costs one billion marks.

At that time, the inflation rate was in the thousands of percent per month. And this at a time without calculators.

Only a few contemporary witnesses, such as the writer Klaus Mann, could enjoy "the macabre joke of inflation": "What an oppressive pleasure to see the world go out of control," he wrote at the time, fascinated. The Germans were now experiencing "the total devaluation of the only value to which a de-godded epoch had truly believed: that of money."

His brother Golo Mann, the historian, was more concerned with the classification of the events. "The devaluation of the German currency was, in its effect, a second revolution, after the first of the war and the post-war period," was his analysis. "It destroyed ancient trust and replaced it with fear and cynicism," he diagnosed, and asked: "What could still be relied on, who could one build on, if such a thing was possible?"

In fact, nothing seemed certain anymore, all order was lost and with it the trust in the republic, democracy, and the future in general. What else could one expect when a large part of the population saw themselves deprived of their savings while the state could get rid of its debts: "The inflation had led basic principles of the rule of law, such as 'good faith', to absurdity," according to the Munich historian Martin Geyer.

A national trauma has remained, which still has an effect today. Inflation anxiety is widespread in Germany, monetary policy here feels more than elsewhere obliged to stability, the experience of 1923 sits deep in the collective memory of the Germans.

But did it have to come to this back then? Or could the catastrophe have been averted? And if so, how?

The switches were set early on, in essence the Great Inflation began with the First World War. The costs for the army and equipment exceeded any imagination, the Kaiserreich paid an estimated 160 billion marks for the war, an astronomical sum. This could only be financed if the Reich procured money in unconventional ways.

To do this, the parliament passed the so-called Currency Laws on 4 August 1914, only three days after the German Reich had declared war on Russia. They fundamentally changed the German money market. The gold coverage of the mark was "suspended for the time being"; in times of war, an "extraordinary increase in the amount of unsecured cash in circulation", as the justification put it, was an "economic necessity". In other words: The German Reich financed the war costs by printing banknotes without interruption.

The volume of cash in circulation increased sharply: from 13 billion marks in 1913 to 60 billion marks at the end of the war. But the printing press alone was not enough to cover the expenses. "As things stand, the only way forward for the time being is to postpone the final regulation of war costs by means of credit into the future," the finance politician Karl Helfferich admitted in 1915.

The Reich became massively indebted to its own citizens, it kept issuing new bonds, a total of almost 100 billion marks. The Germans initially subscribed to these papers almost blindly, in the confident expectation of a quick military victory. State debt soared from 5 to 156 billion marks. "There is a limit where the printing press acts as inflation on the purchasing power of money," the socialist Eduard Bernstein warned in 1918, but such objections fell on deaf ears. The money supply grew steadily, while the goods market shrank.

Too much money meets too little goods: a classic constellation that leads to inflation. It also did not help that the Reich government set maximum prices for important goods of daily need such as grain or coal. Such artificial dams only caused inflation to accumulate and the liquidity flood to be released even more powerfully at the end of the war and economic management.

Thus, the Weimar Republic was not bankrupt from the beginning, but only conditionally creditworthy, the new state was born with the birth defect of inflation. However, at least at the beginning, the devaluation also showed a stimulating effect in its milder form. Because the Mark, which was cheap compared to the Dollar, the Pound or the Franc, boosted the German export economy at the beginning of the Weimar Republic. Industry grew by 20% within a year. The unemployment rate fell to less than one percent in 1922, real wages rose significantly. The "lubricant of inflation", as the Berlin economic historian Carl-Ludwig Holtfrerich put it, revived private economic activity.

The post-war boom is all the more remarkable because at the same time the rest of the world economy sank into deep recession. The USA and Great Britain focused on the stability of their currency and accepted high unemployment rates of up to 20%. The Weimar governments behaved in the opposite way: They bought upswing and full employment at the price of a consumptive Mark.

Although the politicians in Berlin may not have driven inflation consciously, they did not oppose it with much power. The strategy was comfortable for a while, but dangerous, as it turned out.

The enormous budget deficit and the growing interest service restricted the scope of German politics considerably. Above all, the enormous reparations that Germany had to pay for war damage burdened the young republic.

As early as the Versailles Conference in 1919, the German delegates complained that, as a result of the reparations, "every creative impulse, every work ethic, every entrepreneurial spirit would have to be destroyed in Germany for all time"—even though no final sum had been set at that time.

The dispute about the amount only broke out later. In 1921, the Allies estimated the debt at 132 billion gold marks (one gold mark corresponded to the value of the mark from 1913), until 1932 money payments and goods deliveries were made worth an estimated 26 billion gold marks, that is, about ten percent of the then national income annually. In other words: The burden was certainly high, but still manageable.

It was less the amount that destabilized than the ongoing uncertainty about it. Accordingly, the atmosphere within the Reparations Commission was poisonous; in particular, the French, who wanted revenge for the military defeat of 1871, were inflexible.

So it was enough for a relatively small backlog in the delivery of wood, coal and telegraph poles to escalate the conflict in January 1923. The French sent 100,000 men to the Ruhr area, took over the control of the mines and confiscated the coal. "With that, the industrial production of Germany was basically hit in the heart," says Holtfrerich.

An entire region was paralyzed, an important source of tax revenue dried up. The Ruhr area was not allowed to supply any more coal the Reich had to procure the fuel partly at high cost from abroad, paid for with valuable foreign currency. At the same time, millions of people suffered the most severe need.

"I have never seen such crowds of people who are hungry and wandering around," confessed Franz Geyer, the future mayor of Bochum.

Many small children suffered from diseases such as rickets, tuberculosis sometimes took on epidemic proportions. In Mannheim, the lung disease had broken out in a street with 220 households in 43 families.

Who was to blame for the misery was undisputed in public opinion. The French and their uncompromising attitude were identified as the source of all evil. Resistance was organized against them: shopkeepers refused to serve the French. Citizens crossed the street when they met French people.

"The enemy is in the country," commented the "Hildesheimer Allgemeine Zeitung" indignantly about the Ruhr occupation, "he has nestled in the heart of the German economy to drink our heart's blood and destroy our state's existence." The 10,000-mark note issued the year before was given the nickname "vampire note": it showed a man who apparently had a bite wound on his neck.

The value of the mark had already fallen rapidly in 1922, before the French marched into the Ruhr region. The drama unfolded, the creeping inflation (up to 50% devaluation per year) turned into galloping inflation (more than 50% per year) and accelerated into hyperinflation (more than 50% per month). The value of money slipped out of state control.

This loss of value cannot be explained purely by quantitative causes. As so often in economics, expectations played the decisive role. With the nerve-wracking haggling over reparations, confidence in the country's economic future had completely evaporated. The beginning of hyperinflation "is hardly explicable without this loss of confidence in the currency," according to Holtfrerich. As a result, "expectations about future developments in the internal and external value of money" changed for the worse.

A clear sign of this loss of confidence was the almost sudden withdrawal of foreign lenders from the German capital market. They sold Reich bonds en masse.

When Foreign Minister Walter Rathenau was murdered by right-wing extremists on June 22, 1922, all hope of a return to stable conditions was buried. But it was not until early summer of the following year that the exchange rate went into free fall. By mid-October 1922, the mark was already dead, "says Bielefeld historian Helmut Kerstingjohänner."

In December 1922, there were still 2000 marks for a dollar, in April 1923 there were already 20,000 marks, in August over a million. The Republic embarked on the "road to ruin," as the then Interior Minister Wilhelm Sollmann put it: "Even the most resolute can get dizzy when they weigh the fragility of the bridge and the distance to the respective shore of salvation."

In addition to the Reichsbank, at times over 130 other companies were engaged in producing banknotes, 1783 presses were in use, unless the paper was in short supply. Employees brought rucksacks to the payroll office to store the money—and immediately exchanged it for goods.

At Junkers in Dessau, the company paid the workers the daily price for three and a half loaves of bread every morning at nine o'clock. Their wives were already waiting at the factory gate, received the money and hurried to the shops. Because the new dollar exchange rate was published at noon.

Many doctors only accepted natural commodities as fees: sausage, eggs or briquettes. Stores waived price labeling in windows due to constant price increases; when they were forced to do so by Prussian authorities, this only drove prices higher because traders anticipated future increases.

Even cremation became unaffordable for many citizens because its price was linked to that of coal. So people buried the dead conventionally again, a only 50 cm high coffin model was popular, called "nose squeezer" in colloquial language.

People lived in a peculiar tension: On the one hand, they fought a daily battle for survival, for food and fuel. "If we can somehow save the city of Cologne from collapse," said Mayor Konrad Adenauer at the time, "then I will kneel down and thank my creator."

Paradoxically, there was enough goods available. But the stable money was missing to buy them. Germany was threatened, as the future Chancellor Hans Luther said in 1923, "to starve in full barns".

On the other hand, the time is characterized by unbelievable waste. A real buying panic gripped the citizens. People gorged and lived from day to day. "We drink up our grandma's little house," was the popular saying of those days.

What really counted were assets: diamonds and coins, but also antiques, pianos or art; the works of contemporary artists such as Lyonel Feininger, Paul Klee, Max Pechstein or Karl Schmidt-Rottluff were in demand. And whoever had foreign currency was king anyway.

A postal inspector flew up because he caught letters with foreign banknotes: 1717 dollars, 1102 Swiss francs, 114 French francs. The amount was enough to buy two houses, give a piano to a friend, and donate the rest, probably as an indulgence, to the church.

Overall, petty crime increased sharply. Potato fields were looted, bakeries stormed, shop windows smashed. Not only were prices out of control, all values now seemed crazy. In the big cities, dance halls or nude bars opened, cocaine found brisk sales. People enjoyed themselves as if there were no tomorrow. The economist Joseph Schumpeter observed the "disorganizing effects of currency disruption on the national character, morality, and all the ramifications of cultural life."

In this situation, when the mark had been discredited, many cities or companies began to create their own currency and print emergency money. A South German industrial company issued a 500,000 mark note with the sensible saying: "If a briquette is still more expensive, just put me in the oven."

Only a radical currency cut, it was clear, could stop the permanent money devaluation and create orderly conditions again. In mid-November 1923, the government began to issue the so-called rentenmark. It was said that the new currency was backed by the real estate of industry and agriculture, which of course was a fiction. If it had come to a oath, surely no entrepreneur or farmer would have given land for money. But after the exhausting years of currency devaluation, one longed for stability so much that one blindly trusted the new money.

What went down in history as the "miracle of the rentenmark" was in truth a revelation for the German Reich: The state was bankrupt. As always, the price was paid primarily by the citizens.

The fools were all those who had money: savers, holders of government bonds, but above all the rentiers, the citizens who received incomes without working—those who lived on pensions or their capital income. Large parts of the middle class felt expropriated; they practically lost everything they had saved over the years.

But banks, savings banks and insurance companies also suffered heavy losses in equity and remained stuck on paper money. They had to start their business from scratch in 1924.

The winners were, on the other hand, all those who were highly indebted: first and foremost the state, but also private individuals who had bought houses, building land or farms on credit and whose liabilities became worthless due to the switch to the rentenmark. Some industrialists benefited very particularly from inflation.

Hugo Stinnes, the "new Kaiser of Germany", as "Time" wrote, put together a vast empire of companies—heavy industry, newspapers, ships, hotels—built on enormous debts. "The weapon of inflation" Stinnes demanded as early as summer 1922, "must also be used further". In general, factory owners and craftsmen were the winners of the crisis: they had machines and buildings, so real estate, which survived the currency cut.

Most farmers were doing fine. "They had money like hay and threw it around," the writer Lion Feuchtwanger later recalled. Some bought a stable full of race-horses, others an expensive car: "Farmer Greindlberger drove out of the dirty village street of Englschalking to Munich in an elegant limousine with liveried chauffeur," Feuchtwanger described the rural prosperity, "he himself sat in it in a brown velvet waistcoat, with a green hat and chamois."

Germany had never experienced such a fundamental redistribution of assets before, and on the winning side were many who had already been wealthy.

In order to prevent the catastrophe, a lot would have had to happen differently in the decade between 1914 and 1924: it would have required a competent state authority, that is, strong, democratically supported governments that placed value on thrift and arranged themselves better with the Allies. At the same time, the out-side world, in particular France, would have had to take greater account of the difficult situation of the highly indebted republic and act more sensitively. Above all, the Allies would have had to create clarity about the amount of reparations faster.

But the German Reich then fell into a kind of fiscal anarchy. Many Germans became fed up with the bitter reality and left the country—in 1923 the authorities counted three times as many emigrants as the year before—, they turned to sects, some committed suicide. And millions of people radicalized.

Adolf Hitler's rise began not by chance in November 1923, at the height of inflation, when he instigated the so-called Beer Hall Putsch in the Munich Bürger-bräukeller.

The Catalan Germany correspondent Xammar experienced the spectacle up close—shortly before he had interviewed the "future ex-dictator of Germany". "The most important problem today is the high cost of living," Hitler explained in it and promised: "We want to make life cheaper." To do this, the department stores, which were often in Jewish hands, would have to be brought under state control, Hitler demanded and emphasized: "We expect all sorts of miracles from these national department stores."

The journalist from Barcelona expressed himself bluntly at the time about what he thought of his conversation partner: Hitler, according to Xammar, was "the stupidest person we ever had the pleasure of meeting."

Unfortunately, most Germans saw the man soon quite differently.

Summary

Inflation acts system-disrupting, as central functions (price signals) and incentives (property) of the market economy are impaired as well as the functions of money as a value storage, accounting unit and means of exchange. The measurement concepts can only partially capture inflation. ◄

Comprehension Questions

1. Define inflation.
2. Why are inflation and deflation harmful?

Exercise Tasks

1. In an economy, only mobile phones and caravans are produced. Based on the data in the table, calculate the inflation rate for the example quantities car and bread using the consumer price index (Laspeyres).

Year	2010	2020
Caravan price	60,000 €	70,000 €
Mobile phones	10 €	15 €
Number of caravans	1100	1200
Number of mobile phones	900,000	300,000

References

Blanchard, O. (2014). *Makroökonomie*. Pearson Studium.

Blanchard, O., & Illing, G. (2006). *Übungen zur Makroökonomie*. Pearson Studium.

Drost, A., Linnemann, L., & Schabert, A. (2003). *Übungsbuch zu Felderer*. Springer.

Felderer, B., & Homburg, S. (2005). *Makroökonomik und neue Makroökonomik* (9. ed.). Springer.

Friedman, M. (1968). The role of monetary policy. *American Economic Review,58*(No.1 LVIII March), 1–17.

John, K. D. (2004). *Arbeitsbuch Makroökonomik* (12. Aufl.). Schäffer-Poeschel.

Keynes, J. M. (1929). *The economic consequences of the peace* (S. 219–221). Routledge. (First edition 1920).

Mankiw, G. N. (2013). *Makroökonomik* (7. ed.). Schäffer-Poeschel.

Mussel, G. (2009). *Einführung in die Makroökonomik* (10. ed.). Vahlen.

Phelps, E. S. (1968). Money wage dynamics and labour market equilibrium. *Journal of Political Economy,76*(4), 678–711.

Samuelson, P. A., & Solow, R. M. (1960). Analytical aspects of anti-inflation policy; American economic review. *Papers and Proceedings,50*, 177–194.

Siebe, T., & Wenke, M. (2014). *Makroökonomie*. UTB Lucius.

Wagner, H., & Böhne, A. (2003). *Übungsbuch Makroökonomie*. Vahlen.

Further Reading

Eller, R. (Ed.). (2005). *Handbuch derivativer instrumente*. Schäffer-Poeschel.

Forster, J., Klüh, U., & Sauer, S. (2014). *Makroökonomie – Das Übungsbuch*. Pearson Studium.

Mankiw, G. N. (2011). *Makroökonomik* (6. ed.). Schäffer-Poeschel.

Miles, D., Scott, A., & Breedon, F. (2014). *Makroökonomie. Globale Wirtschaftszusammenhänge verstehen*. Wiley-VCH.

Olney, M. L. (2015). *Wiley Schnellkurs Makroökonomie*. Wiley-VCH.

Schröder, H. (2016). *Makroökonomie transparent vermittelt. VWL Grundlagen für Managementscheidungen*. Schröder Consulting.

Monetary Policy and its Implementation by the European Central Bank

5

What Follows Why?

After you have learned the first basic money theoretical relationships and also the topic of inflation in neoclassicism, we want to deal with the monetary policy of the European Central Bank (ECB) in the following as a practical application, whose highest goal is price stability. The knowledge learned here will allow you to form your own opinion about the development of money market interest rates.

Learning objectives

The goal is that you can explain,

- which instruments the ECB
- to pursue which goals
- how to use it and thus
- which effect it has on the money market.

5.1   Advantages of a Unified European Currency Area

There are many reasons that have spoken in favor of creating a European Monetary Union.

1. Fluctuations in exchange rates are eliminated

   This is especially advantageous for the economy. The prices for imports and exports can be planned. Hedging costs and exchange fees are eliminated. For private individuals, the annoying exchange of currencies at the border is eliminated. Prices are quoted in the European Monetary Union (EMU) in one currency, this increases market

C. Conrad, *Applied Macroeconomics*, https://doi.org/10.1007/978-3-658-39315-1_5

transparency. The demanders can compare the prices better, which is why competition increases. It is produced there and the pre-products are purchased where it is cheapest. As a result, European division of labor increases. European markets grow together.

2. The susceptibility to disturbances on the foreign exchange markets is lower. For example, speculators need much more capital to move the euro in one direction than one of the predecessor currencies.

3. Larger currency areas allow for more developed capital markets, more products and lower costs (economies of large scale).

4. Higher seigniorage profits arise because the common currency is more attractive as a reserve, transaction and settlement currency. A large currency becomes the leading currency and is used as a transaction currency. As a result, there is higher demand. The respective central bank prints the money and gets a value for it. If the currencies are invested abroad, interest can be generated.

5. A common European currency strengthens the European identification of citizens with Europe, integration and political cohesion.

5.2   The Founding of the ECB

On December 9/10, 1991, the heads of state and government of the European Community agreed on a European Union that was initially to comprise three pillars: a common foreign and security policy, cooperation in internal and legal affairs, and finally, economic and monetary union (EMU). These were significant historical steps on the way to a political unification of Europe that had never before existed in this form. The preamble of the EU Treaty states: "Determined to take the process of European integration initiated with the founding of the European Communities to a new stage." In European politics, the founding of the European Monetary Union was a success. All EU member states, with the exception of Great Britain, Denmark, and Sweden, decided in due course to join the EMU. The start of the EMU can also be described as successful in terms of the organizational and institutional tasks that had to be solved. Without delay, all of the stages envisaged in the Maastricht Treaty for the establishment of the European Central Bank were able to be implemented. In addition, the EMU fulfilled many tasks and expectations with the introduction of the euro as a single European currency: the transaction or exchange costs of the European currencies with each other fell away. The EU internal market received the missing price transparency through a single European transaction and accounting unit and the European political integration served as an incentive at least in advance for a democratically decisive European monetary policy decided on a country-by-country basis. With the euro, businesses have a constant and therefore predictable accounting unit for their intra-European exports and imports, and the size of the euro currency area protects against the feared currency attacks by speculators. With the introduction of the euro, the second largest capital market in the world was created and the euro area has become more economically independent.

The right way of political integration of Europe has been disputed for a long time. The current European Monetary Union corresponds to the idea of the monetarists to create a political and economic integration by means of a single currency and not to the approach of the economists according to which the single European currency should be the crowning of the political and economic integration (coronation thesis). The political and economic integration now has to be implemented. There is still a lot to do. After all, the euro brings together countries with different economic and political backgrounds without a single government in a currency area. In the following, we want to deal with the numerous unsolved problems of the European Monetary Union.

5.3 National Fiscal Policy

A key problem is the European coordination of national fiscal policies. It is still difficult to understand that the European interest rate policy could not be influenced by hardly bearable state interest charges or that the ECB and its member states would accept the insolvency of one of its members. In principle, the rules of the EMU were clear and restrictively defined.

Art. 123 Treaty on the Functioning of the European Union (TFEU) prohibits the ECB and national central banks from financing public deficits. Here there is a legal interpretation that allows, inter alia, the ECB to buy government bonds on the secondary market because this is not a direct state financing. However, if this provision is interpreted economically, this is an unauthorised state financing that is not covered by the Treaty. Economically, it makes no difference whether the ECB buys the bond directly from the state or indirectly from third parties. If the ECB buys government bonds on the secondary market, it creates a demand for these bonds. Interest rates and thus the costs of government debt will fall and possibly also create a demand if there was no private demand. If market participants know when the ECB buys government bonds, they can buy them before it and use the bid-ask spread at their expense (front-running strategy).

Art. 125 TFEU: "The Community shall not be liable for the obligations of central governments." This is also referred to as the "no-bail-out clause".

Art. 126 TFEU: "The Member States avoid excessive public deficits."

Neither the EU nor its Member States are liable for the obligations of individual EU countries. However, Article 103a (2) of the TFEU does not provide for financial assistance if a Member State is affected by difficulties or seriously threatened by serious difficulties. Although the ECB is independent in its decisions and credit extension to governments is contractually prohibited, European monetary policy is not taking place in a vacuum and is also decided by central bank governors from countries with different economic cycles, economic interests and stability cultures. The non-coordinated fiscal policy is therefore also referred to as the open flank of the EMU. This was confirmed in the case of Greece.

After a strong consolidation of budgetary policy, coupled with some balance sheet cosmetics, a large number of countries have managed to largely fulfill the convergence criteria. Italy and Belgium, however, exceeded the predetermined debt ratio of 1997 with 121.6% and 122.2% of their gross domestic product sustainably and were still accepted. The convergence criteria and the not quite excluded exit of the stability-oriented countries from the EMU ensured a disciplining of these countries in the transitional phase. From 01.01.2001, however, only the Stability Pact can, according to the prevailing opinion, prevent an excessive budgetary policy at the expense of the EMU community. At the instigation of Germany, which served as a stability policy model, the EU member states decided in 1997 on the so-called Stability Pact in the form of two Council Regulations and a Resolution of the European Council. It provides for fines in the form of a decision by ECOFIN, the Council of Economic and Finance Ministers, by qualified majority in the event of a persistent exceedance of the state deficits of 3% of GDP after several intermediate steps. Exceptions are only temporarily possible in the event of a serious economic situation, which must also be determined by ECOFIN by qualified majority. In addition, annual stability and convergence programmes to be submitted by the EMU states on a voluntary basis are to ensure a balanced budget in the medium term. The background to the Stability Pact is the financial policy prisoner's dilemma of a monetary union of states with autonomous national financial policy. The internal political advantages of a state debt benefit only the respective government, while the disadvantages in the form of a deterioration of the creditworthiness of the EMU as a community of all countries have to be borne in the form of increased long-term interest rates (free rider problem). In the Stability and Growth Pact, therefore, a balanced budget or a budget surplus is sought as a medium-term goal.

The decision of the EU Council of Ministers in June 1999 to approve a breach of the ceiling on new government debt in Italy due to a much lower than expected growth rate of gross domestic product was all the more dangerous. The decision of the EU Commission to support Greece's entry into the European Monetary Union on 01.01.2001 despite the still significant failure to meet the convergence criteria in view of a debt-to-GDP ratio of 104.4% in 1999 and the doubts about the consolidation of public finances raised by the European Central Bank is also to be criticized in this context.[1]

In their Stability and Convergence Programs of 1998, the countries planned to further reduce the budget deficit (Belgium, Austria, Portugal, Greece, Germany, Spain, France, Italy and the Netherlands) or to further increase their budget surplus (Luxembourg, Ireland, Finland and Sweden as well as Great Britain and Denmark). The average deficit in the euro area should therefore decrease from 2.3% of gross domestic product to 0.8% in 2002. However, even at this superficial level, some influencing factors were already left out at that time, which is why both the European Monetary Institute and the Deutsche

---

[1] See Conrad, Christian A. (2002).

Bundesbank already saw not only considerable deficiencies in the public finances in the countries' convergence programs for the reference year 1997, but also urgent need for action. Meanwhile, it is known that the postulated targets were almost not achieved by the countries.

When the countries entered the EU, they already used accounting cosmetics to achieve the deficit targets when meeting the convergence criteria. In part, payment obligations were postponed, moved to non-budget-relevant positions, or reserves were dissolved or state assets privatized to generate extraordinary income. In addition, governments increased taxes and fees. State expenditures were reduced—but mainly on state investments and not on state consumption. The EU's public investment ratio fell from 3% in 1991 to 2.2% in 1997. Against the background of the convergence criteria to be met, this development was understandable, but even then it was questionable whether it was sensible and, on the other hand, whether it would be sustainable. It must not be forgotten that the reduction in budget deficits was achieved during a positive economic development and thus also high tax revenues as well as historically low interest rates. For this reason, the European Commission calculated so-called deficit reference values for the individual countries taking into account their respective economic sensitivity. Germany, Greece, France, Italy and Austria would have had to show a deficit of up to around 1% in 1997, Belgium, Denmark, Spain, Ireland, Luxembourg, the Netherlands, Portugal and Great Britain a deficit of between 0 and 1% and Sweden and Finland even a surplus in order to be able to maintain the desired 3% deficit even in the event of a declining economy. The target projections of the Stability and Convergence Programs were not too ambitious: Under the economic conditions of 1997, Italy and Belgium would have needed 15 years and Greece 10 years to reach the debt convergence target of 60% of gross domestic product. Seen in this way, there was already a certain probability at that time that the economic exception rule of the Stability and Growth Pact would be invoked. It must also not be forgotten that even maintaining the debt ratio of 60% at a deficit ratio of 3% is based on the assumption of nominal economic growth of 5%. A significant interest and thus also budgetary risk was therefore to be seen in the high debt levels of Belgium, Italy and Greece.

The ECB already criticized the planned deficit ratios in 1999 as too high to be able to catch up with cyclical tax cuts.[2] Unfortunately, a qualified majority was found in the Council of Ministers all too quickly against a blue letter, which would have come at a very inopportune time for the Schröder government in the year of the Bundestag election campaign. This political decision, which was also referred to as the "decision of the crows"[3], has discredited the European Monetary Union. Since in the end all sanctions of

[2] See ECB, The Implementation of the Stability and Growth Pact, in: ECB—Monthly Report May 1999, Frankfurt a. M. 1999, pp. 49–63, 63 ff.

[3] See Hort, Peter, Coalition of the Crows, in: F.A.Z. from 13.02.2002, p. 3.

the Stability Pact have to be decided by a qualified majority, its importance is called into question. Certainly, a loss of confidence also resulted from the fact that it was precisely Germany as the former stability policy model and initiator of the Stability Pact that first politically undermined the mechanism of the Stability Pact.

5.4   Problems of a Unified Monetary Policy

Monetary policy is overwhelmed by the different economic situations in the individual Euro countries. A uniform Euro interest rate always depends on the average development of all Euro countries. This had the consequence that at the beginning of the currency union the interest rate for Germany was relatively high and for the southern European countries and Ireland too low, which resulted in a sharp increase in consumer and property prices in these countries.[4]

The first interest rate cut on 09.12.1998 to a uniform level of 3% only meant a reduction of 0.3% for Germany, while for Spain it meant a subsidy of 1.75%, for Portugal 2.10% and for Ireland even 3.35%.[5] The result were considerable deviations in the inflation rates between the countries. In most countries with traditionally high inflation rates, the two percent were already exceeded in 1998 and 1999 (Spain: 1999, Portugal and Ireland: 1998 and 1999).

How difficult the transition to a common currency is, if the countries have different economic development and pursue divergent fiscal policy, showed after the financial crisis in the sovereign debt crisis. Countries like Ireland, Spain, Greece and Portugal had pursued an expansive fiscal policy or, as in the case of Ireland and Spain, a credit and real estate bubble. Both led to high demand-driven growth rates associated with corresponding wage and price increases. In terms of monetary policy, interest rates should have been increased and the money supply reduced in these countries, but this was not possible due to the divergent economic development of the eurozone (see Figs. 5.1 and 5.2). After the financial crisis, the strong domestic demand was missing. The states were over-indebted and, due to wage and price increases, no longer competitive. Since there was no own currency, they could not regain their competitiveness through a currency devaluation.

---

[4] See Schrader and Laaser (2010); German Council of Economic Experts (2011) as well as FAZ from 14.09.2011, http://www.faz.net/aktuell/wirtschaft/eurokrise/beamte-in-griechenland-die-ueberfluessigen-11167253.html.
[5] See Joachim Starbatty. (2001, p. 375).

ECB interest rate development
Excerpt from: http://www.finanzen.net/leitzins/

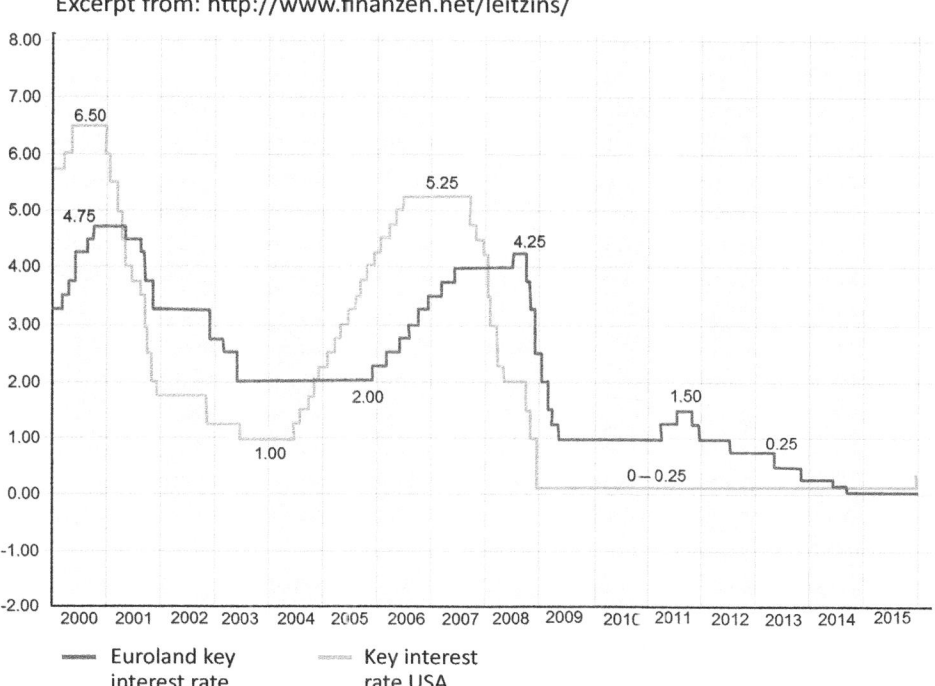

Fig. 5.1 Development of the ECB interest rate in comparison to the US interest rate. (Reprinted with kind permission of finanzen.net GmbH. http://www.finanzen.net/leitzins/)

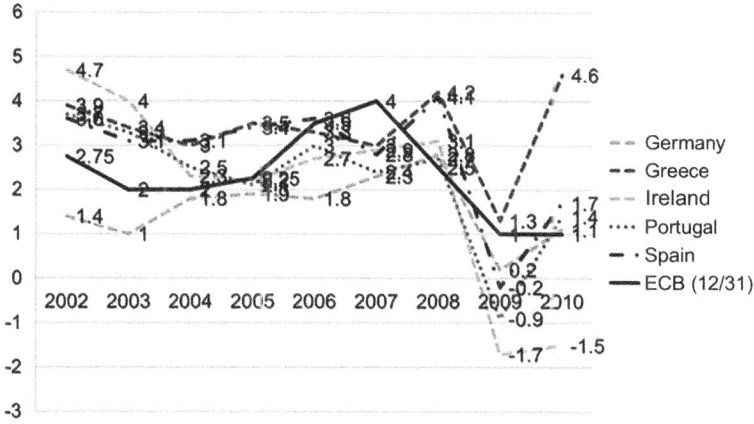

Fig. 5.2 Interest rate and EU inflation rates

5.5   The Missing Political and Economic Agreement of Europe

The ECB also sees sustainable reforms in the labour and goods markets as essential for increasing Europe's growth potential. The still highly segmented or nationally structured bond and stock markets cause transaction costs in the Eurozone to be ten times higher than in the USA. In addition, there are different supervisory regulations and accounting standards. There is also no politically unified government in the Eurozone in contrast to the USA. A non-uniform policy paralyses. The effects of opposite policies counteract each other. This applies not only to financial and economic policy, but also to foreign policy. Although significant progress in integration was made in Amsterdam in 1997 in the areas of internal and legal policy, as well as in foreign and security policy, the competences remained with the member states, there is no Community law. A joint military action by the EU still requires unanimity and the use of national armed forces. A political agreement is gaining in importance after the collapse of the USSR. There is a need for a balancing second political global player next to the USA. A one-sided dominance of the USA in world politics would not find international acceptance in the long term. At present, European politicians are still indebted to the Euro for the incomplete political and economic integration.

Against the background of the foregoing, it becomes clear how important it is that there are idealists and politically independent organisations and individuals who pursue the overriding goal of a stable currency and a political agreement in Europe. European integration has reached a critical point. The step to the monetary union has been taken. Many member states benefited from this. Not least, the reduction in long-term interest rates was a significant reason for the traditionally less stability-oriented countries of the EMU to join in order to benefit from the reputation of the traditionally stability-oriented countries. The long-term interest rates of the traditionally stability-oriented countries were, before the introduction of the Euro, partly 6.5% below those of the less stability-oriented countries.[6] The former less stability-oriented countries were thus able to save billions in state interest payments. Now it is a matter of asserting the overriding European interest as a public good against the national interests of individual states and the interests of other groups. A surrender of national sovereignty is unavoidable here. The public good of Europe can be found everywhere, not only in a stability-oriented budgetary policy, in internal and judicial policy, in the common foreign and security policy or in a subsidy-free internal European competition. What is decisive is that the free-riding behaviour of individual states is prevented, in which this state can secure a higher benefit for itself through non-community-conform behaviour at the expense of the others and thus the community solution with the higher benefit for all can no longer be realised.

---

[6]Annual yields of 10-year government bonds or similar financial instruments, here Italy to Germany in 1985. See Institute of the German economy, Germany in numbers, Cologne 2001, p. 133.

Against this stand the findings of the new political economy. According to the approach of the new political economy, politicians do not usually maximise the common good, but predominantly their own benefit. Political offices grant this benefit in the form of power, prestige and income. In order to achieve the desired offices, the politician has to collect as many votes as possible—one speaks of vote maximisation. This behaviour orientation can be referred to as political expediency or "political rationality".[7] The individual national interests of the member states are therefore in the foreground for the politician. The overriding European interest is only of interest to him if it serves the national interest, as long as he is not elected in a European election.[8]

Summary

The prerequisite for the realization of the benefits of the European Monetary Union is that the currency is stable and therefore accepted in the long term, predictable, that is, without risk surcharges. Furthermore, the economic, wage and financial policy of the countries must be stable and may not differ greatly, because too strong a cost increase (different competitiveness) or cyclical differences can no longer be offset by exchange rate changes. However, as became apparent after the introduction of the euro, many southern European countries did not adhere to this rule. In particular, the lower interest rates after the introduction of the euro were used, as in the case of Greece, for an expansion of the debt. The borrowed money flowed into consumption. Almost every fourth Greek employee worked in the public sector. Greece consumed more than the GDP. The missing goods were imported from abroad and increased the foreign debt. The money was not invested, which was one reason why productivity was lacking in the following years to make the debt service. Due to the high credit-financed state demand, prices and wages rose. In the euro, this competitive disadvantage could no longer be offset by a currency devaluation.[9] ◄

---

[7] A comprehensive theoretical analysis of political rationality can be found in *Frey, Bruno S.* (1981). An empirical verification of further parts of the New Political Economy was carried out by *Meyer-Krahmer.* See *Meyer-Krahmer, Frieder* (1979). An analysis of individual EG policy areas on the basis of the New Political Economy is the subject of *Guerrieri, Paolo and Padoan, Pietro Carlo C.* (1989). The most concise summary of the approaches of the "New Political Economy" is provided by *Krisch, Guy* (1993) and *Franke.* See *Franke, Siegfried F.* (1996). A good theoretical analysis of political voting can be found in *Downs, Anthony* (1968); *Andel, Norbert* (1990), pp. 47 ff.; *Braybrooke, David and Lindblom, Charles, E.* (1963) and *Lindblom, Charles, E.* (1965).

[8] See *Conrad, Christian, A.* (2001) and *Conrad, Christian A.* (2002).

[9] Sachverständigenrat zur Begutachtung der gesamtwirtschaftlichen Entwicklung (2011); Schrader und Laaser (2010) sowie faz.net vom 14.09.2011, http://www.faz.net/aktuell/wirtschaft/eurokrise/beamte-in-griechenland-die-ueberfluessigen-11167253.html.

5.6   Organizations of the ECB

The ECB Council
The Council is responsible for the ECB's monetary policy. The ECB Council is the ECB's supreme decision-making body. It consists of the six members of the Executive Board and the presidents of the national central banks of the Euro area countries.

The ECB Council usually meets twice a month at the ECB's headquarters in Frankfurt am Main.

As part of the two-pillar strategy, it assesses economic and monetary developments and takes monetary policy decisions every six weeks. All national central bank governors have one vote in the ECB Council. Lithuania's entry into the euro area on 1 January 2015 led to an organisational reform to limit the number of members. As a result, a rotation system was introduced for the voting rights of the presidents of the national central banks in the ECB Council.

The Executive Board
The Executive Board consists of the President, the Vice-President and four other members. Its members are elected by the European Council by a qualified majority. The Executive Board is the ECB's permanent executive body. As such, it prepares ECB Council meetings and implements monetary policy in accordance with the decisions of the ECB Council and can issue instructions to national central banks.

Supervisory Board
The Supervisory Board consists of the Chair (appointed for a non-renewable term of five years), the Vice-Chair (elected from among the members of the ECB's Executive Board), four ECB representatives and representatives of the national supervisory authorities.

If the national supervisory authority nominated by a Member State is not a national central bank, then, in addition to the representative of the competent authority, a representative of the respective national central bank may also participate in the meetings.

Conclusion on the Euro Introduction
The balance sheet of the euro so far is, as expected, mixed. Despite many advantages, the long-term problems of an suboptimal currency area without a unified financial policy have been accumulating in recent years. In principle, the euro has, as shown at the beginning, many advantages, but two advantages have also led to disadvantages.

- Advantage: Exchange rate fluctuations are eliminated.

This is especially advantageous for the economy. The prices for imports and exports can be planned. Exchange rate hedging costs and exchange fees are eliminated. For private individuals, the annoying exchange of currencies at the border is eliminated. Prices are quoted in euros in the EU. This increases market transparency. The demanders can better compare the prices, which is why competition increases. Production and pre-orders are made where it is cheapest. As a result, European division of labor increases. European markets are growing together. However, the merger of many different countries into a currency union also results in distribution effects. For example, if you take Germany, Germany traditionally has a high trade surplus. This resulted in a strong currency with a persistent appreciation trend against other currencies, whose countries tended to import more than export. If all these countries are in a currency area, appreciation and depreciation trends even out. That is, from a German point of view, the currency becomes weaker and, for example, from a southern European point of view, stronger. For the German economy, this means an increase in its competitiveness and, as a result, more jobs. For German households, however, this means an increase in the price of their imports or foreign travel. The same is true in reverse for southern European countries.

- Advantage: A common European currency strengthens the European identification of citizens with Europe, integration and political cohesion.

As we have already said, the prerequisite for the emergence of these advantages is, however, that the currency is stable and therefore accepted in the long term, predictable, that is, without risk surcharges. Furthermore, the economic, wage and financial policy of the countries must be stable and may not differ greatly, because too strong a cost increase (different competitiveness) or cyclical differences can no longer be offset by exchange rate changes.

However, as became apparent after the introduction of the euro, many southern European countries did not adhere to this rule. The lower interest rates after the introduction of the euro were used, for example, in the case of Greece, for an expansion of the debt. The borrowed money flowed into consumption. Almost every fourth Greek employee worked in the public sector. Greece consumed more than it produced, that is, more than the Greek GDP. The missing goods were imported from abroad and increased the foreign debt. The money was not invested, which was one reason why productivity was lacking in the following years to make the debt service. Due to the high credit-financed government demand, prices and wages rose. In the euro, this competitive disadvantage could no longer be offset by a currency devaluation.

Monetary policy is overwhelmed by such different economic situations in the individual euro countries. A uniform euro interest rate always depends on the average development of all euro countries. This had the consequence that at the beginning of the currency union, the interest rate was relatively high for Germany and too low for the southern European countries and Ireland due to different economic cycles, which resulted in a sharp increase in consumer and real estate prices in these countries.

This may be one reason why the ECB's asset study (Sect. 2.5) found such distortions between German and Southern European private assets. Ultimately, however, it cannot be ruled out that the differences in wealth are also due to a higher degree of tax evasion, as a result of weaker tax administration in these countries. Otherwise, how could a higher level of wealth have arisen in a country with a lower GDP over the years. At least, from a sense of justice, it must be demanded that these private assets be used to service the debt of the over-indebted countries. Why should German taxpayers pay for the rich Greeks? Not least, the German consumer also bears part of the burden of the euro introduction with the relatively weaker purchasing power of the euro. On the other hand, this is offset by a higher export competitiveness. However, if wages do not rise proportionally, this advantage primarily benefits German corporate owners.

The euro is a historical experiment that brings together economically and culturally different countries into a single currency area. Severe adjustment processes were to be expected. This adjustment requirement currently affects the southern European countries. Since they can no longer devalue their currency against the German one in order to become competitive, they have to lower wages and prices that were previously relatively too high compared to the northern countries. Unfortunately, there is no alternative to such a painful adjustment. Especially the higher competitive pressure resulting from the shared currency with Germany must not lead to a European country financial adjustment. This would be unfair to the northern countries.

5.7   Basics of European Central Bank Monetary Policy

5.7.1   Political Independence

The history of hyperinflations (Sect. 4.3) teaches us that governments often try to finance their spending through central banks when they control them. The result was hyperinflations. For this reason, many central banks are now politically independent. The independence of the ECB is laid down in the institutional framework for the single monetary policy (the Treaty on the Functioning of the European Union, Article 130 of the TFEU, and the ECB Statute).

Neither the ECB's organs nor a national central bank nor a member of its decision-making organs may seek or receive instructions from the organs or bodies of the EU, the governments of the EU Member States or any other bodies. The European Union (EU) and the governments of the Member States undertake, pursuant to Article 130 of the TFEU, to respect this principle and not to attempt to influence the members of the ECB's decision-making organs. The ECB is financially independent and has its own budget. Its capital was paid in by the national central banks of the euro area in accordance with the agreed shares.

There is a distinction between the European System of Central Banks (ESCB) and the Eurosystem. The ESCB, however, comprises the ECB and the national central banks of all EU Member States (Article 282(1) of the TFEU). The Eurosystem, on the other hand, consists of the ECB and the national central banks of the EU Member States that have already introduced the euro. The Eurosystem was designed as a transitional solution as it was assumed when drafting the TFEU that all EU Member States would introduce the euro sooner or later. The distinction between the Eurosystem and the ESCB remains necessary as long as there are EU Member States whose currency is not the euro.

5.7.2   Targets

The primary objective of the Eurosystem is, in accordance with Article 127(1) of the TFEU, to ensure price stability:

> The primary objective of the European System of Central Banks (hereinafter the "ESCB") is to maintain price stability.

In addition, a secondary goal:

> To the extent that this is possible without compromising the objective of price stability, the ECB supports the general economic policy in the Union in order to contribute to the achievement of the objectives set out in Article 3 of the Treaty on European Union.

Article 3 of the Treaty on European Union contains different objectives, including sustainable development of Europe on the basis of balanced economic growth and price stability as well as a highly competitive social market economy aimed at full employment and social progress. Price stability is therefore the primary objective of the ECB's monetary policy. Once this is achieved, it can do everything to create a favourable economic environment and a high level of employment.

In order to support the economic development of the euro area, the ECB wants to smooth out business cycles, which is why monetary policy is conducted as an anti-cyclical monetary policy.

In recession, that is, when aggregate demand is weak, an expansionary monetary policy should stimulate investment. The money supply is increased and interest rates are reduced. This has the consequence that commercial banks can grant more loans and investments are cheaper to finance and due to low demand the prices do not have to rise even if the money supply is increased:

$$M \uparrow, i \downarrow \Rightarrow (p \uparrow) \Rightarrow i \downarrow \Rightarrow I(i) \uparrow$$

In the economic boom, when aggregate demand is greater than supply, the ECB takes the opposite measures. A restrictive monetary policy should reduce demand in order to prevent misallocation and strong price increases. The money supply is reduced and the interest rate is increased. Banks get less liquidity from the ECB and have to raise interest rates on loans:

$$M \downarrow, i \uparrow \Rightarrow p \downarrow \Rightarrow i \uparrow \Rightarrow I(i) \downarrow$$

The ECB Council pursues the objective of price stability by trying to keep the inflation rate below, but close to 2% over the medium term.

The basis of the ECB's monetary policy is its **two-pillar strategy,** which consists of a

- Analysis of economic developments and a comparison with
- The analysis of monetary developments.

The background is that the price level is defined according to the quantity equation on the development of the quantity of goods in relation to the quantity of money, taking into account the velocity of circulation:

$$\underline{M} \cdot v = \underline{Y} \cdot p$$

Quantity equation in growth rates:

$$Y + P = M + V$$

The reference value for the growth of the money supply would be, for example, 4.5% in normal times. The ECB has set an inflation target of below but close to 2%, for example 1.8%. If we assume 2.5% real GDP growth and a slight decrease in the velocity of circulation −0.2%—this results in a growth rate of the quantity equation:

$$M = Y + P - V, \text{ also } 2.5\% + 1.8\% - (-0.2) = 4.5\%.$$

How can the ECB control the money supply?

5.7.3 The Money Creation Process

The Characteristics of Modern Money (Computer Age)
Money today consists not only of coins and banknotes, but mainly of bits and bytes. One also speaks of virtual money. This computer money can be transported around the world in seconds via fibre optic cables. Electronic money can be multiplied (almost free of charge) and very quickly. Electronic money is book money, more precisely sight deposits or sight credit. These are the account balances that you see on your current account (demand deposits), which corresponds to claims on credit institutions or banks.

The central bank has the monopoly on money. However, banks can multiply the central bank's money supply through the money creation process. Only the central bank can increase liquidity by creating additional money. Only she has received the sovereign money monopoly and is allowed to produce money. In addition to the creation of cash by the issuance of banknotes and coins, there is also the creation of sight deposits through the lending of commercial banks. Although the central bank has the monopoly on money, banks can multiply the central bank's money supply through the money creation process. Banks do not keep the money of their customers, which is credited to a checking or savings account, in the safe, but use it to lend it to other customers. The lending of banks with the deposits of customers is one of their essential business principles and economic functions. The credit contribution is made available to the credit customers on an account, for example, to buy a car. In each step, new money is created as a sight deposit and thus the circulating money supply is increased. However, this is not money in the narrower sense, because the banks have lent the money, the liquidity, further, thus do not have it anymore. Only a claim was created and no liquidity, that is, money in the narrower sense. The customers who have deposited their money with the bank get sight deposits, which entitles them to withdraw the liquidity at any time. However, the liquidity has already been passed on as a loan. If the customer withdraws his sight deposits or uses them to buy goods, the bank must make the liquidity available to him again. The banks calculate statistically on the basis of the average customer behavior how much liquidity they have to keep as a reserve. Therefore, every bank becomes illiquid if the customers withdraw all the deposited money at the same time. This is called a bank run. The sight deposits of the customers are seen as money because, like cash in the till, they can be used to buy goods at any time That the bank then has to provide the liquidity for the purchases does not matter from this point of view. Since the customer can pay for goods at any time with the sight deposits, the ECB sees the sight deposits as money.

How does the creation of sight deposits by commercial banks work?

Example of Money Creation
1. **Case banking system with 100% reserve requirement**
   H. Anton deposits 1000 € at the bank. The bank holds 100% reserve in case H. Anton withdraws his money again. Since no money is loaned out here, no sight deposits are created. There is no money creation (see Fig. 5.3a).
2. **Case banking system with fractional reserve requirement**

H. Anton does not immediately withdraw his money, so the bank lends 80% to H. Bose (which makes the money supply 1800 €). H. Bose pays with the money H. Cantor, who deposits the money at bank B. Bank B again holds 20% (160 €) in reserve and lends 640 € to H. Dahmen (which makes the money supply 2440 €) etc. (The process of financial intermediation is a task of the banks). In the process of repeated bank credit, a multiple of the 1000 € is spent. But since always a part is kept as a reserve, the process stops when the 1000 € are completely set aside as a reserve. Nevertheless, the economist Friedrich August von Hayek called this the perverse elasticity of credit supply. On the other hand, the demand from income generation would be missing if the bank did not lend the 1000 € from H. Anton again. H. Anton has operated in a company for 1000 € value creation, so production is generated. The difference is the profit income that accrues to the company owner. But the production from his 1000 € is not opposed to any demand if he saves it, so consumes nothing, but the bank does not lend it and saving can not become investment.

In reality, there is a legally prescribed minimum reserve that has to be deposited with the ECB in proportion to each deposit. The minimum reserve reduces the bank multiplier: The banks have to pay 1% of their short-term liabilities to the central bank as a reserve deposit. In addition, each loan must be backed by an average of 8% equity from the banks depending on the risk. This means that they can lend about 12.5 times their equity. This further slows down the money creation process.

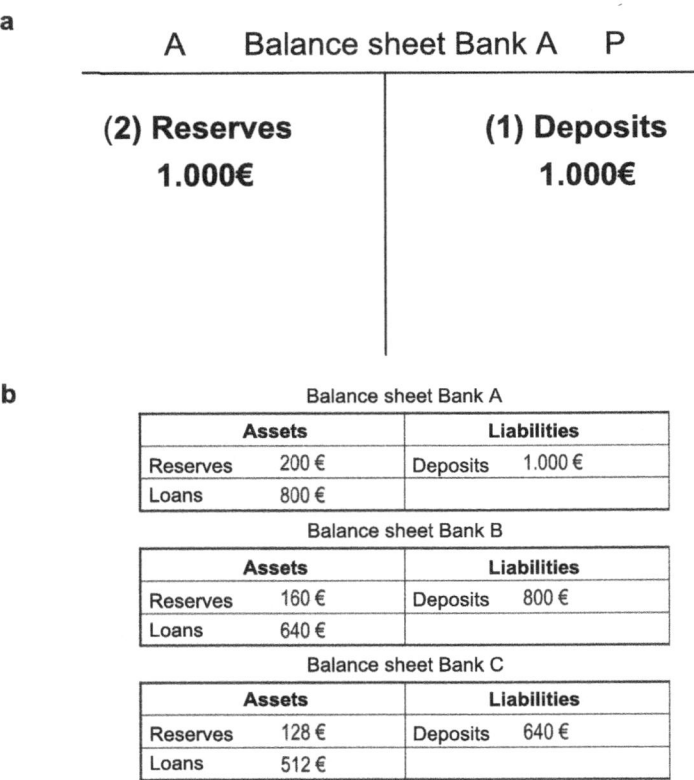

Fig. 5.3   a balance sheet at 100%; b reserve requirement money creation and bank balance sheets. (Figure based on Mankiw, N. Gregory, 2000, p. 539)

The money is brought to the bank. Sight deposits (bank deposits or deposits) arise. Assumption: The money is re-lent by the bank in the same quarter with a 20% reserve requirement, which is why the money supply increases by 80%. This happens in every period, which is why the money supply increases by 80% of the previous bank deposit each time. The money supply, as shown in Figs. 5.3b and 5.4, is multiplied by a factor of 1000 € (money base B) by repeated lending.

The process of money creation can also be represented as an infinite geometric series. With a reserve deposit ratio (R/D) of 0.2, the following applies:

(with C: cash, R: reserve, D: demand deposits, B: monetary base (C + R), LZ: maturity)

$$\textbf{Moneysupply} = \left[1 + (1 - 0.2) + (1 - 0.2)^2 + \ldots\right] 1.000 \text{ €}$$

$$= \frac{1}{0.2} 1.000 \text{ €} = 5.000 \text{ €(infinite geometric series)}$$

Fig. 5.4 Circulation of
money with a 20% reserve
requirement

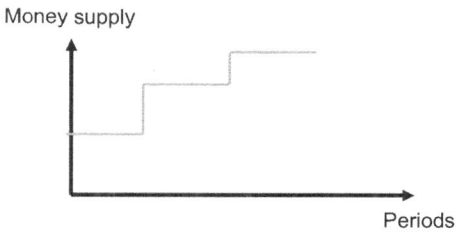

Money Supply Multiplier

$$\Delta M = \frac{1}{R/D} \Delta B$$

A multiplier shows the relationship between a triggering change in size (e.g. change in investment) and the resulting multiple change in the dependent variable. The change in Y is examined if another size changes permanently. The money supply multiplier indicates how much the money supply has increased after the money creation process of commercial banks has expired, given a reserve deposit ratio.

In its monetary policy, the ECB distinguishes between M1, M2 and M3 as so-called money aggregates (see Figs. 5.5 and 5.6). These are the well-known money amounts such as cash and sight deposits (M1), which are extended to other forms of money investment. This includes, outside the banking sector, circulating liquid cash and daily deposits from non-banks. These daily deposits can be converted into cash at short notice. M1 is the money that can be used at any time (purchasing power).

The further the money supply is extended to other investment forms, the lower the probability that the money will be used to purchase goods and thus influence prices. One criterion here is the term of the investment. For example, savings books have a notice period of 3 months and form M2 with term deposits with a term of up to 2 years. This money supply therefore includes M1 plus savings deposits and term deposits with a term of up to two years. A term deposit is money deposited with the bank for a fixed interest and for a certain term. That is why there is also the term fixed deposit. During this period, these term deposits cannot be used, unless a fee is charged. At the end of the

Fig. 5.5 Money aggregates

M1	C	D^1	Cash + non-interest-bearing demand deposits = actual money supply
M2	$C + D^1$	$+ D^2$	Savings deposits with statutory period of notice (3 months) + term deposits LZ up to 2 years
M3	$C + D^1 + D^2$	$+ D^3$	Money market fund shares, repo transactions, bank bonds LZ up to 2 years

The use-oriented monetary aggregate concepts M1, M2 and M3 in the euro area

Status: 31.01.2009 in billion EURO

Currency in circulation	716.9
+ Deposits payable on demand	3,379.2
= **M1**	**4,096.1**
+ Deposits with agreed maturity of up to 2 years	2,377.3
Deposits with agreed + Notice period of up to 3 months	1,596.0
= **M2**	**8,069.4**
+ Repurchase agreements	327.2
+ Money market fund shares	766.4
+ Money market paper and debt securities up to 2 years	221.2
= **M3**	**9,384.2**

Fig. 5.6   ECB money concepts. (Source: Deutsche Bundesbank, Monthly Reports)

term, these term deposits revert to sight deposits. Savings deposits, on the other hand, refer to deposits that are normally open-ended and can only be requested back after the statutory notice period of 3 months. Term and savings deposits can therefore not be used for payments at any time, in contrast to sight deposits. The interest rates for this change with the general interest rate development.

The aggregate M3 also includes other short-term money investments in addition to M2. These include short-term bank promissory notes (original maturity of up to 2 years), money market fund shares issued by money market funds, and so-called repurchase agreements. Bank promissory notes are securities in which the issuing bank undertakes to repay the face value of the promissory note at the end of the term. In addition, the buyer receives interest on his invested capital. A repurchase agreement is a transaction with a repurchase agreement. It serves the short-term financing of the commercial banks by the ECB through open market operations. With open market operations, the ECB grants liquidity to commercial banks against the sale or provision of collateral for claims. As a rule, this transaction is then reversed after 7 days. The money supply M3 is an important indicator for the monetary policy of the Eurosystem.

5.7.4   Process of Financial Intermediation by Commercial Banks

How does our financial system work and what is the role of commercial banks in money and credit supply to the economy? Commercial banks are supplied with liquidity by the ECB through open market operations (see Fig. 5.7). For this they pay the ECB an interest rate. In parallel, they receive liquidity from the public's deposits. These include private households, companies and the state. Commercial banks usually pay interest on these deposits (deposit interest). For the deposits they have to deposit the minimum reserve with the ECB. In turn, they grant loans to the public and charge a higher interest rate for this. In parallel, commercial banks can still provide each other with liquidity via the money market.

This is where the central importance of commercial banks for the economy becomes apparent. The bankruptcy of a commercial bank affects the economy in many ways. Depending on the deposit protection, customers' claims against the commercial bank may be lost. If the bank had provided companies with credit lines, these are no longer available. Both can lead to insolvencies. If necessary, other banks are affected, which either had claims against the commercial bank or against companies that are insolvent due to the loss of deposits or the lack of credit lines. If several commercial banks are affected, this can lead to a financial crisis. For example, during the last financial crisis, it was enough that the banks could not exclude the default of the other banks due to the lack of transparency of the US mortgage derivatives in order to make the interbank market collapse. The banks did not trust each other and did not lend each other money anymore. At the height of the crisis, even transfers were withheld. If you want to get an idea of the effects that the write-downs of the US mortgage derivatives had, you only have to imagine in Fig. 5.3b that banks A, B and C would have to write off their loans. The resulting deficit on the asset side is then offset against the equity of the banks.

In the following, we want to additionally represent in the balance sheets of the participating actors central bank, commercial bank and public the process of financial intermediation described above by the commercial banks (see also Fig. 5.7).

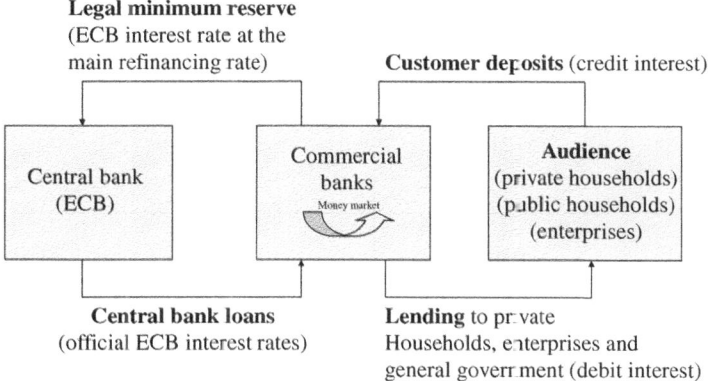

Fig. 5.7 Process of financial intermediation

Commercial banks are supplied with liquidity by the ECB through open market operations. This corresponds to a loan from the ECB to the commercial banks. This loan is reflected as a claim in the ECB balance sheet and as a liability in the balance sheet of the commercial banks (see Fig. 5.8). Commercial banks also receive liquidity through the deposits of the public. This results in a claim of the public against the commercial banks, the deposits or sight deposits, and a liability of the commercial banks towards the public. For this, commercial banks usually pay interest (deposit interest). For the deposits, they must The minimum reserve that must be deposited with the ECB. This creates a liability for the ECB and an asset for the commercial banks. Conversely, commercial banks lend money to the public. This creates a liability for the public and an asset for the commercial banks. The public also has cash. In a wider sense, this is an asset of the ECB because the ECB has issued the cash. The ECB has the cash as a liability on its balance sheet (see also Figs. 5.7, 5.8, 5.9, 5.10, 5.11).

Schematically shown as follows:

$$\text{Money supply}: M1 = C + D = \text{short-term purchasing power}$$
$$\text{Monetary base}: B = R + C(\text{liabilities side of the central bank})$$
$$C : \text{Cash}$$
$$R : \text{Reserve}$$
$$D : \text{Sight deposits}$$

Extract from the consolidated financial statements of the EURO system Status: 27.03.2009 billion EURO

Claims on general government in EURO	37.4	Banknotes in circulation	745.7
Claims in EURO on banks in the EURO currency area of which	661.9	Liabilities to euro area credit institutions denominated in euro	263.8
- Main refinancing transactions 229.9		. . ..	
Gold	217.5		
Receivables in foreign currencies	152.3		
	1,803.1		1,803.1

Fig. 5.8 ECB balance sheet

Fig. 5.9 Central bank

Active (claims)	Passive (liabilities)
- Currency reserves (purchase of foreign currency = money creat on) - Loans to the state (bonds as collateral) - Loans to banks (refinancing)	- Cash - Reserve holding of the Credit institutions R a) Voluntary reserve b) Minimum reserve

Fig. 5.10 Credit institutions (commercial banks)

Active (claims)	Passive (liabilities)
- Loans to non-banks - R (minimum reserve, reserves at the central bank)	- Deposits (Receivables from non-banks Deposits) - Central bank refinancing loans

Fig. 5.11 Non-banks (the public)

Active (claims)	Passive (liabilities)
- Cash C - Receivables from Banks D (demand deposits) Crucial money supply (purchasing power) M = C + D (M1)	- Loans

5.7.5   The Monetary Policy Instruments of the ECB

In monetary policy instruments, one distinguishes between open market operations, standing facilities and the minimum reserve.

5.8   Open Market Operations (As Interest and Monetary Policy)

Open market operations are monetary policy operations that are initiated by the central bank. They aim to provide or withdraw liquidity from banks. There are four categories of open market operations, which differ in terms of objectives, term, frequency and implementation: main refinancing operations, longer-term refinancing operations (maturity 90 days), fine-tuning operations and structural operations (without repurchase obligation; 7 days).

The main refinancing operations are, as the name suggests, the main steering instrument of the ECB and account for around 70% of bank financing.

They correspond to a short-term loan from the central bank to the commercial banks for 7 days with a repurchase obligation, against securities (securities) as collateral. This is also called "repo operations" or "pension operations". The collateral is provided by a time-limited transfer of securities, i.e. with a repurchase agreement or as a collateral loan, i.e. the pledging of securities, which is the current practice of financing German banks via the Deutsche Bundesbank as the executing body of the ECB. The quality of the securities in question is set by the ECB. Eligible securities include government bonds and economic loans. This credit must be paid by the commercial banks with the main refinancing rate, also called the key interest rate.

With the open market operations, the ECB directly controls the money supply M3 (pension or repo transactions). Two types are distinguished here with which the ECB can pass on liquidity to the commercial banks, the interest and the quantity tender. In the **quantity tender**, the interest rate is set by the ECB and the commercial banks ask for the desired amount of money. The distribution repartition takes place proportionally. In the **interest tender**, the banks have to name both the desired amount and the interest rate at which they want to borrow money (currently common with minimum bid rate). The interest and the quantity tender are explained in more detail with an example on the following pages.

In addition, the ECB conducts long-term open market operations with a term of 3 months. They account for around 20% of the refinancing of commercial banks. In addition, there are hourly quick tenders for fine-tuning and final structural open market operations.

5.9   Standing Facilities

The standing facilities are among the monetary policy instruments that banks can use on their own initiative on a daily basis. The standing facilities serve commercial banks to adjust unplanned liquidity shortfalls or surpluses also overnight on a short-term basis. Two standing facilities are distinguished: the deposit facility and the credit facility. The interest rates for this form a interest rate corridor within which the overnight money market rate moves.

Main Refinancing Operations

The main refinancing operations were previously known as the Lombard rate. It corresponds to an overdraft credit for banks. It is short-term and available in unlimited amounts to liquidity shortages of commercial banks. Here too, banks only receive the liquidity against the deposit of collateral.

Deposit Facility

This facility serves commercial banks as a short-term investment opportunity. The money is safe at the ECB. In normal times, the ECB pays an interest on these liquidity surpluses of commercial banks.

The credit facility rate and the deposit facility rate together form an interest rate corridor for the market interest rate. All banks that have collateral can refinance themselves at the ECB at the credit facility rate and invest their money at least at the deposit facility rate.

5.10   Minimum Reserve

The minimum reserve creates a need for central bank money because always a part of the deposits must be deposited with the ECB as a reserve before the rest can be lent as credit and thus new sight deposits can be created. It thus serves as a brake on money creation. By changing the minimum reserve requirement, a long-term money supply gross tax can be levied in this way. The minimum reserve is remunerated with the main refinancing rate (key interest rate).

▶ **Tender of Amount**

In this case, the interest rate is set by the ECB. The participating commercial banks notify the ECB of the amount of money they want to receive at the specified interest rate. The allocation (repartition) is made proportionally. In case of oversubscription, the allocation is made proportionally according to the amount of money requested. The advantage of the amount tender is that the ECB can set the interest rate. The question for the commercial banks is how to position their bids. If they demand too much, they have to invest the excess amount again at the money market at a loss. If they demand too little, they have to borrow money at a higher interest rate.

Example

The ECB wants to allocate 80 billion € to the banks at 2%. 5 banks submit bids (Table 5.1):

You can also calculate the repartition rate (0.4 here) directly and apply it to the bids of the banks to determine the allocation: ◀

▶ **Interest Rate Tender**

This is an auction procedure (American procedure). The commercial banks have to name the desired amount of money and the interest rate to the participating commercial banks at which they want to receive the offered money. The ECB sets a minimum bid rate. The bids of the banks are arranged according to the amount of interest offered. The allocation

Table 5.1 Tender of amount

Banks	Bids in billion €	Shares in %	Repartition	Allocated amount of money	Interest rate (%)
A	50	25	25% × 80	20	2
B	25	12.5	12.5% × 80	10	2
C	25	12.5	12.5% × 80	10	2
D	50	25	25% × 80	20	2
E	50	25	25% × 80	20	2
	200	100	R-rate: 0.4		2

is made according to the amount of interest offered until the money is allocated. If the last amount of money is distributed to several banks, the money is distributed proportionally according to the amount of money requested (repartitioned). The interest rate used last is called the marginal interest rate. The commercial banks do not receive an allocation if they offer too low an interest rate. To find out how the market interest rate has been influenced by the allocated money, the ECB calculates the weighted average interest rate. The advantage of this procedure is that the ECB does not influence the market interest rate by its specification (see also Grögens et al., 2013; Siebe & Wenke, 2014; Blanchard, 2014; Blanchard & Illing, 2006; Wagner & Böhne, 2003; Felderer & Homburg, 2005; Drost et al., 2003; Mankiw, 2013; John, 2004; as well as Mussel, 2009).

> **Example**
>
> The ECB would like to allocate 80 billion euros with a minimum bid rate of 2% (Table 5.2): ◄

Table 5.2 Interest rate

Banks	Bids in billion €	Interest rate (%)	Repartition	Allocated amount of money	Weighted interest rate
B	40	2.3		40	(40 × 2.3%
A	20	2.2		20	+20 × 2.2%
E	20	2.1	50% × 20	10	+10 × 2.1%
C	20	2.1	50% × 20	10	+10 × 2.1%)
D	50	2.0		0	: 80=2.2%

Summary

The ECB's main objective is price stability. For monetary policy purposes, it has at its disposal open market operations, the credit facility, the deposit facility and the reserve requirement. The money creation process is limited by the capital requirements and the reserve requirement. ◄

Comprehension Questions

1. Explain the functioning of interest and quantity adjusters.
2. Describe the money creation process.
3. Why is the independence of the ECB so important for the ECB's objective of price stability?
4. Why are stock prices often rising after ECB interest rate cuts?

Exercise Problems

1. The ECB wants to achieve an inflation rate of 1.8%. GDP growth is expected to be 2% next year. The velocity of circulation remains constant. By how much does it have to increase the money supply M3?
2. The ECB Council decides to inject 25 billion euros into the money market through a main refinancing operation using a rate tender and some time later 30 billion euros through a quantity tender with an interest rate of 3.06%. Five credit institutions (A to E) submit the following bids in billion euros:

Bank	Interest rate Interest rate	Money supply	Mengen tender	Money supply
A	3.07	10	3.06	15
B	3.06	10	3.06	5
C	3.05	10	3.06	10
D	3.05	10	3.06	15
E	3.03	5	3.06	15

Determine:

a) the distribution of liquidity among the banks as well as at the rate tender
b) the marginal allocation rate
c) the weighted average interest rate

5.11   Quantitative Easing, the New Monetary Policy at the Capital Market

▶ Quantitative easing (QE) is when the central bank increases the money supply massively by buying government bonds on the capital market.

There are three goals that are pursued with QE:

1. The increase in the money supply is intended to have an inflationary effect first of all, that is, to fight deflation.
2. Furthermore, the provision of liquidity is also intended to reduce long-term interest rates on the capital market and thus increase the investment readiness of companies. If commercial banks hold the bonds, they would have to invest the excess liquidity again after selling the bonds.
3. This is to support the credit granting of banks to companies.

In January 2015, the ECB decided on a purchase program for government bonds. The main reason for this was the low inflation rates from the ECB's point of view. Up to September 2016, securities worth 60 billion euros were bought each month, with 80% of the purchases to be made by national central banks. This is to keep the loss risk with the nation states, that is, not to redistribute it. The volume thus totals more than one trillion euros. In April 2016, the ECB then expanded the bond purchases to corporate bonds and increased the volume to 80 billion euros per month. The negative deposit rate was increased from 0.3 to 0.4%. In addition, the ECB issued so-called TLTROs (Targeted Longer-Term Refinancing Operations) with a term of up to four years.[10] By extending its bond-buying program until September 2018, the ECB increased its targeted overall volume by €270 billion to €2.55 trillion. Shortly before the end of his term of office, Draghi allowed a new QE program with monthly bond purchases of €20 billion to be approved by the ECB Council in September 2019 against the resistance of Germany, France, Austria and the Netherlands, and lowered the negative deposit rate to minus 0.5%.[11] Due to Covid 19, bond purchases were massively increased to 120 billion euros by the end of 2020. In addition, the Pandemic Emergency Purchase Program (PEPP) was initiated with a volume of 1.35 trillion euros. In December 2020 PEPP was increased by 500 billion EUR to 1,850 billion and extended until March 2022. Reinvestments of the repayment amounts due from PEPP portfolios are to be made at least until the end of 2024.

---

[10] See   http://www.welt.de/wirtschaft/article136673946/Tag-des-Triumphs-fuer-EZB-Chef-Mario-Draghi.html; http://www.finance-magazin.de/maerkte-wirtschaft/kapitalmarkt/ezb-kauft-jetzt-auch-unternehmensanleihen-1375781/ as well as http://www.n-tv.de/wirtschaft/EZB-Geldmaschine-ist-voll-im-Einsatz-article14686981.html.

[11] See https://www.tagesspiegel.de/wirtschaft/geldpolitik-was-die-ezb-entschieden-hat-und-was-das-fuer-sparer-bedeutet/25009332.html.

Case Study Quantitative Easing

Task: Discuss the following article. In doing so, compare and contrast the advantages and disadvantages, or the opportunities and risks, of quantitative easing.

SPIEGEL ONLINE
January 22, 2015, 6:53 p.m.[12]

Quantitative Easing

Government bond purchases—who did it first?

By Christian Rickens

The European Central Bank is breaking a taboo with the purchase of government bonds? Hardly: The so-called quantitative easing has been in fashion for a long time. The German central bank even used it in the seventies.

Hamburg—The purchase of government bonds on a massive scale, as announced by the European Central Bank, only really came into fashion at the turn of the millennium: as a reaction to the weakness of growth and the crisis-ridden economic downturns in the industrial nations.

The Japanese central bank, which has been buying Japanese government bonds in ever new rounds since then, made the beginning with the instrument known as quantitative easing (QE). This has now brought the country an dizzying national debt of more than 240% of annual economic output—by way of comparison: in Greece it is around 170%. But even after almost fifteen years of continuous QE, growth and inflation in Japan are still weak.

After the financial crisis, the US Federal Reserve also began a program to buy US government bonds, which officially expired in October 2014. The balance sheet of the Fed has increased by around $4.5 billion, mainly due to the purchase of debt securities, within five years. And indeed, the USA has recovered impressively from the crisis, according to the latest World Bank forecast, economic growth will be 3.2% in 2015—the Eurozone is only 1.1%.

The picture is similar in the UK: The Bank of England also began buying government bonds in 2009. British growth is also expected to be around 3% in 2015. Impressive for a country whose economy is particularly dependent on the banking sector and was therefore particularly hard hit by the collapse in 2009.

Much less well known is the short-lived flirtation that the Bundesbank had with QE. In 1975, the guardians of the D-Mark bought German government bonds worth DM 7.6 billion from the market. This was then equivalent to one percent of annual German economic output. The goals of the action seem strangely familiar today: interest rates down, growth up. Today, Bundesbank President Jens Weidmann is one of the most outspoken opponents of bond purchases within the ECB Council.

---

[12] Translated from German.

When do bond purchases work—and when not?

What do these experiences say about the prospects and risks of quantitative easing? One thing is certain: In none of the cases has the purchase of government bonds by the central bank led to hyperinflation or even to worrisomely high inflation rates. A concern that is nevertheless widespread in Germany.

What exactly the programs have achieved, however, is difficult to assess. Even in the case of Japan, where the failure of QE seems to be particularly visible, it remains open: Would the economic situation have been worse without bond purchases?

The reverse question arises in the United States and Great Britain: Both countries have recently made an impressive economic recovery. But what share did QE have in this?

The answer that experts can agree on most: Bond purchases by the central bank contribute positively when they fit in with the economic policy of the respective government. In the United States, Presidents George Bush and Barack Obama boosted the economy with debt-financed government spending. The highlight was a check for up to $600 per taxpayer that Bush sent by mail in 2008. The idea is that citizens with low incomes would spend the unexpected money immediately and thus boost the economy. An idea that is currently also being discussed for the eurozone.

A sign against the zombie banks

Above all, however, the United States ensured that the banks weakened by the financial crisis either had to close down or were quickly equipped with fresh capital—if necessary in a kind of forced feeding, administered by the state.

In this way, the country was spared the phenomenon of the zombie banks: credit institutions that are so short of money that they can hardly grant any loans. This in turn hampers investments and thus growth. A problem that affects southern European countries in particular.

Zombie banks have also prolonged the period of weak growth in Japan—together with the notorious reform reluctance of Japanese politicians. Even today, there are only few immigrants in the aging Japan, the labor market is inflexible, women have few career opportunities.

Central bank bond purchases can therefore have the most effect if they are accompanied by appropriate economic policy in the respective currency area. In the US, this meant higher government spending, while in Japan there was a lack of structural reforms.

URL:

http://www.spiegel.de/wirtschaft/soziales/staatsanleihen-programme-anderer-notenbanken-a-1014432.html,

Conclusion

The ECB chose the 2% inflation target itself. The number 2% is arbitrary and many people would understand something else under price stability. According to Art. 123 TFEU, the financing of public deficits is prohibited. If the ECB buys government bonds on the capital market, this has the same effect as if it were to give the money directly to the states. Due to the margin of the intermediary, only the interest rate increases. In expectation that the ECB will buy everything, states get money that they would otherwise not have got from private investors. So it is clearly a circumventing provision. The consolidation pressure on the states decreases, even if they have committed themselves to the restructuring program. Are there any effects at all and if so, what are they? Ultimately, quantitative easing broadens the ECB's zero interest rate policy and money supply expansion from the money market to the capital market. Victims of a zero interest rate policy are savers and also commercial banks. There are redistribution from creditors to savers. Creditors are mainly companies, homeowners and the state. Commercial banks have to reduce their credit and investment margins in the face of very low credit and debit interest rates. In addition, there is the danger of misallocation and speculation bubbles.

The effects are difficult to determine ex post. In the case of the USA, the low interest rate policy of then Federal Reserve Chairman Greenspan is blamed for the US mortgage credit crisis. Despite decades of QE and stimulus programs, Japan's economomy has not recovered to its previous growth level. Instead, government debt has soared. Similar things can be said about the USA, where the central bank massively bought government bonds. Finally, one has to refer to the negative historical experiences that came with a financing of state credit by the central bank. Although the ECB is politically independent like the historical examples of central banks, it nevertheless becomes dependent the more government bonds it buys. The Euro states become more and more dependent on the central bank for financing, so that the ECB cannot withdraw the money from them, it cannot let them fail (too big to fail).

The central question remains whether one can artificially create investments through an expansive monetary policy and extremely low interest rates near zero. Companies will only invest when the return minus risk discount is higher than the market interest rate. This means that investments depend not only on the costs of external capital, but also on the return of investments. And that is determined on the supply side, i.e. neoclassically. In Greece, no one will invest in hotels if the same product, a holiday by the Mediterranean Sea, is offered much cheaper in Turkey. Rather, an expansive monetary policy bears extreme risks.

A targeted expansion of the money supply combined with a zero interest rate policy corresponds to a subsidization of capital. The difference is that subsidies burden the state budget. The central bank can almost create money without cost. However, the purchasing power of the new money displaces that of the existing money, which eventually leads to inflation.

The recent purchase of corporate bonds by the ECB is a contradiction to the principle of a two-tier banking system, in which the central bank pursues the public mandate of price stability and therefore does not work for profit as a public organization, and private commercial banks, which are liable for their equity in the allocation of capital and therefore have to work for profit. Apart from the fact that the central bank's financing of companies leads to distortions of competition, it is also to be expected that the central bank will make more mistakes in this business area, i.e. lose capital, because it has less expertise and is liable not with private equity, but with taxpayers' money. The system is approaching more and more the centrally planned economy.

Overall, the ECB has moved far from the Maastricht Treaty with its policy, so that it is highly questionable whether it does not only interpret its mandate widely, but also exceeds it legally, economically it already does. A problem here is also that these ECB decisions were made within the ECB voting, in which the large countries such as France and Germany, although they are liable for more ECB losses than the smaller countries, had the same voting rights. The problem of Target-II balances has also not yet been solved. Balances from cross-border goods and capital flows are running up. They are not offset. They arise when the Deutsche Bundesbank settles the payment obligations of foreigners. Unlike in the USA, the claims between the central banks are not regularly offset (netting). The claims of the Bundesbank against other national euro central banks amount to 1.245.013.839.004,15 € (as of 31 August 2022).[13]

These balances stem mainly from external trade deficits, which indicate increasing differences in competitiveness between the northern and southern Eurasian states. German goods are ordered from southern Europe, but the Bundesbank pays the bill for German exporters because the importer's money is only passed on to its national central bank.

Thus, the southern European countries have no choice but to lower prices and wages and reduce government spending. At present, however, it does not look as if the politicians want to go that way, and as long as the southern European countries have the majority in ECB votes, ECB policy will not change. However, this would result in a further increase in Target2 balances. Here the German government is called upon to negotiate. And the Bundesbank should define a maximum amount for the Target2 balances that it is willing to contribute. The question of what happens to these claims when a state leaves the euro is still unclear. Opportunities to settle the balances exist, such as an exchange of Target2 claims into national government bonds at market value. Bonds, unlike the Target2 balances, are due for repayment, generate interest

---

[13] See https://www.bundesbank.de/de/aufgaben/unbarer-zahlungsverkehr/target2/target2-saldo/target2-saldo-603478#:~:text=TARGET2%20ist%20ein%20Zahlungsverkehrssystem%2C%20%C3%BCber,rund%201%2C7%20Billionen%20Euro(14.09.2022).

and are tradable on the market. An unorthodox alternative would be for the Deutsche Bundesbank to buy financial assets in the debtor countries in order to reduce the Target2 balances. The long-term hopefully avoidable alternative would be an at least temporary exit of Germany from the euro while retaining the clearing system with the ECB. This would have the advantage that the claims of the Bundesbank to the southern European central banks or the ECB are denominated in euros and could therefore be more easily repaid by the states than the exit of the less competitive southern states. After the euro had depreciated against the new German currency, the products of the southern states would become competitive. There would be current account surpluses, which would result in the repatriation of Target2 balances. ◄

References

Andel, N. (1990). *Finanzwissenschaft* (3. ed.). Mohr Siebeck.

Blanchard, O. (2014). *Makroökonomie*. Pearson Studium.

Blanchard, O., & Illing, G. (2006). *Übungen zur Makroökonomie*. Pearson Studium.

Braybrooke, D., & Lindblom, C. E. (1963). *A strategy of decision*. Free Press.

Conrad, C. A. (2001). Zwei Jahre Europäische Währungsunion: Eine Bestandsaufnahme. *Wirtschaftsdienst, 81*(5), 283–291.

Conrad, C. A. (2002). Die Geldpolitik und die Akzeptanz des Euros. *WiSt (Wirtschaftswissenschaftliches Studium), 31*(2), 97–100.

Downs, A. (1968). *Ökonomische Theorie der Demokratie*. Mohr Siebeck.

Drost, A., Linnemann, L., & Schabert, A. (2003). *Übungsbuch zu Felderer/Homburg*. Springer.

Felderer, B., & Homburg, S. (2005). *Makroökonomik und neue Makroökonomik* (9. ed.). Springer.

Franke, S. F. (1996). *(Ir) rationale Politik?: Grundzüge und politische Anwendungen der „Ökonomischen Theorie der Politik"*. Metropolis.

Frey, B. S. (1981). Theorie demokratischer Wirtschaftspolitik. In M. Fritsch, T. Wein, & H.-J. Ewers (eds.), *Marktversagen und Wirtschafspolitik*. Vahlen.

Grögens, E., Ruckriegel, K., & Seitz, F. (2013). *Europäische Geldpolitik, Theorie – Empirie – Praxis* (6. ed.). UTB.

Guerrieri, P., & Padoan, P. C. C. (1989). *The political economy of European integration*. Barnes & Noble Books.

John, K. D. (2004). *Arbeitsbuch Makroökonomik* (12. ed.). Schäffer-Poeschel.

Krisch, G. (1993). *Neue Politische Ökonomie* (3. ed.). Werner.

Lindblom, C. E. (1965). *The intelligence of democracy*. Free Press.

Mankiw, G. N. (2013). *Makroökonomik* (7. Aufl.). Schäffer-Poeschel.

Meyer-Krahmer, F. (1979). *Politische Entscheidungsprozesse und Ökonomische Theorie der Politik*. Campus.

Mussel, G. (2009). *Einführung in die Makroökonomik* (10. ed.). Vahlen.

Sachverständigenrat zur Begutachtung der gesamtwirtschaftlichen Entwicklung. (2011). Chancen für einen stabilen Aufschwung – Jahresgutachten 2010/2011 Paderborn: Bonifatius. http://www.sachverstaendigenrat-wirtschaft.de/fileadmin/x_ga_2010_11/ga10_ges.pdf.

Schrader, K., & Laaser, C. F. (2010). Den Anschluss nie gefunden: Die Ursachen der griechischen Tragödie. *Wirtschaftsdienst, 90*(8), 537–540.

Siebe, T., & Wenke, M. (2014). *Makroökonomie*. UTB Lucius.

Starbatty, J. (2001). Die EZB muss sich das Vertrauen der Märkte erst noch erwerben. *Wirtschafts-dienst, 81*(VII).
Wagner, H., & Böhne, A. (2003). *Übungsbuch Makroökonomie*. Vahlen.

Further Reading

EZB. (2016). Die Europäische Zentralbank. https://www.ecb.europa.eu/ecb/html/index.de.html. (8. Aug. 2016).
Scheller, H. (2006). *Die Europäische Zentralbank, Geschichte, Rolle und Aufgaben* (2. ed.). EZB. http://www.buba.de/download/ezb/publikationen/ezb_publication_geschichte.pdf. (8. Aug. 2016).

Keynesian Theory

6

What Follows Why?
We now want to deal with the theory that has called into question the neoclassi-cal world of ideals. Neoclassicism was the only valid macro theory until the world economic crisis of 1929 and thus to:

- permanent investment decline
- as a result, overcapacities
- continued mass unemployment
  (approx. 6 million in 1932 in Germany)
- a contraction of consumption, world production and world trade

The governments reacted to the loss of tax revenue with countermeasures by reducing state spending and calling on the population to save. But the situation worsened. Despite price and real wage cuts, there was continued overproduction and mass unemployment. Although people wanted to work more and have a bet-ter supply of goods, unemployment and overproduction persisted. The self-healing forces of the market failed.

Keynesian theory deals with actions, effects and consequences for the economy in exceptional situations, such as in a depression. This theory arose as a result of the world economic crisis of 1929 with investment shortfalls, a glut of goods and mass unemployment, which affected more than 25% of the workforce, and a corre-sponding reduction in consumption. Since, according to Keynes, effective demand is decisive for production, Say's theorem does not apply here, according to which supply creates demand itself. Keynes was the internationally best-known and most influential representative of a demand-oriented macro theory. His main work from

1936 "The General Theory of Employment, Interest and Money" is, after Adam Smith's "Wealth of Nations", the most important economic book. As an introduction to the topic of Keynes and his demand-oriented theory, one of the many videos on You Tube about the great depression of 1929 is recommended.

Learning objectives
You should be able to reproduce the essential content of Keynesian theory and the differences to neoclassicism in your own words and apply them using numerical examples.

6.1   Case Study: The World Economic Crisis

The **circular flow theory** and psychologically oriented **theory** founded by *John Maynard Keynes* under the impression of the world economic crisis (1928–1933) sees the cause of the persistent unemployment in a **lack of demand on the goods markets.** According to Keynes, the effective demand for production is decisive and not the supply as the Say's theorem says. How did he come to this statement? He observed the economic development during the world economic crisis and found some contradictions to neoclassicism. Mankiw summarized the development of the world economic crisis in numbers (see Table 6.1). Discuss in groups what you notice about the development of the macroeconomic numbers. Which development is in contradiction to the neoclassical theory?

Interpretation
Gross national product

First of all, one can see that the GNP falls by more than a quarter from 1929 to 1933. At the same time, the unemployment rate rises from 3.2% to 25.2%. Government spending rises slightly from 1929 to 1931 from 22 billion US dollars to 25.4 billion US dollars and then falls back to 23.3 billion US dollars by 1933. Money supply behaves similarly. It falls from 26.6 billion US dollars in 1929 to 19.9 billion US dollars in 1933, only to rise again. In contrast, prices fall by −2.6% in 1930, by −10.1% in 1931 and by −9.3% in 1932. This is the first contradiction to neoclassicism: despite falling prices, aggregate demand for goods does not increase. On the contrary: demand, i.e. capacity utilization and with it GNP and prices fall at the same time, which is why one speaks of a depression. Demand falls and companies adjust production, which is why GNP and employment fall. Against this background, people consume less despite falling prices because

Table 6.1 Development of the world economic crisis (explanation: real GDP, consumption, investment and government purchases in billion US$ at prices of 1958. Interest rate: "Prime Commercial Paper rate" maturity 4–6 months. Money supply: cash + sight deposits in billion US$. The price level is the GDP deflator (1958 = 100). The inflation rate is the percentage change in the price level series. Real cash balances prices at 1958 in billion US$ as a quotient of money supply and price level multiplied by 100. Savings rate own calculation as a quotient of consumption and GDP). (Source: Mankiw, N. Gregory: Macroeconomics, 4th edition, Stuttgart 2000, p. 330)

Year	1929	1930	1931	1932	1933	1934
Unemployment rate	3.2	8.9	16.3	24.1	25.2	22.0
Real GDP	203.6	183.5	169.5	144.2	141.5	154.3
Consumption	139.6	130.4	126.1	114.8	112.8	118.1
Savings rate	67	71	74	80	80	77
Investments	40.4	27.4	16.8	4.7	5.3	9.4
Government spending	22.0	24.3	25.4	24.2	23.3	26.6
Nominal interest rate	5.9	3.6	2.6	2.7	1.7	1.0
Money supply	26.6	25.8	24.1	21.1	19.9	21.9
Price level	50.6	49.3	44.8	40.2	39.3	42.2
Inflation rate	–	−2.6	−10.1	−9.3	−2.2	7.4
Real cash	52.6	52.3	54.5	52.5	50.7	51.8
Year	1935	1936	1937	1938	1939	1940
Unemployment rate	20.3	17.0	14.3	19.1	17.2	14.6
Real GDP	169.5	193.2	203.2	192.9	209.4	227.2
Consumption	125.5	138.4	143.1	140.2	148.2	155.7
Savings rate	74	71	70	73	71	69
Investments	40.4	27.4	16.8	4.7	5.3	9.4
Government spending	27.0	31.8	30.8	33.9	35.2	36.4
Nomin. Zinssatz	0.8	0.8	0.9	0.8	0.6	0.6
Geldangebot	25.9	29.6	30.9	30.5	34.2	39.7
Preisniveau	42.6	42.7	44.5	43.9	43.2	43.9
Inflationsrate	0.9	0.2	4.2	−1.3	−1.6	1.6
Real cash	60.8	62.9	69.5	69.5	79.1	90.3

they are afraid of losing their jobs. The dismissed employees can no longer consume because there was no social welfare of any significance at that time. The unemployed fed in soup kitchens.

The break in the trend of economic development is due to the first socially oriented program in 1933 under US President Roosevelt, the so-called "New Deal". As a result of this expansionary program, government spending starts to rise again continuously from 1933. With the higher demand, production also increases again.

Savings

If one estimates saving as the difference between the given consumption and the real GDP, it becomes apparent that it tends to fall until 1932 and 1932, but 1934 rises, even though the interest rate has fallen to 1%. Saving seems to develop independently of interest, which is another contradiction to neoclassicism. This also applies to consumption as the remaining part of the income. Savings and consumption fall with production, as the dismissed employees cannot save or consume without income.

Investments

It is striking that the investments of 40.4 billion US dollars in 1929 have almost halved to 4.7 billion US dollars in 1932, despite the fact that interest rates have more than halved from 5.9% to 2.7% in the same period. Falling investments despite falling interest rates are a contradiction to neoclassicism. According to neoclassicism, there is always a balance between investments and savings on the capital market through the market mechanism. If investments fall with given savings, sufficient investments are stimulated by a falling interest rate until I = S again. In the great depression, however, investments did not react to interest rates because companies could not sell their current production and therefore had no reason to invest in expansionary investments. Based on this example, we can see that without the expected return of companies, the interest rate for loans is irrelevant. Here, too, monetary policy cannot influence economic development through interest rate cuts or money supply.

There are four central deviations from neoclassical theory according to Keynes:

1. The income-dependent consumption and saving function
2. The investment function depending on the expected marginal productivity of capital
3. The liquidity preference theory in the money market
4. Rigidities of prices and wages

6.2   Case Study: Keynes and the Relevance of His Theory Illustrated by the Financial Crisis

A Quantum of Keynes[1]

By Jürgen Eustachi

"Never Say Never Again" (1983) is the title of the last James Bond movie starring Sean Connery. John Maynard Keynes died in 1946. His teachings were pronounced dead. But the dead live on. In the face of the death of the economy, as now in the global financial and impending world economic crisis, he is coming back into favor: the man with the golden path that leads out of the catastrophe.

Super agent Keynes is needed whenever the need is greatest. There have only been 2 economists whose names are known as -isms: Karl Marx and Keynes. The decisive difference between Marxists and Keynesians is that the former believe in the demise of capitalism, the latter in the possibility of its salvation. Today, world savior John Maynard Keynes is at least as popular as the powerhouse Daniel Craig in the new Bond: Like Craig, Keynes offers a quantum of comfort--and much more.

Keynesianism is also in good shape more than 70 years after its invention. While the financial crisis is raging like a fireball around the globe and spreading fear and terror, governments around the world are using the instruments that Keynes provided in his main work "The General Theory of Employment, Interest and Money" of February 1936: States are putting together rescue programs for the economy. The Western world is providing 2600 billion euros for the financial sector alone. In addition, there are many state-financed economic stimulus programs, like in Germany.

15 individual measures from securing the credit supply, especially for small and medium-sized enterprises, to the accelerated expansion of transport infrastructure are to trigger investments of 50 billion euros by 2010 and thus mitigate the impending crisis. The goal of creating a balanced budget without new borrowing by 2011 at the latest has been abandoned. This is Keynesianism pure and simple. And it is exactly the right thing to do in this situation. If it should turn out that rescue packages and economic stimulus programs are not enough to tame the crisis, governments will not hesitate to provide more Keynes.

But what can Keynes do better than earlier or later economists? What makes him the Superman of the economy, the Einstein of economics? James Bond comes to the goal with stunts and special effects, which often set aside natural laws of physics. And Keynes's special weapon for cracking economic crises is so brilliant

---

[1] Published in "Die Rheinlandpfalz am Sonntag", 16.11.2008, p. 19. Translated from German.

that it not only suspends previously valid economic laws and teachings, but also makes newer economic and economic concepts look old.

On January 24, 1929, on Black Thursday, the stock prices collapsed massively on the New York Stock Exchange. Panic spread among investors worldwide. The world economic crisis with a wave of corporate bankruptcies and mass unemployment began and only reached the bottom in 1932. In Germany, the Weimar Republic also broke down under the pressure of the economic crisis. Keynes had predicted this and the outbreak of the Second World War precisely. As head of the British financial delegation, he participated in the Versailles Peace Conference in 1919 and unsuccessfully tried to prevent Germany from being burdened with sole war guilt and high reparation payments.

Economists were at a loss in the face of the world economic crisis of the 1930s. The world view of the then neoclassicism was shaped by the belief in the self-healing powers of the market. It assumed that markets would always find their way back to equilibrium on their own if they were not disturbed from the outside, by the state. The neoclassics had further developed the market model of the Scottish moral philosopher and founder of national economics, Adam Smith. The father of the market economy published his main work "Wealth of Nations" in 1776. In it, he set the concept of the "invisible hand" of free markets—the transformation of self-interest into public interest—against the then prevailing mercantilism with strong state interventions in the economy.

A deep crisis lasting as long as after the stock market crash of 1929 should not have existed according to the world view of neoclassicism. This world was not enough for Keynes. Neoclassicism was an intellectual illusion to him. He introduced the previously ignored human factor, psychology, the expectations of market participants as a central element of economic activity. If pessimism prevails, Keynes believes, then every consumer and investor will hold on to his money. The belief in the crisis creates the crisis.

Such a situation also does not help the monetary policy with the reduction of interest rates. Companies do not primarily invest when interest rates are low, but when expected returns from investments in tangible assets are higher than from financial investments, according to Keynes. In a world of fears and uncertainties, the economy ends up in the liquidity trap. Only a state economic policy can free the markets from this trap and fight mass unemployment. For this purpose, the state may also incur debt, which could be repaid in good years. One problem with the implementation of Keynesianism is that in bad as well as in good times, it is easier for politics to incur debt than to repay it.

Keynes, who himself made a fortune on the stock exchange, also saw the dangers of hyper-speculative casino capitalism: "Speculators may not cause any damage as soap bubbles on a constant stream of entrepreneurship. But the situation becomes serious when entrepreneurship becomes the soap bubble on the whirlpool of speculation. If the capital development of a country becomes the by-product of the activities of a casino, work is likely to be done badly." Work is done badly today.

US President Roosevelt's New Deal in the 1930s was inspired by Keynes, who became a star economist. In the 1980s, US President Reagan gave Milton Friedman, a monetarist, a license to kill Keynesianism. Friedman and other neo-liberals propagated their business- and capital-friendly supply policy. But the unrestrained deregulation of financial markets did not bring about the liberation from the evil of state control, but an evil liberation of greed for profit from any control. In the ailing Global casino, now only a good quantum of Keynes helps.

HIS NAME WAS KEYNES—JOHN MAYNARD KEYNES

LIFE

Sir John Maynard Keynes, the most important economist of the 20th century, was a bon vivant and daredevil. He only regretted that he had not drunk enough champagne in his life, he said shortly before his death. He died on April 21, 1946. He was born on June 6, 1883 as the son of the liberal economic professor John Neville Keynes in the eastern English university town of Cambridge.

After his training at the elite institutes Eton and King's College in Cambridge, where he researched and taught himself from 1908, Keynes was a political advisor all his life. That he got the worst grade in economics in the entrance exam for the civil service as a young man, the "Einstein of Economics" explained later that the examiners probably knew less than the examinee.

Keynes, also Lord Keynes of Tilton with a seat in the British House of Lords from 1942, was a successful stock speculator, art collector and member of the then famous liberal Bloomsbury group of writers Virginia Woolf. Between 1908 and 1915 he was in a relationship with the painter Duncan Grant; In 1925 he married the ballet dancer Lydia Lopokova.

QUOTES

"In the long run we are all dead. Economists make it too easy for us when they have nothing more to tell us in stormy times than that the ocean is calm again when the storm has subsided."

"Three things drive people to madness. Love, jealousy and the study of stock prices."

"To assess the future of an investment, we must observe the nerves, hysterics, and even the digestion and weather sensitivity of those people whose actions this investment depends on to a large extent."

"Economics is essentially a moral science and not a natural science."
"Capitalism is based on the strange belief that vile people from vile motives will somehow take care of the general good."

MAIN WORK

"The General Theory of Employment, Interest and Money"; Publisher Duncker & Humblot; 10th revised edition; 343 pages; 38 €. According to the publisher, the book is currently in good economic shape. (jeu)

6.3   The Consumption Function

The consumption function describes the relationship between consumption and income. Consumption is only dependent on the income of the current period, which Keynes clearly differentiates from the neoclassical model, in which consumption depends on interest rates.

For the macroeconomic consumption function, Keynes focuses on the most important influencing factor and postulates that with increasing national income (Y), the total economic **demand for consumption** (C) increases, but disproportionately (**fundamental-psychological law**)

$$\text{applies in general}: C = C(Y), \text{ applies in particular}: \mathbf{C} = \mathbf{Ca} + \mathbf{c'(Y)}$$

for Ca = autonomous consumption (i.e. given as a constant), and $c' = dC/dY =$ marginal propensity to consume or -quote. The marginal propensity to consume indicates how much households increase or decrease their consumption expenditure if income (Y) increases by one unit of currency. For simplification purposes, it is kept constant at 0.8 below. Autonomous consumption is called autonomous because it is not dependent on any other variables, in particular not on income. This means that consumption takes place even without income. In this case, income is financed by savings, i.e. with financial resources from assets. This assumption can only apply to the individual in a narrow sense or to an open economy. In a closed economy, there can be no negative savings rate, as consumption cannot exceed production. The average propensity to consume indicates what percentage of income is used for consumption purposes.

According to Keynes, the consumption function has the following properties (Fig. 6.1):

1. Consumption C always increases with an increase in income
2. autonomous consumption is greater than $0 \rightarrow Ca > 0$
3. marginal propensity to consume is between 0 and $1 \rightarrow 0 < dC/dY < 1$
4. average propensity to consume (C/Y) decreases with increasing income Y

National income (Y)	Consumption (C)	Marginal propensity to consume dC/dY	Average Propensity to consume C/Y
0	20		
50	60	0.8	1.2
100	100	0.8	1
150	140	0.8	0.93
200	180	0.8	0.9

Fig. 6.1 Consumption

Fig. 6.2 Consumption
function

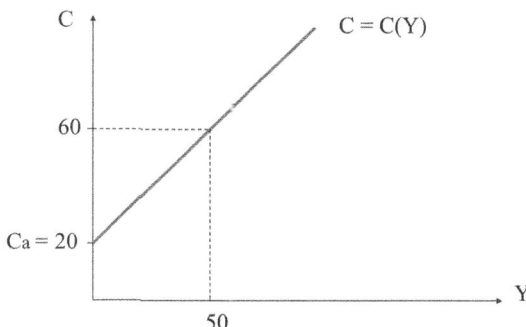

Numerical example: C=Ca+c′(Y) and Ca=20, c′=0.8
   This results in the following graph (Fig. 6.2):

6.4   The Saving Function

Keynes assumes that **saving** is to a large extent **interest inelastic**, while neoclassical economics sees saving as a function of interest:

> There are not many people who will alter their way of living because the rate of interest has fallen from 5 to 4 per cent, if their aggregate income is the same as before.
>   *(Keynes in the "General Theory")*

Discussion: Do you consider this assumption to be realistic? What do you think saving depends on?
   Answer: Saving depends on many factors. One can withhold parts of the income because one expects unexpected burdens in the future (saving out of fear). One can save for a purchase or save to provide for old age. Obviously, a household without income

cannot save. Normally, income hardly changes or is given in the period, i.e. given income, saving depends on interest.

Keynes derives the saving function from the consumption function:

$$Y = C + S$$

$$\Leftrightarrow S = Y - C \text{ it holds}: C = Ca + c'Y \text{ therefore holds for S}:$$

$$S = Y - \left(Ca + c'Y\right)$$

$$\Leftrightarrow S = -Ca + \left(1 - c'\right)Y$$

$$\Leftrightarrow S = -Ca + s' \bullet Y \qquad \textbf{savingsfunction}$$

$$\left(\text{with } 1 - c' = s' \text{ marginal propensity to save}\right)$$

At an income of zero, autonomous consumption Ca corresponds to a negative saving.

The marginal saving inclination indicates how much households increase their savings if income increases by 1 unit.

The average saving inclination indicates how many percent of the income is saved (Figs. 6.3 and 6.4)

$$S = -Ca + s' \bullet Y \text{ Savings Function}$$

$$\mathbf{S = -20 + 0{,}2 \bullet Y \text{ SavingsFunction}}$$

For the numerical example: Ca = 20, s' = 0.2, then:

Planned and realised Y^s - becomes national income (Y)	Savings (S)	Marginal propensity to save dS/dY	Average propensity to save S/Y
0	- 20		
50	- 10	0.2	
100	0	0.2	
150	10	0.2	0.07
200	20	0.2	0.1

Fig. 6.3 Saving

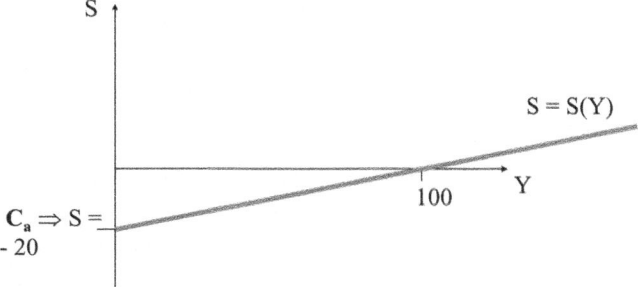

Fig. 6.4 The saving function

The course of the saving curve is interesting. It starts in the negative range because even without income, the household consumes (autonomous consumption). Since $S = Y - C$, negative saving arises. Only with the increase in income does positive saving also increase as $S = s' \cdot Y$. In our numerical example, we need an income of 100 to generate as much positive as negative saving. The saving function then takes the value zero. With an income of 150, the saving function reaches the value 10.

6.5   The Income-Expenditure Model

As we know from the VGR, production generates an income of the same amount. Production represents the supply. The income generates a consumption demand and a saving. The saving represents a demand shortfall because households do not demand goods for this part of the income. To offset this demand shortfall, investment is required as additional goods demand from companies.

If the effective aggregate demand Y^D in the economy consists of the income-dependent consumption demand $C(Y)$ and the autonomous investment demand (I_0), then and only then **there is a goods market equilibrium,** if the firms plan a production as gross domestic product, which is just as high as the resulting from the mirror image income consumption demand and the autonomous investments as effective demand. If the supply plans exceed the income necessary to generate demand or remain behind it, there are **goods market imbalances.**

Conversely, if the investments are given, there is only one economic **equilibrium income Y_0,** which in addition to the investments generates exactly as much demand [C (Y)] that it corresponds to the production Y. Here, the demand shortfall caused by saving is equal to the investments.

The goods market is considered here. The resulting incomes are compared to the expenditures caused by the demand. The effective demand (Y^D) indicates how much is demanded on the market ($Y^D = C + I$).

Two assumptions are made here:

- The investment volume is given
- The capacities are underutilized

If the company's production is on the market as high as the demand, there is a goods market equilibrium. If this is not the case, one speaks of a goods market imbalance.

Fill in the table in Fig. 6.5. At which income is the aggregate demand equal to the supply? Numeric example: $Ca = 20$, $c' = 0.8$, $I_0 = 10$, $Y^D = 20 + 0.8(Y) + 10$

$$S = -20 + 0.2 \, Y \text{ and } C = 20 + 0.8 \, Y$$

Solution

See Fig. 6.6.

Fig. 6.5 Keynes exercise

Domestic product = National income	Planned Consumption	Planned Savings	Planned Investment	Effective Demand
0				
50				
100				
150				
200				

Domestic product = National income	Planned consumption	Planned saving	Planned investment	Effective demand
0	20	- 20	10	30
50	60	-10	10	70
100	100	0	10	110
150	140	10	10	150
200	180	20	10	190

Fig. 6.6 Solution to Keynes exercise

Conclusion

S $(Y\uparrow\downarrow)$ must be equal to I_0 so that the aggregate supply is equal to the aggregate demand. If, for example, I_0 falls to 0, then income must fall to 100 so that S $(100) = 0$. Conversely, Y must rise to 200 if I_0 rises to 20, so that sufficient savings and thus demand decline are generated through income. ◄

Calculation of Equilibrium Income

We calculate the equilibrium income Y_0. This is characterized, as we have seen, by the fact that here the aggregate supply is equal to the demand.

It should therefore apply Y (production) $= Y^D$ (demand)

It applies: $Y^D = C(Y) + I_0$ Furthermore, it applies: $C = C_a + c'Y$

It follows from the goods market equilibrium:

$$Y = C_a + c'Y + I_0$$
$$\Leftrightarrow Y - c'Y = C_a + I_0$$
$$\Leftrightarrow (1 - c')Y = C_a + I_0$$

$$Y_0 = \frac{1}{(1 - c')}(C_a + I_0)$$

Equilibrium income = expenses

Where production Y corresponds to income Y.

If effective demand falls short of or exceeds the demand expected by businesses, there are **economic imbalances.**

An excess supply can, for example, occur if investment demand (e.g. in the world economic crisis) unexpectedly decreases.

For our example, this applies:

$$(C_a = 20, \ c' = 0.8, \ I_0 = 10)$$

$$Y = \frac{1}{(1 - 0.8)}(20 + 10) = 150$$

The equilibrium income is therefore 150.

The derivation of the equilibrium income can also be illustrated graphically:

Given investments, the balance is achieved through income-dependent saving. The saving curve starts in the negative range because, due to autonomous consumption, the household consumes even though it has no income. At an income of zero, there is thus an excess demand of 30, which results on the one hand from the autonomous consumption of 20 and on the other hand from the additional investment demand from companies. Only with the increase in income does the positive saving as $S = s' \cdot Y$ also increase. This results in a demand shortfall. The excess demand is reduced. In our numerical example, we need an income of 100 to generate as much positive as negative saving. In addition, however, there is still the excess demand from companies that invest. At an income of 150, the saving function reaches the value 10, so that as much demand shortfall has arisen from the saving as is needed to cover the additional demand from companies, i.e. the investments. This is the equilibrium income. If income continues to rise, more demand will be lost through the income-dependent increased saving than additional demand from companies is added, resulting in a shortage or excess supply (Fig. 6.7).

The numerical example makes it easy to see that, under the assumptions made, only a balance exists if **the planned savings of households are exactly as large as the planned investment demand of companies.**

The so-called **equilibrium condition** is:

$$S(Y) = I_0$$

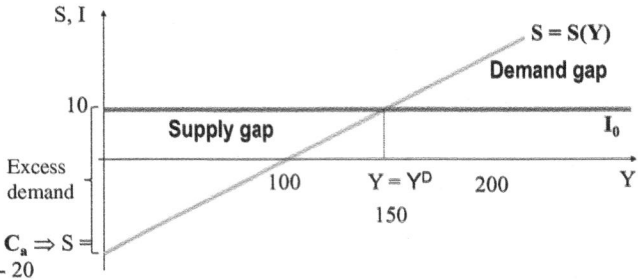

Fig. 6.7   Balance of saving and investing

This also makes it understandable that, from a Keynesian perspective, **savings demand shortfall** is something that must be compensated for by an appropriately large investment demand on the part of businesses, if equilibrium is to be maintained. In a depression, investment falls away because economic expectations are poor. But despite this, people still save, and usually save even more (out of fear). The result is an oversupply in the goods market.

We want to illustrate this relationship in another diagram (see Fig. 6.8). Here, on the x-axis, we have the supply, i.e. production, which is synonymous with income. The line of symmetry or 45 degree line always has the same distance from the x- and y-axes. This means that all points on this line are equilibrium points. The supply (x-axis) and demand (y-axis) are equal in size. If the demand curve is above the equilibrium line, there is more demand than supply in the goods market; if it is below, there is more supply than demand.

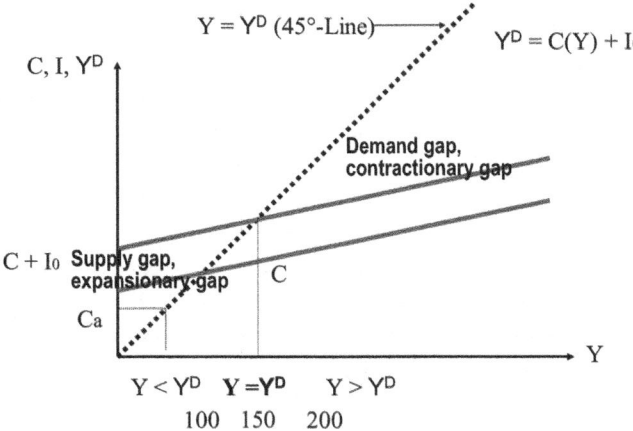

Fig. 6.8   Aggregate supply and demand with Keynes

As demand components, we have consumption and investment. Consumption rises proportionally to income, while investment is added as a constant. The point at which the total demand curve thus generated intersects with the line of symmetry then indicates the equilibrium between supply and demand. Here we have the equilibrium income (150).

The graphical representation makes it clear that there is an oversupply if actual production is greater than equilibrium income (e.g. 200). There is then a so-called **contractionary gap.** Market forces close this gap by reducing production due to unplanned inventory in order to avoid oversupply. The graphical representation also makes it clear that there is an excess demand if actual production is less than equilibrium income (e.g. 100). There is then a so-called **expansive gap.** Market forces close this gap because—given free capacity—companies increase production from their profit interest in order to satisfy the excess demand. There is thus a tendency towards equilibrium, but with corresponding adjustments in production and employment.

How is this relationship to be seen in terms of the demand shortfall caused by saving? If we now have a supply from the companies and thus an equal income that is less than the demand, an excess demand or a supply gap is created. Since the income is too low to generate sufficient demand shortfall through saving. This is an expansive gap because, due to the excess demand and underutilization of capacity, companies expand production until equilibrium income is reached. With the increased production, income and thus saving and the associated demand shortfall increase until at equilibrium income the supply of goods is equal to the demand for goods. If production is too high, too much saving and thus demand shortfall is generated through the same income. The supply is greater than the demand, which corresponds to a contractionary gap. Companies adjust their supply to demand and reduce it. Employees are dismissed. Income decreases and with income saving and the associated demand shortfall decrease until equilibrium is reached between supply and demand.

In Keynes, supply does not create its own demand, as the Saysche Theorem claims, but demand determines production. Investment and savings are not brought into agreement via interest rates as in neoclassicism, but via real production adjustments, which implies losses in prosperity and unemployment.

As will be shown with the money demand function, a key difference with Keynes is that money can also be held as cash without creating demand (speculation motive), and thus also not invested.

John Maynard Keynes:

Given the psychology of the public, the level of output and employment as a whole depends on the amount of investments. The theory can be summed up by saying that, given the psychology of the public, the level of output and employment as a whole depends on the amount of investment. I put it in this way, not because this is the only factor on which aggregate output depends, but because it is usual in a complex system to regard as the *causa causans* that factor which is most prone to sudden and wide fluctuation.[2]

---

[2] See Keynes, John Maynard (1937, p. 121).

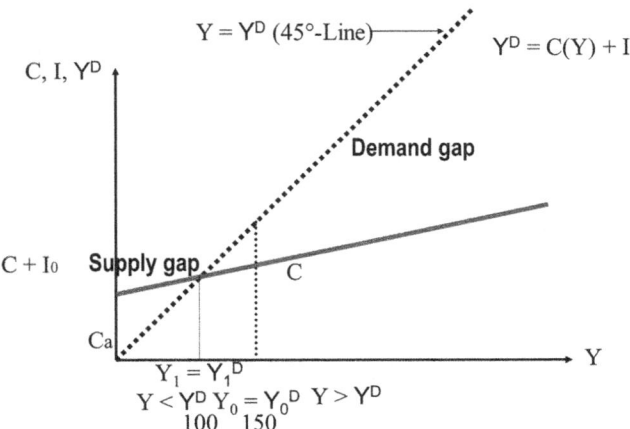

Fig. 6.9 Aggregate demand gap in Keynes

Situation World Economic Crisis

What happens if, as in the world economic crisis, investment demand collapses due to poor economic expectations? (Fig. 6.9).

If investment demand falls, the additional demand from companies in the amount of 10 is missing. The result is a demand gap. At this high income, too much is saved, which results in too much demand being lost. If this situation persists, companies will reduce production to match it with the demand. Employment and income will fall by 50. Only at an equilibrium income of 100 is the saving, that is, the demand loss, sufficiently reduced, so that again supply equals demand. This corresponds to the situation of persistent unemployment during the global economic crisis.

In Keynes, investments are given autonomously, which is why there can only be one equilibrium income. If I unexpectedly decreases, e.g. due to the pessimism of an economic crisis, the income is too high due to $S(Y)$, $S(Y)>I$, which is why there is too little demand at the corresponding gross domestic product. There is an oversupply. If the state does nothing, companies would restrict their supply until the lower equilibrium income is reached. This would be the depression associated with unemployment. The state must prevent this by timely compensating for the external demand decrease. If the mood has improved again, I increases and the necessary original demand exists again, so that the state can then reduce its demand.

In neoclassicism, saving is positive because an equilibrium $I = S$ always arises and thus investing means growth (Fig. 6.10).

Fig. 6.10 Equilibrium
of saving and investing in
neoclassicism

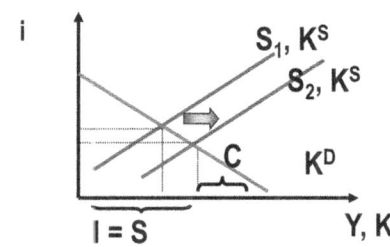

Fig. 6.11 Equilibrium of
saving and investing by Keynes

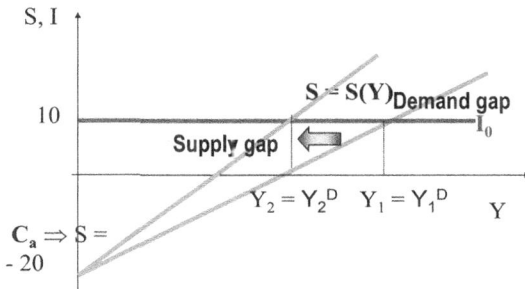

For Keynes, saving, on the other hand, means a drop in demand, which leads to a
decrease in national product and income (Fig. 6.11).

6.6   Expenditure and Tax Multiplier

We have already seen that a 10 decrease in investment leads to a 50 decrease in production and income. And vice versa. What is the reason for this? What is the effect of a permanent increase in autonomous investment expenditure or government expenditure on
the level of equilibrium income?

In the case of underutilized capacity, an increase in ΔI from an existing equilibrium
creates an expansionary gap (see Fig. 6.12), which is closed by an increase in production (ΔY). New employees are hired who receive an income. These employees will
consume their new income partly. So Y will not only increase by ΔI, but by a multiple,
because each increase in income also leads to an increase in consumer demand. However, this multiplier effect only works in the situation of excess supply, that is, underutilized capacity, because the infrastructure for the increase in employment is already
available. Work is lacking without capital, that is, machines that are productive. If general demand is increased in a situation of utilized capacity, this will only lead to price
increases in the short term.

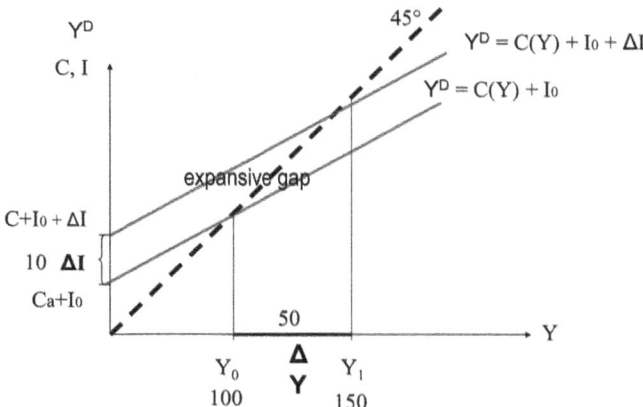

Fig. 6.12 The expansionary gap

In the following, we want to calculate the so-called **investment multiplier.** This indicates by how much GDP increases if net investment increases by ΔI, with autonomous consumption and the marginal consumption rate remaining constant.

$dY = 1/s \, dI$, where: dY = change in national income; s = marginal savings rate; dI = change in investment.

Effect of the Investment Multiplier or Expenditure Multiplier
(also applies to an increase in government spending):

The expenditure increase ΔI leads to income in the corresponding amount $\Delta Y = \Delta I$ and additionally $\Delta I \cdot c'$ in the second year, additionally $(\Delta I \cdot c')^2$ in the third year, etc. The companies react to the over-demand and hire the new employees one year later:

Example for a consumption rate of 0.8:

$$\Delta Y = \Delta I + 0.8 \, \Delta I + 0.8 \, \Delta I^2 + 0.8 \, \Delta I^3 + \ldots$$
$$\Delta Y = \left(1 + 0.8 + 0.8^2 + 0.8^3 + \ldots\right)\Delta I$$
$$\Delta Y / \Delta I = 1 + 0.8 + 0.8^2 + 0.8^3 + \ldots \text{ (infinite geometric series)}$$

Formula for the infinite geometric series (application as with the money multiplier):

$$\frac{\Delta Y}{\Delta I} = \frac{1}{(1 - c')}, \text{ d. h.} \frac{1}{(1 - 0.8)} = 5$$

This means that an increase in investment or expenditure by 1 € leads to an increase in equilibrium income of 5 €. Demand creates demand (in the world economic crisis).

We now want to derive the investment multiplier generally. For the goods market and equilibrium income, it applies:

$$Y = C(Y - T) + I + G_0$$

We form a total differential (all variables that do not change drop out, the rest is captured as a change):

(1)$dY = c' \, dY + dI \Leftrightarrow$ (2)$(1 - c')dY = dI$

$$dY = \frac{1}{(1 - c')} dI \frac{1}{(1 - c')} = \frac{1}{s'} \text{ is the investment multiplier}$$

$$= \text{Value of the reciprocal marginal propensity to save}$$

The same applies to the government spending multiplier:

$$\text{bei } Y = C(Y - T) + I_0 + G$$

Total differential (all variables that do not change drop out, the rest is captured as a change)

(1) $dY = c'dY + dG \Leftrightarrow$ (2)$(1 - c')dY = d$

$$GdY = \frac{1}{(1 - c')} dG$$

$$\frac{1}{(1 - c')} = \frac{1}{s'} \text{ is also the government spending multiplier}$$

$$= \text{Value of the reciprocal marginal propensity to save}$$

(or **general expenditure multiplier**)

Conclusion

The value of the investment multiplier (expenditure multiplier) is determined by the level of the reciprocal marginal propensity to save. In other words, the less households save from the new income, the greater the demand effect and thus the impact on equilibrium income. ◀

Example

for $c' = 0.8$, $\Delta I = 10$:

$$\Delta Y = \frac{1}{(1 - 0.8)} 10 = 5 \cdot 10 = 50$$

$1/(1 - 0.8) = 1/0.2 = 5$ investment multiplier

This means that an increase in investment or expenditure by 1 € leads to an increase in equilibrium income by 5 €. ◀

For the tax multiplier it applies:

at $Y = C(Y - T) + I0 + G0$

$$(1) \; dY = c'(dY - dT) \Leftrightarrow (2)(1 - c')dY = -c'dT$$

$$dY = -\frac{c'}{(1 - c')}dT$$

An increase in taxes thus leads to a reduction in equilibrium income, as consumption is steered away from income as demand. It is striking that in the tax multiplier, in contrast to the expenditure multiplier, not 1 is in the denominator, but the marginal propensity to consume, which is less than one (e.g. 0.8). It must be taken into account that d T is negative in the case of a tax reduction. I.e. with c' = 0.8, a reduction in taxes by 1 € increases equilibrium income by 4 €. (0.8/0.2 = 4). The expenditure multiplier would be 5. This is due to the use of income by private households. They do not spend it 100%, but save, which means a reduction in demand. If the state allows citizens to have more income through a tax cut, this will have less effect than if it increases government spending, because these will have a 100% effect on demand. This relationship has led economists Haavelmo to consider combining the expenditure multiplier and the tax multiplier, i.e. the state increases taxes and the government spends the money completely. There is a net effect of 1, because taxation prevents households from saving. The income that would have been saved is spent by the state, creating demand.

Then the following applies to a tax-financed increase in government spending:

$$\frac{dY}{dG} + \frac{dY}{dT} = \frac{1}{(1 - c')} - \frac{c'}{(1 - c')} = 1$$

Haavelmo Theorem

Tax-financed spending increases increase income or gross national product by the same amount.

Politically, however, this approach was rarely implemented because it is hardly possible to convey to voters that it is better if the state spends their money. However, credit-financed spending increases are popular as state demand policy because voters do not feel affected. Who pays back the loans in the future is open (Fig. 6.13).

Graphic representation of the multiplier effect using the **equilibrium condition I=S**

Summary

Unlike in neoclassicism, in Keynesian theory, the consumption and saving functions are income-dependent. Saving is not interest-related. As a result of the autonomous consumption share and the autonomous investments, aggregate supply and demand can therefore diverge if, for example, investments unexpectedly decline, as during the world economic crisis. Keynesian theory is demand-oriented. The oversupply then leads to capacity and production reductions, i.e. permanent unemployment, while an overdemand leads to production expansions with corresponding welfare gains and jobs. ◀

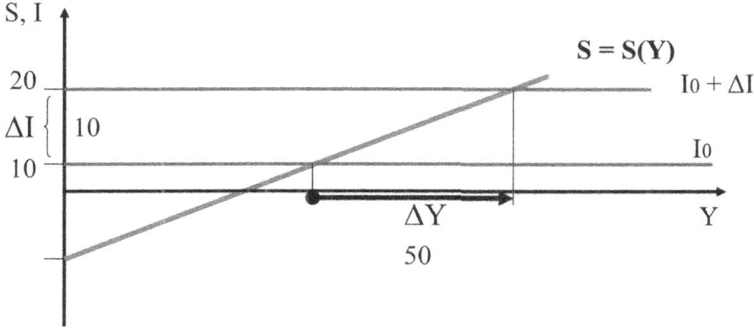

Fig. 6.13 The investment multiplier

6.7   Interpretation of Keynesian Demand-Oriented Policy

Politically, the state expenditure multiplier and the Keynesian theory were abused for the election campaign. Politicians interpreted it as a blank check for credit-financed government spending increases. If demand increases lead to economic growth, tax revenues would also increase and the loans would be repayable. Unfortunately, this Münchhausen effect is not found in reality because demand increases only lead to price effects and not to growth at fully utilized capacities. Rather, there are wage and price increases, which have a negative effect on competitiveness in an open economy.

What do consumption and GDP depend on? We remember the VGR: $Y = C + I + G + Ex-Im$. These are all expenditure components. Does production therefore only depend on demand? Do we therefore only have to increase demand to generate growth? In retrospect, this equation always applies (ex post), but the goods must be produced beforehand and in the open economy, exports can be decisive for demand. However, it depends on the competitiveness of a country, more precisely whether it has an attractive offer to trade.

We remember Robinson and Friday. First Robinson is alone and takes care of himself. He doesn't have a demand problem, but a supply problem, because he has to take care of himself. Then Friday comes along and the first division of labor is created. Friday now catches fish while Robinson specializes in hunting. In the evening they exchange their food. Both offer their products and ask for those of the other. Both have the basic needs for food, but only if they have produced an offer themselves, can they also pay for their needs, their demand.

For Ludwig Erhard, above all hard work and in the first years the renunciation of the fulfilment of personal consumption needs were decisive for the economic boom in Germany after the war (quote "There are no miracles"). What is decisive is that goods which create utility are created, only in this way does prosperity arise. Demand which does not satisfy any utility is a waste of resources (e.g. house building in the desert). If the production capacities are available, it can happen in the short term that demand lags behind supply or in longer-term exceptional situations like in the world economic and financial crisis (depression), then state demand must be increased. In the long term, however, the Say's theorem applies. Supply creates its own demand.

Examples of Economic Development

China

There were many unsatisfied needs in China with more than one billion people. Only the market-based reforms created internationally competitive production. Wages were extremely low by international standards. Labour-intensive products were produced. One can argue about what a fair wage is. But if the Chinese had not started to offer interesting goods to the outside world on this basis, they would never have been able to demand foreign goods. Only when production existed was both demand and income available or income to pay for demand. Foreign machines could be acquired. Productivity, production know-how and product quality increased and with them wages. The same development took place, for example, in Korea. After all, the basis of the economy is the exchange of goods and the goal is the satisfaction of needs. Today, more and more Chinese can afford cars.

Africa

In Africa, the problem is that there is no internationally competitive production here to exchange goods, so there is also no affordable demand.

Greece

After joining the Euro, Greece, like Germany after reunification, pursued a credit-financed expansive fiscal policy. The Greek governments were able to benefit from nearly halved interest rates after joining the Euro. A lot of money flowed into construction projects (including the Olympics) and the payment of public servants. Domestic demand rose sharply, with it the economic growth and as a result the wages and prices. Greece was no longer competitive and unemployment rose, as well as the debt problem, while growth declined. Is this a demand problem? From the perspective of the Greek economy, but it is an offer problem from an economic point of view. Without an offer that meets the interests of buyers, Greece can not sell anything and can not finance its needs. The Greek unemployed also have needs, so demand, which they can no longer pay without a job. With the high wages compared to other countries and productivity, they can not create an offer to pay their demand. There is a great demand here, but there is no production to pay for it. Greece is therefore unproductive and can not service its debts. ◀

1. Explain in your own words the difference between Keynes and neoclassicism.
2. How does the expenditure multiplier work?
3. Is the Say's Theorem wrong?

1. In a Keynesian economy, the consumption function is given by $C = 300 + 0.60$ (Y-T). Planned investment is 200, government spending and taxes are each 100.
   a) Represent the planned aggregate demand as a function of income.
   b) What is the equilibrium income, that is, the income at which aggregate supply is equal to aggregate demand?
   c) What is the new equilibrium income if government spending is increased to 150?
   d) Assume the government wants to achieve an equilibrium income of 2350. How high would government spending have to be then?
2. We want to investigate how the saving behavior of households affects Keynes. The following functions are given: $Y = Ca + c '(Y) + I_0$ with $Ca = 30$, $c' = 0.6$, $I_0 = 20$.
   a) Calculate the equilibrium income from the income-expenditure function.
   b) What effects does this have on equilibrium income if households save more to, for example, provide for bad times, and autonomous consumption decreases by 10?
   c) How does saving in equilibrium change?
   d) Why is the result of b) and c) referred to as the savings paradox ("paradox of thrift")?

6.8   The Investment Function

Investments have two essential economic properties. First, they are additional demand from companies and second, they increase the capital stock and thus also productivity or production capacity. Investments make up the second block of aggregate demand.

So far we have considered Keynesian investments to be autonomous, that is, externally influenced, and thus given Keynes sees the investment demand of companies in relation to the market interest rate and the expected marginal productivity of the capital used (= return = r).

In **private investment decisions**, the **profitability** depends on the consideration of whether future revenues can cover the incurred expenses and expected costs, that is, whether future net revenues exceed the acquisition costs of the machine.

Q = future expected net revenues

R = discount factor that reduces net proceeds to the amount of the purchase price, i.e. the profitability or marginal productivity of capital (corresponds to the internal rate of return).

Purchase price $= Q_1 + \frac{Q_2}{(1+R)^1} + \cdots + \frac{Q_n}{(1+R)^{n-1}}$

Although Keynes's investments are also dependent on the market interest rate, they are specified by the expected marginal productivity of capital, and thus also psychologically influenced.

Numerical example: A machine has an expected life span of 2 years and costs 1000 €. The investor expects net income of 500 and 540 €. The profitability (marginal productivity) of capital is then:

$$1000 = 500 + \frac{540}{(1+R)} \Leftrightarrow R = 8\%$$

The Y-axis shows both the capital market interest rate and the investment projects, arranged according to their profitability. The investment demand curve is derived from the quantity and the investment volume (Fig. 6.14).

Investments are carried out until all investment projects for which the capital costs i are less than the profitability have been implemented. With a high market interest rate, only investments with a high marginal productivity of capital (return) are carried out. With a low interest rate, investments with low returns are also carried out. Companies invest as long as the profitability is higher than the interest rate, i.e. i = r. This makes investments dependent on the capital market interest rate given the profitability: I = I (i).

Even with a zero interest rate, investment demand does not rise above a certain amount, as only investments are carried out whose earnings value is at least as high as the acquisition costs. Alternatively, the money can be invested in the capital market:

i > r ⇒ Investment on the capital market
r > i ⇒ Investment

Fig. 6.14 Keynesian investment function

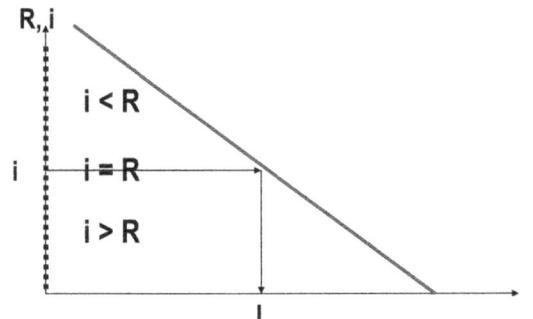

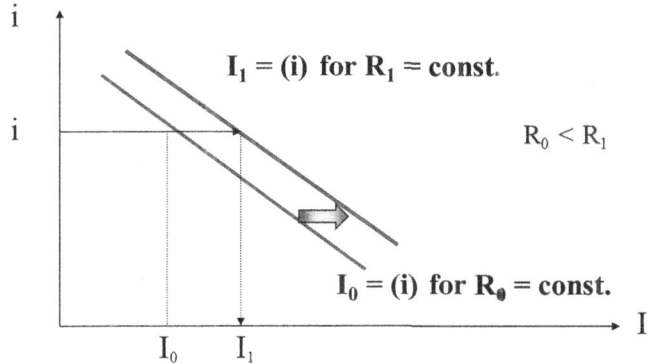

Fig. 6.15 Rising expectations and investments

If the **expected** return on investment projects, that is, the marginal productivity of capital R, rises, the function shifts to the right. Then, at the same interest rate i_0, more is
invested. The same applies vice versa, which was one of Keynes's explanations for the
world economic crisis of 1929 (Fig. 6.15) (see also Siebe & Wenke, 2014; Blanchard,
2014; Blanchard & Illing, 2006; Wagner & Böhne, 2003; Felderer & Homburg, 2005;
Drost et al., 2003; Mankiw, 2013. John, 2004 as well as Mussel, 2009).

6.9   Excursus: Interest Rates in Practice, the Yield Curve

On the financial market for loans and investments with regard to the term in the money
market and the capital market (banking terminology) is distinguished. The so-called.
Money market, the term money up to one year. The interest rate is determined here
mainly by the monetary policy, as the central bank usually only lends short-term. On the
capital market, the term of the term money is greater than _ year and is determined by
the interest and inflation expectations of market participants.

The relationship between the term of a risk-free investment, which is equivalent to a
loan to a third party with the best creditworthiness (AAA), and the interest rate is called
the yield curve. In the case of a normal course of the yield curve, the interest rates rise
with the term. In the case of the inverse interest rate curve, it is the other way around (see
Fig. 6.16).

How can the course of the yield curve be explained?

Explanations for the Yield Curve
1. **Liquidity preference hypothesis**
    A long-term commitment reduces the flexibility of the investor. The investor has to
    pay a liquidity premium. The longer he does not have access to his money, the higher

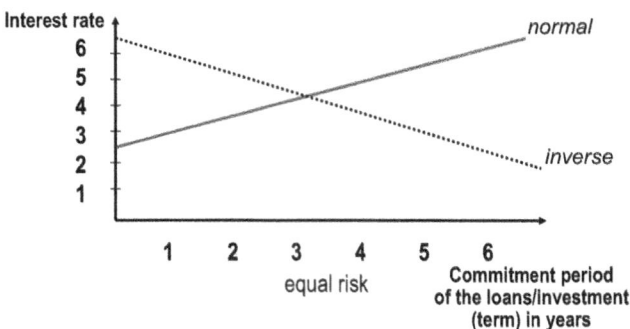

Fig. 6.16 The yield curve

the liquidity premium. Therefore, the interest curve rises over time. The waiting loss as an interest explanation of neoclassicism also falls under this.

2. **Expectation hypothesis**

But how can one explain inverse curves or changing interest rate curves? Expectations play a role here. If investors expect rising real interest rates, for example, due to future growth, they will invest their money short-term and push down the short-term interest rate. At the short end, the supply will rise while it falls at the long end. Inversely, borrowers will try to borrow money long-term to secure the relatively low interest rates. At the long end, the demand will rise and at the short end it will fall. Both lead to a steeply rising interest rate curve.

If investors expect rising inflation, they will invest their money short-term and wait for a risk compensation. Inversely, borrowers will try to borrow money long-term. This will also lead to a sharply rising interest rate curve.

But if they expect a phase of economic weakness in the future, and thus falling real interest rates, capital providers will try to secure the relatively higher interest rate long-term and invest long-term. The supply will rise at the long end and fall at the short end. Borrowers will try to borrow money short-term. The demand will rise at the short end and fall at the long end. That is why one can often observe inverse interest rate curves before recessions. Inversely, sharply rising interest rate curves are often a sign of an upswing.

3. **Market segmentation hypothesis**

The interest rate curve consists of different market segments at different maturities, each of which is determined by different providers and demanders. For example, one could explain a relatively low interest rate at 10-year maturities because there is a continuous high capital oversupply by life insurers. However, the long-term capital demand of home financing and state financing fluctuates. Many people only invest for a short time due to the uncertainty of whether they will still need their money. In the money market, i.e. short-term, the interest rate is determined by the monetary policy of the ECB.

Other Factors Influencing Interest

For risky investments there are. depending on the risk, so-called risk premiums. For example, risk-free government bonds have a so-called AAA rating. This is an external rating that is awarded by American rating agencies.[3]

6.10   The Capital Market Equilibrium

What Follows Why?
After we have dealt with the Keynesian basics of consumption, saving and investment as well as the goods market equilibrium in the income-expenditure model, we now want to turn to the central markets in the Keynesian model, the capital and money market. The famous IS-LM model, which we will present below, is an interpretation of Keynes' theory by Hicks.[4]

Learning objectives
The goal is for you to be able to explain the functioning of the Keynesian money market and the capital market and to calculate the equilibrium combination of interest and income in the IS/LM model.

The so-called IS curve is the geometric locus of all combinations of real income and interest that achieve an equilibrium of supply and demand in the capital market. Here, investment (I) and saving (S) are in equilibrium, which explains the name IS curve. Saving corresponds to the demand shortfall from the part of household income that is not consumed. To achieve a goods market equilibrium, we need investments of the same size as additional demand. It must hold that I = S. Investing, like in neoclassicism, depends on the interest rate. But saving, according to Keynes, depends on income, which is why there can be no market equilibrium mechanism here. The IS curve is rather the geometric locus of all combinations of real income and interest that achieve the same level of saving and investing and thus an equilibrium of supply and demand in the capital market.

We are looking for a curve that tells us when the capital supply, that is saving, and the capital demand, that is investment, are in balance and thus also the goods market.

It applies:

$$S = S(Y)$$
$$I = I(i)$$
$$S(Y) = I(i)$$

---

[3] See Eller, R. et al. (eds.) (2005).
[4] See Hicks, J. R. (1937).

A system of equations with three equations and four variables is solvable if one assumes the value of a variable Y as given. We start with a given income, with which we can determine the savings according to the saving function (see Fig. 6.17). Now we need the same investments on the Y-axis. Via the investment function we can now determine the interest rate that causes investments in the required amount. Now we actually already have the income-interest rate combination that causes equilibrium in the capital market and indirectly in the goods market. To derive a curve, however, we still have to bring the interest rates into a quadrant with the income, which is why we reflect the interest rate on a 45-degree line. In the last, fourth quadrant, the first intersection of income and interest rate results, which causes equal savings and investment volumes. With the next income, the corresponding equilibrium interest rate is then obtained in the same way. The IS curve as a straight line is thus determined.

The expectations of companies with regard to future economic development are also reflected in the IS curve. If the expected return on investment deteriorates, the investment curve shifts inward and with it the IS curve (Fig. 6.18).

For Keynes, the interest rate on the capital market is predetermined by the equilibrium interest rate on the money market, which we will discuss in the next chapter. The money market determines the interest rates on the capital market. On the capital market, production and thus income adjust until an equilibrium point on the IS curve and thus an equilibrium between investment and saving on the capital market is reached. How does the adjustment process work? If the given interest rates are too high for the existing national income as in case 1 (see Fig. 6.18), then I (i) < S (Y). Too little is invested so that the demand corresponds to the supply of national product. The companies react to this underdemand by adjusting their supply, that is, producing less. In parallel, income decreases, so less is saved. National product decreases and with it S (Y) until I (i)= S (Y) applies again.

In the second case, the opposite applies. Interest rates are too low, which is why investment demand is greater than what is necessary to match production to consump-

Fig. 6.17 Construction of the IS curve

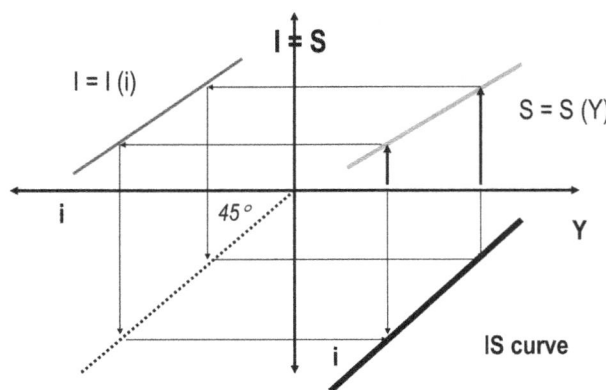

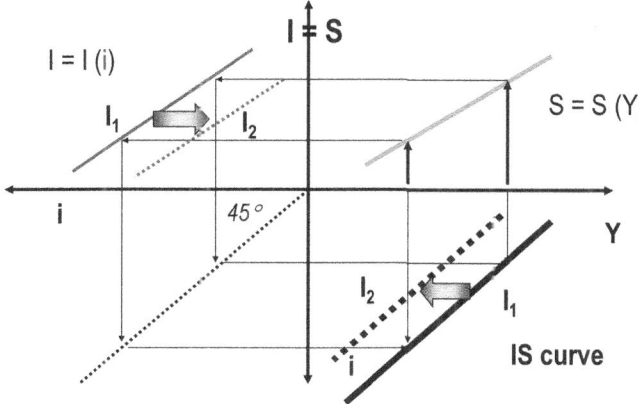

Fig. 6.18 Graphic example: Reaction of the IS curve to a decline in investment expectations

tion. The additional investment demand is greater than the demand decline caused by saving. Since Keynes assumes underutilization of capacity, businesses will increase production and hire employees in the short term. This increases the national product, and therefore also income. With income, saving also increases, and therefore the decline in demand, until the level of investment demand by businesses as additional demand is reached. The equilibrium national product is reached. In the IS model, the interest rate is given and the national product adjusts. The interest rate is determined in the money market, however (see Fig. 6.19).

Fig. 6.19 The IS curve

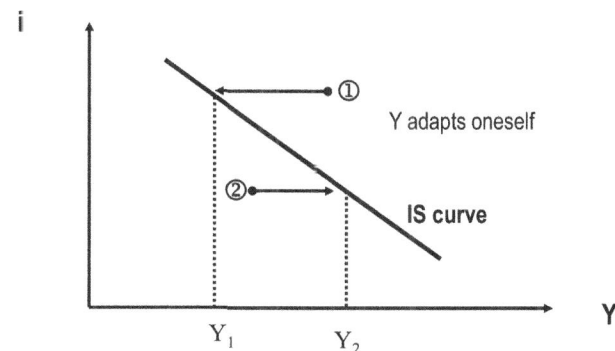

6.11   The Money Market Equilibrium

The interest rate, which determines the level of aggregate income in equilibrium
through the investment function, is the **price of liquidity** and is determined on the
money market in accordance with the money supply and the money demand. For the
further model-based considerations, Keynes assumes for the monetary sector of the
economy:

1. the **money supply (M)** is an **autonomous, exogenously determined size** that can be
   changed by the central bank if necessary. This implies:

$$M = \text{const.}$$

2. The **money demand (L)** is exerted by the **non-banks** (public).
3. The demand for money depends on the **purposes** for which the non-banks use money
   (new!!!).

The **money functions** are:

a) medium of exchange function (as in neoclassicism)
b) unit of account function and (as in neoclassicism)
c) store of value function in competition with fixed-interest securities **(new!!!)**

To 1. The Transaction Cash Demand
As far as money is needed for exchange purposes (L_T) (Liquidity), the demand, i.e. the
demand, depends on how large the value of the exchanged **production volume** (Y) is
and how high the cash holding coefficient (-duration) based on the payment habits of the
public is k (Fig. 6.20).
     then is $L_T = k \cdot Y$

To 2. The Speculation Cash Demand
The operation of bond markets

Fig. 6.20 The transaction
cash demand

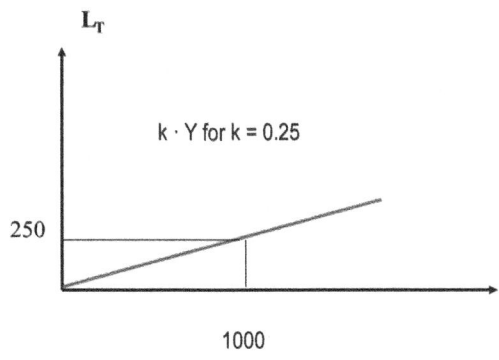

L_T

$k \cdot Y$ for k = 0.25

250

1000   Y

In Keynes, households can hold their money as cash or invest in securities, so-called bonds. More well-known than bonds are savings books. On them, the household can invest money and get it interest-bearing at the market interest rate. The notice period is three months. However, professional participants in the capital markets do not use savings books, but fixed-rate bonds. Issuers of such papers, i.e. the debtors, are companies and states. These papers promise the owners a fixed annual interest payment for the term until the capital is repaid at the end. If the papers are issued, the security price corresponds to 100 and the interest rate to the market interest rate. The yield corresponds to the interest rate divided by the price and thus the market interest rate at emission. After that, the security is traded on the bond exchanges. A new price is formed as a market price. The yield of a security (WP) adapts to the current interest rate level. If securities are sold, the price falls and with it the yield and the interest rate level, vice versa. For simplification reasons, fixed-rate securities with an infinite term are assumed here.

Example: A WP costs 100 € on the day of issue and is interest-bearing at 5%. The return is then 5%, which corresponds to the general interest rate. If the general interest rate rises to 10%, the 5%-bond will only be sold at a price of 50 €, because this corresponds to the market return of 10%.

$$\text{Yield } (5\,\%) = \frac{\text{nominal interest or coupon interest (5)}}{\text{rate (price) of the security (100)}}$$

$$\Uparrow\Downarrow \text{ Yield } (10\,\%) = \frac{\text{nominal interest or coupon interest (5)}}{\text{rate of the security } \Downarrow\Uparrow \;\; (50)}$$

The investor can either hold his money in cash or invest it in fixed-interest securities (government or corporate bonds). If he invests in securities, he has the advantage that he receives interest. The disadvantage is that the price of his security can fall. He then has, like with shares, a price risk.

The return on his securities investment depends on the price development of his papers and in turn on the development of the general interest rate. If interest rates rise, i.e. also the capital market yields of fixed-interest bonds, and he has already invested in securities, the price of his security falls. He would then have done better to hold the money in cash and buy the security later at the higher return. If market interest rates fall, the price of his security rises.

The return of a security adjusts to the current market interest rate. Furthermore: If securities are sold, the price falls and with it the return and the market interest rate rise, vice versa.

For the price value it applies:

$$\textbf{Market value} = \frac{\text{nominal interest}}{\text{current interest level}} \times \text{nominal value} = \frac{i_0}{i} \times \text{nomnal value}$$

$$\text{Market value} = \frac{5\%}{10\%} \times 100 = \frac{1}{2} \times 100$$

Fig. 6.21 The speculative
cash demand

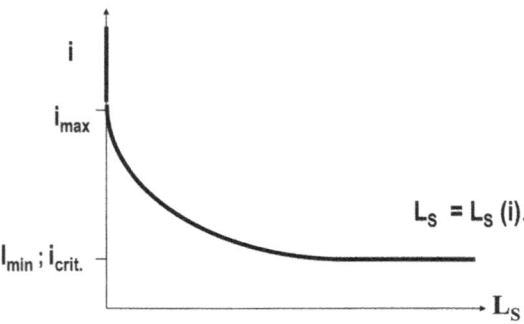

The investor must weigh the advantages and disadvantages of a security purchase. The interest income is offset by the risk of a price loss. When will an investor therefore invest in fixed-interest securities? If the interest income is higher than the expected price loss.

We want to know at what interest rate i the interest income is greater than the expected loss.

Interest income $>$ current price $-$ expected price

$$i_0 \bullet \text{nominal value} > \frac{i_0}{i} \bullet \text{nominal value} - \frac{i_0}{i_n} \bullet \text{nominal value}$$

$\Leftrightarrow 1 > \frac{1}{i} - \frac{1}{i_n} / + \frac{1}{i}$ (Nominal exchange, with the sign reversed)

$\Leftrightarrow i > \frac{i_n}{1+i_n}$ i.e. if the average expected interest rate is 5%, the critical interest rate is 4.76% (0.05/1.05).

$i = market\ interest\ rate,\ i_0 = nominal\ interest\ rate,\ i_n = expected\ interest\ rate$

This means that if the current interest rate is 3% and the investor expects an average interest rate of 5%, he will not invest, but wait until the interest rate has exceeded 4.76%. Then he invests all his money in securities. Since every investor has different expectations regarding the future average interest rate, this results in a curve for the demand for speculation money (see Fig. 6.21).

If the interest rate falls, the critical interest rate will be undershot by more and more investors, which is why more and more investors sell their securities because they want to hold money to achieve a higher return later or to avoid losses in value. If the interest rate is low, it is likely that it will be higher in the future, which would result in losses in value for investors if they bought now. The demand for speculation money rises. They speculate on falling prices. Conversely, if the interest rate rises, more and more investors will speculate on rising prices and buy securities. If the interest rate is high, it is likely that it will be lower in the future, which would result in gains in value for investors if they bought now. It pays to buy securities because the interest income is greater than the expected losses in value. The demand for speculation money falls.

This **speculative demand for money** thus leads, in addition to the income-dependent transaction money holding L_T, also to an **interest-dependent holding of money** for which the following applies:

$$L_S = L_S(i)$$
$$(-)$$

It is assumed for their course of action that

1. beyond a certain maximum interest rate i_{max} no economic subject is anymore ready for liquid asset holding **(money demand $L_S=0$),** i.e. all investors have already invested in securities because their critical interest rate is exceeded, i.e. the interest income exceeds the expected stock losses for all investors.
2. beyond a certain minimum interest rate $i_{min}, i_{crit.}$ the demand for money for speculative purposes is **completely interest elastic,** i.e. all money goes into the cash register to stay liquid (liquidity preference function in the so-called liquidity trap). The investors fear stock losses. I.e. the low interest rate does not compensate the expected stock losses.

There is another type of money demand with Keynes, the so-called precautionary cash demand for unexpected expenses. The possible unexpected expenses depend on the lifestyle, i.e. on the income that makes it possible. In reverse, an increasing interest rate has a negative effect on the precautionary cash demand, because the investor has to forego the interest investment to keep the cash register. However, the precautionary cash demand can be neglected due to its small scope. Furthermore, interest and income affect it like the transaction and speculation cash demand. Like the transaction cash demand, it depends positively on the income (unexpected expenses) and like the speculation cash demand, negatively on the interest as an opportunity cost. Therefore, it is not significant.

To illustrate the speculative demand curve, it can be practically derived in a group by asking who would invest 1000 € for ten years at a fixed interest rate. Start with a very low interest rate, e.g. 2%. Usually nobody reports here. This means that the speculative cash demand is infinitely large. If this is the interest threshold after which no one buys securities, this would be the critical interest rate. All money is kept in the cash register, no one buys securities. If you now slowly increase the interest rate, more and more investors will buy securities. Until finally, at an interest rate of, for example, 10%, all investors have bought securities and no money is left in the cash register. I max is the maximum critical interest rate of the investors. If it is exceeded, all investors have invested in securities and the speculative cash register is empty. Conversely, i min is the minimum critical interest rate of the investors. If this is undershot, all investors have exited the securities and only speculative cash demand is left.

The following **supply and demand functions** therefore apply to the monetary sector:

$$M/p = \text{autonom}$$
$$1.\ L_T = k \cdot Y$$
$$2.\ L_S = L_S(i, -)$$
$$L = k \cdot Y + L_S(i)$$

The demand for money therefore consists of two components:

- Transaction cash demand, i.e. demand for money for transactions, exchange: money for goods (consumption). The transaction cash demand is dependent on Y and k;
- Speculative cash demand, i.e. demand for money for the later purchase of fixed-interest securities. The investors speculate on interest rate increases. It is negatively dependent on interest. The lower the interest rates, the more investors expect higher interest rates in the future and want to keep cash.

The **equilibrium condition** therefore reads:

$$3.\ \mathbf{M/p = k \cdot Y + L_S(i)}$$

So now we have a given money supply and two money demand. The one, the transaction demand for money, is income-dependent and the speculative demand for money is interest-rate dependent. To determine the money market equilibrium, one must therefore find the combinations of income and interest rates that generate the same amount of money demand as there is supply. The so-called LM curve is the geometric locus of all combinations of income and interest rates that bring about a balance of supply and demand in the money market. The name means equality of L, the money demand ("demand for liquidity") and the money supply M ("money"). How do you determine the LM curve, so the money market equilibrium?

As with the IS curve, with four variables (L_T, L_S, Y and i) and three equations, the determination of the money market equilibrium is possible if one assumes the value of a variable to be given (see Fig. 6.22).

In the LM curve, we take i as given and derive the speculative demand for money from this with the corresponding given function (1). The leg of the isosceles triangle shows us the actual money supply M/p. We deduct the speculative demand and get a remainder that is left over for the transaction demand for money (2). We now need a transaction demand for money that is exactly as large as the money not needed by the speculative demand for money, so that equilibrium between money supply and money demand is achieved. Since the transaction demand curve is in a different quadrant, we have to reflect it, but this time so that the remaining amount of money to be assigned to the transaction demand is on the y-axis. Therefore, we reflect at the hypotenuse of the isosceles triangle (3). The other leg of the triangle represents the money supply, which now shows us the remaining part for the transaction demand in reverse order. Starting from this, we can now derive the income associated with the transaction demand function. So the same amount of transaction demand will arise as is needed to demand the

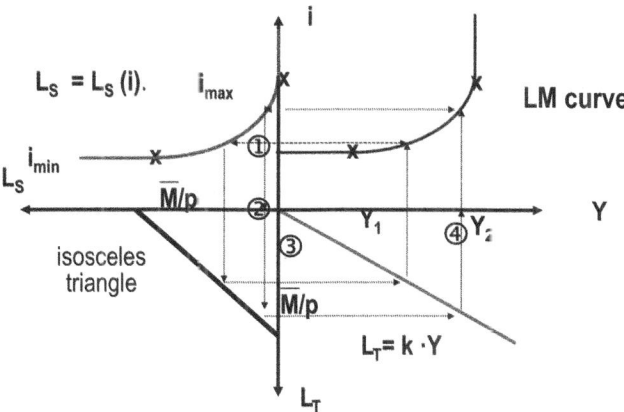

Fig. 6.22 The money market equilibrium curve

part not needed by the speculative demand (4). We have thus determined the first inter-est-income combination at which the money supply is equal to the money demand on the Keynesian money market. We can derive further points by always taking a differ-ent interest rate as given and then deriving the speculative demand for money from this and then distributing the remainder to the transaction demand for money with the corre-sponding income."

The Formation of the Equilibrium Interest Rate

As already mentioned, Keynes' interest rate is formed on the money market, which then initiates the adjustment process via income to an IS equilibrium and thus also to a goods market equilibrium on the capital market. How is the equilibrium interest rate formed on the money market? (Fig. 6.23).

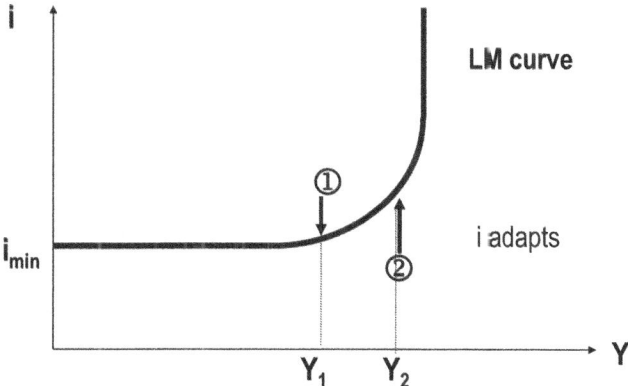

Fig. 6.23 The adjustment processes of the LM curve

1. **Case (1):** All **points left** (e.g. Y_1 and i_0) of the LM curve represent income—interest—combinations in which a **money-overhang** exists **(M>L)**. The **actual cash holding is higher than** the one **planned (wanted) cash holding** at the given interest rates and income level **(M>L)**. The interest rate is higher than the critical interest rate of some investors, which is why they buy these securities. In order to reduce the too high liquidity, economic subjects increasingly **demand securities.** The investors hold more cash in their portfolio than they would like to, which is why they buy securities. The resulting over-demand for interest-bearing papers makes the **prices rise,** which is equivalent to a reduction in the **yield.** The yield of all securities in circulation is called the market yield. It represents the market interest rate. As a result, the market interest rate falls when investors buy securities.

$$\Downarrow \text{Yield} (10\%) = \frac{\text{nominal interest or coupon interest}}{\text{rate} \Uparrow}$$

With falling interest rates, the demand for cash increases, according to the speculation cash demand function, until the point corresponding to the income is reached on the LM curve. There the actual cash holding is as high as the planned cash holding. The speculation cash demand has risen along with the falling interest rate until it is equal to the given transaction cash demand plus the money supply.

In short:

Interest rate too high for equilibrium L_S $(i, -)$, L_T (Y), i.e. $L < M$

$$\Rightarrow \text{Purchase of securities} \Rightarrow \text{Prices} \uparrow \Rightarrow i \downarrow$$

2. **Case (2):** All **points to the right** (e.g. Y_2 and i_0) of the L/M curve represent income—interest—combinations in which there is a **demand for money** **(M<L)**. The **actual cash holding is lower than** the one **planned (wanted) cash holding** at the given interest rates and income level **(M<L)**.

The interest rate is lower than the critical interest rate of some investors, which is why these WP sell. To get liquidity, the economic subjects **sell securities.** The investors hold less cash in their portfolio than they would like at the low interest rate, which is why they sell securities. The resulting oversupply of fixed-income securities causes the **prices to fall,** which is equivalent to a **rise in interest rates.**

$$\Uparrow \text{Yield} = \frac{\text{nominal interest or coupon interest}}{\text{rate} \Downarrow}$$

With rising interest rates, the demand for cash falls according to the speculation cash demand function until the point corresponding to the income has been reached on the LM curve. There the actual cash holding is as high as the planned cash holding. The speculation cash demand has fallen with the rising interest rate until it is equal to the given transaction cash demand together with the given money supply.

In short:
Interest too low for equilibrium L_S (i, −), L_T (Y), i.e. L > M

$$\Rightarrow \text{Sales of securities} \Rightarrow \text{Prices} \downarrow \Rightarrow i \uparrow$$

Why does the LM curve rise in the middle section? In other words, why does an increase in income lead to an increase in interest rates. What happens in the money market when income increases at a given money supply?
The equilibrium condition for the money market is:

$$M/p = L_T(Y, +) + L_S(i, -)$$

If income rises, so does the demand for transaction money, because households need more money for their purchases. I.e. the interest rate must rise, so that with the same amount of money, a balance between money supply and money demand can be formed. Only with a higher interest rate does the demand for speculative money decrease, thus providing room for a higher demand for transaction money. Only with a higher interest rate is there enough money for the demand for transaction money.
There is another more practical explanation. With rising income, the demand for transaction money also rises. In order to get the money needed for the higher income into the till, investors sell securities, causing prices to fall and, with them, the yield— i.e. the general interest rate—rises. Only with a higher interest rate can the demand for speculative money decrease in favour of the demand for transaction money.

6.12   The IS/LM Model

How do the money and capital markets work together? The money supply is given. Together with the liquidity preference in relation to income (LT, transaction motive) and interest (LS, speculative motive), the money market equilibrium curve LM is formed. The interest rate is determined on the money market. Depending on income, it adjusts until:

$$M/p = L_T(Y, +) + L_S(i, -).$$

In Keynes, the interest rate is determined on the money market, which determines the level of investment. Income adjusts accordingly.
   The saving function shows the saving inclination in relation to income and the investment function shows the capital demand in relation to interest, and both together result in the IS curve. Income adjusts accordingly on the capital market.
   While for the capital market and the money market a large number of equilibrium income—interest—combinations were determinable, there is **only one income—interest—combination** that guarantees **equilibrium for both areas at the same time.** This is determined by the **intersection of the IS and LM curves.**

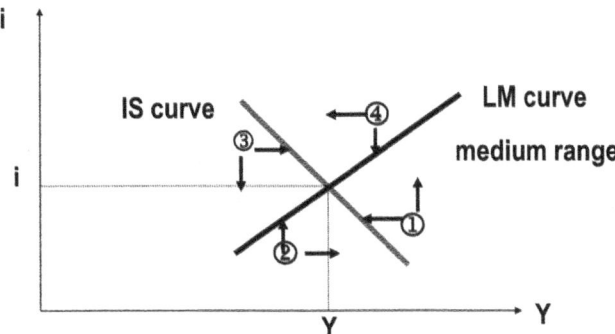

Fig. 6.24 Equilibrium processes in the IS/LM model

In principle, four non-equilibrium combinations are possible. The first point (1) in Fig. 6.24 is **below the LM curve.** The interest rate is therefore too low for the given income in a money market equilibrium. The return on securities is too unattractive, which is why there is an excess demand for speculative cash. Investors sell securities to satisfy their demand. Stock prices fall. This increases the return on securities and thus the general level of interest rates. There is a tendency towards the equilibrium interest rate, which is represented by the arrow.

The first point is also **above the IS curve.** This results in an excess supply in the capital market. The investment demand is too low at the interest rate given by the money market to demand the capital supply S (Y) predetermined by national income through investments I (i). This results in an excess supply in the goods market, so that companies reduce their supply. National income and gross national product fall as a result of the multiplier effect, as companies lay off employees and they consume less and therefore demand less. There is therefore a tendency towards the equilibrium national product, which the arrow symbolizes.

For the other points there are corresponding tendencies towards the equilibrium interest rate and equilibrium national product. If the interest rate is above the LM curve, it is too high for the given income. Households want to hold less speculative cash and invest their money in securities at the high interest rate. They buy securities. Stock prices rise, which reduces the return on securities and thus the general level of interest rates.

If the point is below the IS curve, the interest rate is too low for an equilibrium between saving and investing. If the interest rate is too low, investments are too high, that is, higher than saving, which corresponds to an excess demand on the goods market. Companies expand production. National income and thus saving as a demand shortfall rise until an equilibrium between saving and investing and thus also a goods market equilibrium between demand shortfall and additional demand is reached.

In principle, the capital market could be in equilibrium (I = S), but not the money market. Then the interest rate on the money market would also adjust, that is, change,

Fig. 6.25 Areas of the LM
curve

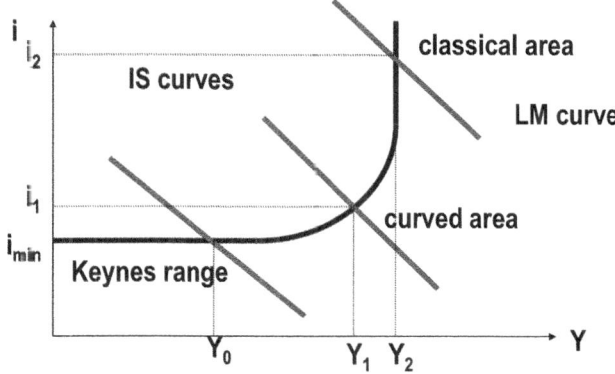

which in turn would have the consequence of an adjustment process of the capital market
to the new interest rate level. Depending on whether the interest rate is then above or
below the IS curve, there is an undersupply or oversupply on the goods market with a
corresponding adjustment process.

The IS curve can intersect the LM curve in three areas (Fig. 6.25):

1. **Classical area:** the interest rate is so high that all investors have already invested in
   securities, the speculation account is empty. The demand for money is independent of
   interest rates as in neoclassicism.
2. **Curved area** (normal case): higher income leads to higher interest rates, as the
   demand for the transaction account must decrease for the demand for the speculation
   account. If income increases, households sell securities to have the money available
   for the transaction account. Prices fall, which increases the return on securities and
   thus the general interest rate.
3. **Keynes area or liquidity trap:** If the critical interest rate is below that of all investors
   (i_{min}), the demand for the speculation account is 100 percent elastic. Investors only
   want to keep cash and not invest in securities, which is why interest rates can not fall
   further. The critical interest rate is constantly low, i.e. in this area income can increase
   without interest rates rising, as households have enough money in the cash register
   (see also Siebe & Wenke, 2014; Blanchard, 2014; Blanchard & Illing, 2006; Wagner
   & Böhne, 2003; Felderer & Homburg, 2005; Drost et al., 2003; Mankiw, 2013; John,
   2004 as well as Mussel, 2009).

Summary

The money supply is given. Together with the liquidity preference in relation to
income (L_T, transaction motive) and interest (L_S, speculation motive) the money market equilibrium curve LM results. The interest rate is formed on the money market.

The saving function shows the saving inclination in relation to income and the investment function the capital demand in relation to interest. The intersection of the IS-LM curve thus determines the equilibrium income, at which the money and capital markets are in equilibrium. It is $I = S$, with which then also the goods market is in equilibrium (after a possible adjustment process). ◀

Comprehension Questions

1. Explain the adjustment process to the equilibrium interest and income combination if the interest rate is to the right or below the LM curve.
2. Explain the adjustment process to the equilibrium interest and income combination if the interest rate is to the left or below the IS curve.
3. Why is there a range of the LM curve that is infinitely interest-elastic? How do investors behave here?

Exercise: Determination of the Equilibrium Income at the Money Market

1. In the context of a Keynesian model world, the following are given:
   autonomous money supply: **460 Mrd. €**
   Cash holding coefficient: **0.2**
   Interest-dependent speculative cash demand:

   $$L_S(i) = {}^{180}/_i \text{ for } 1 \leq i \leq 10$$
   $$\text{for} = 0.99 \; L_S(i) = \text{perfectly elastic}$$
   $$\text{for } i \geq 10 \; L_S(i) = 0$$

   Determine the level of equilibrium incomes
   for $i = 1$; 1.5; 2 and 3.

2. Assume that the following Keynesian conditions apply to the German economy:
   The consumption function is: $C = 300 + 0.60 \, (Y - T)$
   The investment function is: $I = 300 - 50i$. The money demand function is $L = Y - 200i$. Government spending and taxes are each 100. The money supply M corresponds to 2000 and the price level P is equal to 4. Determine the equilibrium interest rate i and the equilibrium income Y.

3. Assume the following keynesian frame conditions for the German economy. The consumption function is: $C(Y) = 60 + 0.5 \, Y$. The investment function is: $I(i) = 50 - 500i$. Government spending is 40. The money demand function is $L \, (Y, i) = Y - 4000i$. The money supply M is 800 and the price level P is 4.
   a) Determine the equations for the IS and LM curves.
   b) Determine the equilibrium interest rate i and the equilibrium income Y.
   c) What is the equilibrium investment and consumption in equilibrium income?

Fig. 6.26 Derivation of the aggregate demand curve

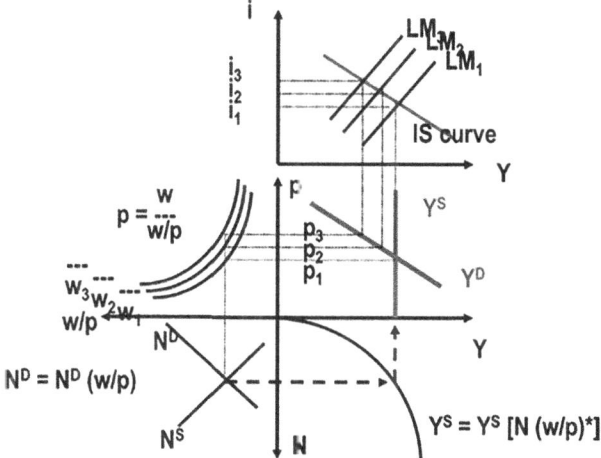

d) Assume that income (or GDP) would be 350 at the equilibrium interest rate. Describe the situation in the money and goods market. How would income and interest rates adjust to reach equilibrium?

6.13   A general Keynesian Aggregate Model (Neoclassical Synthesis)

What Follows Why?
In order to be able to derive macroeconomic statements, we still need a Keynesian total model that includes all markets. The so-called neoclassical synthesis is not strictly Keynesian. It was developed by some economists after Keynes. However, it makes it possible to include the normal economic situation, thus creating a generally applicable overall model.

Learning goal
The goal is that you are able to explain the functioning of the Keynesian overall model and to calculate the equilibrium combination of interest and income. In addition, you should be able to explain which economic policy is required in which situation.

In the so-called neoclassical synthesis, the neoclassical supply sector, i.e. the labour market and the production function, is combined with the demand-oriented Keynesian

Fig. 6.27 b Effect of price
level increases on the LM
curve

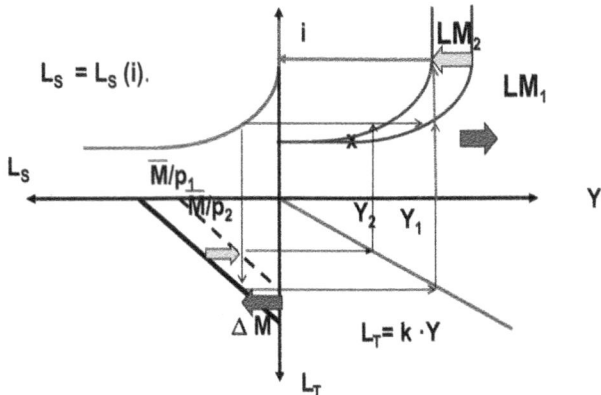

IS/LM model for the money and capital markets (see Fig. 6.26). We remember that the Keynesian IS/LM model is demand-oriented because, unlike in neoclassicism, the quantity demanded is always automatically demanded.

Says's theorem does not apply and, if investment demand, for example due to sudden negative expectations (decreasing marginal productivity of capital), is too low, there may be oversupply. This is the case in a depression.

New is the III. Quadrant, which determines the price level. Here the neoclassical supply function meets the demand function derived from the IS/LM model.

It is asked how the equilibrium income in the IS/LM model changes if the overall economic price level changes. The price level is only found in the IS/LM model at the real money supply. For the money market equilibrium, the following must apply: $M/p = L_T$ $(Y, +) + L_S$ $(i -)$. If the price level increases, the real money supply M/p decreases. This shifts the LM curve because the money supply is an exogenous variable. In order to find a new equilibrium on the money market, the interest rate must be higher at a lower real money supply (see Fig. 6.27a), so that households demand less speculative cash and/or the national product or income is lower (see Fig. 6.27b), so that the transactions cash demand also decreases. In other words, economic actors try to offset the lower real money supply by selling securities. As a result, prices and yields of the securities, i.e. interest rates, rise. Higher interest rates on the money market lead to an imbalance on the capital market. The interest-dependent investments decrease, which creates an undersupply on the goods market through the decreasing investment demand. Companies adjust their supply by reducing it. There is a negative multiplier process in which production and income decrease equally. The equilibrium and the equilibrium income shift to the left.

Price level increases

$(M/p\uparrow)\downarrow$ i.e. for the process to the new money market equilibrium $M/p = L_T (Y, +) + L_S$ $(i -)$ the following must apply:

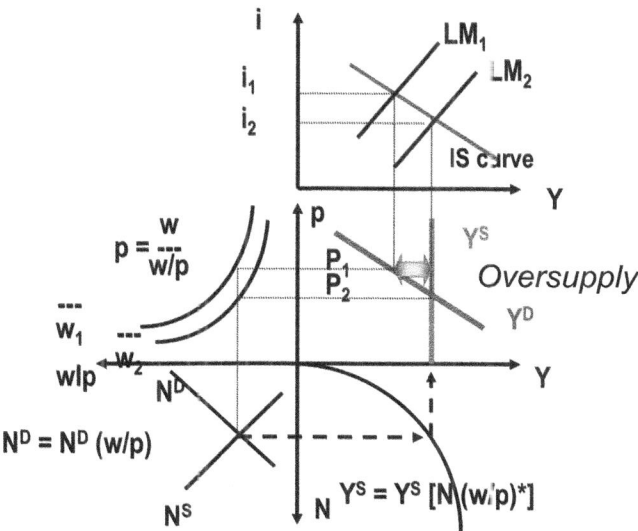

Fig. 6.28 The Keynes effect

$$L_T(Y \downarrow) \downarrow + L_S(i \uparrow) \downarrow \Rightarrow i \uparrow \Rightarrow I(i \uparrow) \downarrow \Rightarrow Y^D \downarrow$$

The LM curve therefore shifts to the left, which also shifts the equilibrium income in the IS/LM model to the left. Thus, the aggregate demand decreases when the price level increases[5].

Exercise

Calculation of the goods demand function

Suppose that the demand for money function in Germany is $L(Y, i) = 3Y - 200i$, the saving function $S(Y) = 0.6\,Y$ and the investment function $I\,(i) = 6 - 60i$ are empirically determined.

a) The real cash is $M/P = 5$. What are then real income and interest?
b) Assume that the money supply is 30. Now you can calculate the goods demand function Y^D.

---

[5] If one were to keep the equilibrium income Y1 constant, the new LM curve would show that the interest rate would have to rise so far that the speculative demand for money has declined in favor of the unchanged transactional demand for money.

Keynes Effect: Equilibrium Process at Price Deviations

Equilibrium process: Let us assume that the price level is above the equilibrium price level (see Fig. 6.28). Due to the small real money supply M/p, the interest rates must be higher in the money market equilibrium than in the overall equilibrium in order to reduce the speculative demand for cash and lower income so that the transactions demand for cash is reduced. This means that the LM curve must lie to the left of the equilibrium LM curve. Since the interest rates are too high, the investment demand is too low on the goods market and there is a surplus of goods. As a result, prices fall and the real money supply increases again. The investors have more money than they want to hold and buy securities, which is why the prices rise and the yield and thus the market interest rate fall. Since the interest rates fall, the investment demand and thus the demand for goods rise until the equilibrium income is reached again. The LM curve shifts to the right until the equilibrium LM curve is reached again.

This indirect relationship between price level and demand for goods via the real money supply induced LM curve reduction is called the **Keynes effect.**[6] In the end, a doubling of the money supply leads to a doubling of the price level and vice versa. With twice as much money, economic actors buy securities. The interest rates fall, the investments rise and there is a corresponding over-demand, which causes a price level increase until the old real cash is restored.

$$\textbf{Keynes} - \textbf{effect}: \textbf{p} \downarrow \Rightarrow \textbf{M/p} \uparrow \Rightarrow \textbf{B}^{\textbf{D}} \uparrow \Rightarrow \textbf{i} \downarrow \Rightarrow \textbf{I(i)} \uparrow \Rightarrow \textbf{Y} \uparrow$$

6.14   Keynesian Economic Policy in the Normal Situation

6.14.1 Expansive Credit-Financed Fiscal Policy

IS: $S(Y) = I(i) + G$

The effect of the demand for capital is like the spending multiplier:

$$m = \frac{1}{1 - c'}, \text{ with } c' = \frac{dc}{dY}$$

It corresponds to the change in equilibrium income.

The state asks for capital on the capital market in the amount of the planned state expenditure G. At the same time, the state expenditure is increased by the credits. In the capacity underutilization, the additional demand leads to an immediate increase in production. People are hired again and consume with their additional income. The multiplier works (see Fig. 6.29).

---

[6]The positive effect of an increase in real asset values of households on consumption at falling prices is also referred to as the Pigou effect.

Fig. 6.29 Expansive fiscal policy in the IS curve

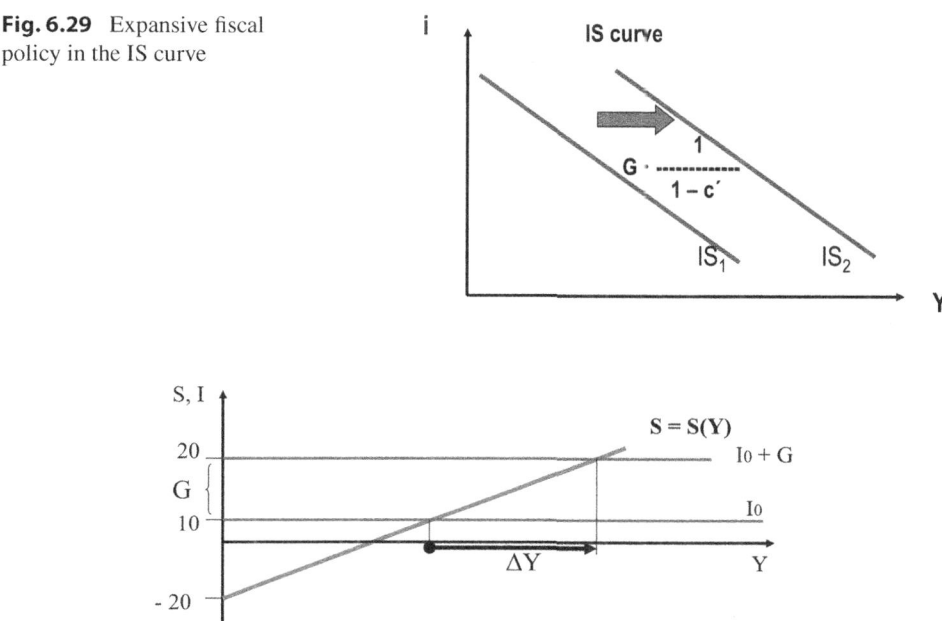

Fig. 6.30 The expenditure multiplier for credit-financed expansionary fiscal policy. (Graphical representation of the multiplier effect using the **equilibrium condition I+G=S**)

Unlike in neoclassicism, capital supply does not depend on interest, but on income. (S = S (Y) see Fig. 6.30). Production increases and thus also income and household savings. This automatically leads to a larger capital supply. Interest does not have to rise to generate more capital supply. The capital market is in equilibrium when: Capital supply = capital demand. The IS curve shifts to the right.

We again consider the two cases for fiscal policy in which the state finances its expenditure either through loans or through taxes (Fig. 6.31).

1. The credit-financed increase in government spending (G) leads to a corresponding demand for capital and goods, which is why the IS curve shifts to the right. The shift to the right corresponds to the government expenditure multiplied by the expenditure multiplier derived for investment **(1).**

Given a certain amount of money, the interest rate must rise in order for the speculative demand for cash to decrease and thus make money available for the increased transactional demand of those with higher incomes. For this reason, securities are sold and their prices fall, corresponding to an increase in yield and market interest rate. Private investment is displaced by the increased interest rate due to government spending.

We still have a positive demand increase due to government spending. The demand for goods curve shifts to the right due to the increased government demand, but to a

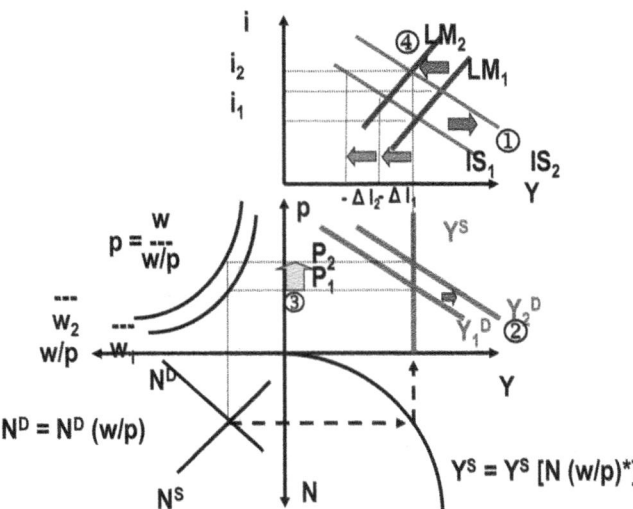

Fig. 6.31   Credit-financed expansionary fiscal policy in the normal situation

lesser extent, as the demand for investment is weakened by the higher interest rate on the money market **(2)**.

Given a certain amount of production, prices increase **(3)**.

If coffee used to cost 2 euros, the household could buy 50 coffees with 100 euros. Now the price has risen to 4 euros, meaning it needs additional 100 euros to buy the same amount of coffee. If the price level increases, so does the isoline, because households are not subject to money illusion. The real money supply decreases. Now one can buy less with their money than before.

Since households have less money in their cash, they have to sell securities to get money. The price of securities falls and the interest rate increases.

4. The price increase causes a reduction in the real money supply, which is why the LM curve shifts to the left until the equilibrium level S $(Y) = I (i) + G$ is reached again at the given income **(4)**. Higher prices therefore lead to a higher interest rate.

The demand for investment is increasingly displaced by the demand for government spending as the interest rate rises.

This effect continues until as much private investment demand has been displaced as government demand has increased, thus resulting in the same effect as in neoclassicism **(Total Crowding Out)**.

    1. $G \uparrow \Rightarrow Y \uparrow \Rightarrow L_T(Y \uparrow) \uparrow + L_S(i \uparrow) \downarrow = M/P$, that means $i \uparrow \Rightarrow I(i) \downarrow$

    2. $p \uparrow \Rightarrow M/P \downarrow = L_T(Y \downarrow) \downarrow + L_S(i \uparrow) \downarrow$, that means $i \uparrow \Rightarrow I(i) \downarrow$

Excursus open economy

At this point, a brief look should be taken at the effects of a credit-financed expansive fiscal policy in the normal situation in an open economy. As shown above, such a policy leads to wage and price increases and interest rate increases in the event of fully utilized capacities. As a result, the country's competitive situation deteriorates. This deterioration can only be compensated for by a flexible exchange rate that reduces prices in foreign currency. If this is not possible, for example in a currency union, the capital import will increase due to the higher interest rates and thus a balanced balance of payments will be established (see Sect. 6.19), but the debt will increase and employment will fall. This was also the problem of Greece in the Euro crisis, which had previously carried out an expansive credit-financed fiscal policy.

6.14.2 Expansive Tax-Financed Fiscal Policy

There is also a total crowding out with tax financing. Government spending is financed by revenue from higher taxes. Thus, consumption and savings no longer depend on real income, but on disposable income, that is, the remainder that is left after deducting from income. Household income thus decreases by the real tax contribution. The demand thus decreases by the part that households would have consumed from the income. Here, income is taxed, that is, both consumption and savings. That is why the higher government demand goes at the expense of (compared to credit financing, less strongly) increased interest rates both at the expense of investments and through the reduction in consumption at the expense of private demand.

There is also a total crowding out in the case of state financing. With a consumption rate of 80%, this part of private demand is displaced from the outset. Thus, the private demand decreases as a result of the higher state demand. The rest of the income that households would have saved, i.e. not demanded, represents additional demand. The IS curve therefore also shifts to the right in this case. However, the effect is weaker than in the case of credit financing. With a consumption rate of 80%, i.e. around 20%. For the 20% additional demand, there are the same effects as for the previously presented state demand increase financed by credit. This 20% effective demand increase increases the overall demand. However, since capacities are utilized, there are only price effects. The LM curve shifts to the left. Interest rates rise and private investments are displaced until the original equilibrium income is restored. As in neoclassicism, the private demand (consumption and investment) is displaced by the state.

The difference between the two financing alternatives lies in the fact that, as a result of borrowing, only investment demand is displaced, while state financing goes at the expense of both investments and consumption, and that the demand effect is lower. However, when capacities are utilized, there are only price increases and crowding out. There are no employment effects.

As a result of the higher demand effect, credit-financed state expenditure increases therefore have stronger interest and price effects than state-financed.

However, if one looks at fiscal policy as a whole, it is ineffective. It can neither generate growth nor employment. The crowding out, i.e. the displacement of private investment by the state and the price increases, are rather negative effects. ◄

6.14.3 Expansive Monetary Policy

In this case, the amount of money is increased by the central bank. In this way, more money comes into circulation. With the money not needed for the transaction account or the speculation account, households buy securities. The price of the securities rises, the yield and the interest rates fall. The LM curve shifts to the right **(1)**.

In order to remain in equilibrium in the money market, when there is a higher amount of money, interest rates must fall and/or income must rise, so that the higher demand for money for speculation and the higher demand for money for transactions are offset by the higher money supply (see Fig. 6.32).

If interest rates fall, investments become more profitable. Investments increase. Due to the increased demand for investment, the overall economic demand and thus also production increase **(2)**.

The given level of production increases the price level. **(3)** The real money supply decreases due to the rising prices (Fig. 6.33).

Prices rise until the LM curve is back in its original place. The nominal wage has also adjusted, as there is no money illusion. The real money supply decreases due to the ris-

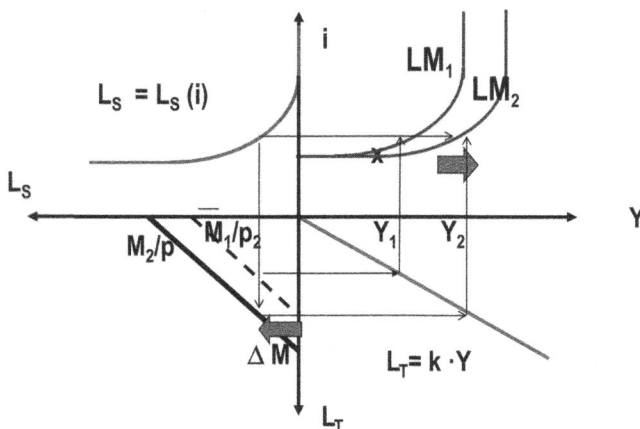

Fig. 6.32   Shift of the LM curve due to expansive monetary policy

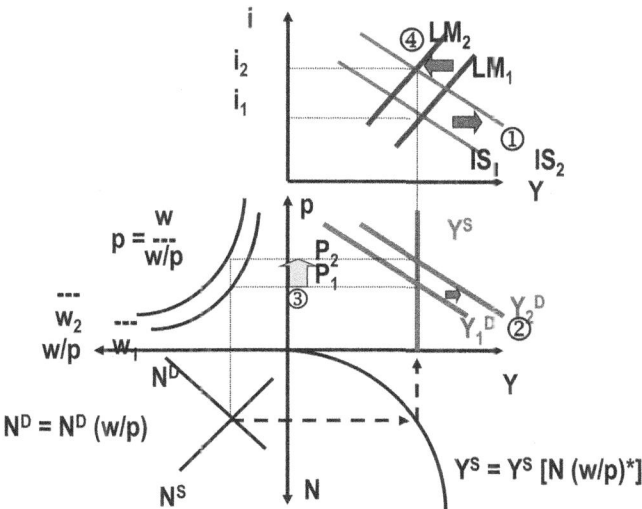

Fig. 6.33 Effect of expansive monetary policy

ing prices. Now the opposite effect occurs as described before. If the money supply is increased, the price level also rises accordingly. The result is the same interest rate and a higher price level, so there is also no difference in monetary policy in the economic normal case compared to neoclassicism.

Conclusion

In the normal situation of fully utilized capacities, the effects in the neoclassical and in the Keynesian model are identical. ◄

6.15   Keynesian Explanations of Depressions

6.15.1 The Great Depression and the Financial Crisis

We remember the overview of the development during the world economic crisis of 1929 at the beginning of Chap. 6. Prices fell, but demand did not increase. It is also striking that investments from 40.4 billion US$ in 1929 fell to 4.7 billion US$ in 1932, almost one tenth, even though interest rates fell from 5.9% to 2.7% in the same period, more than halved. Falling investments despite falling interest rates are a contradiction to neoclassicism. According to neoclassicism, there is always an equilibrium between investments and savings on the capital market through the market mechanism. If investments fall at a given savings, sufficient investments are stimulated by a falling interest rate until I = S again. But in the Great Depression, investments did not react to interest rates because companies could not sell their current production and therefore had no reason to invest in expansionary investments. Interest rates fell, but investment demand continued to fall. Here Keynes developed his famous investment trap as an explanation.

However, interest rates fell to only 1.7% by 1933, which was still a high interest rate in view of this crisis. Keynes answered the question of why they did not fall further with the so-called liquidity trap.

The Financial Crisis

The Financial Crisis was triggered by American home loans. The volume of loans to bad debtors, so-called subprime mortgages, rose from $35 billion in 1994 to $600 billion in 2006 to $800 billion in 2007. With the increased volume, lending practices became more and more lax. This is how people got loans who had neither income, jobs nor assets (so-called NINJA-loans: no income, no job and no assets). The loans were usually brokered by brokers for commissions in relation to the amount of the loan. Only they had direct contact with the borrowers. The lender, a US bank, sold the loan with others to a US investment bank. The investment bank structured the loans into a loan bundle, so-called collateral debt obligations (CDO) with different loss absorption in different risk tranches, the default risk of which was classified by a rating agency. These ratings were based on the portfolio approach, according to which risks that are correlated differently balance each other out. This is based on historical estimates or statistics of US home loans. Most of this long-term house financing was bought by banks in property companies (conduits), which,equipped with little equity, refinanced themselves short-term via so-called commercial papers (CP) on the money market and thus with lower interest rates, which represented a high maturity transformation. In the event that refinancing was not successful, the banks had to provide liquidity lines, which, however, did not appear on the balance sheet as contingent liabilities and did not have to be backed with equity.[7]

The first write-down on CDOs occurred in February 2007 at HSBC for $10.5 billion. Finally, in March 2008, the volume of bad subprime loans was estimated at up to $600 billion. More and more write-downs on CDOs had to be made. As a result of the write-downs and the lack of transparency of the CDOs, not only did the demand for CDOs collapse, but also for the CPs on the money market. In the end, the banks stopped lending each other money because it was not transparent how many bad subprime loans the loan-seeking banks had and thus how at risk of bankruptcy they were. The promised liquidity lines were utilized by the property companies. This led to an unexpected outflow of

---

[7]See Shiller, Robert (2007); Gold, Gerry/Feldmann, Paul (2007); Muolo, Paul/Padilla, Matthew (2008); Woods, Thomas E. (2009); http://www.amazon.de/s/ref=ntt_athr_dp_sr_1?_encoding=UTF8&field-author=Financial%20Crisis%20Inquiry%20Commission&search-alias=books-de-intl-us&sort=relevancerank. Financial Crisis Inquiry Commission (2010) and Conrad, Christian, A. (2010).

liquidity from the banks and the banks had to take the loans on their balance sheets and back them with equity.

Most of the real estate loans were still being serviced, but the market for CDOs had collapsed, so that the banks had to write off the irrational market prices, up to 70% according to IFRS and US GAAP (fair value accounting). There were bank runs and bankruptcies. This development culminated in the partial illiquidity of US investment bank Bear Stearns in March 2008. Bear Stearns was acquired by JP Morgan for $1.2 billion along with a $29 billion loan from the US Federal Reserve. After this government-initiated bailout, the markets calmed down. The risk of a large financial institution failing was apparently averted. This was particularly important for the markets due to the high volume of credit default swaps (CDS) outstanding.

However, the system break was triggered by the insolvency of the fourth largest investment bank, Lehman Brothers, in September 2008. With Lehman's bankruptcy, US politics became unpredictable. The financial markets could no longer foresee the occasional, discretionary dropping of individual banks. The confidence of market participants was completely lost. Lehman was "too big to fail", i.e. a threat to the system. A standstill in financial flows could only be prevented by massive state intervention, including the nationalization of many banks. Many newspapers compared the development on the financial markets with the crisis of 1929. Although there was no depression comparable to that of the time, a credit crunch and a massive slump in the real economy could not be prevented.

For our further considerations we want to establish the following. In the financial crisis one could observe an order intake drop of up to 40% (see Fig. 6.34). Against this background, investments were no longer profitable for the companies. The investment demand broke away. In addition, the investment demand became inelastic with respect to interest rates because, due to the poor expectations, the interest rates could fall but the companies still did not invest. The capacities of the companies were not utilized and they also do not expect an improvement of the demand situation. As in 1929, this led to an investment trap as Keynes calls it.

6.15.2 The Investment Trap
Order intake in the financial crisis

Due to the pessimistic expectations of the companies, the investments have collapsed. The investment function is completely interest inelastic. Even interest rate cuts do not trigger a new investment decision. The IS curve shifts downward and becomes a parallel to the Y-axis. Due to the lack of demand, prices fall. The real money supply increases and the LM curve shifts to the right. Since people now have more money, they buy securities. This purchase causes the stock price to rise and the return, that is, the market interest rates to fall. However, the Keynes effect does not work in this case. The interest rate cuts do not lead to an increase in investment, as the investment function is completely interest inelastic (6.35).

New orders index in the manufacturing sector
Working day and seasonally adjusted value (X-12-ARIMA)
Volume index 2005 = 100

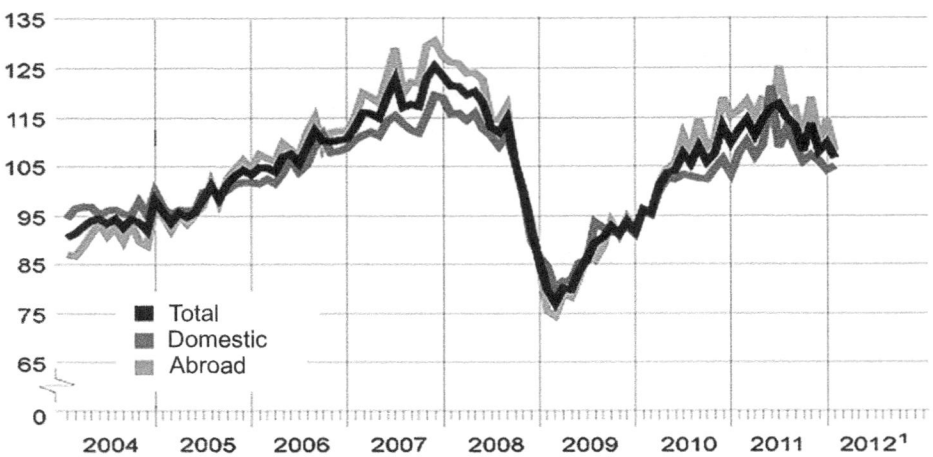

Selected economic activities lt. Eurostat Regulation (EC) No 1893/2006.
Preliminary result.
[1] Including January 2012.
© Federal Statistical Office. Wiesbaden 2012

Fig. 6.34 Order intake in the financial crisis. (Source: Federal statistical office, https://www.destatis.de/DE/ZahlenFakten/GesamtwirtschaftUmwelt/VGR/VolkswirtschaftlicheGesamtrechnungen.html)

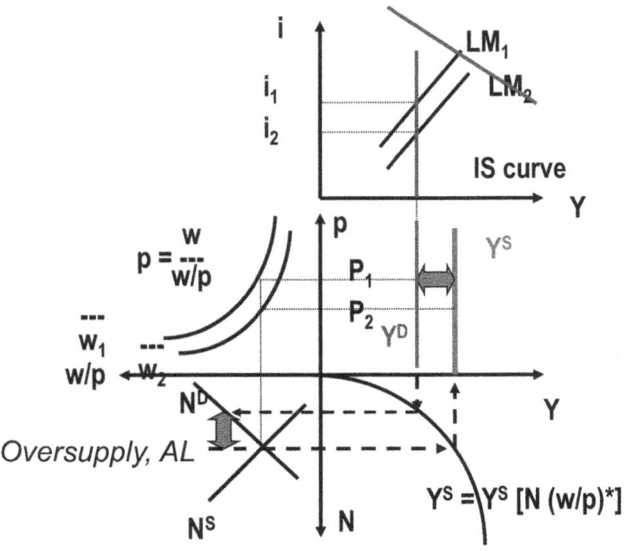

Fig. 6.35 Keynes effect and expansionary monetary policy in the investment trap

The effective demand decides about the demand for labor. Only as many employees are needed as are necessary for the production of the decreased demand. Before the depression, the companies produced according to the condition marginal product of labor equal to marginal costs, that is, the real wage. But since they cannot shut down production, they are now oriented towards the effective demand, that is, demand-oriented. So there was a switch from supply orientation to demand orientation. Since demand falls, unemployment rises. The companies have sales problems and only ask for the work they need for the effective demand, that is, the demand for labor falls. The labor supply is based on the real wage, which has remained the same. There is an oversupply of labor as a difference between labor supply and labor demand. Since the Keynes effect does not work due to the interest-independent investments, a situation of stable unemployment arises.

Conclusion

Due to the oversupply, prices are falling and, as a result, interest rates are falling due to the shift in the LM curve, but this does not lead to an increase in investment demand. Unlike in neoclassicism, demand does not increase despite lower interest rates and prices. The Keynes effect does not work.

As long as pessimism prevails, a stable situation of unemployment arises. Unlike in neoclassicism, the market mechanism does not work. The state must intervene to prevent economic damage. An expansive monetary policy is ineffective in the investment trap, as investments do not respond to lower interest rates.

Based on this example, we can see that without expected returns of companies, the interest rate for loans is irrelevant. Here, too, monetary policy cannot influence economic development through interest rate cuts or money supply. ◀

6.15.3 The Liquidity Trap

In the situation of a depression, interest rates usually fall until the equilibrium interest rate is reached and sufficient investment demand and, conversely, investment goods demand have been generated. However, in the liquidity trap, the interest rate cannot fall below the so-called critical interest rate, as investors in the money market no longer buy securities, but only hold cash. The Keynes effect does not work. The behavior of investors is explained as follows (Fig. 6.36):

1. Explanation
The LM curve has a kink (liquidity trap or Keynesian range) and the critical interest rate is below. The demand for money is infinitely elastic. For economic subjects, the interest rate is exceptionally low, so that they fear high price losses on fixed-income securities and therefore prefer to hold cash. The speculation account rises to infinity. That is, they want to put all the money they get into the speculation account and not hold any securi-

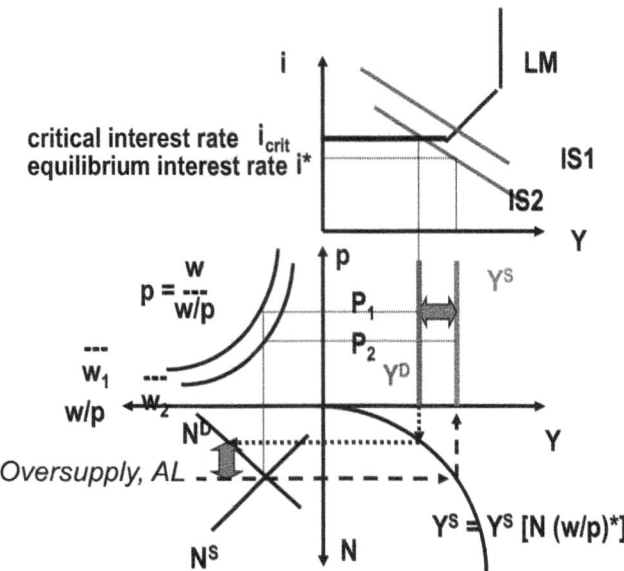

Fig. 6.36 The liquidity trap

ties. They expect that the interest rate can only rise and thus the price losses are higher than the price gains.

2. Explanation
In large depressions, people hold cash and do not invest. There is a fear that the invested capital will not be returned. During the financial crisis, Deutsche Bank CEO Josef Ackermann said that all investors were holding cash. He even spoke of an "investor strike".

Interim conclusion: At the critical interest rate, investors expect the future interest rate to be higher than the missed interest income from the non-investment. Therefore, they hold cash to avoid price losses. Investors also hold cash because they are afraid of the risk of investment. They even expect defaults due to insolvency. They then buy neither corporate nor bank bonds. For this reason, the interest rate cannot fall and companies and banks cannot refinance. There is a so-called credit crunch.

The interest rate necessary for a goods market cannot be established. The corresponding monetary policy of the central bank as a demand stimulation is ineffective. All additional money is held in cash. Even the Keynes effect does not work, because a higher real cash is not used to buy securities, because the households are afraid of price losses due to rising interest rates or fear of losing their investment if the debtors have to file for bankruptcy in the depression, such as companies or banks.

Effective demand determines employment demand. Only as many employees are needed as are necessary to produce the goods demand. Prior to the depression, companies produced supply-oriented profit-maximizing according to the profit maximization condition "marginal product of labor equals marginal cost", that is, the real wage. But since they could not shut down production, they now orient themselves to effective demand, that is, they are demand-oriented. So there was a switch from supply-orientation to demand-orientation. Since demand falls, unemployment rises. Companies have sales problems and only ask for the work they need for effective demand, i.e. employment demand decreases. The labor supply is based on the real wage, which has remained the same. There is an oversupply of labor as a difference between labor supply and employment demand. Since the Keynes effect does not work due to interest-independent investments, a situation of stable unemployment (Fig. 6.37) arises.

An increase in the money supply (**expansive monetary policy**) does shift the LM curve to the right, but all additional money is hoarded by investors in the cash register. The speculative cash demand is infinitely interest-elastic. With falling income, investors do not buy securities as usual at a given money supply, which is why interest rates do not fall and why investments and thus demand cannot increase. The Keynes effect does not work.

Prices have fallen and thus the real money supply has increased. In this way, the LM curve shifts to the right. Although the real money supply has increased, economic subjects do not buy securities. They hold their money. As a result, interest rates do not fall and the equilibrium interest rate cannot equilibrate. The speculative demand for cash is infinitely interest-elastic. Investment and demand do not increase. There is also unemployment here.

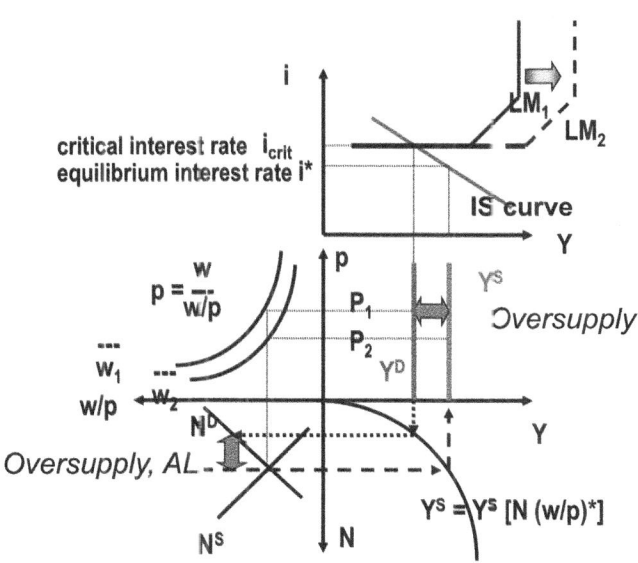

Fig. 6.37 Expansionary monetary policy in the liquidity trap

Summary

In the Keynesian model, interest rates are set by the money market. In phases of depression, interest rates are generally low. At the critical interest rate, investors expect the future interest rate (return) to be higher than the missed interest income from not investing. They therefore hold cash to avoid losses in value. In crisis situations, such as the world economic crisis of 1929, investors also have extremely poor expectations. Investors hold cash because they are afraid of the risk of investment. They not only expect losses in value due to interest rate increases, but also defaults due to insolvency. They then buy neither corporate bonds nor shares.

In a situation of depression, interest rates usually fall (as in neoclassicism) until the equilibrium interest rate is reached and sufficient investment demand (as capital demand) and, conversely, investment goods demand have been generated (usually: decrease in underdemand $\rightarrow$ p $\downarrow$ $\rightarrow$ M / p$\uparrow$ $\rightarrow$ WP$\uparrow$ $\rightarrow$ i $\downarrow$ $\rightarrow$ I (i)$\uparrow$).

In the liquidity trap, however, the interest rate cannot fall below the critical interest rate, because investors no longer buy securities on the money market, but only hold cash (absolute liquidity preference). The interest rate necessary for a goods market equilibrium cannot be achieved.

In this situation, the state must actively promote the economy through expansionary fiscal policy. ◄

6.16   Keynesian Economic Policy in the Depression

6.16.1 Credit-Financed Expansionary Fiscal Policy in the Investment Trap

Expansive fiscal policy is a financial policy measure of the state. The basic idea is as follows: In the depression, the state must replace the missing private demand with state demand by increasing government spending. The state goes to the capital market, asks for capital and spends it, which corresponds to the effect of an equal increase in investments. As long as the demand for capital also increases production and thus income at the same time, the supply of capital also increases as savings depend on income (Fig. 6.38).

The increased government spending increases production and thus income. With the higher income (production), the transaction demand for cash also increases. Households need more money to buy the increased number of goods. To get this money, they have to sell securities. The sale leads to lower prices and thus an increase in the return of all securities in circulation, which corresponds to the market interest rate. But since we are in a depression, investments are not interest-related. Entrepreneurs do not invest because their capacities are underutilized. They cannot sell their production, so they do not want to expand it. For this reason, the increased interest rates cannot displace private investment (no crowding out). Where there is nothing, nothing can be displaced. The problem or disadvantage becomes an advantage.

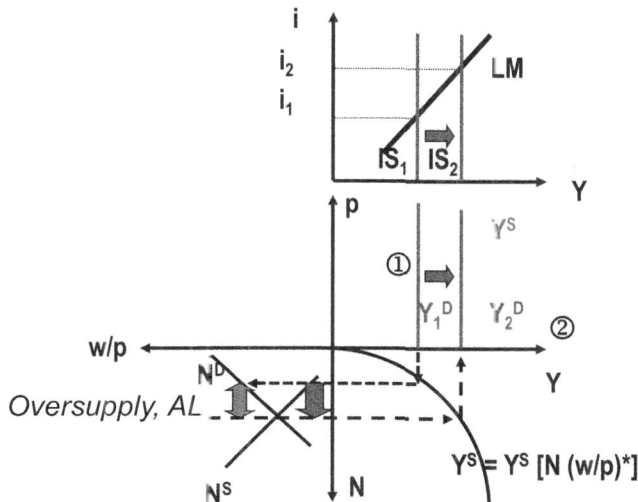

Fig. 6.38 Credit-financed expansionary fiscal policy in the investment trap

However, the price level does not rise, as there is underutilization of capacity during the depression. Due to the low demand, prices tend to fall rather than rise. In this way, the price decrease is offset. Prices remain stable. The LM curve does not shift to the left and remains constant, there is no crowding out. There is rather a crowding in of private investment. Due to the lack of sales, the companies already had bankruptcy in sight. Now, thanks to the government demand, they have orders again. The capacities are utilized again. As much is offered by the companies at utilized capacities as is demanded. The mood improves. Investments are worthwhile again. The economy is stimulated and the aggregate demand increases.

On the labor market, due to the increase in production, there is an increase in employment. The companies now need the workers they previously laid off to satisfy government demand. Full employment is created on the labor market.

The state has replaced the private demand. Due to the good mood in the economy, as a result of the crowding in, the companies again expect that the goods offered will be sold again. They therefore inquire on the labor market again according to the profit maximization condition $dY/dN = w/p$. The crowding in also causes the IS curve to shift back to its original position.

The state's demand for capital leads to an increase in the interest rate through the increased national product ($G\uparrow \Rightarrow Y\uparrow, \Rightarrow i\uparrow$, since $M/P = const. = L_T(Y)\uparrow + L_S(i)\downarrow$). However, due to the inelastic demand for investment, the interest rate increase does not lead to a displacement of private investment. There is rather a crowding in. Since the economy is in a depression, the capacities are underutilized, which is why there are no price increases and thus no shift of the LM curve to the left. The multiplier effect is unchecked.

Example for $c' = 0.8$, $\Delta G = 10$:

$$\Delta Y = \frac{1}{(1 - 0.8)} 10 = 50$$

On the contrary, since the economy is in a pessimistic mood (negative expectations), the unexpected increase in demand can lead to further investments, i.e. further demand, beyond the spending multiplier. The government intervention thus causes a tendency towards full employment equilibrium (crowding in).

$$\Rightarrow Y \uparrow \Rightarrow L_T(Y \uparrow) \uparrow + L_S(i \uparrow) \downarrow = M/P, \text{ normally } i \uparrow \Rightarrow I (i) \downarrow \text{ but here } I = \text{const.}$$

6.16.2 Expansive Tax-Financed Fiscal Policy in the Investment Trap

In the case of tax financing, there is also no crowding out. However, here it is the income that is taxed, i.e. both consumption and savings. However, government spending acts as a demand one hundred percent, as the state does not save, so that the spending multiplier is one. There is no crowding out because there are hardly any investments and these are interest-independent. According to the so-called Haavelmo theorem, therefore, an expansionary fiscal policy financed by taxes is also suitable for combating depression. However, the effects are much lower than in the case of an increase in government spending financed by credit.

6.16.3 Credit-Financed Expansive Fiscal Policy in the Liquidity Trap

In the situation of a depression, interest rates usually fall until the equilibrium interest rate has been reached and sufficient investment demand and, conversely, investment goods demand have been generated. However, in the liquidity trap, the interest rate cannot fall below the so-called critical interest rate, as investors in the money market no longer buy securities, but only hold cash. Investors buy neither corporate nor bank bonds. For this reason, the interest rate cannot fall and companies and banks cannot refinance. There is a so-called credit crunch (Fig. 6.39).

The state replaces the missing private demand with public demand by increasing government spending accordingly. The state goes to the capital market, asks for capital and spends it, which corresponds to the effect of an equally large increase in investments. As long as the demand for capital also increases production and thus income at the same time, the supply of capital, which depends on income, also increases through saving. The effects are the same as with expansive fiscal policy in the investment trap.

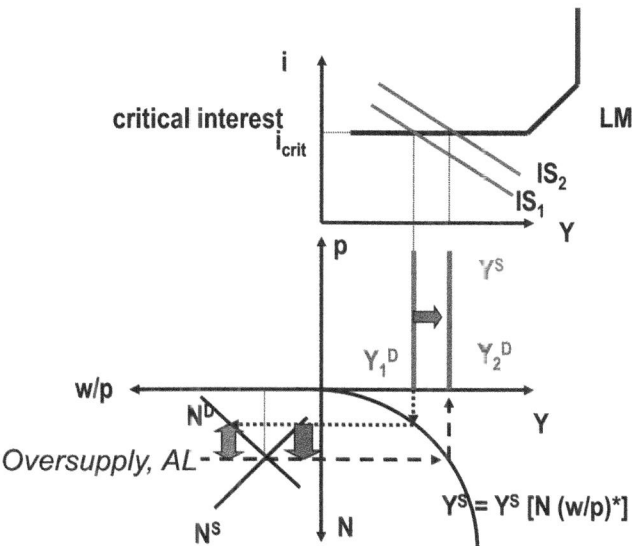

Fig. 6.39 Credit-financed expansive fiscal policy in the liquidity trap

Increased government spending increases production and thus income. With the higher income (production), the transaction cash demand also increases. Households need more money to buy the increased number of goods. In order to get this money, they would actually have to sell securities. In the liquidity trap, however, they do not own securities, but only keep cash. The speculation cash is full of money. In order to make their purchases, they do not have to sell securities, but can rely on the money in the speculation cash. Since no securities are sold, the interest rate does not rise and thus no private investments are displaced (no crowding out). The disadvantage of the liquidity trap thus becomes an advantage.

Why does the interest rate not rise with the increasing demand in the liquidity trap, as is the case in normal situations? On the capital market, the supply of capital is given by saving and grows with increasing income, which is why not necessarily a higher interest rate is necessary for a higher income to reduce the demand for speculation cash in favor of the transaction cash, because investors have enough cash. They just don't want to buy securities. Without a liquidity trap, the interest rate would have fallen further with falling income, because less transaction cash is needed and investors would have bought securities with the surplus money.

However, the price level does not rise either, as there is underutilization of capacity during the depression. Due to the low demand, prices tend to fall. So seen, the price decrease is compensated. Prices remain stable. The real cash box remains constant, so the LM curve does not shift to the left. There is no crowding out. Rather, there is a crowding in of private investment. Due to the lack of sales, the companies already had bankruptcy in sight. Now, thanks to the government demand, they have orders again. The capacities are utilized again. As much is offered by the companies with utilized capacities as demanded. The mood rises. Investments are worthwhile again. The economy is stimulated and the aggregate demand rises.

On the labor market, due to the increase in production, there is an increase in employment. The companies now need the previously dismissed workers again to satisfy the government demand. There is full employment on the labor market.

The state has replaced the private demand. Due to the good mood in the economy as a result of the crowding in, the companies again assume that the offered goods will also be sold again. They therefore ask on the labor market again according to the profit maximization condition $dY/dN = /p$. The crowding in also causes the IS curve to shift back to its original position.

Conclusion

As with the investment trap, there is no displacement of private investment without an interest rate increase. Rather, there is a crowding in. Since the economy is in a depression, the capacities are underutilized, so there is no price increase and thus no leftward shift of the LM curve. The demand multiplier works unchecked. ◀

Example

for $c' = 0.8$, $\Delta G = 10$:
◀

$$\Delta Y = \frac{1}{(1 - 0.8)} 10 = 50$$

On the contrary, since the economy is in a pessimistic mood (negative expectations), the unexpected increase in demand can lead to further investments, i.e. further demand, beyond the spending multiplier. The state intervention thus causes a tendency towards full employment equilibrium.

$$\Rightarrow Y \uparrow \Rightarrow L_T(Y \uparrow) \uparrow + L_S(i = \text{const.}) \downarrow = M/P, \text{ d. h. } \Rightarrow I(i) = \text{const.}$$

6.16.4 Expansive Tax-Financed Fiscal Policy in the Liquidity Trap

If the state's expenditures are financed in the liquidity trap through taxes, there is also no crowding out. However, income is taxed here, i.e. both consumption and savings. But government spending acts one hundred percent as demand, because the state does not save, so there is a net effect in the amount of the saved taxes. With a marginal propensity to save of 20%, the multiplier is one. There is no crowding out because interest rates do not rise due to the liquidity trap. According to the so-called Haavelmo theorem, a state-financed increase in state demand is also suitable for combating depression. The effect with tax financing is much lower than with credit financing as in the investment trap.

6.17   Keynesian Economic Policy

The IS curve and the LM curve have different elasticities depending on the economic situation:

1. Good Economic Situation/Boom Situation/Classical Area

The interest rate is so high that all investors have already invested in securities, the speculation fund is empty. The demand for money is independent of the interest rate as in neoclassicism. Due to the good economic situation, the IS curve is relatively interest-elastic and the LM curve is inelastic. (High economic situation: high interest elasticity of the IS curve, low (or no) interest elasticity of the LM curve).

The demand for money is, as in classical economics, only dependent on income, which is why one speaks of the classical range here. With the interest rate i_2 all investors have invested in securities (see Fig. 6.40). There is no speculation demand for money. The interest rates are so high that it is not expected that they will rise significantly. In the classical range, investments are very interest-sensitive. Everything is invested and expectations are positive. In the boom situation, the demand is greater than the supply. This can cause prices to rise over time (inflation). It can also lead to over-investment, as companies want to expand their capacities due to the high demand. Investments often take more than one year to be realized. The problem is that companies cannot see what competing companies are investing. Overcapacities and over-investments are the result, which can then cause a downturn. The bigger the boom, the bigger the downturn.

Which policy is most useful in this situation? A restrictive fiscal policy does not work. Although demand, production and income would fall in the short term and thus also the transaction demand for money, the economic actors would immediately invest the remaining money in securities, which would cause the interest rate to fall and the very interest-sensitive investments to rise, thus offsetting the decrease in government demand.

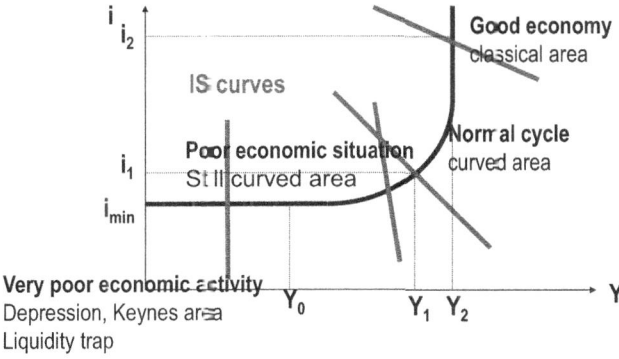

Fig. 6.40 Elasticities and business cycles of the IS and LM curves

A restrictive monetary policy is effective in this situation. In this way, the money supply is reduced. Monetary policy is more effective than fiscal policy, because due to the economic optimism, all money is used to purchase securities But then the interest rates rise when the money supply is reduced (e.g. restrictive monetary policy of the ECB). Because all investors have invested in securities, they have to sell securities to the same extent as the money supply decreases. The prices of securities fall and the interest rates rise. Investments are interest-elastic, so investments decrease sharply, which has a dampening effect on demand.

Conclusion on economic policy: Restrictive monetary policy to mitigate price effects. $Y^D > Y^S$

2. Normal Economy (Curved Area)

In this area, demand and supply are in equilibrium. All capacities are utilized. Here is a total crowding out of fiscal policy, because Y^S is given and interest and price effects lead to the same displacement of private demand as in neoclassicism (see Sect. 6.14). An expansive monetary policy only leads to price and wage increases.

In this situation, no intervention should be made by the policy, as it is not necessary and only leads to crowding out, that is, the displacement of private investment or consumption demand by the state.

Conclusion on economic policy: No policy required.

3. Poor Economy (Recession)

If investors still buy securities, we are therefore not yet in the liquidity trap and investments are still interest-sensitive, an expansionary monetary policy is successful. The investors buy with the additional money that they do not need at given or lower income, securities. The prices rise, with the result that the yield of all securities in circulation, ie the market interest rate, falls. The investments respond to the lower interest rates and generate an expansive demand effect.[8]

Conclusion of economic policy: Expansionary monetary policy.

4. Bad Economy/Keynesian Area/Liquidity Trap and/or Investment Trap

In this area, the economy is in a depression. On the market, demand is smaller than supply. We have no interest elasticity of the IS curve and infinite interest elasticity of the LM curve. In this extreme case, money supply increases do not lead to lower interest rates and are also ineffective due to the non-interest-elastic investments (investment trap). Fiscal policy is most effective in this extreme case, as no investments are displaced in the extreme case (income can rise without interest rates rising [liquidity trap of the LM curve]).

---

[8]This requires that there are enough investments with a positive return. This may, for example, in an open economy with lack of competitiveness is not the case.

Expansive fiscal policy is the only way to get out of the liquidity and investment trap. The credit-financed variant is better than the tax-financed one. By increasing taxes, households have income taken away, which reduces private household consumption (private consumption demand is displaced). However, the disadvantage of this policy is that the state's debt increases. Such a policy is only justified as long as there is a depression, i.e. a persistent underdemand associated with deflation (price reduction tendencies). Capacity utilization must be very low and expectations very negative. Otherwise, if government spending increases, prices and wages may also increase. The country loses competitiveness. Due to the lower competitiveness, production and employment decrease and the state can no longer repay its debt.

Conclusion on economic policy in the depression: Credit-financed expansive fiscal policy YD<YS

6.18   Expansive Monetary Policy with Rigid Wages

Rigid wages lead to a stable unemployment equilibrium in Keynes.

In this model, there is the special feature of the curved YS curve. With rising price levels and constant nominal wages, real wages decrease, which increases the supply of goods. However, from a certain low real wage, the YS curve bends back, as workers begin to restrict their supply of labor.

From the equilibrium income, there can also be an excess demand on the labor market. The equilibrium of the goods market is given by the intersection of the YD and YS curves.

There is no dichotomy. I.e. by an increase in the money supply, the labor market and the equilibrium of the goods market can be established through the falling real wage, since money illusion is assumed for the employees. The LM curve shifts to LM_2. The interest rate falls, which is why investments increase and with them the aggregate demand and the price level with the demand. As a result, the real money supply decreases, which is why the LM curve moves back to LM_3 Nevertheless, full employment has been established by the lower real wage level (Fig. 6.41) (see also Siebe & Wenke, 2014; Blanchard, 2014; Blanchard & Illing, 2006; Wagner & Böhne, 2003; Felderer & Homburg, 2005; Drost et al., 2003; Mankiw, 2013; John, 2004 as well as Mussel, 2009).

Summary

Keynes manages to explain the world economic crisis with sustainable demand shocks. These are exceptional situations, but they are sustainable, so they can also damage in the long term, because stable under-demand situations can arise in which companies permanently restrict their supply. We can conclude that only fiscal policy is successful in the investment trap and in the liquidity trap. Furthermore, the

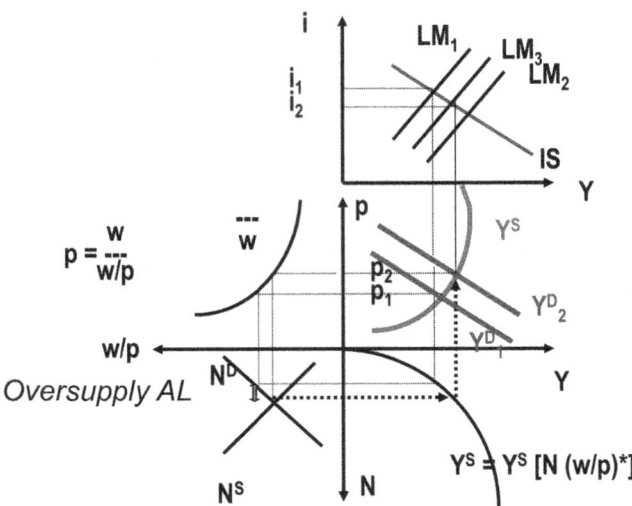

Fig. 6.41 Expansive monetary policy with rigid wages

economic situation depends on which area the LM curve is cut by the IS curve: In this case, the credit-financed fiscal policy is more successful than the tax-financed one, as no private consumption demand is displaced.

Monetary policy only acts as an anti-cyclical monetary policy to weaken the business cycles.

Recession: expansive monetary policy: $M\uparrow$, $i\downarrow \Rightarrow (p\uparrow)\Rightarrow i\downarrow \Rightarrow I(i)\uparrow$ as well as

Boom: restrictive monetary policy: $M\downarrow$, $i\uparrow \Rightarrow p\downarrow \Rightarrow i\uparrow \Rightarrow I(i)\downarrow$

An anti-cyclical fiscal policy has turned out to be counterproductive (see Sect. 7.3).

◀

Finally, the differences between Keynes and neoclassicism should be summarized once again:

Neoclassicism	Keynes
1. Consumption and saving are interest-dependent	Income-dependent
2. Money demand is income-dependent	Income- and interest-dependent (speculation cash demand)
3. Investments are marginal productivity-dependent and interest-dependent	Autonomous or interest-dependent and dependent on the expected return (marginal productivity of capital)
4. Flexible prices and wages	Rigid prices and wages possible, therefore also over- or under-demand

Neoclassicism	Keynes
5. Monetary policy ineffective dichotomy	Monetary policy effective in boom and recession no dichotomy
6. Supply-oriented, Say's Theorem applies	Demand-oriented Say's Theorem does not apply
7. Always market equilibrium	Possible stable disequilibria such as investment trap and liquidity trap, therefore in exceptional cases:
8. No state intervention	State intervention

Comprehension Questions

1. Explain why monetary policy is ineffective in the investment trap. Why does the overall necessary demand not occur by itself?
2. Explain why monetary policy is ineffective in the liquidity trap. Why does the overall necessary demand not occur by itself?
3. Explain how the recent financial crisis is comparable to the situations described by Keynes.

Exercise Tasks

1. In the fictional country of Utopia, the model of neoclassical-Keynesian synthesis applies. Given are:
   Production function $Y = 4N^{1/2}$,
   Labor supply function $N^S = 1/2$ w/p,
   Savings function $S = 0.2Y$,
   Investment function $I = 2 - 20i$ and
   Money demand function $L = 6Y - 30i$.
   Calculate the equilibrium values for employment, real income, nominal wages, the price level and the interest rate for the money supply $M = 28.8$.
2. Draw the effect of an expansionary fiscal policy in the Keynesian aggregate model in the investment trap.
3. Draw the effect of an expansionary fiscal policy in the Keynesian aggregate model in the liquidity trap.

6.19 The Mundell-Flemming Model of the Open Economy

What Follows Why?
How do the above-mentioned economic policy measures work in the open economy? This will be examined below.

Learning goal
You should be able to explain the effects of an expansionary fiscal policy on the balance of payments in relation to monetary policy.

Mundell and Flemming wondered if, in general, one could increase employment while maintaining balance in the external economy by combining an expansive fiscal policy with an expansive monetary policy. The background to this is that they wanted to avoid exchange rate changes through economic policy, for example because they were in a system of fixed exchange rates (Fleming, 1962 as well as Mundell, 1962).

First, the conditions for balance in the external economy must be determined. The condition for a balanced current account is that the balance of the balance of payments (Ex-Im, the other sub-accounts are neglected) must be equal to the balance of the capital account (capital exports-capital imports), so that demand for and supply of currencies can be equalized.

The so-called Z-curve is then the geometric combination of all interest rates i and incomes Y, at which the balance of payments is equal to the capital account, that is, the current account is balanced, without imbalances causing exchange rate changes. Here, exports are given and imports depend positively on income. Capital exports are also given and capital imports depend positively on the domestic interest rate. This means that one also assumes that the price level in Inland and abroad is given and constant. Furthermore, the financing of fiscal policy plays no role in the model and there is an underutilization of production capacity, so that production can be expanded immediately in the event of increased demand. It applies:

$$\text{Ex} - \text{Im}(Y) = \text{Capital}_{\text{Ex}} - \text{Capital}_{\text{Im}}(i_{\text{inl.}})$$
$$+ \qquad\qquad\qquad\qquad +$$

Otherwise, the well-known Keynesian IS-LM model applies.

For the formation of income on the goods market, the following applies:

$$Y = C(Y) + I(i) + \text{Ex} - \text{Im} + G$$

Assumption: The exchange rate, the foreign national product or income and the domestic and foreign price level are constant.

For the money market, the following applies:

$$M = \text{konstant} = L(i_{\text{inl.}}, Y)$$

For the capital account, the following applies:

$$K_{\text{Saldo}} = K(i_{\text{inl.}}, i_{\text{ausl.}} = \text{constant})$$

In order to generate a balance between the capital imports which increase in the capital balance sheet as income Y increases, interest rates must also increase. There are two possible combinations (see Figs. 6.42 and 6.43):

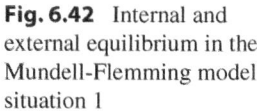

Fig. 6.42 Internal and external equilibrium in the Mundell-Flemming model situation 1

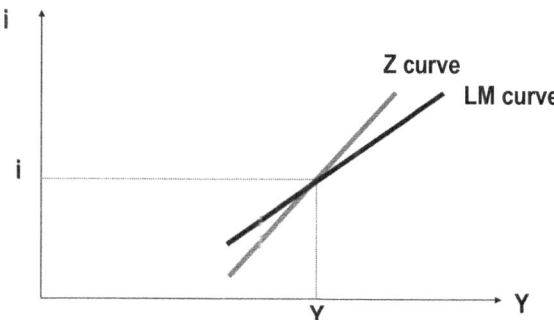

Fig. 6.43 Internal and external equilibrium in the Mundell-Flemming model situation 2

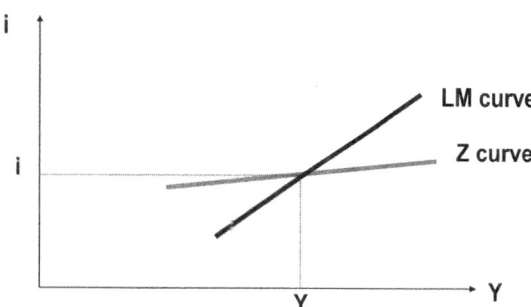

Thus, the balance as the intersection of the LM and Z curves depends on the interest rate responsiveness of foreign capital supply and the interest rate responsiveness of liquidity demand. Liquidity demand must decrease with the rising interest rates, so that money becomes available for the transaction account, which increases with income.

Expansive Fiscal Policy Situation 1

If the interest rate increase in the IS-LM model to the new equilibrium is less than necessary to adjust the balance of payments (see point 1 in Fig. 6 44), there is a passivation of the balance of payments, since the balance of payments deficit can not be offset by a correspondingly high capital import due to the increased import resulting from the income increase. Here, a restrictive monetary policy is necessary to establish an overall equilibrium. The interest rate increase leads to an increase in capital imports and offsets the balance of payments deficit (see Fig. 6.45).

Expansive Fiscal Policy Situation 2

If the interest rate rise in the IS-LM model to the new equilibrium is greater than necessary to adjust the balance of payments (see point 1 in Fig. 5.46), this activates the balance of payments, since the balance of trade deficit due to the increased income imports by capital imports was offset too much capital was imported, so there is an apprecia-

Fig. 6.44 Expansive fiscal policy in the open economy

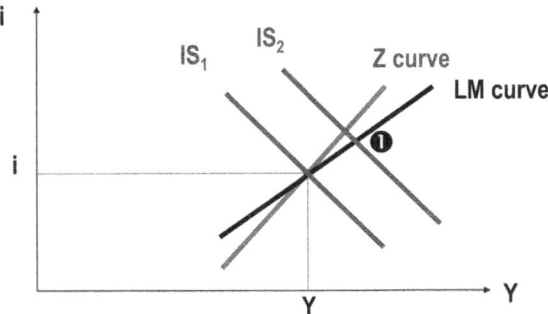

Fig. 6.45 Adjustment of the balance of payments by restrictive monetary policy situation 1

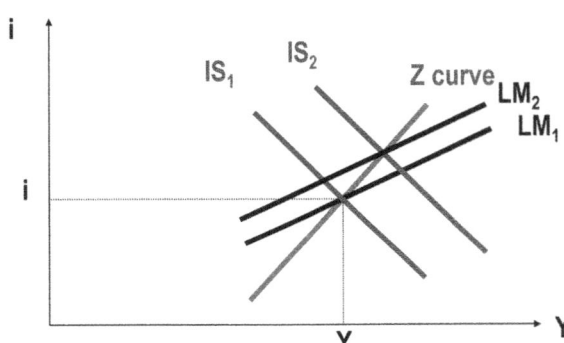

Fig. 6.46 Expansive fiscal policy in the open economy situation 2

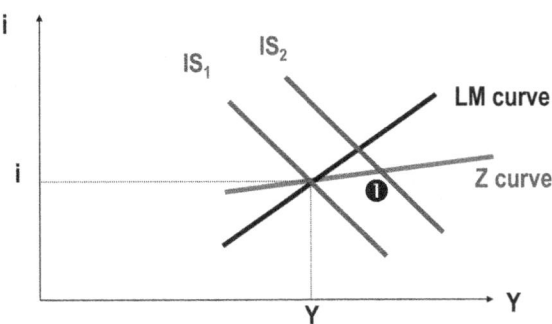

tion tendency. Here, an expansive monetary policy is necessary to establish a general equilibrium. As a result, the interest rate falls, the capital import falls until equilibrium is reached (see Fig. 6.47). The economic policy described to adjust the balance of payments or exchange rate adjustment tendencies is called the Mundell policy mix.

Criticism of the Mundell-Flemming Model
1. The assumptions of the model rarely apply in reality. There is only capacity underutilization, so that there are no price increases in the country—as already shown—in the

Fig. 6.47 Adjustment of the balance of payments by expansive monetary policy

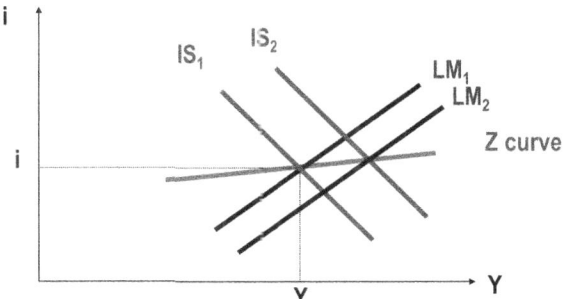

depression or in a very severe recession. Normally, the price level changes of monetary and fiscal policy would have to be taken into account, which would lead to different results. In the normal situation, there would only be price effects and no increase in gross domestic product or income.

2. The interest rate effect is limited to the Keynesian money market equilibrium, that is, to the LM curve. With income and the resulting increased savings, the supply of capital increases. In the normal situation, at fully utilized capacities, the price effect would lead to a leftward shift of the LM curve and thus to even higher interest rates and there would be no growth because investment would then decrease. There would be a total crowding out, that is, the displacement of private investment by the state.

3. The debt problem is ignored because it is assumed that gross domestic product and thus tax revenue will increase. This only applies in the case of capacity underutilization and then it is not growth, but a restoration of the old status quo with then higher debt.

4. The model is comparatively static. The feedback effects of domestic economic policy from abroad are not taken into account.

Questions for Understanding

1. How does an expansive fiscal policy affect the balance of payments? Distinguish between the different cases.
2. How can one achieve a balance of payments despite an expansive fiscal policy?
3. How realistic is the Mundell-Flemming model?

References

Blanchard, O. (2014). *Makroökonomie*. Pearson Studium.

Blanchard, O., & Illing, G. (2006). *Übungen zur Makroökonomie*. Pearson Studium.

Conrad, C. A. (2015). Incentives, risk and compensation schemes: Experimental evidence on the importance of risk adequate compensation. *Applied Economics and Finance, 2*(2), 50–55.

Conrad, C. A., & Stahl, M. (Eds.). (2000). *Risikomanagement an den internationalen Finanzmärkten*. Schäffer-Poeschel.

Conrad, Christian, A. (2010). Morality and Economic Crisis - Enron, Subprime & Co. disserta: Hamburg.

Drost, A., Linnemann, L., & Schabert, A. (2003). *Übungsbuch zu Felderer/Homburg*. Springer.

Eller, R. et al. (Hrsg.). (2005). *Handbuch Derivativer Instrumente*. Schäffer-Poeschel.

Felderer, B., & Homburg, S. (2005). *Makroökonomik und neue Makroökonomik* (9. Aufl.). Springer.

Financial Crisis Inquiry Commission (2010). The Financial Crisis Inquiry Report: Final Report of the National Commission on the Causes of theFinancial and Economic Crisis in the United States. Washington, D.C.

Fleming, M. (1962). Domestic financial policies under fixed and floating exchange rates. *IMF Staff Papers,9,* 369–379.

Gold, G., & Feldmann, P. (2007). *A house of cards – From fantasy finance to global crash*. Lupus Books.

Hicks, J. R. (1937). Mr. Keynes and the ‚Classics': A suggested interpretation. *Econometrica,5*(2), 147–159.

John, K. D. (2004). *Arbeitsbuch Makroökonomik* (12. Aufl.). Schäffer-Poeschel.

Keynes, J. M. (1936). *The general theory of employment, interest and money*. Macmillan. reprinted 2007.

Keynes, J. M. (1937). The general theory of employment. In E. Johnson & D. Moggridge (Hrsg.), The collected writings of John Maynard Keynes.*Royal Economic Society* (Vol. 14, 109–123). Cambridge University Press.

Mayr, B. (2007). Das ABC der Kreditderivate. *Treasury Log,5,* 16–19.

Mankiw, G. N. (2013). *Makroökonomik* (7. Aufl.). Schäffer-Poeschel.

Mundell, R. (1962). Capital mobility and stabilization policy under fixed and flexible exchange rates. *Canadian Journal of Economic and Political Science,29,* 475–485.

Mussel, G. (2009). *Einführung in die Makroökonomik* (10. ed.). Vahlen.

Muolo, P., & Padilla, M. (2008). *Chain of blame: How wall street caused the mortgage and credit crisis*. Wiley.

Shiller, R. (2007). *The subprime solution: How today's global financial crisis happened, and what to do about It*. Princeton University Press.

Siebe, T., & Wenke, M. (2014). *Makroökonomie*. UTB Lucius.

Wagner, H., & Böhne, A. (2003). *Übungsbuch Makroökonomie*. Vahlen.

Woods, T. E. (2009). *Meltdown: A free-market look at why the stock market collapsed, the economy tanked, and government bailouts will make things worse*. Regnery.

Further Reading

Forster, J., Klüh, U., & Sauer, S. (2014). *Makroökonomie – Das Übungsbuch*. Pearson Studium.

Grögens, E., Ruckriegel, K., & Seitz, F. (2013). *Europäische Geldpolitik, Theorie – Empirie – Praxis* (6. ed.). UTB.

Keynes, J. M. (2009). *Allgemeine Theorie der Beschäftigung, des Zinses und des Geldes* (11. ed.). Duncker & Humblot.

Mankiw, G. N. (2011). *Makroökonomik* (6. ed.). Schäffer-Poeschel.

Miles, D., Scott, A., & Breedon, F. (2014). *Makroökonomie, Globale Wirtschaftszusammenhänge verstehen*. Wiley-VCH.

Olney, M. L. (2015). *Wiley Schnellkurs Makroökonomie*. Wiley-VCH.

Schröder, H. (2016). *Makroökonomie transparent vermittelt: VWL Grundlagen für Managementscheidungen*. Schröder Consulting.

Business Cycles in Theory and Practice

7

What Follows Why?

Fluctuations in the economy are primarily a large economic and business problem of fluctuations in demand and only very limited by economic policy. In the following lecture section we want to analyze the economic phenomenon and the impact on the economy and show the reasons for economic fluctuations.

The task of economic theory has two main tasks. It should explain fluctuations in the economy observed in reality and thus provide a basis for economic policy recommendations at the same time. The following chapter examines the aspect of economic policy relevance of older and newer economic theories. Under new economic theories, theories are understood in this context, which were developed after 1950. A selection of theory contributions was created, which does not claim to be complete, but at least approximately reflects the most important developments. Some older theories were also included, which are of particular importance.

Learning objectives

You should be able to explain the essential effects, interdependencies and causes of economic fluctuations in your own words.

7.1 The Economic Phenomenon of Business Cycles

The non-seasonal fluctuations of aggregate demand observed in reality are referred to as business cycles. They manifest themselves in an increasing and decreasing utilization of production potential. Business cycles and growth are tendentially interdependent. The net investment demand will be in the subsequent periods to the growth of production

C. Conrad, *Applied Macroeconomics*, https://doi.org/10.1007/978-3-658-39315-1_7

potential and as income to consumption demand. In the narrower sense, the distinction between business cycles and growth is therefore artificial. The empirical time series of gross domestic product always contain both growth and business cycle components.[1] Business cycles differ greatly in terms of their fluctuations, amplitude and length of time as the distance between two peaks. The actually observable developments of gross domestic product show irregular developments, from which, in addition to the stylized sinusoidal cycles, a wealth of other fluctuations can be filtered out.[2]

Fluctuations in the utilization of production potential are associated with high welfare economic costs. In the underutilization phase, part of the value-added potential is idle. People are unemployed and therefore without income and socially integrating task. In the boom phase, inflation is particularly threatening, which is difficult to control due to its interdependencies and time lags and causes severe allocation and distribution distortions.[3]

An estimate of the economic costs of business cycles carried out by the National Bureau of Economic Research for the USA over a period of 35 years resulted in a loss of growth of 2%.[4]

In view of the business cycle phenomenon, two questions arise from a theoretical perspective: first, why do changes in aggregate demand for production capacity occur at all, and second, how can the cyclical nature of this development, in particular the exist-ence of turning points, be explained? A theory of the business cycle therefore has the task of explaining the causes and relationships of economic fluctuations. But in order to minimize the welfare economic costs of these fluctuations, it should also be able to pre-dict the development of national income and to derive from the explanatory approaches instruments for smoothing out fluctuations for economic policy.

The "stylized facts" compiled by SCHEBECK and TICHY in 1984 adequately describe the business cycle phenomenon. The business cycle is characterized above all by the procyclical development of the investment rate, nominal wages, the profit rate, prices and short-term interest rates, real wages and the countercyclical development of the adjusted wage rate.[5] These "stylized facts" are to serve as a yardstick for assessing the business cycle theories presented here: on the one hand, a realistic theory must not contradict these facts, and on the other hand, a theory claiming general validity should be able to explain many of these facts.

Fig. 7.1 is used to illustrate the fluctuations in economic activity.

---

[1] However, developments are conceivable in which the net investments are equal to zero. The production potential would then remain unchanged. Fluctuations in the utilization of production potential would then be a pure business cycle phenomenon.

[2] See Albers, Willi et al. (eds.) (1976, pp. 479 ff.).

[3] See also Zarnowitz, Victor (1997, pp. 1 ff. and 25 ff.).

[4] See Ramey, Garey and Ramey, Valerie A. (1991).

[5] See Schebeck, Fritz and Tichy, Günther (1984).

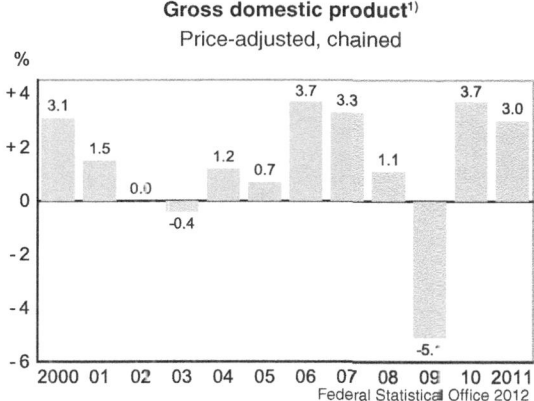

Fig. 7.1 Fluctuations in gross domestic product. (Source: Federal Statistical Office, https://www. destatis.de/DE/ZahlenFakten/GesamtwirtschaftUmwelt/VGR/VolkswirtschaftlicheGesamtrechnungen.html)

▶ **Economic Activity**
  are fluctuations in the utilization of production potential.

▶ They are expressed in cyclical fluctuations in gross domestic product (a measure of the annual production output of an economy) around the level required for the normal utilization of production potential in an economy (Fig. 7.2).

  After an **1. upswing** in economic activity, there is an overheating of existing supply capacity (**2. boom**) due to aggregate demand.

▶ Suppliers react to this.

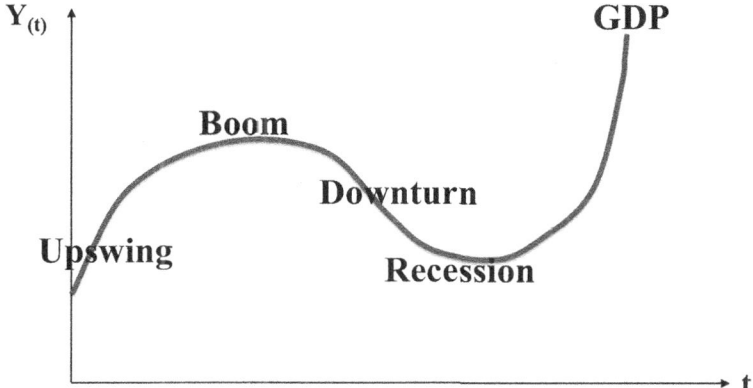

Fig. 7.2 The stylized economic cycle

▶ **Definition**

1. increased demand on the factors (overtime),
2. reduction in stock or increase in orders and/or
3. inflationary price increases.
4. capacity expansion, new hires

▶ And after a **3rd downturn** there is underutilization of production capacity due to the cyclically declining demand.

This is then referred to as a **4th recession**.

Most widespread definition: at least two consecutive quarters of negative growth, i.e. declining GDP. In this phase of the economic cycle, numerous insolvencies, mass unemployment and short-time work, i.e. cyclical unemployment and usually only small inflationary price increases occur.

▶ The intensification of the recession is the **Depression** as a prolonged stagnation (underutilization of production capacity) with deflationary tendencies.

Types of business cycles according to length:

1. Kitchin 3–4 years,	2. Juglar 7–10 years and	3. Kondratieff 50–60 years
e.g. the internet		e.g. the railway

Business cycle indicators.

Leading Indicators: For example, investment, the purchasing managers' index and the ifo business climate index are leading indicators compared to GDP, while consumption is a lagging indicator (lagging indicator).

Above all, changes in investment are a decisive *example:*

Investment changes in Germany	GDP
1957/8 0.3% → 4.2%↑	5.9% → 4.1%↓
1959/60 11.3% → 7.3%↓	7.5% → 8.8%↑

To create the ifo business climate, around 7000 companies from the manufacturing, construction, wholesale and retail sectors are surveyed monthly. Companies are asked about their assessment of the current business situation and their expectations for the next six months. The business climate is formed as a transformed average of the business situation and expectations (see Fig. 7.3).[6]

---

[6] See http://www.cesifo-group.de/de/ifoHome/facts/Survey-Results/Business-Climate/Geschaeftsklima-Archiv/2016/Geschaeftsklima-20160525.html. (Query from 19.06.2016).

ifo Business Climate Germany[a]

Seasonally adjusted

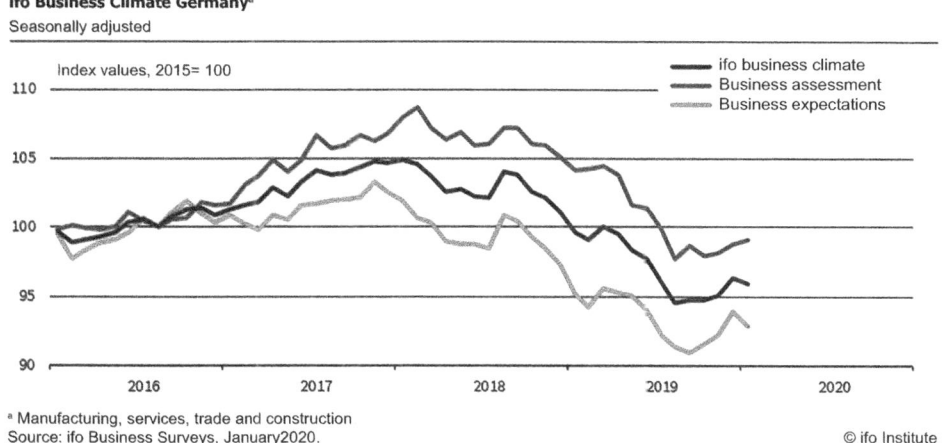

ᵃ Manufacturing, services, trade and construction
Source: ifo Business Surveys, January2020.   © ifo Institute

Fig. 7.3 The ifo business climate index. (Source: Ifo Institut, http://www.cesifo-group.de/de/ifoHome/facts/Survey-Results/Business-Climate/Geschaeftsklima-Archiv/2016/Geschaeft-sklima-20160926.html)

You can derive a business climate index from the business climate index by relating the assessment of the current situation to expectations. A good current situation and positive expectations then result in the boom phase (see Fig. 7.4).

7.2   Dynamic Keynesian Approaches: The Hicks Supermultiplier

Starting from Keynes, fluctuations in autonomous investment and multiplier effects (continued effects of demand increases) and accelerator effects (demand increases at fully utilized capacities lead to investments) lead to economic fluctuations, as shown below using the Hicks supermultiplier (1950).

SAMUELSON[7] was the first in 1939 to combine Keynes's demand multiplier and investment accelerator into a model of a demand-dependent investment function and in this way generate regular fluctuations in aggregate demand. However, the disadvantage of Samuelson's business cycle model is that the fluctuating gross domestic product does not follow a growth trend, but moves towards or to a constant value depending on the

---

[7] See Samuelson, P. A. (1939).

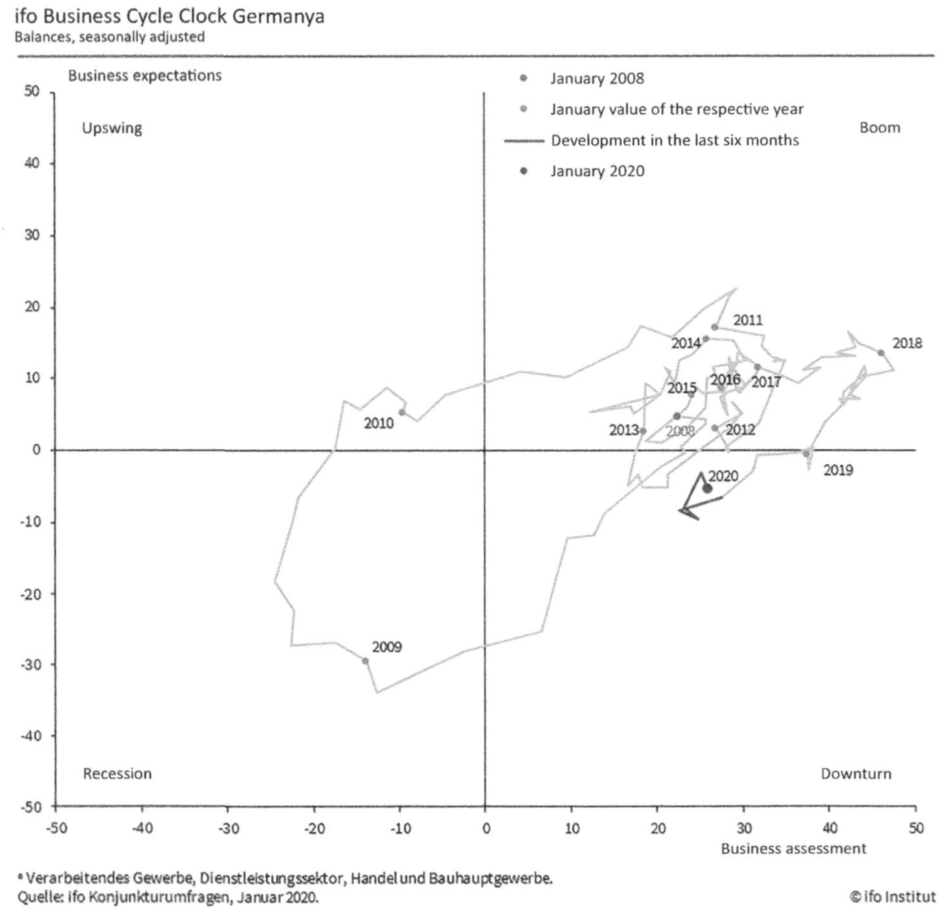

ifo Business Cycle Clock Germanya
Balances, seasonally adjusted

Fig. 7.4 The ifo business climate clock. (Source: Ifo Institute, http://www.cesifo-group.de/de/ifoHome/facts/Survey-Results/Business-Climate/Geschaeftsklima-Archiv/2016/Geschaeft-sklima-20160926.html)

parameter constellation, or moves away from it in the case of explosive fluctuations. Finally, HICKS[8] succeeded in 1950 in explaining the fluctuations in the utilization of a constantly growing production potential observed in reality by taking into account induced and autonomous investments[9]. HICKS combines a simple consumption func-

---

[8] For the Hicks supermultiplier, see Hicks, J. R. (1950); Tichy, G. (1995, pp. 11 ff.); Assenmacher, Walter (1998); Teichmann, U. (1997, pp. 11 ff.); Wagner, A. (1990, p. 222) and Ott, A. (1963, pp. 196 ff.).

[9] All investments that are not caused by a change in demand, i.e. long-term planned investments such as public infrastructure investments and innovations.

tion and an accelerator into a dynamic Keynesian approach. The system is in dynamic equilibrium when gross domestic product grows at the same constant rate as autonomous investments.

HICKs[10] (1950) combines the consumption function $C_t = c\,Y_{t-1}$ and the accelerator $I_t^{ind} = \beta \cdot (Y_{t-1} - Y_{t-2})$. Through the consideration of induced and autonomous investments $I_t^{aut} = A_0 \cdot (1 + w)^t$ [A_0: initial value, w: constant growth rate of autonomous investments] HICKs is able to explain fluctuations in the utilization of a continuously growing production potential.

$$Y_t = C_t + I_t^{ind} + I_t^{aut} = c\,Y_{t-1} + \beta \cdot (Y_{t-1} - Y_{t-2}) + A_0 \cdot (1 + w)^t \Leftrightarrow$$

$$Y_t = \frac{I_t^{aut}}{1 - \frac{c + \beta\,\beta.}{(1+w) + (1+w)^2}}$$

Figure 7.5 shows the autonomous investment expenditure and, above that, the other components of national product formation, which would develop according to line Y_t, i.e. the long-term equilibrium path, in the absence of business cycle fluctuations and external disturbances. This is the imaginary equilibrium path of real national product, which grows at the same constant rate as the autonomous investments. Induced investments have no capacity effect. Y_t^S, max represents the capacity limit (full employment) and Y_t^D, min the disinvestment lower limit. The capacity limit and the disinvestment lower limit form an upper and lower boundary, within which the growing gross domestic product moves. On the disinvestment lower limit, the investment demand corresponds to the uniformly growing autonomous investments.

The actual development of gross domestic product presents itself as an oscillation[11] around the long-term growth path of gross domestic product. If gross domestic product is in the initial equilibrium at time t_0 due to a positive exogenous demand shock, it will reach its temporarily highest value at t_1, which is limited by the growth of production potential (path A). Due to the accelerator effect $I_t^{ind} = \beta \cdot (Y_{t-1} - Y_{t-2})$ a constant growth rate is a prerequisite for constant demand. The mere decline in the growth of demand can thus already initiate a downward process. The lower limit of this contraction process is reached when investments have declined to the level of omitted reinvestments. The induced investments have shrunk to zero due to the drop in demand and gross

---

[10] For the Hicksian supermultiplier, see Hicks, J. R. (1950); Tichy, G. (1995, pp. 11 ff.); Assenmacher, W. (1998); Wagner, A. (1990, p. 222) and Ott, A. (1963, pp. 196 ff.).

[11] Due to the choice of β: $1 < \beta < (1+\sqrt{s})^2$ these are explosive oscillations.

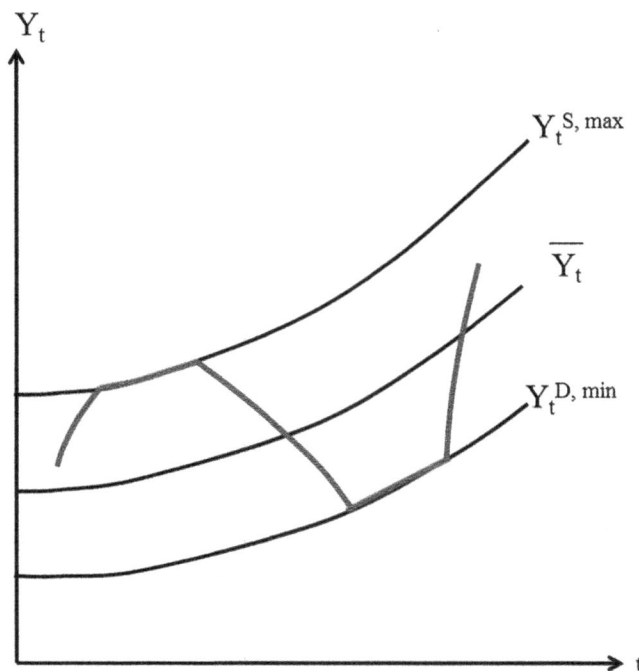

Fig. 7.5 Growth cycles of the Hicks model. (See Wagner, A., 1990, p. 224)

domestic product growth is determined solely by autonomous investments and the share
of consumption. The upward process is initiated by the investment demand induced
by the growth of autonomous investments. As soon as $Y_{t+1} > Y_t$ again, investments are
induced.

The greatest deficiency of this model is the neglect of the monetary side (investments
are not interest-dependent). Price level changes are left out as a business cycle determinant.
An excess demand does not have negative consequences as a result. Furthermore, the
demand-induced investments have no capacity effect. HICKS, however, illustrates the
dynamic importance of changes in demand. This can be used to explain the sinusoidal fluctuations observed in reality around an ascending gross domestic product growth
path. On the other hand, HICKS does not provide an explanation of how the growth rate
of autonomous investments assumed by him comes about.[12] But he himself admits that

---

[12] "Public investment, investment which occurs in direct responce to inventions, and much of the
'long-range' investments (as Mr. Harrod calls it) which is only expected to pay for itself over a
long period, all of these can be regarded as Autonomous Investment for our purpose" Hicks J. R.
(1950, p. 59).

the growth rate of autonomous investments need not be constant and can even be greatly reduced:

> One of the most dangerous things that can happen (and on one occasion, at least surely has happened) is that autonomous investment itself is severely checked by financial break-down.[13]

Based on the model by HICKS, there have been numerous further developments. CHEN-ERY has designed an investment function that depends on both demand and capacity utilization and takes into account the capacity effect of past investments.[14] GOODWIN develops an overall model in which consumer demand consists of an autonomous and an income-dependent part. From the model by GOODWIN, business cycles with very realistic properties emerge, with each cycle initiating the following one. The cycles do not run out, nor do they—in contrast to the model by HICKS—lead to explosive oscillations that would require the introduction of ceilings. In addition, the type of oscillation is not dependent on the initial conditions or the model coefficients.[15] The missing endogenization of the money market was provided by PHILLIPS and the of the labor market by BERGSTROM. PHILLIPS is able to show the stabilizing influence of output-dependent price changes triggered by wage reactions in his model.[16] Building on the PHILLIPS model, BERGSTROM endogenizes the labor market by means of a production function. In accordance with the profit maximization conditions in perfect competition, the marginal productivity of capital determines the demand for capital and the marginal productivity of labor determines the demand for labor, thus also determining the level of interest and wages. Other things being equal, wage increases lead to an increase in the supply of labor, but also to a decrease in the demand for labor and thus a decrease in gross domestic product. The income decline acts through the multiplier.[17]

Conclusion

The economic policy conclusions that can be drawn from this model correspond to those of the further developed theory of Keynes. The state must compensate for fluctuations in demand through autonomous demand impulses.

---

[13] Hicks J. R. (1950, p. 129).

[14] See Chenery, H. (1952) and Assenmacher, Walter (1998, pp. 186 et seq.).

[15] See Goodwin, R. M. (1951) and Assenmacher, Walter (1998, pp. 120).

[16] See Phillips, A. (1961); Teichmann, Ulrich (1997, p. 17) and Assenmacher, Walter (1998, pp. 117).

[17] See Bergstrom, A. (1962); Teichmann, Ulrich (1997, p. 17) and Assenmacher, Walter (1998, p. 18).

Therefore, **discretionary countercyclical fiscal policy** is necessary:

Recession: credit-financed increase in government spending, dissolution of reserves, tax relief

Boom: Restrictions on government spending, tax increases, setting aside in reserves ◄

However, HICKS' model also shows the sensitivity with which the economy reacts to changes in demand in the dynamic process. Taking into account the now known practical problems of detecting and implementing state demand management, this also results in a warning against discretionary economic policy. A one-time (one-period) increase in demand by the state would correspond to a general economic decline in demand in the following period (c. p.), thus initiating a downward process. At the same time, the model shows the risks of discretionary economic policy.

7.3   Neoliberals Versus Keynesians, A Synthesis

The approach of countercyclical fiscal policy was practiced worldwide in the 1960s until the mid-1970s. It found its way into the Stability and Growth Act of 1967, which is no longer applied today. This policy was also practiced during the government of former Federal Chancellor Schmidt. However, there were significant implementation problems. There were first of all the problem of correctly interpreting the business cycles. The question of when a recession was taking place that required an increase in government spending was not easy to answer because the cycles did not run schematically. Then it often took too long for the economic measures to be implemented, so that often the increase in government demand only took effect when the economy was already in an upswing. However, the decisive problem was the one-sided implementation of the concept of countercyclical fiscal policy. The expansion of government spending in the recession was easy for politicians, but not the saving in the boom. But even in the boom, ministers want to increase their budgets if tax revenue is high. Also politically, spending cuts in the boom were not popular. Politicians feared loss of votes if they cut government spending for their citizens. This had the consequence that the debt in the recession was increased by the expansive fiscal policy, but not reduced again in the boom. So in the end it was the far-reaching interpretation of Keynesian theory of depression that was responsible for the sharp increase in government debt in the 1960s and 1970s.

Monetarism or "neoliberals" (supply-oriented)

As a countermovement to the discretionary demand-side economic policy of the 1960s and 1970s, monetarism developed with its main representative Milton Friedman and generally with neoliberalism as an extremely market-optimistic economic orientation.

They put forward the thesis that, due to the numerous implementation problems (recognition, planning, implementation and impact lag) and the difficulty of clearly identifying the cause responsible for the respective business cycle development, fiscal policy should be used in the long term and not discretionarily in the short term.

Neoclassicism and in particular the quantity theory ($M \cdot v = Y \cdot P$) became the prevailing doctrine again. The main task of monetary policy is to ensure price stability and it may only help to cushion external shocks in exceptional cases. Real gross domestic product growth cannot be artificially generated by an expansive monetary policy.

The neoliberals proceed from the "policy inefficiency hypothesis". Consequently, the influence of policy on the economy is to be kept as low as possible. The future environmental conditions are unknown. The market participants therefore make decisions under uncertainty. The state must not increase this uncertainty by a "non-constancy" of economic policy. Rather, what is required is a rule-based approach in the form of clear, long-term policy programmes based on a comprehensible, order-compliant concept, i.e. order-based rather than process-based policy.

The state should only intervene in a depression, i.e. in the event of persistent underutilisation of production potential due to lack of demand, otherwise an upturn will not occur in the foreseeable future. Clear rules and framework conditions must be created, including for monetary policy.

What remains is the **rule-based anti-cyclical monetary policy:**

In the long term, for example, the ECB is oriented towards production potential, but in the short term also towards its utilisation or GDP, i.e. in the.

Recession it lowers interest rates and increases the money supply in order to give the economy expansive impulses and in the.

Boom increases interest rates and tightens liquidity to prevent an overheating of the economy as well as price increases in order not to endanger its inflation target.

Recession: expansive monetary policy: $M \uparrow, i \downarrow \Rightarrow (p \uparrow), \Rightarrow i \downarrow \Rightarrow I(i) \uparrow$ as well as.

Boom: restrictive monetary policy: $M \downarrow, i \uparrow \Rightarrow p \downarrow, \Rightarrow i \uparrow \Rightarrow I(i) \downarrow$

With the neoliberal orientation, the demand-oriented economic policy was replaced by the supply-oriented economic policy. Now the focus was again on the profit or return expectations of companies, because the creation of jobs should take place supply-oriented and not demand-oriented. The goal of the supply-oriented economic policy is therefore to improve the investment conditions and to increase the expectations of winners:

1. Less state and more market and competition:
   a) Reduction of bureaucracy and deregulation b) Privatization of public companies c) Reduction of subsidies d) Reduction of government debt
2. Reduction of payroll taxes

Neoliberal	Keynesian
Markets tend to equilibrium; they are stable and efficient (market optimists)	Markets and their equilibria are unstable and inefficient (market pessimists)
Markets should therefore be deregulated	Markets should therefore be regulated
Policy inefficiency hypothesis, rule binding of politics	State must correct market, Policy efficiency
Bidding conditions for companies are crucial	Demand in the goods markets is crucial
Labour market is largely autonomous	Labour market is derived from goods markets
Economic framework is crucial, regulatory policy	State intervention is crucial, process policy
Long-term oriented	Short-term oriented

Fig. 7.6 Comparison of Neoliberals and Keynesians

3. Reductions in social benefits to a minimum → Hartz IV ↓, labor supply ↑
4. Simple tax system with low rates
5. Price stability: Orientation of the money supply on the GDP → otherwise inflation results

Political applications (partially): USA Reaganomics, GB Thatcherism, BRD reforms by Chancellor Schröder "Agenda 2010".

Figure 7.6 shows the differences between Keynesian and neoliberal economists:

7.4   Growth Determinants as Business Cycle-Triggering Factors

7.4.1   Technical Progress

A fundamental real-economic initial ignition that justifies a long growth trend is characteristic of the starting point of almost all major stock market bubbles. These are product or process innovations that are not the maturity of known technologies, but rather extraordinary technical progress that results in a sustainable increase in productivity. Often one speaks of a "new era". Schumpeter (Joseph Alois Schumpeter 1883–1950) speaks of "creative destruction". The old production methods are replaced by new, better ones and the economy as a whole is raised to a higher level of productivity. The profits of the companies that use the new technology or produce the new products increase. A new wave of growth as a discontinuous business cycle, a sustainable boom of real growth, arises. Due to the length of these cycles, they would correspond most closely to the so-called Kondratieff waves. Schumpeter developed his business cycle theory from the two central dynamic competition functions.

Innovation Function

For the growth process of an economy, the dynamic character of competition is of particular importance. Dynamic competition is, according to Friedrich August von Hayek, a search and discovery process.[18] Hayek characterizes competition as a procedure for discovering facts that would remain unknown or at least unused without it. For Hayek, competition is above all evolutionary. This applies to process innovations as well as product innovations, where innovation is generally understood to mean the economic realization of an invention, also called invention. In the expectation of above-average remuneration by the market, the entrepreneur continuously searches for more cost-effective production methods and new products for which a potential market demand exists. For this purpose, he carries out research at his own risk or economically evaluates the research results of others. The market and thus ultimately the demander as a consumer or further processing producer decide on the success of a process innovation or product innovation.

Function of Imitation

According to Joseph Schumpeter, competition presents itself as a process of innovation and subsequent imitation.[19] The successful innovation of the pioneer entrepreneur gives him a competitive advantage over the entrepreneurs who have maintained their old production structure. From this competitive advantage results in an above-average profit, which then encourages other entrepreneurs to imitate the innovation or finally forces them to do so if they do not want to be displaced from the market. This leads to the spread of newer, resource-saving production methods and thus to the comprehensive implementation of technical progress and, with this, to economic growth. The functions of innovation and sanctions thus support each other in dynamic competition.

Schumpeter derives his dynamic theory of economic cycles from the function of innovation and the function of imitation.[20]

Phase: Equilibrium State

The prerequisite for a boom are new productive combinations with which an above-average profit can be achieved. These productive combinations are so fundamental that they influence the entire economy. This makes possible:

---

[18] See Hayek, Friedrich August von (1969).

[19] See Schumpeter, Joseph Alois (1993).

[20] See Schumpeter, Peter (1939).

- above all product and process innovations (e.g. Internet), fundamental innovations such as the assembly line,
- new sources of raw materials or intermediate products and the
- exploitation of new markets, e.g. by the abolition of the "Iron Curtain", i.e. the division between East and West, as well as
- organizational corporate reforms (AG, new stock market forms, such as the New Market, etc.).

These profit potentials are implemented by a dynamic entrepreneur (possibly also inventor) with the support of a dynamic, risk-taking banker. Together they realize the profit from technical progress (innovation function). Because they are the first to implement the more productive combinations, they have a temporary monopoly on the market and can reap the pioneer profits, which lead to phase 2.

Phase: Imitation (Upswing and Boom)
The pioneer profits lure many entrepreneurs to imitate (imitation function). They imitate the more productive combinations. For this they have to invest. Since there are many who invest, the overall economic demand increases. There is an economic euphoria. The boom is initiated. Due to the higher demand, prices and profits of companies increase not only in the area of new production combinations. Further investments are stimulated.

$\Rightarrow$ Investments (I) $\uparrow$, Demand $(Y^D)\uparrow \Rightarrow$ Prices (P)$\uparrow$, Profits (G)$\uparrow \Rightarrow$
Investments (I) $\uparrow$

Phase: Erosion of Pioneer Entrepreneur Profits (Downturn)
The high demand leads to rising prices for the raw materials. Wages and interest rates, i.e. the cost of capital, also rise, which is why the profit margins sink. After the investment period of the investments, the new supply of the imitators comes onto the market. Competition and the new supply lead to falling prices. Investments are significantly reduced, which reduces demand and initiates the recession.

- Competition of imitators $\Rightarrow$ Prices (P) $\downarrow$, profits (G) $\downarrow$ as well as
- Rising costs for raw materials, labor and capital (interest rates)

$\Rightarrow$ Profits (G) $\downarrow \Rightarrow$ Investments (I) $\downarrow$, demand $(Y^D)\downarrow$, prices (P)$\downarrow$

Phase: Creative Destruction (Recession)
In the recession, demand is greater than supply. Production cuts and unemployment are the result. Gross domestic product falls. The oversupply of new production combinations displaces the companies with the old non-competitive production methods or products from the market. The companies that have not imitated have to file for bankruptcy.

In this way, technical progress is enforced. This is a necessary process. Schumpeter speaks of the "life elixir of capitalism". No economic policy is necessary. On the contrary, a credit-financed fiscal policy would artificially keep the non-competitive companies in the market, which is not desired.

Schumpeter explains the long cycles caused by fundamental economic changes. A Schumpeterian business cycle would be, for example, the upswing at the end of the 1990s caused by the Internet boom and the New Market, followed by a similar recession, but also a new economic structure, especially in the service sector.

However, the creative product and process innovations have, in addition to the positive effect in the form of increased productivity, also a negative side effect. Although they destroy, as Schumpeter points out, the old, no longer efficient economic structures, this also implies structural unemployment.

7.4.2   The New Growth Theory

Under the term of the new growth theory, various newer theories are summarized, which aim to endogenize the growth-determining factors, thus dissolve the traditional separation of business cycle and growth theory. It turns out—also empirically—that the business cycle influences the growth trend.[21] Based on Schumpeter's efficiency-increasing effect of creative destruction, for example, from the approach of AGHION and PAUL[22], it follows that, under certain assumptions, the growth rate of gross national product also increases with the intensity and frequency of recession.[23]

The approaches of the new growth theory are concerned with the endogenization of the determinants of innovation waves, fluctuations in the level of technical and organizational knowledge or changes in the capital stock, but not with their effects on the business cycle as a fluctuation in the utilization of production potential.[24] Based on these approaches, only indirect conclusions can be drawn for economic policy. For example, the approach of SHLEIFER results in a warning against restrictive stabilization policy in boom phases, because in this approach companies only realize their investments in times of high demand, because they have the liquidity for the implementation of the invention due to the higher coverage ratios here. A stabilizing restrictive policy would indeed com-

---

[21] See Ramey, G. and Ramey, V. A. (1995). "Business cycle theory and growth theory have traditionally been treated as unrelated areas of macroeconomics", which is why it is often assumed that "growth and business cycle volatility are unrelated" Ramey, G. and Ramey, V. A. (1995, p. 1138). See also Franz, Wolfgang et al. (1999).

[22] See Aghion, P. and Saint-Paul, G. (1993).

[23] See to the approaches of the new growth theory the overview of Ramser. Ramser, Hans Jürgen (1997).

[24] See Ramser, Hans Jürgen (1997, pp. 219).

pensate for this procyclical effect, but at the same time reduce the demand for innovation, i.e. technical progress and economic growth, by throttling the overall demand.[25]

Even in the model of STIGLITZ (1994), boom phases have positive feedback on innovation activity. STIGLITZ justifies this with learning effects at high capacity utilization, which stimulate invention and the fact that a company will invest more in research and development if it expects high demand. In addition, he also represents the argument of SHLEIFER that—with the exception of capital market imperfections—companies only have the liquidity necessary for research and innovation in boom phases.[26]

The contribution of the new growth theory to economic policy has so far been small. However, this research direction promises significant new insights, especially with regard to the financing effects of discretionary stabilization policy. The government's demand for capital through deficit spending and alternative tax financing affects the innovation activity of companies directly through its feedback effects on the distribution of current and future consumption between generations. Since the innovation activity of companies depends positively on the expected returns in a secure environment, a redistribution policy to the detriment of corporate profits and an unpredictable discretionary economic policy that creates an uncertain situation are likely to have a negative effect on innovation activity and thus growth.

7.5   Overinvestment Theories and Experiments

Overinvestment can also be a cause of economic fluctuations. The key problem for companies is that when making their investment decisions, they do not know how stable the increase in demand is and to what extent competitors are expanding their capacities. As a company, they have to agree on how much each company invests and how much the capacity should be extended. Since such coordination does not exist, companies must approach demand with their production plans. It always comes back to overcapacity and undercapacity. In the upswing, demand is rising ($Y^D \uparrow$). As a result, prices and profits rise ($p \uparrow$, gains $\uparrow$). It is invested ($I \uparrow$). There is overcapacity as markets must first coordinate all business plans. Capacities must be reduced again in the adaptation process. Here, too, there are exaggerations, since the capacity reduction as well as the capacity was not coordinated. A similar process in microeconomics is also called pork cycle or cobweb theorem. An example is the overinvestment theory of Karl Marx, which builds on technical progress as a stimulus to the economy.

---

[25] See Shleifer, A. (1986) and Ramser, Hans Jürgen (1997, p. 200).

[26] See Stiglitz, J. E. (1994) and Ramser, Hans Jürgen (1997, pp. 221).

The Overinvestment Theory with Technical Progress By Karl Marx[27] (1818–1883) or the Law of the Tendency of the Rate of Profit

Technical progress needs capital for implementation. Marx divides capitalists into owners of the means of production and workers who make a living from their labor. Labor-saving technical progress allows the capitalists higher productivity and thus a higher rate of profit. They invest (accumulation of capital), the demand increases, and the upswing comes. The higher productivity leads to increased competition and thus to a fall in prices and thus also the rate of profit. Labor forces are released by technical progress (impoverishment of the proletariat, formation of an industrial reserve army). As a result, in addition to oversupply, demand is also falling. The dismissed workers can no longer consume anything. It comes to a downturn. The capitalists eliminate each other due to high oversupply in the ruinous competition (recession). The supplier concentration increases (concentration of capital). The rate of profit rises again (upswing) and the process starts from scratch until the collapse of the capitalist system (dictatorship of the proletariat and planned economy) comes.

However, Marx's fears did not materialize in Germany. Through the formation of the unions, the unilateral became a bilateral monopoly on the labor market; the workers no longer competed with each other driving pay down. Strikes were possible. Due to the now balanced distribution of power, the unions can enforce wage increases. Demand increased and there was no sales problem. In addition, product innovation led to a new demand for labor that could be paid for productivity-related wage increases. Existing purchasing power and the re-employed previously released work thus led to an ever-higher level of prosperity.

Overinvestments Caused by Demand and Interest Rates Changes, Evidence from Two Behavioral Experiments

Companies invest if they can make more profit with more production. Increased prices or cost cuts might be reasons for an augmented profit margin and thus trigger investments. This article analyzes the causes of overinvestment and thus investment cycles with two behavioral experiments (experimental simulation, behavioral modeling). Increases in demand and cuts in interest rates are examined as possible causes for overinvestment, which lead to corresponding increases in profits and thus trigger investments. If economic actors make mistakes in managing capacity, overinvestment can result. The problem is that the market participants do not know by how much their competitors are increasing their capacities and the price only reacts once the capacities are on the market. What if the market players systematically make mistakes because they are not behaving rationally or because they do not have all the information, such as the capacity increases of their competitors? Applying behavioral economics, this essay analyzes the economic

---

[27] See Marx, Karl (1864) and Stavenhagen, Gerhard (1969, p. 157).

behavioral dispositions using models to identify the mistakes actors make in groups (collective error hypothesis). The goal of the chapter is therefore to test if increases in demand can lead to overinvestment due to errors made by market participants and if interest rate cuts can lead to overinvestment due to errors made by market participants

The existing literature and studies are presented and compared to the experiment presented here. Next the experimental design of the study is explained. Finally, the results are present-ed and the conclusions drawn (Conrad, 2022).

Related Literature

It usually takes a while before capacities can be increased when companies invest. The production facilities must be financed, purchased, delivered and integrated into production. Price increases that lead to overinvestment due to delays in expanding supply are primarily seen in the market for raw materials (Humphreys, 2012). Mining projects take five to ten years to complete. Conversely, mine production is difficult to throttle so that the capacities can continue to be used for production as long as the prices are above the variable costs (Glöser-Chowhound et al., 2017).

This is in contradiction to the Efficient Market Hypothesis. This hypothesis assumes that all accessible price-relevant information of the past, present and future are known. The efficient market hypothesis in financial market theory was undisputed until the mid-1980s. Since rational behavior is assumed in principle, irrational behavior or wrong decisions do not influence the price (Fama, 1970; Menkhoff & Röckemann, 1994; Shleifer, 2000; Sloan & Stern, 1988). However, the spot prices, but also the future prices, can not take into account the investment decisions of the market participants.

Conversely, there is a direction in economics that repeatedly emphasized the difficulties in adapting supply and demand. As early as 1966, Leontief (1966) pointed out that time lags between supply or demand reactions can massively impair the achievement of market equilibrium. This connection found its way into economics as the cobweb theorem (Ezekiel, 1938; Waugh, 1964).

High raw material prices lead to high investments and capacity expansions and low prices lead to low ones, which increases the probability of over- and undersupply. Market expectations play a decisive role in investment decisions (Humphreys, 2012), which is why future prices also have an influence here. These behavior errors in capacity planning were demonstrated in 1992 by Kampmann's market behavior experiments (Kampmann, 1992; Kampmann & Sterman, 1996).

Using experiments with students who played the company, Kampmann and Sterman (1996) obtained an overshoot of production at fixed given prices with a subsequent downward adjustment of production as a recession, i.e. boom and bust cycles. They stated that firms have great difficulties catching up with demand due to production delays and the continuous accumulation of inventory imbalances. Kampmann (1992) found out that the increase of prices apparently induces the firms to further increase output. And Glöser-Chowhound et al., 2017 point out that market participants also need information about the other participants. A balance between supply and demand cannot be achieved even in simple markets (Zame, 2008). Shachat and Zhang (2012) conducted experiments with students with reference to the Cobbweb Theorem and found out "that sellers do a miserable job of making optimal investment decisions…."

Knut Wicksell lays the blame for boom and bust cycles at the doorstep of the monetary policy decision-makers and their inappropriate decisions regarding interest controls (see also Sect. 8.2.7). In the boom the interest rates are too long to low, creating overinvestments as collective error. The reaction of the central bank is too late and too harsh, creating not just the boom but also inadvertently the bust (Wicksell Hypothesis) (Grosskettler, 1989; Wicksell, 1922, 1968).

All these studies show that there appear to be undesirable developments in the markets because not all information is available or correctly applied. The concept of bounded rationality was developed in response to this information problem, implying limited information processing capacities as opposed to complete rationality. A decision that maximizes utility is rationally limited if it takes account of information access and processing (Simon, 1959).

Experimental Design

We want to answer two questions:

A. Can increases in demand due to systematic errors by companies lead to overinvestment or can companies interpret the price signals and collectively manage the expansion of capacity correctly?
B. Could interest rate cuts trigger overinvestment because companies misinterpret higher profit margins and expand capacity?

The purpose of this chapter is therefore to test the two hypotheses:

A. Increases in demand can lead to overinvestment due to errors made by market participants
B. Interest rate cuts can lead to overinvestment due to errors made by market participants

Two behavioral experiments on MS Teams were carried out online with the help of Excel. Increases in demand (game A) and interest rate cuts (game B) were examined as possible causes of corresponding increases in unit profit and thus a trigger for investments.

The two experiments, A and B, were conducted in the summer 2021 and winter semester 2021/22. There were 95 participants in seven groups in game A and 87 students (six groups) in game B, who were participants of different Business Bachelor courses (macroeconomics and political economy) at the University of Applied Science HTW at Saarbrücken, Germany. The task of the students was to invest capital like a manager of a company. The participants were asked to maximize the profit, which is the obligation of a manager as agent for a principal (company owner resp. shareholder). Maximal profit in the group resulted in 10€ real money as variable compensation. The rules were explained to the students before starting the experiment.

Experiments
Game A: The Effects of Increases of Demand on Investments
The goal is to test the following hypothesis: Increases in demand can lead to overinvestment due to errors made by market participants.

The model used was that of a simplified company. Each company (represented by a player) had in the beginning a production capacity (PC) of 500,000 units. The games started with sales (S) of 10 million euros, at a price (P) of 20 euros and cost of 15 euros (C). Thus, the test subjects sold 500,000 goods with their individual company, making a profit (PR) of 2.5 million euros ($PR = S - C\ PC$) with an equity (EQ) of 10 million. Each company had to decide on its investment (I). There were delays in expanding the range. For example, investments of 2.5 million euros (two rounds of the game) brought 50,000 increased production capacity in 2 years, or 1 million euros more sales at a price of 20 euros (40% or 50 euros per unit of production capacity, $PC_{t+2} = PC_t + I_t/50$). Investments decreased equity, while profits increased it. Demand and capacities were included in the price. The ratio between demand and capacity was multiplied by the price of the previous period ($P_t = D/PC\ P_{t-1}$). Due to the delayed supply increases, the prices only react to the investments after two rounds. Once production facilities were installed they could no longer be dismantled, so the increase in capacity was irreversible. Whoever had the most equity after 10 rounds won and received 10 euros. The demand was changed and entered by the game master. The game began with a demand equal to supply.

Results
Figure 7.7 shows the increases in demand in rounds 5, 9 and 13. As a result, the prices in Fig. 7.8 increased and with it the average unit profits ($UP = PR/PC$) in Fig. 7.9. Figure 7.10 shows the investments of the players. The investments were initiated by the increase in demand or the price and unit profit increases, which were always too high, as can be seen in the subsequent sharp drop in prices and thus also average unit profits (Fig. 7.9). All groups showed similar behavior.

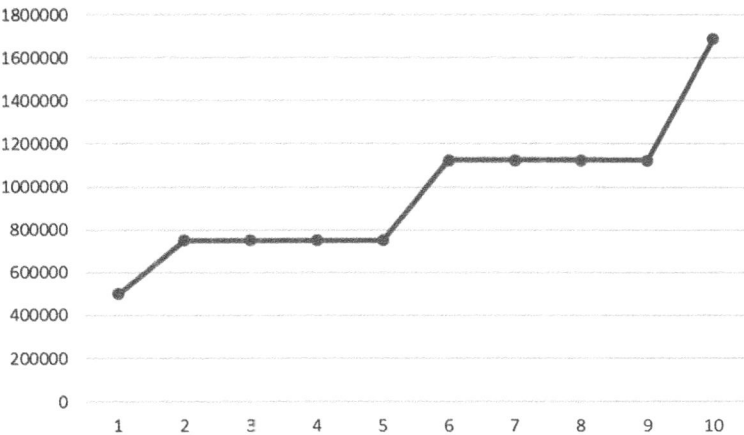

Fig. 7.7   Demand per player in units

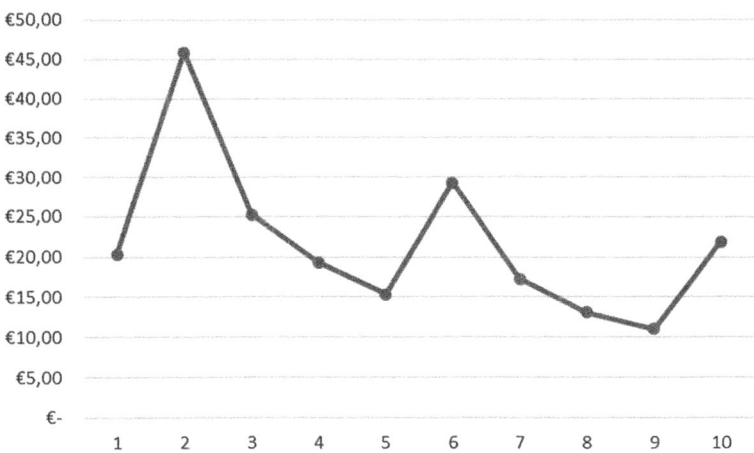

Fig. 7.8   Prices

Conclusions for Game A.

The first game shows the fundamental problem of non-coordinated supply adjustment among the companies. Game A's hypothesis was supported by the behavioral test. The increase in demand led to price increases, which signaled increases in profits. The companies (test subjects) increased their capacities, but did not know how much their competitors were increasing their capacities. This led to collective errors. The capacities were increased too much, resulting in investment cycles. First there was an upswing when capacity was being built up and then a downturn when prices fell as a result of overcapacity and companies hardly invested any more.

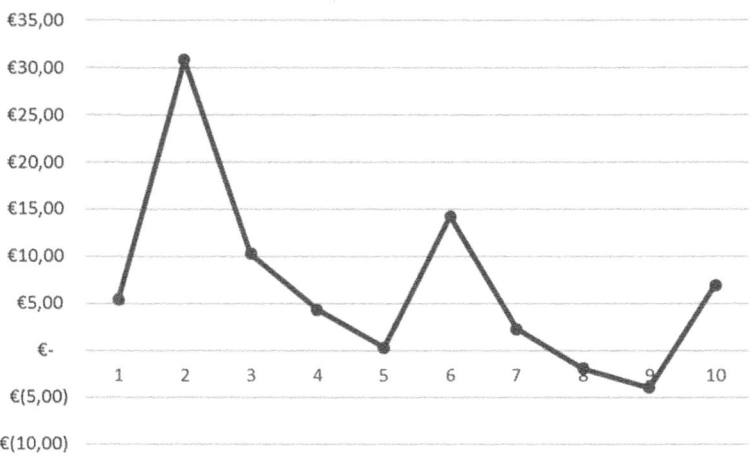

Fig. 7.9   Unit profits

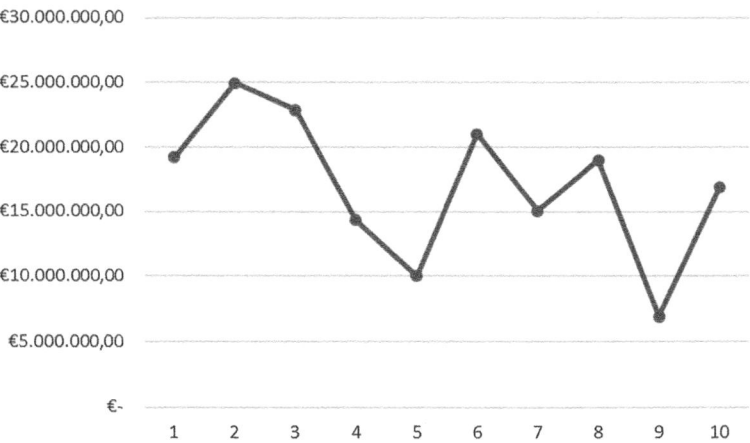

Fig. 7.10   Sum of investments

Assuming a profitable equilibrium, an increase in demand creates an oversupply. And even without an increase in demand, there was a tendency towards overinvestment due to the profitable starting position. The increase compared to the original state, however, clearly shows the influence of the increase in demand. Due to a lack of experience, players tended to over-invest. After the game, the test subjects said that they had underestimated the influence of other market participants on the success of their own investment decisions. In practice, the experience with capacity adjustments should not be much higher than in the Excel games, since managers change in the company and the adjustment processes take years (Thaler, 1989).

Game B: The Effects of Interest Rates on Investments

The aim is to test the following hypothesis: Interest rate cuts can lead to overinvestment due to errors made by market participants.

The model used was that of a simplified company. As before, every company had to make decisions about its investment. Each company (represented by a player) had in the beginning a production capacity (PC) of 500,000 units. New was that the investments were financed by debts. Starting debt capital was 20 million euros. At an interest rate of 5%, the companies paid 1 million euros in interest. The games started with sales (S) of 10 million euros, at a price (P) of 20 euros and cost of 15 euros (C). At a price of € 20, sales were € 10 million. The companies sold 500,000 goods in the first round, making a profit of 1.5 million euros (PR) after deducting the production costs of 15 euros (C) and the 1 million euros in borrowing costs (BC) (PR = S − C PC − BC). Each company had to decide on its investment (I). There were delays in expanding the range. For example, investments of 2.5 million euros (two rounds of the game) brought 50,000 increased production capacity in 2 years, or 1 million euros more sales at a price of 20 euros (40% or 50 euros per unit of production capacity, $PC_{t+2} = PC_t + I_t/50$). The investments directly increased the borrowed capital and the interest to be paid (in addition to the 15 euros production costs per unit), the remaining profit increases the equity. Demand and capacities were included in the price. The ratio between demand and capacity was multiplied by the price of the previous period ($P_t = D/PC\ P_{t-1}$). Due to the delayed supply increases, the prices only react to the investments after two rounds. Once production facilities were installed they could no longer be dismantled, so the increase in capacity was irreversible. Whoever had the most equity after 10 rounds won and received 10 euros. The demand and interest rates were changed by the game master. The game began with a demand equal to supply. The demand was again entered by the game master up to round 6 as equal to supply.

Results

The first round started with 5% interest. The demand had not changed. In the second round the central bank cut interest rates to 2% and in the third round to 0%. The demand was only increased in round 6 (Fig. 7.11). The interest rates were reduced from round 2 (see Fig. 7.12). This led to a sharp increase in investments (Fig. 7.13). The increase in capacity (Fig. 7.14), which was delayed by two rounds, then pulled the price (Fig. 7.15) down, and thus also the average unit profit (UP = PR/PC) Fig. 7.16). All groups showed similar behavior.

The central bank's reaction to possible inflation was also tested. In the sixth round demand increased by 50% (Fig. 7.11). The prices also rose (Fig. 7.15). There was another increase in investments (Fig. 7.13). The central bank reacted too late to the increased prices (Wicksell assumption) and first raised interest rates to 5% in the eighth round and then to 10% in the ninth and tenth round in order to stop inflation (Fig. 7.15). The higher borrowing costs lead to bankruptcies, as equity dropped massively (Fig. 7.17). It is also interesting that the test subjects barely learned from their mistakes

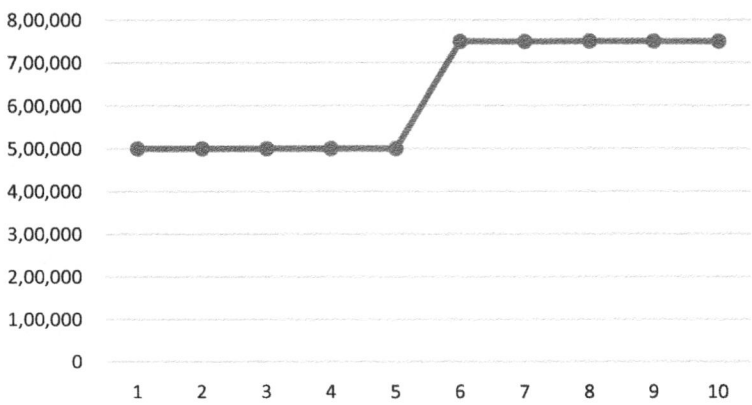

Fig. 7.11 Demand per player

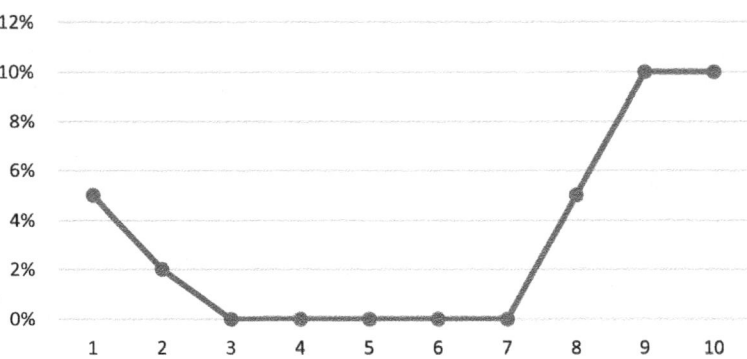

Fig. 7.12 Interest rates

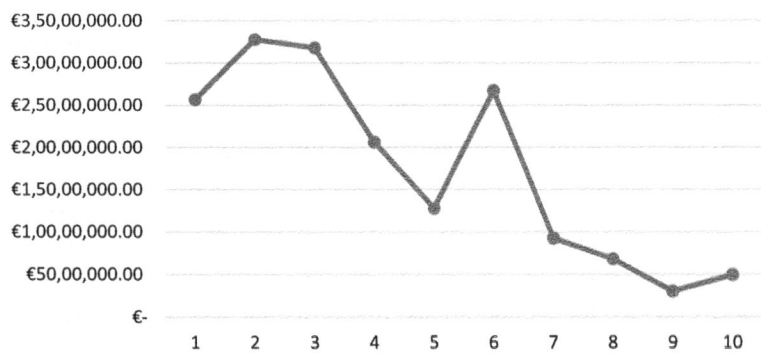

Fig. 7.13 Investments

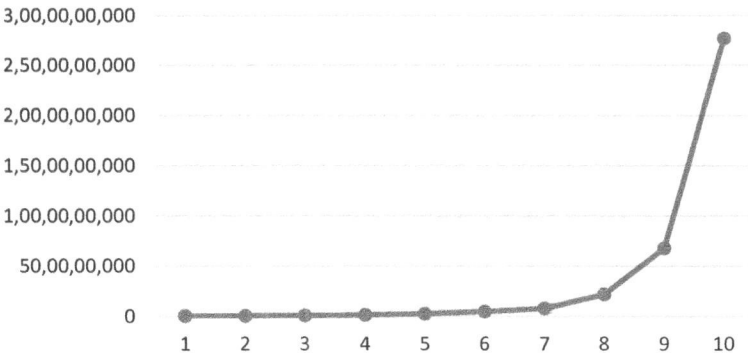

Fig. 7.14   Production capacities

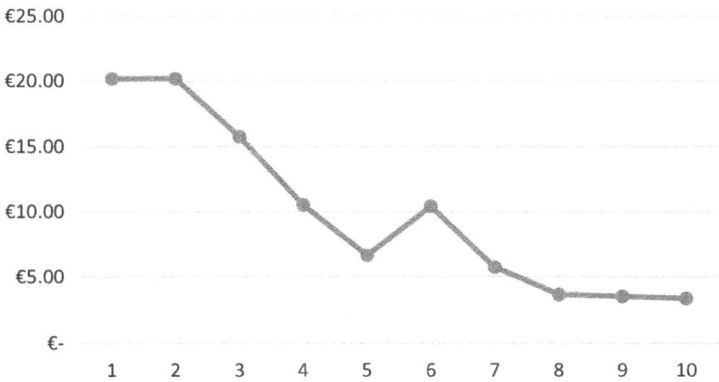

Fig. 7.15   Prices

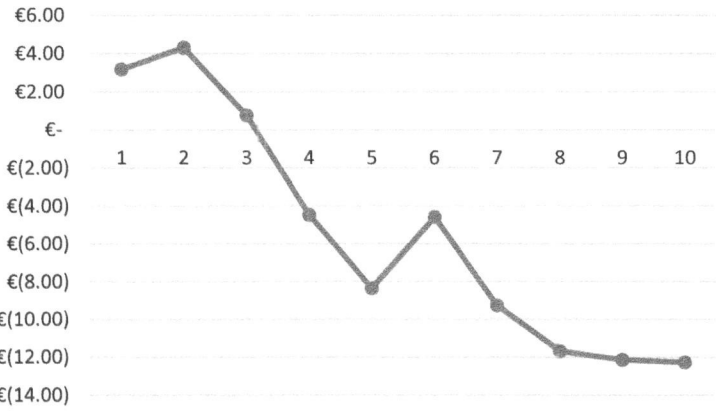

Fig. 7.16   Unit profits

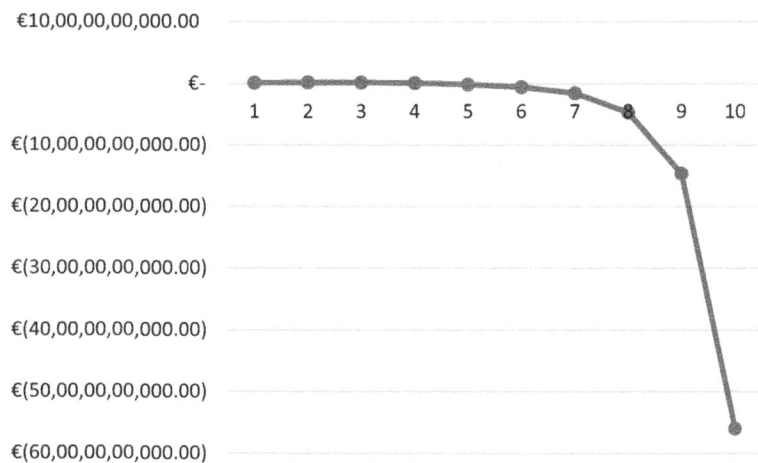

Fig. 7.17 Equity of the companies at the end of each round

with a tendency to overinvest throughout the game. In practice, there would be a reduction in supply through exit from the market, i.e. bankruptcies.

Conclusion Game B.
The experiments confirmed the hypothesis. The interest rate cuts led to unit profit increases. The companies increased their capacities even though prices had not increased. The rate cut thus led to collective errors.

The increase in demand and the associated increase in unit profit also led to overinvestment. The central bank reacted too late and finally raised interest rates too sharply, resulting in massive bankruptcies because the companies were too indebted during the low interest rate phase. Here, too, there was a collective error. The actors assumed that interest rates would remain low. This phenomenon was seen in the financial crisis. The real estate buyers were unable to pay the interest rates that had risen as a result of the Fed's decision, which ultimately triggered the first loan defaults and thus the crisis (Conrad, 2020).

In game B the participants said that the lack of any borrowing costs had triggered a strong psychological impulse in them to access, i.e. to invest. Apparently similar processes take place as those in discounts or closing out sales.

Final Conclusion
In our behavioral experiments increases in demand and cuts in interest rates increased unit profits, which led to uncoordinated and thus collectively too high investments. The result was also a misallocation of resources (capital). This made it possible to demonstrate collective errors that led to overinvestment and investment cycles (boom and bust

cycles) and which can be relevant to the economy. Central banks and companies should take this into account when making their decisions. The results of our experiments show that interest rate cuts not only stimulate investment to protect the economy from a recession, but can also encourage overinvestment. A low interest rate policy should therefore not last too long and, above all, the central bank must make clear the time limit for subsidizing borrowing costs. Otherwise the central bank risks bankruptcies and a new recession (boom and bust cycles). In addition, central banks should monitor investment behavior in order to identify overinvestment in good time. In the event of overinvestment, the central bank has to raise interest rates at short notice in order to prevent the economy from overheating and thus the subsequent sharp slump. The central bank must not hold inefficient companies in the market with artificially low borrowing costs (low interest rate policy). The overcapacities have to be eliminated from the market so that the supply can adapt to the demand.

The experiments show the fundamental problem of uncoordinated supply adjustment and a tendency on the part of market participants to neglect the behavior of other actors and to underestimate the influence of the market on their own investment decisions (undervalue of external influences). A company can do everything right on an individual economic level, but fail on the macroeconomic one. The games presented are therefore also suitable for manager training. Students can gain experience in economic interrelationships, which will protect them from wrong decisions in their later professional practice.

The results support the Wicksell hypothesis and the above-described findings by Kampmann and Sterman (1996) and Kampmann (1992) and Shachat and Zhang (2012) but contradict the Efficient Market Hypothesis.

7.6   Distributional Conflicts to Explain Fluctuations in the Business Cycle: The GOODWIN Model

The question that was not answered despite the expansion of the HICKS model by BERGSTROM is which factors influence wage development. Here is a basic problem of business cycle theory. If an economic factor is endogenous, new, to be explained influence factors arise. However, in order to maintain the clarity of the model and thus its explanatory value, it is advisable to consider the influence factors isolated and to use a new model. The development of wages is addressed by another model by GOODWIN.

Goodwin develops a model of interdependent, nonlinear differential equations in 1967. In his model, he is able to explain cycles, growth and distribution simultaneously.[28]

---

[28] For the GOODWIN model, see Goodwin, R. M. (1967, pp. 54 ff.); Heubes, J. (1986, pp. 86 ff.); Kurz, Rudi (1986); Teichmann, Ulrich (1997, pp. 18 f.) as well as Wagner, A. (1990, pp. 225 ff.).

Two sinusoidal oscillations of the wage rate (q, hunter population[29]) and the employment rate (b, prey population) result from his model equations, which are offset by one phase. A complete business cycle can be modelled, which also depicts the empirically observable, anti-cyclical development of the adjusted wage rate as well as the pro-cyclical development of the profit and investment rate. According to GOODWIN, his model confirms the instability of capitalist economic systems pointed out by MARX. High profits induce entrepreneurs to accumulate capital. However, by the additional demand for labour, they worsen their negotiating position, which is why they can no longer maintain the given functional income distribution. The investment increase sinks and the downward process is initiated. Business cycle stability and full employment can thus never be realized.

Goodwin's model is based on the following assumptions:

1. real variables (e.g. real wages), the inflation rate is not part of the model;
2. steady technical progress and steady growth of the labor supply or population (constant growth rates).
3. Extremely classical saving function: The wage income is completely consumed by the workers, while the profits are saved and invested by the companies in full. So at any time I = S, the goods market is always cleared. Goodwin cycles are pure growth and employment fluctuations.
4. constant capital coefficient: Capital and production grow at the same rate (limitational production function).
5. The growth rate of the real wage and the employment rate are positively correlated. This means that in times of high employment in the economic boom, the unions demand sustainable real wage increases. They can also better enforce wage increases in the economic boom because the companies can realize high profits due to the good order situation and therefore want to prevent a strike. Empirically, GOODWIN is based on the correlation of wage and employment development discovered by PHILLIPS in 1958.

This results in two interdependent differential equations:

for the change in the employment rate applies:

$$\Delta b = \left[1/v - (m + n) - q/v\right] \cdot b \qquad \text{or also} \qquad \Delta b/b = \Delta K/K(m + n)$$

for the wage rate applies:

$$\Delta q = \left[f \cdot b - (g + m)\right] \cdot q \qquad \text{or also} \qquad \Delta q/q = f\,b - (g + m)$$

---

[29] The hunter population (wage rate) develops in dependence on the prey population (employment rate) with a time lag of one phase. The designation of hunter and prey population originates in biology, which had established a similar correlation for predators (e.g. lynxes) and prey (e.g. rabbits) (so-called LOTKA-VOLTERRA equations).

m   Growth rate of labor productivity
n   Growth rate of labor
q   Wage rate
v   Capital coefficient (K/Y)
b   Employment rate (labor demand/labor supply)
g, f   Constants.

This results in two sinusoidal oscillations that are offset by one phase. The hunter population (wage rate) develops in dependence on the prey population (employment rate)
with a time lag of one phase. The designation of hunter and prey population comes from
biology, which had found a similar correlation for predators (e.g. lynxes) and prey (e.g.
rabbits) (so-called Lotka-Volterra equations) (Fig. 7.18).
    Four phases can be distinguished:

A. Boom
   The wage share has reached its lowest value, with the profit share mirroring this with
   the highest amplitude. According to the classical savings assumption, profits are completely invested. Due to the high demand for investment, production increases and so
   does employment (assumption $K/A = $ constant). $\rightarrow$ Transition phase to B: Due to the
   increase in employment (beute population), unions increase wages (jäger population),
   resulting in a decrease in the profit share. Consequently, investments and the growth
   of the employment rate also decrease. The growth rate of the national product slows
   down.
B. Rezession
   The growth in the employment rate has stopped ($\Delta b = 0$). The profit share has
   reached its average value. However, due to the time lag, the wage share is still growing. $\rightarrow$ Transition phase to C: With the growth of the wage share, the profit share con-

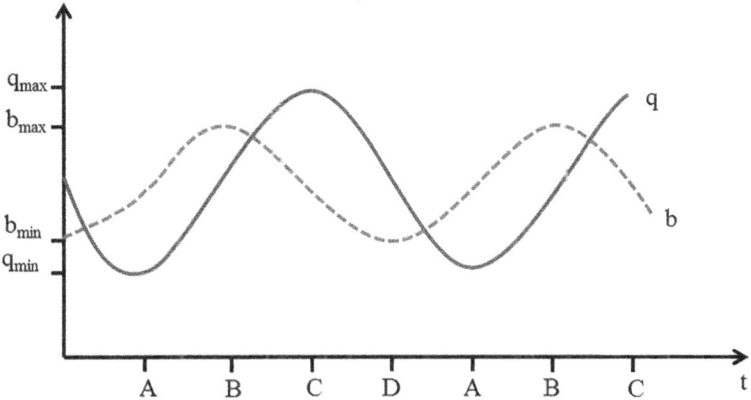

Fig. 7.18 Goodwin cycle. (q [wage rate], b [employment rate])

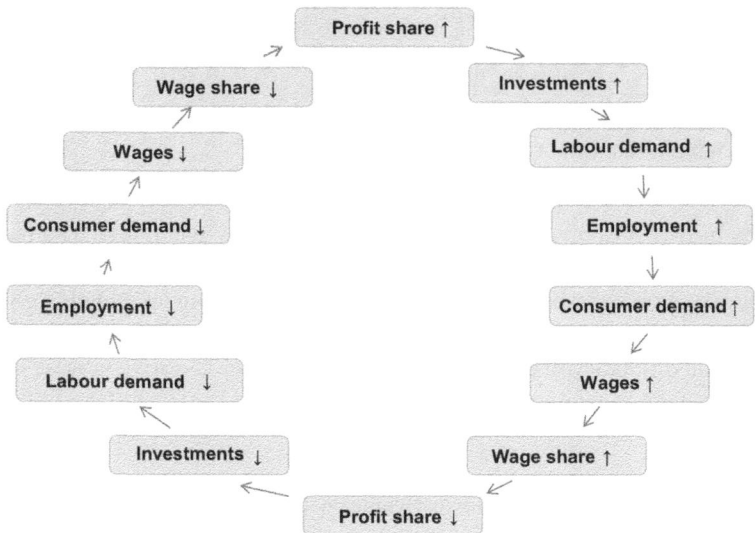

Fig. 7.19 The Goodwin distribution cycle

tinues to decline and, as a result, so do investments. The point $\Delta b = 0$ was exceeded, and now there is a decrease in employment. Now the unions react and dampen their wage demands, which reduces the growth of the wage share.

C. Depression

The growth in the wage share has stopped ($\Delta q = 0$), which also stops the decline in the profit share. → Transition to D: The employment rate has reached its average value, but is still declining because the growth in the labor force is greater than the increase in employment caused by the growth in investments (increase in the profit share).

D. Economic recovery

The decline in the employment rate has stopped ($\Delta b = 0$), as the increase in employment caused by the growth in investment corresponds to the growth in the labor force. → Transition phase to A: The wage rate continues to fall due to the time lag, thus increasing the profit rate and investments. The employment rate increases, as the increase in employment caused by the growth in investment is greater than the growth of the labor force (Fig. 7.19).

Conclusion

The Goodwin model explains the empirically observable anti-cyclical development of the adjusted wage rate and the pro-cyclical development of the profit and invest-ment rate. According to GOODWIN, his model confirms the instability of capitalist economies pointed out by MARX. High profits make entrepreneurs accumulate capital. However, the additional demand for labor deteriorates their negotiating position, so they can no longer maintain the given functional income distribution. The increase in investment decreases and the downward process is initiated. Cyclical stability and full employment can thus never be realized. In addition, the Goodwin model explains the—contrary to the predictions of MARX and RICARDO—observable relatively constant profit rate at rising real wages.

However, GOODWIN's business cycle theory is one-sidedly focused on distributional struggles. Exogenous demand shocks, expectations, price development as well as monetary and fiscal policy are not taken into account. Investments are not interest-dependent. The assumption of an extremely classical saving function is also to be classified as unrealistic. The model is only designed for the capacity effect of investments. Investments do not have a demand effect on the goods market. Fluctuations in the workers' consumption demand have no effect, as the capacities are assumed to be always utilized. In view of these constellations, the model is unrealistic. The model explains growth, employment and distributional fluctuations endogenously, that is, without the use of exogenous influencing factors. However, it cannot explain the fluctuations in the utilization of production potential observed in reality: since I = S is always assumed, there is neither under- nor over-demand. Goodwin cycles are therefore pure growth and employment fluctuations. Employment and wage share are constant in the long run. However, all absolute values grow.

Since, as in Hicks' model, the state was not included in this model, no immediate economic policy conclusions can be drawn. In GOODWIN's model, however, the state is not even indirectly integrated into the model via an exogenous influence on demand. GOODWIN's business cycle fluctuations are distribution-determined. However, government redistribution policy would, in this model, due to the reduction in profits and thus also in investments, only brake the business cycle upswings. The same applies due to the crowding out in credit-financed expenditure policy, as WOLFSTETTER shows in his model.[30] Automatisms are required to reduce the amplitude of the oscillations. A progressive tax on income from profits would dampen the cycle. In addition, the state is required as a mediator of distributional conflicts, for example in the form of a concerted action. However, due to the assumption of the extremely classical investment function, any diversion of profit income to wages slows down the growth process and thus also the economic upswing at the same time. Nevertheless, a stabilization of the positive development of growth and employment could be achieved if, according to the model, the unions increased wages less strongly or if the tax revenue surpluses were used for investment purposes. A pure redistribution tax always has a growth- and employment-reducing effect, unless the workers also save and thus offset the investment reduction of the profit recipients.

---

[30] See Wolfstetter, E. (1982) and Assermacher, Walter (1998, pp. 229 et seq.).

GOODWIN's economic theoretical achievement lies mainly in the endogenization of wage development, with which he included distribution policy in the business cycle policy consideration spectrum. GOODWIN's model was constructively extended by DESAI and POHJOLA. DESAI[31] endogenized expectation formation processes, whereas POHJOLA[32] by transforming the continuous differential equation system of GOODWIN into a discrete difference equation system and by changing the wage formation hypothesis[33] succeeded, depending on the parameter constellation, to model stable equilibria without oscillations, multi-period cycles and indeterminate chaotic development of national product. The studies of POHJOLA show that all results of the GOODWIN model are also valid for discrete distribution of economic variables. In reality, there are both discrete economic variables, such as tariff agreements, and continuous variables, which should predominate in general, since market decisions leading to price formation (including investment decisions), are usually made decentralized by many economic subjects at different times. ◄

7.7   Shocks and Price Rigidities: New Keynesian Macroeconomics and Neo-Keynesian Macroeconomics

Classical theory assumes that prices react quickly and quantities delayed. Since there is no auctioneer who determines an equilibrium price in a tâtonnement process ex ante, a simultaneous market equilibrium at equilibrium prices is rather the exception than the rule. Empirically, it can be observed that prices do not fluctuate countercyclically, as would actually be assumed. Even in periods of underutilization, companies do not reduce wages despite layoffs. On goods, labor and other markets, the respective prices react only very slowly—in the extreme case, short-term not at all—to surpluses in supply and demand.[34] Two main criticisms of the older Keynesian approaches are the incomplete decision-logical linking and the neglect of the feedback of the rationing of quantities on other markets. The New Keynesian Macroeconomics[35] therefore picks up the Keynesian assumption of fixed prices and wages and takes into account the mentioned criticism points in the model conception. In the New Keynesian Macroeconomics, prices and

---

[31] See Desai, M. (1973) as well as Assenmacher, Walter (1998, pp. 223).

[32] See Pohjola, M. T. (1981) as well as Assenmacher, Walter (1998, pp. 233).

[33] In Pohjola, the real wage rate is—based on empirical studies—dependent on the average labor productivity multiplied by a factor depending on the employment rate.

[34] See Gerfin, H. and Möller, J. (1980b, p. 201).

[35] For the New Keynesian Macroeconomics see Malinvaud, E. (1977), Barro, R. J. and Grossmann, H. I. (1976); Gerfin, H. and Möller, J. (1980a); Gerfin, H. and Möller, J. (1980b); Barro, Robert J. (1971); Clower, R.W. (1965); Heubes, Jürgen (1991, pp. 65 ff.) as well as Rothschild, Kurt, W. (1981).

wages do not react in the short to medium term. Exogenous demand or supply shocks disturb the market equilibrium and cause the rationing of the opposite supply or demand side, without prices or wages being able to bring about an immediate compensation.

New Keynesian macroeconomics considers two markets, the goods market and the labor market. The entrepreneurs are suppliers in the goods market and demanders in the labor market, while the workers are demanders in the goods market and suppliers in the labor market. Both have given expectations about quantities and prices that are based on the previous period. Prices and wages reflect expectations and therefore only react delayed. If the economic subjects are rationed in their demand or supply plans, this has an impact on their decisions in other markets (spill-overs). The shocks propagate as a multiplier process.

Example

An exogenous demand shock rationes the entrepreneurs as suppliers. The consequence will be that they first reduce the supply in the goods market and then also the demand in the labor market. Unemployment arises. If the workers are rationed as suppliers in the labor market, they will reduce their demand in the goods market, which will ration the entrepreneurs as suppliers again. The vicious circle continues. There are mutual demand reductions of decreasing tendency, with the respective rationings being much higher than if prices and wages were to adjust as in the classical cobweb theorem (cobweb theorem). ◄

Demand shocks are sudden, large changes in private investment, government spending, and/or exports. Here, *Keynesian unemployment* arises. Supply shocks are fluctuations in the price-unit cost relation caused by variations in the nominal wage, the price level of goods, and/or labor productivity. Classical unemployment is formed. In this case, part of the demand reduction caused by the demand reduction on the labor market is absorbed on the goods market by the original supply reduction. However, overall, a lower short-term equilibrium national product still results than if prices and wages were to adjust. The business cycle is a temporal sequence of demand or supply rationing caused by exogenous shocks on the supply or demand side. Business cycles arise, which are reflected in short- to medium-term fluctuations in the utilization of production potential. In the long run, the market equilibrium is restored by price reactions.

A significant representative of New Keynesian Macroeconomics is Malinvaud. The originally static model of Malinvaud led to false conclusions in that only an undersupply of government demand had negative consequences for the economy as a whole, but not an oversupply. Finally, there are, it is assumed, at least in the short term, no demand- and supply-determined price changes. Not least for this reason, Malinvaud dynamized his static approach in a second model, while also endogenizing some variables and giving up the assumption of fixed prices and wages. The following conditions apply: The labor supply is constant. Consumption depends positively on consumption in the previous period and negatively on the unemployment rate. The production function is linear limitational and determined by the factors labor (constant, first bottleneck), labor productivity and production capacity as the second bottleneck and rationing variable. The aggregate demand consists of consumption demand and investment demand, which is delayed by one period and influenced positively by the return on labor (labor productivity—real wage) and the utilization of capacity. Depending on the real wage and production capacity, four temporary equilibria emerge, the development of the real wage depending on the respective regime.

In classical unemployment, the real wage decreases with the increase in unemployment; in pent-up inflation, it increases due to the demand surplus on the labor market. Due to the oversupply of goods in Keynesian unemployment, both the nominal wage and the price level decrease due to unemployment and the oversupply, so the real wage remains constant. In the Walrasian equilibrium, neither the nominal wage nor the price level change, as no market side is rationed. In the medium term, only two stable equilibria emerge, in which the real wage does not change: the Keynesian regime and the Walrasian equilibrium. In the Walrasian equilibrium, the stability is maintained by the fact that a positive work incentive effect and a negative underutilization of capacity effect offset each other in the investment demand. However, a disturbance of this equilibrium, which will certainly occur at some point, automatically initiates a development towards one of the three regimes, so that the Walrasian equilibrium can also be considered unstable, and thus in the long term all combinations lead to the Keynesian regime.

In the Keynesian regime, the further development of the national product depends on the combination of the nominal wage rate and the adjustment parameter of the capital stock. Two possible developments result. In the first case, there is a monotonic approach to a stable equilibrium, and in the second, more likely case, a much longer-lasting approach to the stable Keynesian equilibrium with damped oscillations of the national product around the equilibrium national product, i.e. with cyclical fluctuations until the Keynesian equilibrium is reached. At this point, no endogenous cyclical fluctuations can occur or be explained any more, so that the persistence problem also arises in New Keynesian macroeconomics, as will be the case in the still to be analysed New Classical macroeconomics: in order to explain the continuity of the cyclical fluctuations, exogenous shocks must be used. A complete business cycle cannot be explained, which is why both theories are also not to be counted as business cycle theories in the narrower sense.

The procyclical investment and profit ratios observed in reality result from the model of New Keynesian macroeconomics as an automatic consequence of changes in the cost-revenue relations. Prices, wages and interest rates will also behave procyclically, but with a time lag. Although positive shocks can also be simulated with New Keynesian macroeconomics, it is again a one-time deviation from equilibrium with a subsequent tendency towards a new static equilibrium.

A new distribution of roles in wage policy results from New Keynesian macroeconomics. According to New Keynesian macroeconomics, neither the trade unions (employers and unions) nor the state can be solely responsible for full employment. In wage policy, the trade unions have to make sure that the situation of classical unemploy-ment does not arise, whereas in the situation of Keynesian unemployment the state is obliged to carry out stabilization policy in the form of autonomous demand increase. The flexibility of wages downwards is to be restored by deregulation of the labor market (e.g. by opening clauses). The approach of New Keynesian macroeconomics provides another justification for the need for discretionary state demand management, but it does not solve the problems of recognition and implementation that arise in practical economic policy. On the contrary, exogenous demand shocks that occur abruptly require even faster economic policy recognition and reaction than a situation of permanent unemploy-ment. However, this model leads to false conclusions in that only an underdose of state demand has negative consequences for the economy as a whole, but not an overdose. Finally, there are, by assumption, at least temporarily no demand- and supply-determined price changes. The persistence problem arises again. The business cycle is explained exogenously and not self-contained. Although positive shocks can also be simulated with New Keynesian macroeconomics, it is always, as with New Classical macroeconomics, a one-time deviation from equilibrium with subsequent tendency towards a new static equilibrium. Continuous exogenous shocks are required to model a business cycle. How-ever, this would then correspond to the boom being the normal state of the model in t_0.

In the context of further developed **neoclassical macroeconomics**, a number of newer approaches have been developed with the aim of microeconomically foundation the Keynesian assumption of price rigidity. Two causes, price adjustment costs and infor-mation asymmetries, are to be presented below as representative of this direction. If one does not assume perfect competition, but at least in partial markets supply monop-olies, it can—as MANKIW and BALL[36] show—lead to price adjustment delays if the price adjustment costs are higher than the increased prices of intermediate goods due to an expansive monetary policy. The companies calculate their prices from the outset so that they have enough room for manoeuvre in the event of smaller changes in the inflation rate in order to avoid an expensive price adjustment, be it in advertising bro-chures or with outstanding goods. Under this assumption and even with rational behav-iour, changes in the money supply can lead to a change in the relative price structure, which in turn has real employment effects. Furthermore, there is a double asymmetry in price adjustments. On the one hand, only large changes in the money supply or inflation lead to a price adjustment, and on the other hand, companies only adjust prices when the price calculation deteriorates as a result of monetary policy, i.e. with an expansive mone-tary policy. Consequently, the real effects on employment and national product are great-est when the price reductions of the intermediate goods do not have to be passed on by the companies, i.e. with a very restrictive monetary policy. Furthermore, they are expan-sive and thus act counter to the reduced demand for investment due to the increased interest rate level.

---

[36] See Mankiw, G.N. (1985) as well as Ball, L. and Mankiw, N.G. (1994).

This approach is criticized for only taking into account the price adjustment costs, but not the adjustment costs of production and employment. In addition, the positive employment effect of the restrictive change in money supply is likely to be offset by the negative effect of the decreased demand for investment. The value of these models therefore lies primarily in the economic justification of the old Keynesian hypothesis that prices are downward rigid and upward flexible.

The second central neo-Keynesian research direction[37] examines the effect of the asymmetric distribution of information between companies as borrowers and lenders (ie mainly banks), assuming that companies are equity-rationed because they cannot find equity investors due to information asymmetry and the resulting higher risk. In order to expand employment and production, they therefore have to take out loans. Since the lenders want to secure their capital in time, that is, to withdraw it from the company, they—according to this approach—bring about bankruptcies earlier than equity investors. The risk of capital loss increases in the recession, which is why credit rationing takes place in this phase of the business cycle. This approach explains the procyclical development of real wages observed in practice: although productivity increases in the recession due to the release of inefficient production factors, there is still an oversupply of labor on the labor market because companies cannot expand their employment due to credit rationing. A restrictive monetary policy can intensify the recession here due to the negative feedback on the credit supply. In contrast, an expansive monetary policy cannot change the long-term equilibrium because, in turn, the marginal productivity determines the real wage, thus also creating an asymmetry in the effects of restrictive and expansive monetary policy.

These newer approaches, due to the partial non-neutrality of monetary policy, initially call for discretionary fiscal policy, in particular for expansive monetary policy during a recession. But they also indirectly show the dangers of mismanagement. If one assumes—as the monetarists do—unknown or changing time delays in the mechanisms of action, the interventions can increase the economic instability due to the asymmetry of effects: an expansive monetary policy that only takes effect when the economy is no longer in recession, but in the upswing or boom phase, mainly causes inflation and hardly any positive real effects. A subsequent deflationary policy would then have a much more contractionary effect on national product and employment.[38]

The incorporation of mathematical chaos equations into equilibrium systems (chaos theory) underlines this conclusion. It turned out that, depending on the initial parameter constellation, solutions moving away from equilibrium, i.e. chaotic solutions, are possible in addition to cyclical solutions. However, if neither the parameter constellation in

---

[37] See Stiglitz, S.E. and Weiss A. (1992) as well as DeLong, B.D. and Summers, L. (1988) as well as Homburg, Stefan (1996, pp. 64).

[38] See Kugler, Peter (1998, p. 32).

the initial situation can be determined exactly nor the economic policy instruments can be dosed exactly, the risk of mismanagement is all the greater.[39]

7.8   Political Business Cycles: Nordhaus' Political Business Cycle Model

Nordhaus' approach is based on the "New Political Economy". According to the approach of the New Political Economy, a politician does not maximize the common good, but rather his own utility. Political offices grant this utility in the form of power, prestige and income. In order to achieve the desired offices, the politician must collect as many votes as possible—one speaks of vote maximization.[40] Positive economic indicators can be used as a political success indicator and secure the approval of voters. If the politician assumes the controllability of the economy, he will try to use the instruments available to him in such a way that the economic indicators are best at the time of the election. Already from this behavioral hypothesis, the existence of politically caused business cycles can be concluded. However, until the publication of Nordhaus' business cycle model, the approach of the New Political Economy lacked the mathematical behavioral model with which politically initiated business cycles could be derived and explained endogenously.[41]

The one by Nordhaus[42] The economic indicators used are inflation and unemployment. Every voter is directly affected by inflation in his role as a consumer of goods. He is directly affected by unemployment if he loses his job. He can also be indirectly affected if he feels threatened by it, that is, if he expects to lose his job in the future as well. Nordhaus lists various reasons for a trade-off between inflation and unemployment. First, a low unemployment rate creates a higher overall demand, which also affects the price level. Second, the higher overall demand is associated with higher strike costs as

---

[39]The use of non-linear behaviour functions based on mathematical chaos theory in neo-classical growth models usually only leads to stable solutions in exceptional cases, so that the empirical explanatory power is to be rated as very low. See Teichmann, Ulrich (1997, p. 24).

[40]A comprehensive theoretical analysis of political rationality can be found in Frey, Bruno S. (1981). An empirical verification of further parts of the New Political Economy was carried out by Meyer-Krahmer. See Meyer-Krahmer, Frieder (1979). An analysis of individual policy areas of the European Community on the basis of the New Political Economy is the topic of Guerrieri, Paolo and Padoan, Pietro Carlo C. (1989). The most concise summary of the approaches of the "New Political Economy" is offered by Krisch, Guy (1993) and Franke. See Franke, Siegfried F. (1996). A good theoretical analysis of political voting can be found in Downs, Anthony (1968); Andel, Norbert (1990, pp. 47); Braybrooke, David and Lindblom, Charles, E (1965).

[41]See Frey, B.S. and Lau, L.J. (1968).

[42]For Nordhaus' business cycle model, see Nordhaus, William D. (1975): The political Business Cycle, in: Review of Economic Studies, Vol. 42 (1975, pp. 169–190).

opportunity costs of lost sales due to production shortages. These make the employer accept the workers' wage demands. Nordhaus also attributes a short-term trade-off to the workers' adaptive reactions to unemployment and inflation and the effects on the price level. With high unemployment, they reduce their wage demands. The reduction in production costs leads to a reduction in prices, which in turn leads to a reduction in wage demands. With inflation, workers realize the reduction in real wages late and therefore adjust their wage demands late as well. The long-term "Phillips curve"[43] is thus steeper than the short-term "Phillips curve" (see Figs. 7.20 and 7.21).

Within the "Phillips curve", the politician can choose combinations of inflation and unemployment. However, this is only possible as long as the money illusion persists. If the economic subjects have adapted their expectations (adapted), the short-term Phillips

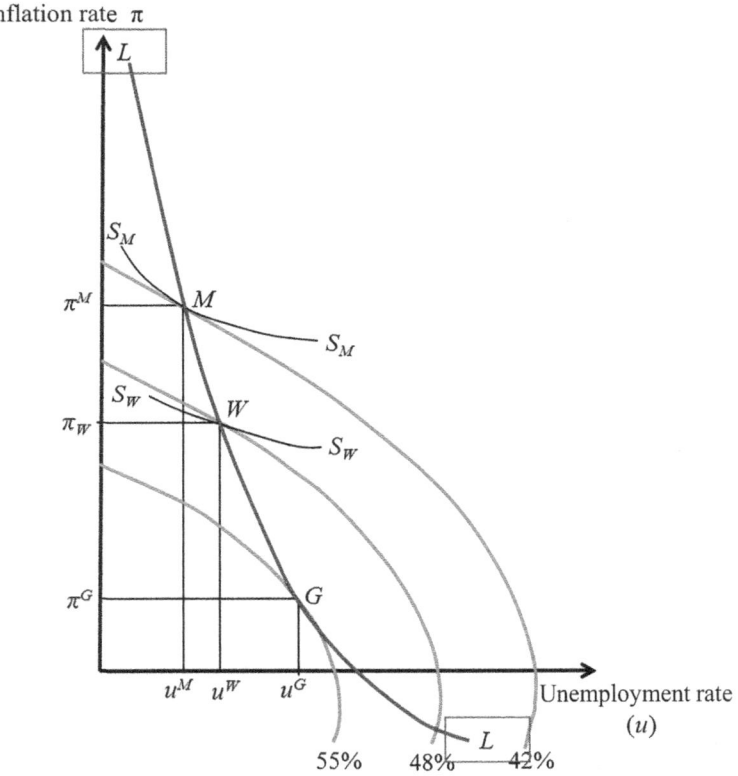

Fig. 7.20 Long-term policy strategies. (See Nordhaus, William D., 1975, p. 177)

---

[43] Here Nordhaus refers to the econometric estimates of Menil and Enzler for the USA. See Menil, George and Enzler, Jared J. (1972).

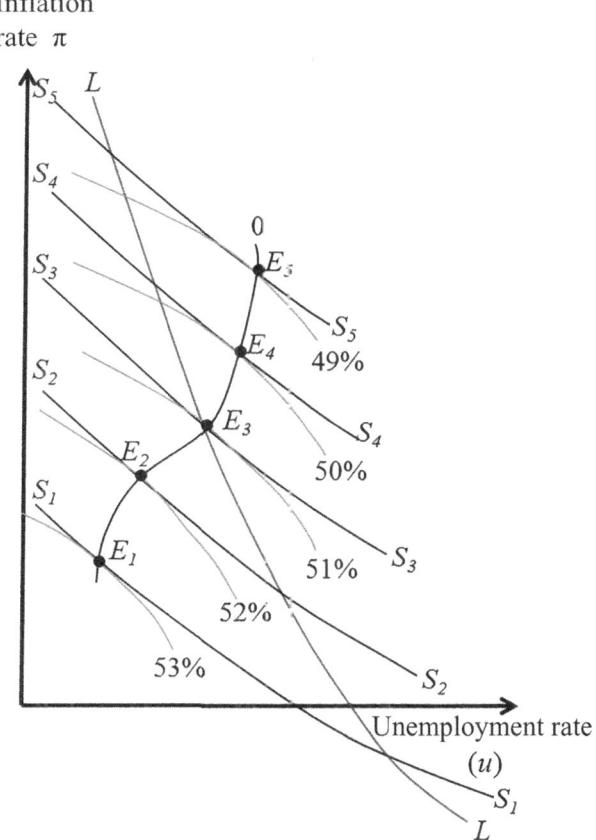

Fig. 7.21 Short-term election results. (See Nordhaus, William D., 1975, p. 179)

curve shifts upwards. The politician chooses the maximum number of votes. The decisions of the individual citizens to re-elect the government are made depending on the satisfaction of the expectations of the citizens: Improvements in economic indicators are rewarded with votes. In this case, improvements and deteriorations in the election period are less important than recent developments. Consequently, it is vote-maximizing for the governing party to take restrictive measures at the beginning of the election period and expansive measures at the end of the election period. After expansive measures, the short-term Phillips curve shifts from below to above. If the government does not pursue a restrictive policy after the election, it must increase the inflation rate more than in the first election period in order to reduce unemployment despite higher inflation expectations. The new, worse combination of unemployment and inflation is evaluated by the voters with a lower approval (measured in votes), which is why the governing party cannot maintain this policy for long. At point E_3 the system is in long-term equilibrium: Both by an expansive and by a restrictive policy before the election the government would lose its majority (see Fig. 7.20). After its re-election, the government therefore has to try to reach the original Phillips curve with the old inflation expectations through a restrictive policy. The discretionary, politically motivated interventions generate business cycles.

Thus, in democracies, the average unemployment rate is below and the average inflation rate is above the general welfare optimum (W, see Fig. 7.21) for the current and future generations due to the overemphasis on the present. Furthermore, from the time preference of the voters, a tendency can be derived for government politicians to value today's positive economic developments higher than future ones. Nordhaus concludes that politicians tend to maximize current wealth at the expense of future generations' wealth. Nordhaus business cycles also occur in centrally planned economies. Since these are usually one-party systems that govern dictatorially, the cycles will only occur at the times when the government needs short-term support from the population. For the governing party, it is vote-maximizing to implement restrictive measures at the beginning of the election period and expansive measures at the end of the election period (Nordhaus model).

NORDHAUS' assumptions and conclusions are mostly plausible. The model endogenously explains the emergence of political business cycles and thus shows the dangers of political interference in the economic process. NORDHAUS found his theory confirmed for Germany, New Zealand and the USA. He determined small political business cycles for France and Sweden, while the probability of political influence on the business cycle was low in the other cases he examined.[44] However, NORDHAUS' model assumes controllability of the economic indicators unemployment and inflation. The business fluctuations do not arise from macroeconomic mismanagement, but from political manipulation intentions. However, this only marginally diminishes the importance of the model, since politically induced fluctuations would only occur irregularly in the event of mismanagement.

NORDHAUS discusses several alternatives in his basic essay that could reduce political fluctuations. The simplest option would be to shorten the election periods to take account of voters' forgetfulness. However, there would be a risk that the government period would not be long enough for a long-term, strategically oriented policy and that policy would therefore only be oriented towards the short term. In addition, there would be inefficiencies in administration due to the frequent change of government. Refreshing the information level of voters again and again seems to be an unrealistic alternative in view of the low interest of people in past events (present preference). It is particularly interesting that the demand for political independence of central banks and even of finance ministries (in the area of short-term expenditure decisions) can be derived from this model. NORDHAUS sees this as a disadvantage, however, in that monetary and fiscal policy as a political instrument to implement the wishes of voters is lost. This

---

[44] Australia, Canada, Japan, Great Britain.

statement contains a certain contradiction to the criticism of politically caused business cycles inherent in the model. Political and economic rationality (expediency) are rarely identical. Another alternative would be to reduce the inclination of the Phillips curve, i.e. the short-term trade-off between unemployment and inflation, for example by means of price and wage freezes or by automatic induction or inflation compensation. With the exception of inflation compensation, these measures are not compatible with a market economy. They would be market- and therefore system-destroying. Automatic wage induction or indirect inflation compensation, as in the Italian Scala Mobile, would lead to less resistance to inflation and thus ultimately to inflation acceleration. NORDHAUS himself tends to prevent manipulation of voters by exploiting their short-term memory through greater transparency and wider participation in the political decision-making process.

The following theories are presented and examined for their pro-cyclical policy statements, which, contrary to the Keynesian, non-Walrasian theories, are based on an inherent market stability or an automatic market equilibrium mechanism. Here, the monetarist theories and the New Classical Macroeconomics are essentially to be credited with their further developments.[45]

7.9   Monetary Policy as a Cause of the Business Cycle

7.9.1   The Interest Rate Spread Theorem By Knut Wicksell

Wicksell (1851–1926) attributes cyclical fluctuations to the wrong decisions of monetary policymakers, i.e. the central banks (at that time still commercial banks)in controlling interest rates. (Wicksell Hypothesis)[46]: Based on these approaches, the following model can be developed. The profitability of investments, i.e. the marginal productivity of capital (or internal rate of return), increases due to external influences (e.g. due to technical progress).

1. The central bank does not react or reacts too late (see Fig. 7.22), which is why the internal interest rate (return on investment) is above the money interest rate. The central bank's interest rate (i) is therefore below the return on investments and below the equilibrium interest rate (i*), which would bring about a balance of supply and demand. There is therefore an excess demand for capital. The result is that more is

---

[45] See Conrad, Christian (1999, pp. 188–220), as well as Stavenhagen, Gerhard (1969).

[46] See Grossekettler, Heinz (1989, pp. 203 ff.); Wicksell, Knut (1898, pp. 109 ff.) as well as Wicksell, Knut (1922, p. 231). For Wicksell, the monetary policy decision-makers are the commercial banks.

Fig. 7.22 Upswing caused by
the central bank not reacting

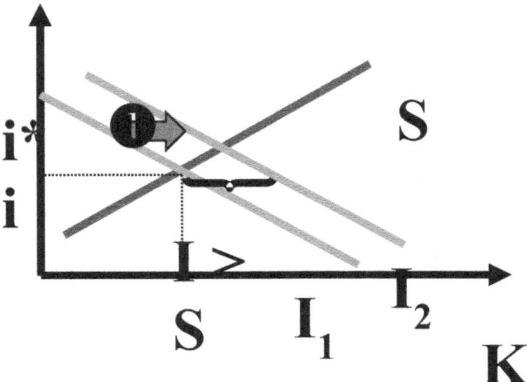

invested than saved. The demand shortfall caused by saving is less than the additional
demand caused by the investments of the companies. Due to the excess demand, an
upswing occurs. The central bank does not increase the interest rate, which is why the
equilibrium interest rate i* is not reached.

$\Rightarrow$ I > S $\Rightarrow$ Upswing ($\Rightarrow$ equilibrium interest rate i* > i, see Fig. 7.22).

2. Due to the excess demand, the costs of pre-deliveries (labor and intermediate products) increase, which is why the internal interest rate falls.
3. Since the aggregate demand is greater than the supply, the price level rises. In
   response to the price increase, the central bank raises interest rates, so that the internal
   interest rate is now below the money rate ($\Rightarrow$ equilibrium interest rate i* < i, see Fig.
   7.23). As a result, investments are smaller than savings. I.e. the central bank reacts
   wrongly and thus triggers the recession ($\Rightarrow$ I < S $\Rightarrow$ recession). The interventions of
   the central bank in the market thus cause economic fluctuations, as the market mechanism is disturbed.

Fig. 7.23 Recession caused
by delayed reaction of the
central bank

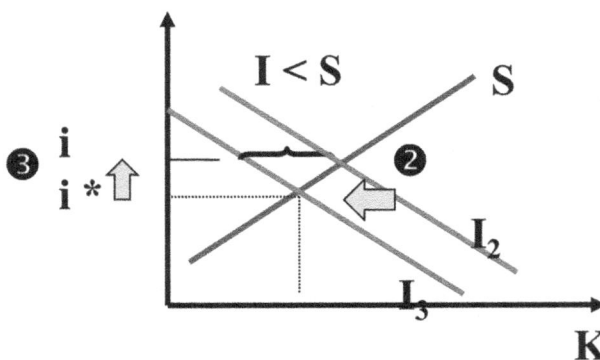

7.9.2   Hayek's Perverse Elasticity of Credit Supply

Friedrich August von Hayek (student of Wicksell), on the other hand, blames the uncontrolled money supply development for the economic overheating in his theory of economic cycles.[47] Due to the uncontrolled money creation process, there is too much money supply.

In the money creation process of banks, they lend the sight deposits of their customers (deposits) to third parties, creating new sight deposits (see Sect. 5.7.3). The money is taken back to the bank and can be lent out again. Hayek refers to this unlimited lending as the perverse elasticity of credit supply.

Due to the money creation of banks through lending, there is no increase in interest rates, even though the demand for capital has increased. The investments are therefore larger than the savings, which is why the demand on the goods market is also greater than the supply ($\Rightarrow$ I > S). There is an upswing. There is an uncontrolled upswing because more money is lent than saved.

Due to the excess demand, the costs of pre-deliveries (labor and intermediate products) increase, which is why the internal interest rate falls and prices in general rise. Now the lenders increase the interest rates to get a compensation for inflation, which is why the internal interest rate is now below the money interest rate and many investments are no longer profitable. There are investment ruins and write-offs. The demand for investment by companies does not compensate for the decline in demand for savings by households ($\Rightarrow$ I < S $\Rightarrow$ downturn).

Conclusion

Wicksell and Hayek show the dangers of central bank interventions. The central banks prevent the natural market mechanism of the money market from correcting over- and undersupplies. This criticism speaks for the rule-based monetary policy, which is oriented towards the growth of production potential. Only in exceptional cases does a central bank intervention in the money market appear justified. If the central bank intervenes, it bears responsibility for the business cycle. The central bank must monitor credit and money circulation.[48]

The intervention of the central bank with interest rate cuts in the money market is standard, as Fig. 7.24 shows. Since the appointment of its central bank president Draghi, the ECB has pursued an expansionary monetary policy. After the interventions in the course of the financial crisis and the sovereign debt crisis, Draghi is now trying to combat deflation and stimulate economic growth with an expansionary monetary policy. This is also served by his program to buy government bonds. In this way,

---

[47] See Hayek, F. v. (1935).
[48] See Conrad, Christian, A. and Stahl, Markus (2003, pp. 685–693).

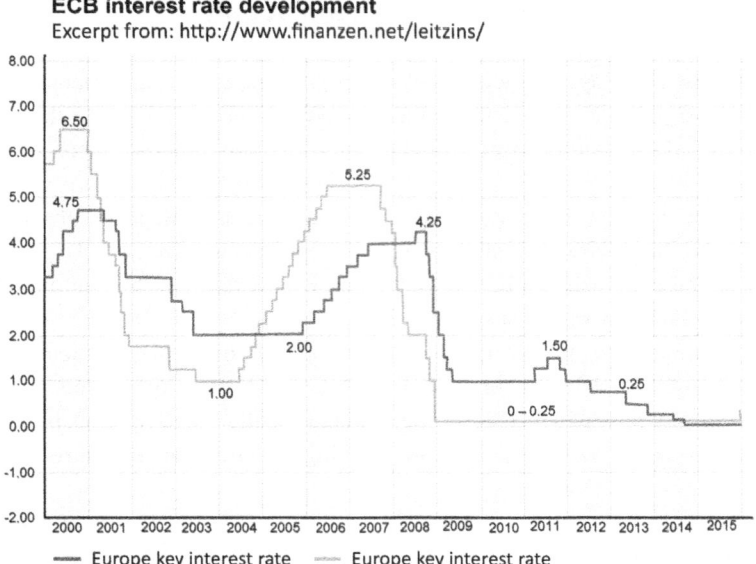

Fig. 7.24 Development of the ECB and US interest rate. (Reprinted with kind permission of finanzen.net GmbH. http://www.finanzen.net/leitzins/)

not only money is pumped into the market, but the banks are also forced to grant loans to companies by the lack of government bonds as an investment opportunity. Furthermore, the purchase of government bonds on the capital market should also lower the credit interest rate. Since the crash of the financial crisis, the USA has also pursued an expansionary monetary policy. ◀

The following chapter uses the example of the USA to examine to what extent an expansionary monetary policy can cause speculative bubbles.

7.9.3   Case Study: US Monetary Policy in the Tension Field of Stock Market Development

Task

Read and discuss the following case study on US monetary policy. To what extent can monetary policy of a central bank affect asset prices? Does the central bank have a responsibility here?

Since 1994, the Federal Reserve has supplied the American economy with plenty of liquidity against the background of productivity gains of the economy at that time

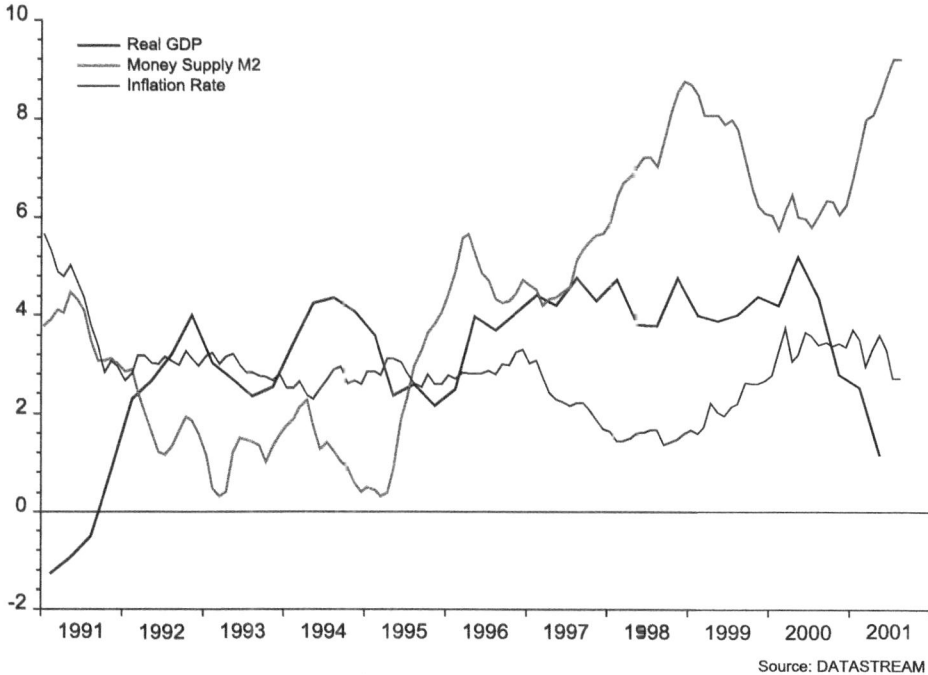

Fig. 7.25 Real growth (bottom right), inflation rate (middle right) and money supply M2 (top right)

referred to as the "New Economy". However, the money supply growth (see Fig. 7.25) disproportionate to the real GDP in recent years not only supported the productivity forces of the American economy, but also an unprecedented stock price inflation.

From September 1994 to March 2000, the S&P 500 gained more than 250%, corresponding to an annual return of around 25%. The Russia crisis and the subsequent bankruptcy of the hedge fund LTCM[49] in autumn 1998 turned out to be only short-term breaks[50]. Already in the period after the crash of October 1987, Greenspan saved the US stock market through his pragmatic steps to lower interest rates. In 1998 he succeeded for a second time by organizing a rescue operation for the LTCM hedge fund. In addition, he saved the world financial system from a severe crisis. However, the verbal

---

[49] See Gerhard Single and Markus Stahl (2000), pp. 1060–1066.

[50] See: Conrad, Christian A. and Schoett, Harry (2000), pp. 151–159.

statements and actions of the US central bank differed widely in 1997 and 1998. As early as 1996, Greenspan warned of an "irrational exuberance" (irrational exuberance) when the Dow Jones 30 Industrial Average stood at 6600 points. Just as the then development trends in US growth and inflation rates rather suggested a more restrictive policy, the Fed decided in view of the strong share price decline in the US stock market in autumn 1998 for three interest rate cuts. From September 28 to November 17, 1998, the Federal Funds Target Rate was lowered by a quarter percentage point from 5.5% to 4.75% (Fig. 7.26).

Only these interest rate cuts by the American Federal Reserve Bank could stop the downward trend on the stock markets. What could have prompted Greenspan to make this interest rate cut?

We remember the monetary policy of the American central bank in the run-up to the stock market crash of 1929, which was followed by a long-lasting global economic crisis. To what extent the American monetary policy contributed to the speculative excess in the 1920s and the stock market boom before the year 2000, divided economists then as today. It is undisputed that the initial phase of both boom movements was accompanied by an expansive monetary policy. Since 1921, the last year of the restrictive monetary policy introduced to combat post-war inflation, the central bank lowered the discount rate from 6% in 1921 to 3.5% by mid-1927. For a more restrictive line there was then,

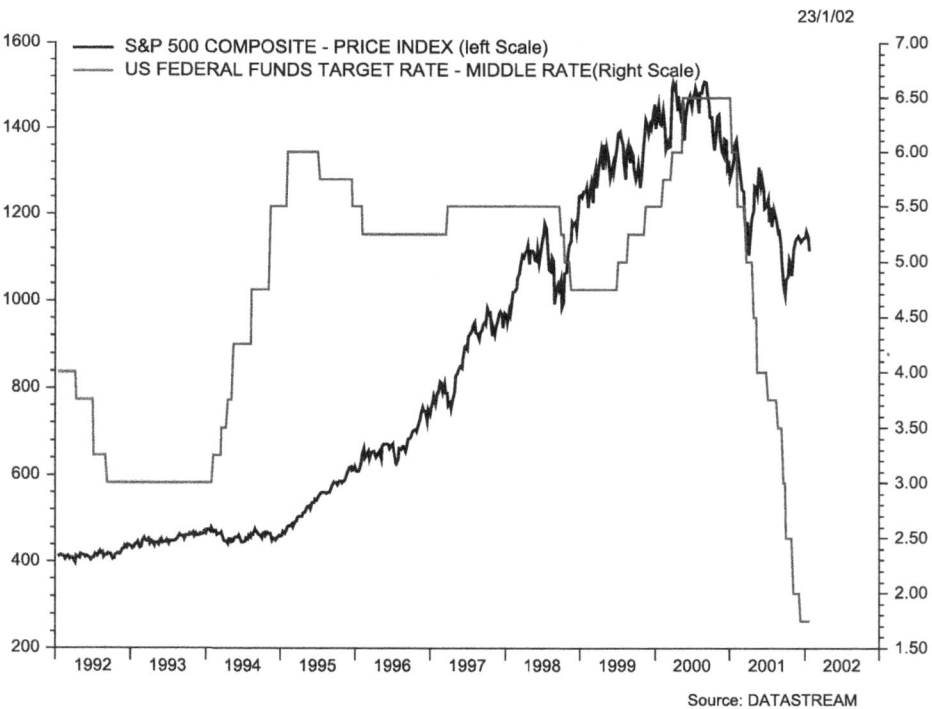

Fig. 7.26 Stock index S&P 500 (left scale) and Fed Fund Rate (right scale)

according to the traditional inflation concept, no reason. The growth rates of commodity prices were consistently below the critical tolerance thresholds. The growth of the money supply M1 developed largely in parallel with real gross domestic product, so that the risk of a pent-up money surplus that could be directed to consumer goods in the short term was relatively low. The actual inflation and credit creation took place in the securities sector. The then broker loans reached around 8.5 billion US dollars in 1929, around 10% of market capitalization. When some members of the American money supply sensed the danger posed by the securities credits, it was already too late to stop the speculation carousel. When the central bank finally decided to intervene, the three discount rate increases by a total of 1.5% to 5% in summer 1928 were not enough to brake the speculative movement. This is hardly surprising in view of the partly more than 10% interest rates on the Brooker loans, which were mainly fed by industrial companies and foreign banks. Even the warning of the central bank president Roy Young that central bank money must not be misused for credit-financed speculation, but only for productive purposes, went unheeded, so that the US central bank finally raised the discount rate again on 9 August 1929 from 5% to 6%.[51] The decisive blow, however, as it would only two months later to find out.[52]

In the light of the world economic crisis of 1929, the interest rate cuts Greenspans are understandable. The interest rate cut signal, however, could not only stop the downward trend in the stock market, but also stimulated in addition, the speculation of investors.[53] Since the first interest rate cut was made outside the regular meeting cycle, has earned the Fed-Chairman Alan Greenspan—the—questionable—reputation of the savior, who would not allow in the future that the capital markets fall sharply below its present level. This implicit bail-out guarantee encouraged investors really, the technology stocks between autumn 1998 and the first quarter of 2000 to quadruple.[54] Thereafter, however, was the Federal Reserve (Fed) in a with 1929 comparable dilemma. The unleashing of speculation and the furious development of Internet stocks in the winter of 1999/2000 were no longer to be stopped by the meantime transition to a more restrictive monetary policy. Only the increase in the Federal Funds Target Rate showed in April 2000 on the US stock exchanges. But there was the S & P 500 already at around 1500.

In the course of this interest rate increase, the price bubble finally burst for technology stocks in March 2000, just as it had in the 1920s. From its high of 5050 points on March 10, 2000, the American technology exchange Nasdaq lost more than 60%. The

---

[51] See Clarke, Stephen (1967).

[52] The monetary circumstances of the crash of 1929 investigated in particular Termin, Peter (1976) as well as Friedman, Milton and Schwartz, Jacobson (1965).

[53] See Conrad, Christian, A. and Schoett, Harry (2000).

[54] See Interview with Markus Stahl and Christian Conrad, published under the title: With the technology values, it is like horse racing, experts see further correction needs in the stock market, in: Frankfurter Allgemeine Zeitung, No. 120, 24 May 2000, pp. 31–32.

downturn also affected the classic standard values. After the previous excesses in consumption, a recession could also threaten the US economy. In contrast to 1929, the US Federal Reserve reacted immediately and drastically. In the course of 2001, the Fed lowered the key interest rate in eleven steps to 1.75% in the end. In terms of dynamics, the interest rate cut trend exceeded the key interest rate cuts in the run-up to the world economic crisis of 1930 to 1933.[55]

The Fed justified its very expansive monetary policy with the increasing economic weakness in the course of 2001. It referred to the declining consumer confidence and the cautious investment willingness of many companies. In addition, there was further deterioration in sentiment in connection with the terrorist attacks of September 11, 2001. The Fed also openly discussed the weakness of the US stock market and the question of how the investors' losses could affect their demand.

Such comments on monetary policy as well as the reaction patterns of interest rate policy impressively demonstrate that the development of the stock market was a central factor for the monetary policy of the US Fed. In contrast to other central banks, the US Fed is not only given the goal of price stability, but also—among other goals—the goal of an appropriate economic growth. How these goals are filled and weighted according to the respective economic situation is left to the Fed.

In Japan, too, the money supply aggregates had been growing much faster than GDP in the mid-1980s. When plans for a tightening of monetary policy were already on the table, the Bank of Japan was forced, by the global stock market crash in October 1987, to contribute to the stabilization of world financial markets through the maintenance of monetary expansion. While Wall Street and the European exchanges needed a longer time to digest the price declines, the Japanese stock index Nikkei 225 quickly rose to new heights. From October 1987 to December 1989, it rose by another 80%. At the beginning of 1990, the bubble then burst. In the following years, the Nikkei index lost up to 70% of the December 1989 price level.[56]

After discussing in the case study the influence of monetary policy on asset values such as stocks, we want to take a closer look at this relationship in the following.

7.9.4   Review of Monetary Policy Goals

7.9.4.1 Asset Bubbles as an Indicator of Invisible Inflation

In many cases, the central bank is forced to mitigate emerging problems in the financial system and the real economy through the printing press and devaluations. The history

---

[55] See Christian A. Conrad and Markus Stahl (2000a), pp. 25.

[56] See Daxhammer, Rolf and Schmied-Wörle, Tatjana (2000, pp. 45–58).

of money is rich in examples in which an excessively expansionary monetary policy was the financial breeding ground for an inflation of capital market prices (asset inflation), without leading to rapidly rising consumer prices. Often, the final result was severe crises in the financial system, the undermining of the external and internal value of the currency, and an overextension of public finances. Already in 18th century England, a speculative stock price bubble had shaken the financial markets.[57] Under the chairmanship of John Blunt, the South Sea Company was commissioned to convert government debt and pension payments into its own shares with fixed dividend payments. Although the exact conversion plan was not made public, a run on South Sea Company shares began in early 1720. The share price rose from 128 British pounds to 1050 British pounds between January and June of that year. The entire English stock market was caught up in the speculation fever. The speculation mania was driven by the money creation of the banks, which issued new securities against low securities. In France, it was the Banque Generale founded by John Law, a predecessor of the present central bank, which offered similar services to the French crown as the South Sea Company. When Louis XIV died in 1715, he left his successor Louis XV with an extremely high debt of 2.4 billion livres. John Law relieved the royal finances by issuing shares of the Banque Generale and the Mississippi Company against the deposit of government bonds. The speculation in these shares led to a regular popular movement in the autumn of 1719. The now renamed Banque Royal, John Law's bank, financed the speculative excesses with the ongoing issue of paper money, which was no longer covered by the bank's gold reserves.[58] In the end, the assets of the stock and paper money owners in England and France had been largely destroyed by the uncontrolled money supply of the then private central banks.[59]

The inflation measures used by central banks mainly include consumer prices and producer prices. Price developments in the financial sector or prices for assets (asset prices) are thus systematically excluded by the measurement method.[60] It is thus possible that excessive money production initially does not result in rising prices for consumer goods, but in price increases for assets. If only consumer prices are considered, an invisible inflation can arise. However, for long-term, steady and balanced economic growth, price distortions in the financial sector are just as harmful as unchecked price inflation in goods. Price distortions in the markets for assets can lead to serious misallocations in the real economy and ultimately endanger the financial system as the central addressee and transmission belt of monetary policy.

---

[57] For the South Sea Bubble, see Chancellor, Edward (1999, pp. 58–95).

[58] For the Law financial scandal, see Kiehling, Hartmut (2000, pp. 19–29).

[59] Gold investments could be promising in such a scenario. See Mezger, Markus and Stahl, Markus (2001a, pp. 372–378) and Conrad, Christian, A. and Stahl, Markus (2002).

[60] See Mezger, Markus and Stahl, Markus (2001b, pp. 15–22).

A stock market boom is supported by excessive money supply from the central bank. The board game "Monopoly" can serve as a simple example here. After an initially very slow start with rather low price offers for streets in negotiations between the players, in the final phase of the game absurdly high amounts are achieved for streets. The background to this phenomenon is neither the special strategic performance of the few who have become rich nor the luck or misfortune when throwing the dice. The key to the explanation is the popular "Chance" field. If you go over "Chance" you get 4000 units of money extra.

The "Los" playing field, which bestows blessings, means nothing more than that the amount of money held by the players per player and round is increased by 4000 units of money. With 5 players and 15 rounds, the amount of money increases by 300,000 units of money. The original amount of money is 30,000 units of money per player; with 5 players, that's a total of 150,000 units of money. After 15 rounds, therefore, three times as much money (150,000 + 300,000 = 450,000) is available from the "Los" money source. So it's no wonder that in bilateral price negotiations between the players over individual streetscapes, increasingly higher bids and revenues are generated as the game progresses. The asset price bubble, originally limited to the real estate sector, continues to grow larger and larger.

The connection between the development of the money supply and asset prices has been examined in several empirical studies. They show, for example, that in addition to an increase in productivity in the Japanese economy and an increased demand for real estate in Tokyo, the expansive monetary policy was responsible for the sharp increase in stock, art and real estate prices in Japan in the second half of the 1980s. It was expressed primarily in increased lending by banks.[61] Various analyses[62] show a positive correlation between the two variables, which can be interpreted in different ways:

1. For example, the productivity of companies could have increased, leading to increased profits for publicly traded companies and, as a result, stock prices. In this case, the central bank would have simply expanded the money supply in parallel with the increase in real production.
2. If the central bank increases the money supply or lowers the interest rate directly, this can lead to a reduction in the long-term interest rate as a discounting factor for expected corporate profits, which corresponds to a higher present value. As a result,

---

[61] See Ito, Takatoshi and Iwaisako, Tokuo (1995).

[62] See International Monetary Fund 2000 and *Baks, Klaas und Kramer, Charles* (1999).

stock prices rise. This connection can be easily illustrated. If one disregards the thesaurized profits, the return on a share for a period can be represented as follows:[63]

$$\text{Yield price gain in \% dividend in \%}$$

$$r_k \quad = \quad \frac{p_{t+1} - p_t}{p_t} \quad + \quad \frac{D_{+1}}{F_t} \tag{7.1}$$

$$= \frac{p_{t+1} + D_{t+1} - p_t}{p_t} \tag{7.2}$$

(where p is the price of the stock [course] and D is the dividend represent.) t stands for the period).

In the allocation equilibrium, the stock return must correspond to alternative investments, so also the return of government securities. It can therefore be seen as a minimum return—with a constant return of government securities and stock price. The Equ. (7.2) can be resolved according to p_t, that is the stock price. We get:

$$p_t = \frac{p_{t+1} + D_{t+1}}{1 + r_k} \tag{7.3}$$

In order to increase the statement of the Equ. (7.3), we make two simplifying assumptions. First, dividends grow at a constant rate g and secondly capital gains are also constant. As a growth rate of D, g can also be deducted from the discount factor rk. Then it applies:

$$p_t = \frac{D}{r_k - g} \tag{7.4}$$

Consider the constellation $r_k' = 10\%$ (0.1), g'= 0.05 and D'= 2 US\$, we get for.

$p_t = 2$ US\$/(0.1 − 0.05)=40 US\$. With this equation, the effect of a interest rate cut on the price, that is, the interest elasticity of the price, can be derived. We leave all other numbers unchanged and reduce the interest rate r_k from 10% by 40% to 6%. As a result, the price rises by 160 US\$ (400%) to 200 US\$. The interest elasticity of the stock price is therefore 10, an effect that would certainly not have been expected to this extent.

3. Lower interest rates mean lower financing costs for companies, which in turn increases their profits, which also leads to an increase in the share price. Let us assume that the financing structure of German companies consists of 70% equity and 30% equity, then a interest rate cut as a result of an expansive monetary policy from

---

[63] See Braley, R. (1983). Actually, all future periods must be included. However, this is not done here due to the limited forecast horizon in reality.

5% to 1% with an assumed equity return of 10% would lead to an increase in company profits of 93.33% ($70 \times 4\% = 2.8$, equity return: $3 + 2.8 = 5.8$).

4. If the money supply is increased sharply, the portfolio of investors shifts in favor of cash holdings. Investors want to restore their desired portfolio ratio between cash and equity investments and therefore ask for more shares. The price of shares then rises like the price of other goods. This is an expression of inflation, as the real productivity of listed companies has remained unchanged.

We can thus conclude the following: If the return of bonds as a competing capital investment has a significant impact on stock prices, then this also applies indirectly to monetary policy as an interest-determining influence. As shown, in his theory of the business cycle, Friedrich August von Hayek[64] attributes the perverse elasticity of the banking system, i.e. the uncontrolled development of the money supply, to the business cycle overheating. Knut Wicksell[65] attributes it to the wrong decisions of the monetary policy decision-makers in interest rate control. A setting of the benchmark interest rate below the equilibrium interest rate of supply and demand in the capital market causes an inflation of the money supply, more precisely a shift in the goods-money exchange relation in favor of money. Due to the low interest rate, the demand for credit increases. New sight deposits are created through increased lending. The velocity of circulation and thus the money supply increase. Since the cash position of the investor has increased relative to the value of securities, portfolio reallocations occur. The new money flows into the stock markets and drives up prices. Due to the function of interest as a comparison return and discounting factor, an artificial interest rate subsidy not only leads to an increase in stock prices, but also to an excessive allocation of resources in equity values, which can lead to overheating.[66]

In addition, there are self-reinforcing effects: the rising stock prices (and/or real estate prices) signal potential profits and represent collateral for the banks with which they can operate credit and indirectly money creation. There is a self-reinforcing upward process on the stock exchange. Refinancing promises (bail-out as lender of last resort) in case of liquidity shortages, such as those of the International Monetary Fund or the central banks, increase the security of speculation and thus support such development (moral hazard problem[67]). In addition, the low interest rate promotes the credit-financed purchase of shares. However, the bubble can not expand indefinitely, as the price spiral and the rising stock market turnover bind more and more of the available liquidity.

---

[64] See Hayek, Friedrich August von (1929, pp. 81).

[65] See Wicksell, Knut (1928, pp. 231); Wicksell, Knut (1898, pp. 101 ff.), as well as Grossekettler, Heinz (1989, pp. 203 f.).

[66] See Conrad, Christian A. (2000, pp. 135–146).

[67] Moral hazard ("moral hazard" or "moral risk", is an incentive for the individual (individual) to behave against or at the expense of the general public (collective).

At the latest when the entire money supply is absorbed by the stock exchange, the market capitalizations of the shares begin to fall under their own weight. Price declines trigger a kind of chain reaction of further forced liquidation. The crash is there.[68] The same applies to the real estate market.

7.9.4.2 The Consequences of Asset Bubbles

If the high stock prices do not reflect the permanently achievable company profits, but mainly the exaggerated expectations of a majority of the stock market participants, this can lead to misallocations of resources in the economy, if the companies issue new shares or bonds at the inflated prices and make unprofitable investments. This is how the bubble at the technology stock exchanges has led to a general over-dimensioning of the real investments in this sector by March 2000.[69] Here the theories of Hayek and Wicksell apply. Too much liquidity and a reduction of the interest rate below the equilibrium interest rate favour speculation bubbles. Over-investments, which had to be written off afterwards, were also characteristic of the real estate bubble in the USA, Spain and Ireland before the financial crisis. Money at no charge strengthens the willingness to take risks. In addition, investors are taking higher risks in the search for yield due to the lack of alternatives. This was also a reason for the financial crisis.

Economic resources would thus have been partly misdirected. Investors and lenders would then be confronted with painful losses. If, for example, the banking system were to be affected by high equity holdings or by extensive credit commitments from defaults in this sector, then there could be crisis-like developments in the credit economy. Since the lending capacity of the banking system is a direct function of equity, write-downs caused by write-downs could lead to growing restrictions on lending. The economy could then suffer from a paralyzing credit crunch (Credit Crunch) in the banking sector. After the burst of the stock market bubble, for example, the Japanese economy was confronted with this situation. Although the Japanese central bank virtually gave away the money, Japanese companies had a hard time getting bank loans because the banks lacked equity. There was also a credit crunch as a result of the financial crisis.

The infection of the real economy by a bursting stock market bubble takes place—in addition to the way via the banking system (credit crunch)—also via the wealth effect of consumption. If the airy stock market gains dissolve into thin air again, only one fiction should be lost. But like all fictions, stock market fictions can also deeply intervene in real economic life. Consumers who have no fears whatsoever during the stock market boom to overburden their household budgets for months in the expectation that they will be able to settle the due installments from stock market gains overnight have considerable difficulty meeting their obligations after a crash. New acquisitions are no longer pos-

---

[68] See Conrad, Christian A. and Stahl, Markus (2000b, pp. 24–32).
[69] See Stahl, Markus (2000).

sible. Based on the rising value of their own shares and participation, entrepreneurs and their companies also take out loans for additional investments to a greater extent during the stock market boom. Overnight they become doubtful debtors to whom the bank cancels the loans. There can be a vicious circle of consumption restraint, investment stop, production restriction, wage losses, mood deterioration and renewed consumption and investment restriction.

The strength of the wealth effect is shown in the following example calculation:

Example

The consequences of a ten percent correction of stock prices are calculated under the assumption of a five percent wealth effect. With a market capitalization of around 16 trillion US dollars in the USA (NYSE index values: 12.8 trillion US dollars, NASDAQ index values: 3.2 trillion US dollars) reached at the end of April 2001, such a 10% correction represents a destruction of wealth on the order of 1.6 trillion US dollars. Consequently, due to the wealth effect of, for example, 5%, consumption would decrease by 80 billion US dollars. Total private consumption in the USA amounted to approximately 6800 billion US dollars in the year 2000. The wealth effect therefore implies a decrease in private consumption of approximately 1.1%. Since consumption grew by approximately 7.8% in nominal terms in the year 2000, this is a quite significant order of magnitude. However, the margin of error for this estimate is large, since empirical studies put the wealth effect at 2% to 10% of consumption. For a 10% decline in the stock market, the decrease in consumption could therefore be 0.47% (2% wealth effect) or 2.3% (10% wealth effect). Regardless of the exact size of the wealth effect, however, it remains clear that a drastic stock market crash, for example, on the order of 30%, could have a very sustainable impact on the economy. In the best case, the decrease in consumption would be around 1.5%, but in the pessimistic case it could already be as high as 7%.[70] ◀

The resource misallocations resulting from too expansive monetary policy thus cause massive wealth losses and economic downturns after the bubble bursts. In addition to resource misallocation, massive allocative redistribution effects can also be observed. They are added to the speculative effects of expansive monetary policy, which the monetary policy creates through artificially low interest rates. Even without a negative real interest rate due to inflation, there are massive distributional effects in favor of debtors and to the detriment of creditors, such as savers, which can endanger the population's pension provision over a longer period of time.

---

[70] See Conrad, Christian, A. and Stahl, Markus (2002).

7.9.4.3 Conclusion

The hitherto common objective is that central banks should ensure price stability. In this respect, they would also have to control inflationary risks resulting from the revaluation of equity and the corresponding increase in private household consumption. With regard to the capture of inflation potential, at least concepts for measuring instruments should be thought of which include a more comprehensive range of prices than the current development of the price of the basket of goods. In the case of an intertemporal interpretation of the concept of inflation, in addition to current consumer prices, future price developments could also be taken into account, which are derived from asset price changes. Estimates can be made on the basis of the correlation between stock market capitalization and aggregate economic consumption. Central banks would thus consider an indicator of prices when considering their monetary policy target, which would include not only current consumer prices but also price developments in the asset markets. The development of asset prices would thus become part of monetary policy control.

So far, the price development in the stock and real estate markets has not been included in the monetary policy target. There are reasons for this. Monetary policy can only be oriented towards measurable indicators if it wants to remain predictable. In contrast to consumer price indices, however, there are neither empirically recognized values for the overall economic effect of asset price distortions nor are there any figures by means of which one could determine a deviation or imbalance. An empirically-mathematical proof of a stock market bubble will never be possible ex ante, as stock prices always contain expectations about the uncertain, unforeseeable future. Ultimately, central banks cannot determine the fundamentally correct price level of stocks any better than the multitude of market participants who determine the price level in the markets every day through their purchase and sale decisions.

The central bank could also come under pressure if it were accused of destroying equity or real estate assets or of unduly constricting the money supply to the real economy and thereby slowing the economy, in order to counteract an unidentified stock market bubble. However, the opposite accusation, that central banks represent the interests of speculators, which the US Federal Reserve is exposed to, also damages the reputation of a central bank.

In principle, a bubble cannot be exactly determined, but it can at least be suspected. The central bank should first check whether there is a fundamental reason for the exorbitant price increase, which will usually be the case. If the stock exchange under consideration is representative of the economy as a whole, the central bank should on the one hand compare the growth rates of the stock market indices with the historical values and on the other hand with the current growth of gross domestic product. If it finds a sustainable historical or relative increase here, the suspicion of a bubble is likely. Stock exchanges with a history can be measured against past periods, stock exchanges with economic representativeness can even be measured against gross domestic product. The starting point here is the question of whether a stock exchange representative of an economy as a whole can grow stronger over a longer period of time than the economy as a whole.[71]

7.9.5   Empirical Verification of the Effects of a Zero Interest Rate Policy On Risk Behavior[72]

The Japanese central bank, the Federal Reserve Bank (Fed), and the European Central Bank are applying an extreme form of expansive monetary policy in which interest rates are lowered to zero percent or even lower for an extended period of time (zero interest rate policy). This monetary policy is controversial and its effects are hardly researchable because the influence of monetary policy on the economy cannot be isolated. Too many other factors are also at play.[73] In addition, the development of growth rates in Japan is raising doubts as to whether there are any positive effects when the zero interest rate policy is applied over an extended period of time. Rather, this policy of cheap money is held partially responsible for bubbles on the stock market[74] all the way to the financial crisis. The accusation is that money is wasted and used for risk-taking when it costs nothing.

Historically, the question is very controversial as to how far a central bank can generate real growth through monetary policy instruments. Monetarism under Milton Friedman rejected this. Monetary policy is only to serve the purpose of ensuring price stability and may only help to cushion external shocks in exceptional cases. Real gross domestic product growth cannot be artificially generated by an expansive monetary policy. Hayek and Wicksell even held the central bank responsible for boom and bust cycles. (Wicksell, 1922; Wicksell, 1898; Hayek, 1935; Friedman & Schwartz, 1969).

Against this background, the effects of interest rate cuts on investment behavior are experimentally examined in this chapter. The method consists in simulating investment decisions under different capital costs. Does the risk appetite of borrowers change if the cost of borrowed capital changes? In Chap. 2 the existing literature and studies are introduced and compared with the experiment carried out. Chap. 3 then explains the

---

[71] See Shleifer, Andrei (2000b), p. 21 as well as Stahl, Markus and Conrad, Christian A. (2000, op. cit., pp. 415–422).

[72] See Conrad, Christian A. (Conrad, 2019).

[73] See for instance Nishad Nishad, Pankaj (2018).

[74] See Conrad, Christian, A. and Stahl, Markus (2002).

experimental design of the study. Finally, the results are presented (Chap. 4) and the conclusions drawn (Chap. 5).

Previous Knowledge

"The more money there is, the better it is for the economy," is the conclusion of most studies on quantitative easing (Gagnon, 2016) and "the lower, the better" for the interest rate. For a long time it was self-evident that nominal interest rates could not fall below zero. This barrier was referred to as the "lower bound." Since the financial crisis, however, scholars have been discussing how the lower bound can be exceeded in order to achieve more economic impulses.

There have been numerous studies on zero interest rate policy or negative interest rate policy. For example, Cúrdia estimates that in the United States, GDP would have fallen by half a percentage point during the recession if the Fed had lowered the interest rate to -0.75% (Cúrdia, 2019). However, the question arises as to what other consequences arise from the subsidization of loans by the central bank. If money is cheap, it can be wasted like any other product. Others argue that low interest rates could lead to asset bubbles by encouraging financial market participants to take on too much risk (Conrad & Stahl, 2002; Caruana, 2013; Feldstein, 2013; Stiglitz, 2016) At low interest rates, investors may try to offset the lower interest income with more risk (Hannoun, 2015). This mechanism is called search for yield. When financial institutions enter into long-term commitments (e.g. pension funds and insurance companies), they come under pressure to achieve the return they have promised for their liabilities. If they only achieve a low interest rate of return on their assets, they may be forced to take on more risk (Rajan, 2005; De Nicolò et al., 2010).

Empirical studies show (e.g. for Spain Maddaloni & Peydró, 2010; Ongena et al., 2009), that credit standards tend to loosen when interest rates decline. Maddaloni et al. (2009) show that credit standards are loosened when the overnight rate declines. De Nicolò et al. (2010) found in a study on US bank policy a negative relationship between the monetary policy rate and the ex-ante risk. The average internal risk rating of banks and the spread over the policy rate decline with rising monetary policy rate. They also examined the relationship between the interest rate and the ratio of the bank's risk-weighted assets to total assets of US commercial banks and bank holding companies based on their quarterly financial statements. They find a strong negative relationship between real interest rates and the risk of the bank's assets. The relationship is weaker when the bank's capital is low.

The expansive monetary policy and the low interest rates, especially the long-term, were held responsible for the credit boom and the excessive risk-taking. The context is as follows. Lower interest rates lead to higher asset values of the borrower, which in turn allows for higher and cheaper credit. Analytical models (Stiglitz & Weiss, 1981) show increased risk-taking when interest rates decline and vice versa a shift to higher quality and more secure investments when interest rates rise.

An easy and cheap money supply promotes risk-taking, which leads to asset bubbles. A later collapse of such bubbles could harm the real economy. If they occur in the housing market, they can lead to write-downs of the claims of the credit institutions and thus to credit bottlenecks, which can seriously affect the real economy (Conrad & Stahl, 2002; Claessens et al., 2012; Mian et al., 2015). Cheap central bank money is seen as the cause of the US housing bubble. The relatively low interest rate in the USA in the period 2001–2004 led to a rapid increase in house prices and the indebtedness of private households (Lansing, 2008; Hirata et al., 2012).

Expansive monetary policy is cited as one of the reasons for the global financial crisis. Sustained low real interest rates and liquidity surpluses led to a boom in asset prices, and collateralized loans and lured financial institutions to take on increased risk and a higher debt-to-GDP ratio. If central banks had raised rates earlier and more aggressively, and if they had preempted this risk-taking, the consequences of the outbreak would have been much less severe (Borio & Zhu, 2008; De Nicolò et al., 2010). In addition, one-sided bonus-based compensation systems encourage excessive risk-taking and were thus another cause of the financial crisis (Conrad, 2015). Claessens and Kose call for further research to be done on how monetary policy affects risk-taking and, as a result, asset prices (Claessens & Kose, 2013).

In this chapter, a simple incentive-based experiment based on roulette is described to investigate investment behavior in relation to credit costs. There have been several experiments with roulette, but with the aim of studying the game behavior (Rubio, Hernández & Santacreu) and the estimation behavior (Rubio et al., 2010). In 2015, there was a roulette experiment that simulated one-sided bonus compensation systems (Conrad, 2015).

Experimental Design
Roulette has the advantage of transparently offsetting the risk of losses through higher payouts. The experiment was conducted with 107 students from various business administration bachelor's programs at the HTW University in Saarbrücken. The students played 3 rounds of roulette (A, B, and C) with three games each. They could bet on red or black, on one of the three thirds of the 36 numbers, or on a number. The winning number and color were determined by the roulette wheel. If it was zero, the game was repeated and not registered. The payouts were distributed according to the probability of winning ($\times 2$, $\times 3$, $\times 36$).

The task was to invest borrowed capital like a company manager. The participants were asked to maximize the profit, as this is the task of a manager as an agent for the principal (owner or shareholder of the company). The maximum profit in the group led to 10 € real money as a variable compensation. In order to reduce behavioral changes due to learning effects, the game consisted of three rounds with three games each. Learning effects should therefore occur early on with little impact.

In order to simulate investment behavior with different interest rates and thus capital costs, decision-makers were exposed to three different investment situations. In round

A they were allowed to borrow up to 10,000 € at 10% interest, in round B at 5% and in round C at 0%. Losses and profits were credited in full. The payouts could be reinvested and were accumulated in each round and then the borrowed capital was deducted. The results of rounds A, B and C were added and the player with the highest result was rewarded with 10 € real money. The rules were explained to the students before the start of the experiment. The students were asked to check the calculations of the other after each game. This simple experiment shows clear results.

Results

The average amount of borrowed capital increased from €5439.93 in Round A to €9931.78 in Round C, an increase of 81.03%. The average amount of capital put into play increased from €7211.05 in Round A to €14,244.15 in Round C, an increase of 97.53% (see Figs. 7.27 and 7.28).

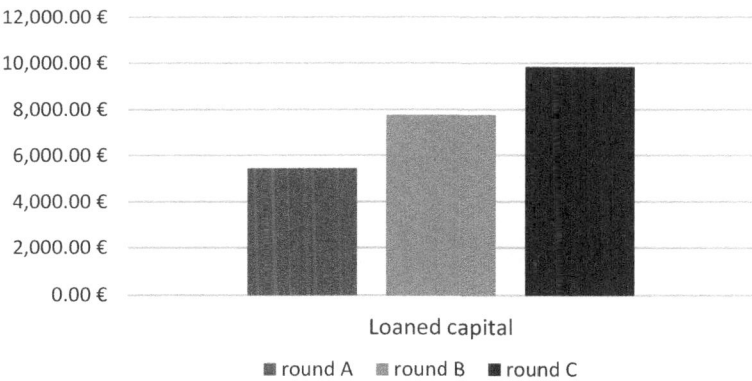

Fig. 7.27 Average amount of borrowed capital

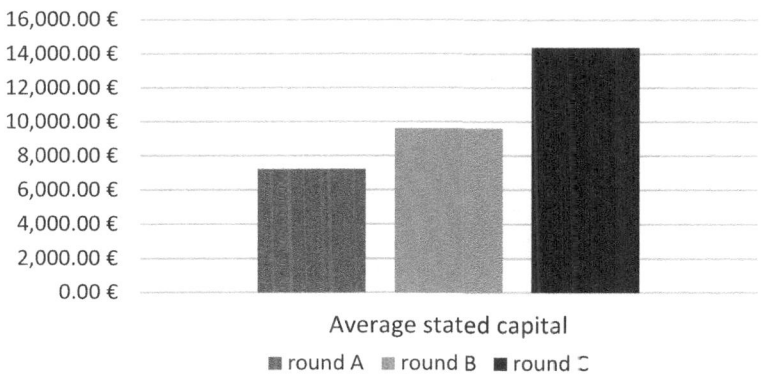

Fig. 7.28 Average amount of capital put into play

What was the risk behavior? The maximum possible profit (calculated as the product of the specified capital and the possible payout multiplier) increased continuously in all three games from 37,483.12 € in round A to 98,754.77 € in round C, i.e. by 163.46% (see Fig. 7.29). The significantly higher standard deviation in round C shows that some players were more willing to take significantly higher risks than the average (see Fig. 7.30).

If we use the maximum possible profit in relation to the specified capital as an indicator of risk appetite, risk appetite increased by 33.27% from 5.20 in round A to 6.89 in round C (see Fig. 7.31). The same trend is shown by the risk indicator maximum possible profit in relation to equity. Risk appetite increased from 6.90 in round A by 46.67% to 10.04 in round C (see Fig. 7.32).

What were the results? How successful were the investors in setting up their capital? The average profits of round A and B with 10% and 5% interest rate remained quite similar (A: €51.68 and B: €63.60), while the students in round C achieved an average loss of €297.66 (see Fig. 7.33).

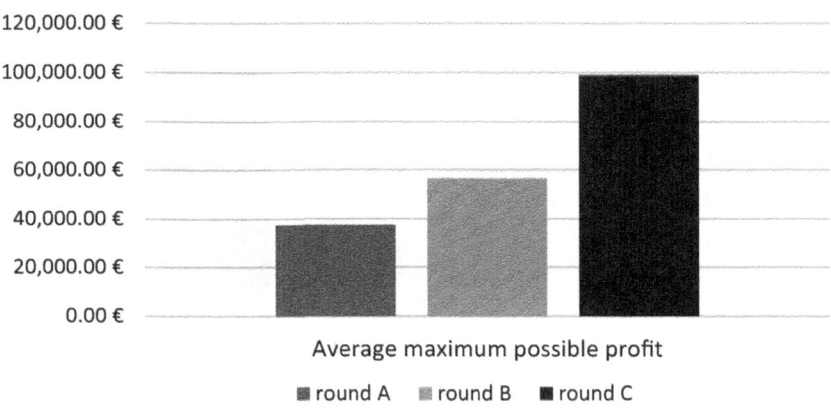

Fig. 7.29 Average maximum possible profit

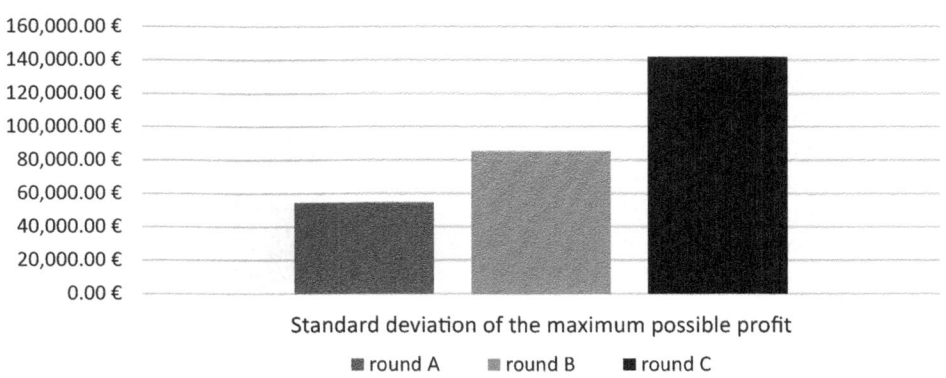

Fig. 7.30 Standard deviation of the maximum possible profit

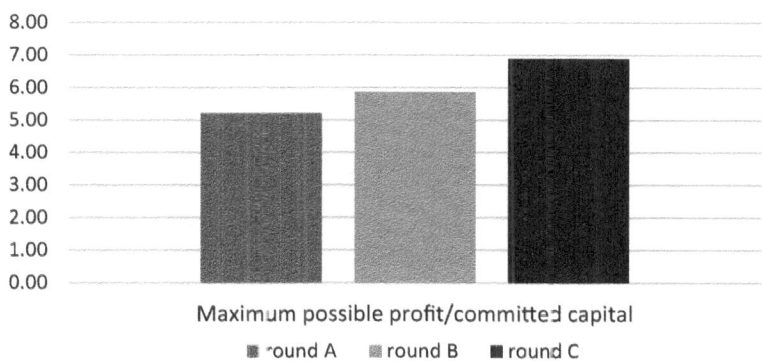

Fig. 7.31   Maximum possible profit in relation to the capital employed

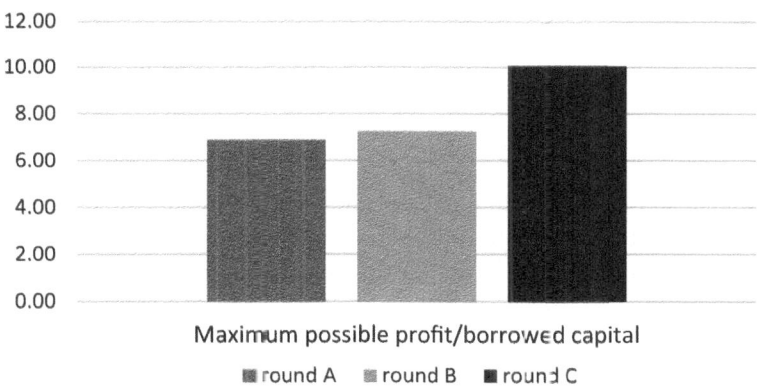

Fig. 7.32   Maximum possible profit in relation to the borrowed capital

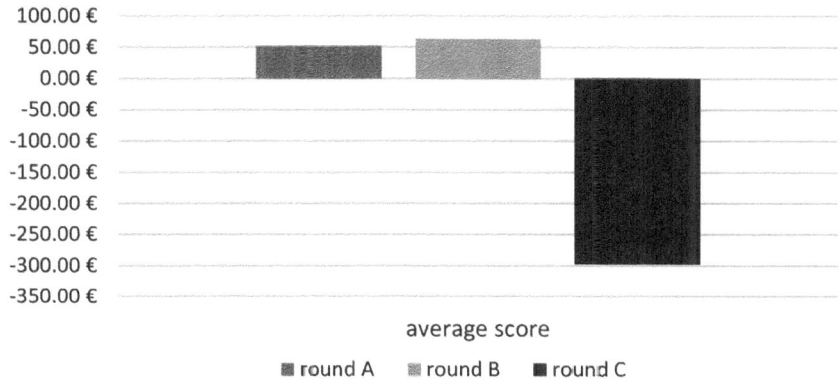

Fig. 7.33   Average player result

Overview Statistical Data

	Round A	Round B	Round C
Average loaned capital	5430.93 €	7759.81 €	9831.78 €
Average set capital	7211.05 €	9617.37 €	14,244.15 €
Average maximum possible profit	37,483.12 €	56,466.74 €	98,754.77 €
Standard deviation of maximum possible profit	54,490.10 €	85,157.77 €	141,764.15 €
Maximum possible profit/set capital	5.2	5.87	6.93
Maximum possible gain/loaned capital	6.90	7.28	10.04
Average player result, +profit, -loss	51.68 €	63.60 €	−297.66 €

Interestingly, as the interest rate as a foreign capital cost decreases, risk-taking behavior increases continuously, so that proportional effects of foreign capital costs on risk-taking behavior result. However, the strongest reaction was found at an interest rate of zero, at which no capital costs were incurred.

Conclusions of the Experiment
The experiment showed that falling interest rates promote the taking of risks. With the decreased interest rate as a foreign capital cost, the taken risk increased weakly but continuously. Risk-taking behavior increased sharply when the interest rate reached zero. The experiment showed excessive risk-taking behavior when no capital costs were incurred. Without capital costs, the average result of the game was a net loss, while previously a small profit was made. If capital is free, people seem to react less rationally. This finding supports the hypothesis that an extremely expansive monetary policy with low, zero, or negative interest rates promotes financial bubbles and over-investment or misinvestment in the real economy. Bank and non-bank investors are less cautious and rational, the lower the capital costs are, and extremely irrational and careless if no costs are incurred at all.

When interest rates are lowered, the risk in the financial system increases. The lower the cost of capital, the higher the return on equity can be increased by debt (leverage effect). With externally financed real estate, the financing costs decrease, which allows a higher purchase price. Real estate prices will rise. Thus, economic actors can be encouraged by low interest rates to take excessive risks in their search for returns, which can lead to the formation of asset bubbles in the stock and real estate markets. If the bubbles are financed by loans, there can be write-downs at the banks in the event of a crash, and as a result, credit crunches and severe economic downturns can occur, as in the Great Depression of 1929 (stock market crash) or the financial crisis of 2008 (US real estate crisis).

In addition, it has been shown (Conrad, 2015) that one-sided incentive systems lead to excessive risk-taking by managers. If they are involved in the profits but not in the losses, they take high risks that lead to losses in the long term at their employers. Low interest rates allow high profits to be generated through strong debt. Such one-sided compensation systems were a reason for the financial crisis.

After the financial crisis, many central banks relied on quantitative easing (QE) to support economic growth. To lower the long-term cost of capital, they bought large amounts of long-term bonds, creating liquidity and lowering long-term capital costs. Some central banks have even slightly pushed short-term interest rates below zero to stimulate the economy. However, the slow economic recovery, especially in Europe, and the risks associated with such a policy, as shown in this chapter, call into question the usefulness of QE bond purchases.

Japan's example should make us think. Japan is a pioneer of zero interest rate policy and quantitative easing. In 2001 and 2013, the Bank of Japan introduced quantitative easing and zero interest rates. Neither was able to sustainably boost the economy nor increase inflation (Drozd, 2018). When pursuing an inflation target, it is often forgotten that we are in a long phase of globalization with falling import prices. In particular, the goods produced in China depress the prices of many consumer goods.

The question remains why the long period of low interest rates in Japan did not lead to a second bubble. A bubble requires a constant inflow of liquidity that is financed by loans. After the real estate and stock market crash in Japan in the 1980s, Japanese banks still had a lot of bad loans on their books. They were not recapitalized, and therefore they lacked the equity for real estate and corporate loans. Rather, one spoke at that time of a credit crunch, because the Japanese banks and the real economy hardly granted any loans due to the lack of equity, which is why the economy stagnated at a low level. Dell'Ariccia et al. (2013) showed that the extent of bank capitalization seems to be an important factor for the recovery. They found that a well-capitalized bank is more willing to grant loans, reduce its supervision and take more risks when interest rates are lower, while a highly indebted, low-capitalized bank does the opposite (Dell'Ariccia et al., 2010; Claessens & Kose, 2013). If the ECB wants to promote the European economy, it would be better to work towards writing off bad loans and recapitalizing European banks.

Aside from the shift to higher-yielding assets, there are many market distortions due to central bank intervention. If the interest rate is below the inflation rate, there are redistribution effects from creditors to debtors. Insurance companies and pension funds do not have enough income to meet their obligations. Money market funds may not earn enough to cover their operating costs. The population's retirement becomes a problem because there is a lack of interest income. Banks lack float income from lending and the margin between investment and lending rates. Negative investment rates are not usually enforceable in the market and at a refinancing rate of zero there is also no high credit margin (Arteta et al., 2016). Therefore, a reduction in interest rates means a reduction in net interest margins—the difference between banks' lending and deposit rates. In several studies, a positive relationship has been found between short-term central bank interest rates and net interest margins. A low interest rate environment affects the profitability of banks (Claessens et al., 2016; Borio et al., 2015).

In the bank survey from April 2016, a decline in European bank profits due to low interest rates and quantitative easing was already observed (Arteta et al., 2016). If banks do not have income, there is also a lack of equity to weather crises. Therefore, zero interest rate policy is counterproductive. When the central bank buys corporate and government bonds, it also displaces commercial banks from this market, since it lacks the know-how to manage corporate risks. The financing of companies by state organizations is not market-oriented, but typical of central planning economies.

All studies assume an interest rate sensitivity of investments. As we know from the world economic crisis of 1929, this does not have to be the case. If expectations of the return on capital are negative, interest rates would have to be so negative that they more than offset the losses of the investment. But then it would be less risky for companies to not invest the borrowed money, but to consider the negative interest rates of the central bank as a safe return.

The expectations for the return on capital do not have to be negative solely because of the poor economic expectations, but can also be due to a lack of competitiveness. For example, despite zero interest rates, no one would invest in Greek hotels if the comparable Mediterranean vacation in Portugal is much cheaper due to lower labor costs.

Falling interest rates, on the other hand, always affect stock and real estate prices. On the one hand, they are the alternative investment to bonds and, on the other hand, they can be financed by loans. If the cost of credit decreases, the present value of real estate and stocks increases. The demand for stocks and real estate, and thus also the price, will increase. The profit of the companies increases due to lower interest rates on external financing, which also increases the demand for stocks and thus the price.

In summary, it can be said that the side effects of an extremely expansive monetary policy such as a zero interest rate policy, a negative interest rate policy or quantitative easing are so great that such an intervention in the markets is only justified in a Keynesian depression situation (Great Depression) like 1929 and 2008 and only for a limited time. We can only warn against the most recent proposals that propagate the decoupling of cash from electronic money and call for the devaluation of cash against the electronic currency in order to be able to lower interest rates further into the negative range (Assenmacher & Krogstrup, 2018). This would have negative consequences that are not foreseeable.

7.9.6 The Effects of Money Supply and Interest Rates on Stock Prices, Evidence from Two Behavioral Experiments

What is the impact of interest rate and monetary policy on the stock market? Some studies find a positive impact of expansive monetary policy on stock prices others prove the opposite. The following chapter examines the effects of monetary expansion and interest rate changes on investment behavior on the stock market by illustrating two behavioral experiments with students (Conrad, 2021). In our experiments the increase of money supply and the decrease of interest rates had a direct positive impact on share prices. These findings support the hypothesis that extreme expansive monetary policy with low, zero or negative interest rates encourage financial bubbles on the stock market. To avoid a crash the exit from such a policy must be slow. As happened in 1929, crashes can damage the financial system and the real economy. Central banks must take this into account in their monetary policy.

Introduction

After the financial crisis and now in the Covid-19 crisis many central banks turned to quantitative easing (QE) to support economic growth. In order to reduce long-term borrowing costs they purchased massive and unprecedented amounts of long-term bonds, which created liquidity and decreased the long term borrowing costs. Some central banks even pushed short-term interest rates slightly below zero to stimulate the economy. But the slow recovery, especially in Europe, has raised questions about the benefits of QE bond purchases versus their detriments and whether their effectiveness has reached a limit. What is the impact of such an expansive monetary policy on the stock market? Empirical studies contradict each other. Some find a positive impact of expansive monetary policy on stock prices others prove the opposite. Against such a background this chapter examines the effects of monetary expansion and interest rate changes on investment behavior on the stock market by illustrating two behavioral experiments with students. The existing literature and studies are presented and compared to the experiment presented here. Next the experimental design of the study is explained. Finally, the results are presented and the conclusions drawn (Conrad, 2021).

Related Literature
Theoretical background

A positive correlation between the two variables money supply and stock prices can be interpreted in three different ways. Firstly, there is an ex post correlation when the stock prices increased due to higher productivity in real economy and the central bank provided the money needed to prevent deflation. Secondly, an increase in money supply, e.g. liquidity, leads to portfolio adoptions on the part of the stockholder, to realize the desired proportion of liquidity and assets. The stockholders have more money to buy assets, which leads to an increase in stock prices providing a constant amount of stocks. Thirdly, increased money supply leads to lower interest rates and thereby lowers the discount rate on future cash flows from an enterprise's expected profits. Interest is a main part of production and investing costs of enterprises, therefore lower interest rates means higher profits (Baks & Kramer, 1999; International Monetary Fund, 2000). In addition, others argue that low interest rate policy could lead to a buildup of leverage, or asset bubbles by encouraging excessive risk taking by financial market participants (Caruana, 2013; Conrad & Stahl, 2002; Feldstein, 2013; Stiglitz, 2016). Confronted with low interest rates bank and non-bank investors may switch to excessive risk in order to compensate the smaller interest income (Hannoun, 2015). The mechanism is called "search for yield". If financial institutions have long-term commitments (such as pension funds and insurance companies) they come under pressure to earn the yield they promised on their liabilities. If they obtain only a low interest return on their assets they might be forced to go in risk (De Nicolò, Dell'Ariccia, Laeven, & Valencia, 2010; Rajan, 2005) and purchase stocks instead of bonds. Unilaterally constructed bonus-based compensation schemes encourage excessive risk-taking and were one reason for the financial crisis (Conrad, 2015). However, only one paper examined the effects of interest rate cuts on investment behavior. This behavioral experiment with students showed that decreasing interest rates encourage risk-taking (Conrad, 2019).

The roots of the boom and bust cycle theory go back to Hayek and Wicksell. Friedrich August von Hayek holds the tremendous elasticity of the banking system and the unregulated money supply development responsible for the economy overheating (Hayek, 1935, 1976). Knut Wicksell on the other hand, lays the blame at the doorstep of the monetary policy decision-makers and their poor decisions regarding interest controls (Grosskettler, 1989; Wicksell, 1922, 1968). A set interest level on the capital market below that for the supply and demand balance causes an expansion of the money supply. In specific, the exchange relation of goods to money tips in favor of money. The demand for credit increases because of the low interest level. New current account deposits come into existence through the increased credit. The speed of money circulation increases, and with it the money supply. There is a shift in portfolios, since the value of the investor's liquidity increases relative to the stocks owned. The new money flows into the stock markets and pushes the stock prices ever upwards. Because the interest functions as both an asset yield and a discount factor it brings about an artificial interest reduction in an upswing of the stock price as well as an excessive resource allocation in stock value. This effect can cause the system to overheat. The higher stock prices signify profit potential and represent security to the banks that allows them to grant credit and thus indirectly create money. A self-propagating upward movement is created on the stock market, which supports a boom through excessive liquidity supply from the central banks. Should the central bank reverse interest rate decreases, the same effect in the reverse direction will occur (Conrad, 2000).

Empirical studies

There are empirical studies about the impact of interest rates on stock market prices. According to Thorbecke (1997), stock prices decline by 0.8% if federal funds rate increases unexpectedly by 1%. Rigobon and Sack (2004) estimated that stock index S&P 500 loses 1.7% because of 3-month rate increases of 0.25% and found a higher effect for Nasdaq index (2.4% decrease).

   Trust Kganyago and Victor Gumbo tested the long-term relationship between money market interest rates and stock market returns in Zimbabwe from April 2009 to December 2013. The estimation model controls for money supply growth rate, inflation, volume of manufacturing index, crude oil price and political stability. They found evidence of a strong and statistically significant inverse causal relationship between money market interest and stock market returns (Kganyago & Gumbo, 2015).

   The relationship between money supply development and asset prices has been examined in several empirical studies. Using the increase in Japanese stock, art and real estate prices in the second half of the 1980s as an example, empirical studies have shown that the catalyst for the bubble was an expansive monetary policy in conjunction with a productivity increase in the Japanese economy and an higher demand for real estate in Tokyo; all of which expressed itself in more credit given by the banks (Ito & Iwaisako, 1995). In the first half of the 1990s the prices mostly fell back to their original level. Ito and Iwaisako (1995) establish further, that the increase in prices can be explained with fundamental changes in data only until 1987, at which point the bubble took on a life of its own. By Homa and Jaffee (1971) had already found a significant and systematic relationship between stock prices and money supply as represented by deposits and currency. Rozeff (1974) showed that both money supply and M1 aggregate can impact stock prices; a finding which was later supported by Flannery and Protopapadakis (2002). Lastrapes (1998) estimates that stock prices fall off by 2.4% if M1 is reduced by 1%. Safar and Siničáková (2017) prove statistically significant influence of money supply on stock market indices in the US and EU. Pícha (2017) found an influence of money supply on valuation of S&P 500 indices with a 6 month lag. According to the International Monetary Fund further analyses show a positive correlation between the variables money supply and stock prices (Baks & Kramer, 1999; International Monetary Fund, 2000). However, other studies have come to contradictory conclusions. Black (1987) found that changes in money supply do not influence stock prices. Campbell and Ammer (1993) came to the conclusion that money supply has only minimal effect on stocks prices.

   How can these controversial findings be explained? We have fundamental method problems here. The scientific content of the predominantly Granger-based econometric studies has to be questioned. Because of the risk of false results, the Granger test is discouraged if the variables under study are extremely volatile (Irwin & Sanders, 2012). For highly volatile variables such as stock prices, a lack of covariance stationarity was found, which does not provide a condition for the regression of time series (Conrad, 2020; Frenk, 2011; Pagan & Schwert, 1990; Phillips & Loretan, 1990; Schlecker, 2014). Due to innumerable influencing factors on supply and demand, we have a strong multi-causality here in which the individual influencing factors cannot be filtered out precisely. If causal variables are not extracted, Granger tests can show correlations that are not present (spurious regression). The same applies to purely random correlations, which may arise in particular in the case of short observation periods or incorrect time intervals (Frenk, 2011).

Against this background, we decided to analyze the relationship between money, interest rate and stock markets with a behavioral experiment as an alternative scientific method. This should give additional evidence.

Experimental Design

We want to answer two questions:

A. How does the investor react on the stock market if the money supply is changed? Some studies find a positive impact of expansive monetary policy on stock prices while others prove the opposite. However, as most studies show a positive impact we use this as hypothesis.
B. How do the investors react on the stock market if the save interest rate of bonds as an alternative investment is changed and how is the profit of the stock market companies, and therefore also the dividends influenced by the interest rate as cost of borrowed capital? We test the assumption of the portfolio-theory that not only risk but also yield is decisive for the allocation of invested capital.

The purpose of this chapter is to test the hypothesis that:

A. an increase of money supply leads to higher share prices and encourages bubbles with a subsequent crash when money supply is reduced (boom and bust cycle).
B. interest rates influence capital allocation as per the portfolio-theory that capital follows the yield. Thus, bonds are the alternative of shares and vice versa. A decrease in the interest rate should therefore lead to higher share prices and vice versa. Interest rates also influence the cost of capital borrowed from the enterprises. Therefore, lower interest rates lead to higher profits and dividends.

How do the money supply and interest rates affect investment behavior? The methodology was to simulate investment decision making on the stock market under different money supply and interest rates. We conducted two experiments, A and B:

Two experiments, A and B, were conducted in the winter semester of 2019/20 with different groups but were terminated due to the Covid 19 pandemic. There were 56 participants in game A and 43 students in game B, who came from different Business Bachelor courses at the University of Applied Science HTW at Saarbrücken, Germany. Most investment capital is controlled and allocated by agents for third persons. There are family offices, investment firms, fund managers and the managers of companies. The task was to invest capital like an investment agent or a manager of a company. The participants were asked to maximize profit, which is the obligation of a manager as agent for a principal (company owner resp. shareholder). Maximal profit in the group resulted in 10 € real money as variable compensation. The rules were explained to the students before starting the experiment. The students were asked to check each other's calculations after each game.

Game A: Money supply and stocks

Game A aimed to examine how money supply affects the demand for stocks. Apart from stocks, there was only the alternative of holding money as liquidity without interest. The shares did not distribute any dividends.

Students were to invest their money in stocks or hold cash. Ten shares in the fictional corporation Rancom LC with a nominal value of €100 each were added per round. The shares were auctioned every round. The students were informed of the additional amount of money that they had at their disposal each round as a result of the monetary policy of the central bank. They could sell or buy the shares through the lecturer who would auction them off (stock exchange). The highest bids were accepted. The respective maximum price was set as the share price. Sales were served first and settled according to the available bids. Up to round 5 the money supply was doubled. The last two rounds it stayed the same.

Game B: Interest rate and stocks

Game B aimed to examine how interest rates affect the stock's attractiveness as an alternative investment. Two factors affect the investor here. On the one hand, the interest rate is the return on bonds as safe investment, and on the other, it determines the cost of debt and thus also the profit and dividend of the stock corporation. Students were to invest their money in stocks or fixed deposits. There was an initial stock of 0 shares in Rancom LC with a nominal value of €300 (€300 equity and €600 debt). Each round, €1000 were added per player and 10 shares were auctioned off so that stocks and money increased roughly proportionally. The return on capital employed was a constant €60, or 6.67%. The interest rates, which the central bank set as the base rate, were communicated to the students every round. Likewise, the price to earnings ratio and the dividends changed every round in accordance with the change in the cost of debt of Rancom AG. Representing the earnings situation, the students were informed of the dividend yield as a 50% distribution of the profit. Students could invest an amount of money at the relevant interest rate, or sell or buy the shares through the lecturer who would auction them off. The highest bids were accepted. The respective maximum price was set as the share price. Sales were served first and settled according to the available bids. At the end of each round the interest and dividends were added as yield to the invested capital.

These simple experiments show clear results.

Results

Game A: amount of money and stocks

Figure 7.34 shows the development of the money supply and the average bid as share prices and Fig. 7.35 the development of the liquidity on hand (which is the average cash held by the students at the end of each round) and the average share bids of the students. We can see a positive relation between money and share price. In addition, the mere stop of monetary expansion in round 5 created a stock market crash if we look at the average bids which would be relevant for the stock market development. Starting in round 5 we

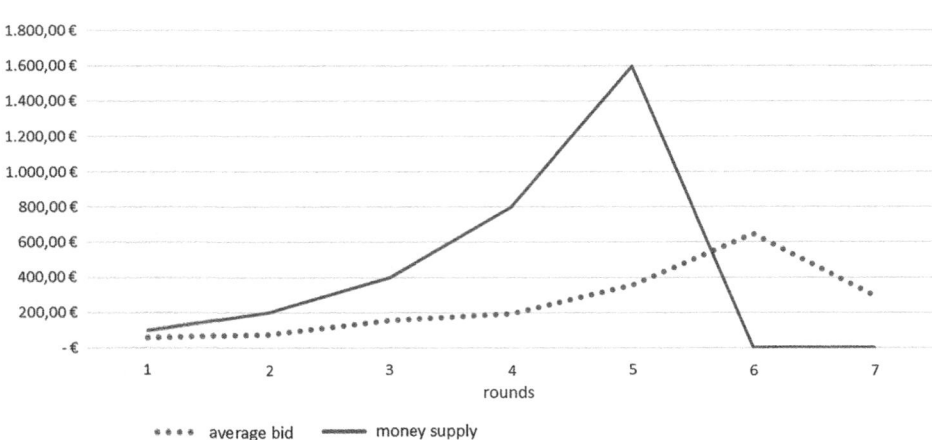

Fig. 7.34 Money supply and average bid

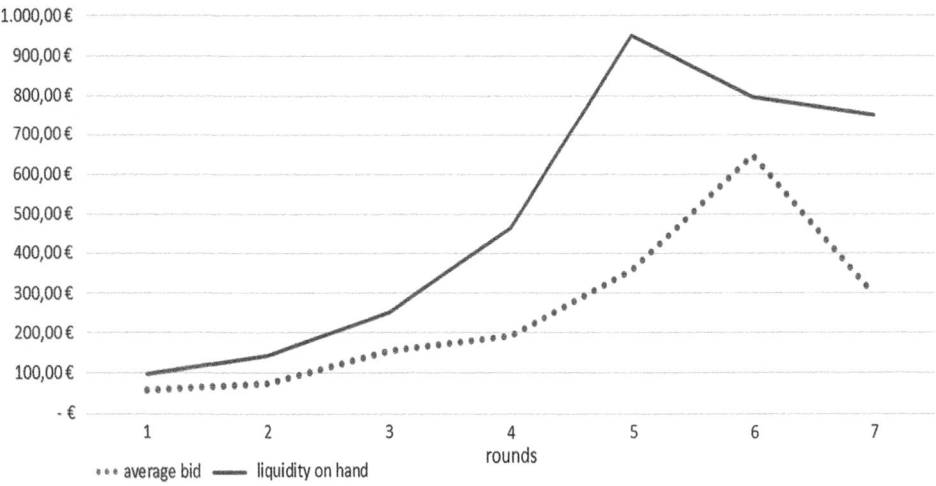

Fig. 7.35 Liquidity on hand and average share bids

see a slow reaction of the bids. Even though the money supply drops the bids first stay high.

Conclusion Game A

In our experiment money supply had a direct positive impact on share prices. The hypothesis was not disproven and seems to be true. Central banks have a strong responsibility for the stock market if they increase the money supply disproportionately to the real production. If there has been an expansive monetary policy followed by increasing stock prices, the exit of this policy must be done slowly, otherwise a crash might follow.

Game B: interest rate and stocks

The interest rates were first decreased and then increased (see Fig. 7.36). The dividends were adapted according to the changed-borrowing cost of Rancom LC due to the changes in the interest rate (Fig. 7.37), also the price to earning ratios were adapted (Fig. 7.38).

Share prices were clearly driven by the interest rate reduction, which resulted in higher earnings and dividends (Fig. 7.37). The students adjusted their portfolio according to the changed yield relation between shares and fixed deposits even though the shares were more risky. The sharp increase in interest rates in round 7 led to a stock market crash (see Fig. 7.30) due to quick portfolio adjustments (see Fig. 7.39). And the crash resulted in a strong decrease of the asset value of shares (see Fig. 7.40).

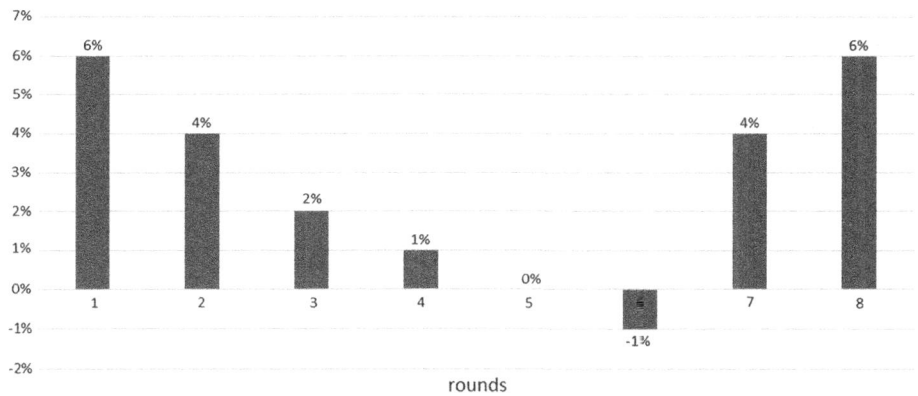

Fig. 7.36   Interest rates

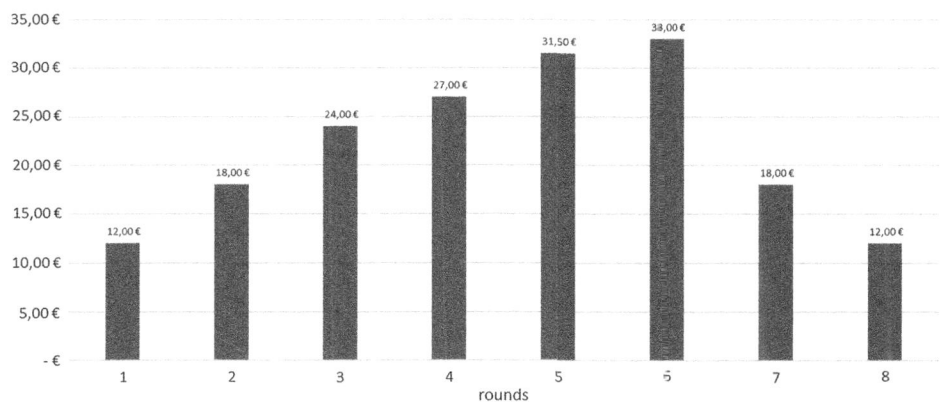

Fig. 7.37   Dividends

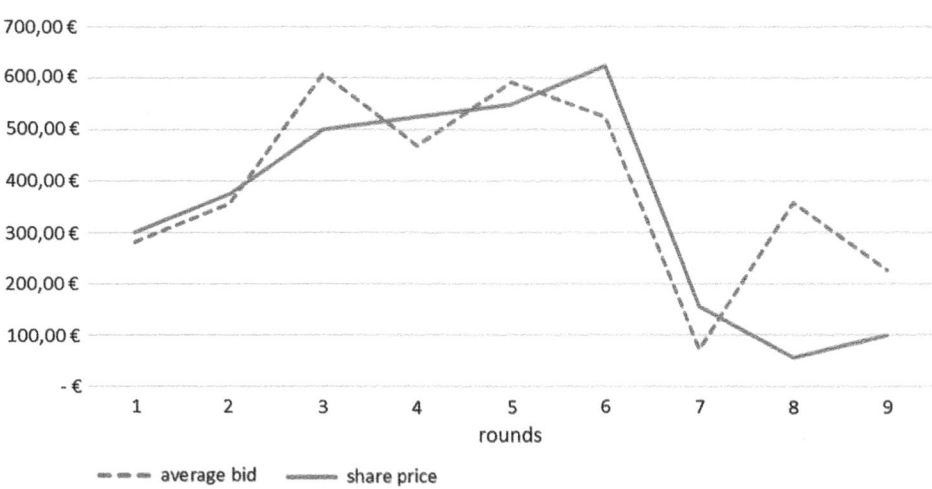

Fig. 7.38 Average bids and share prices

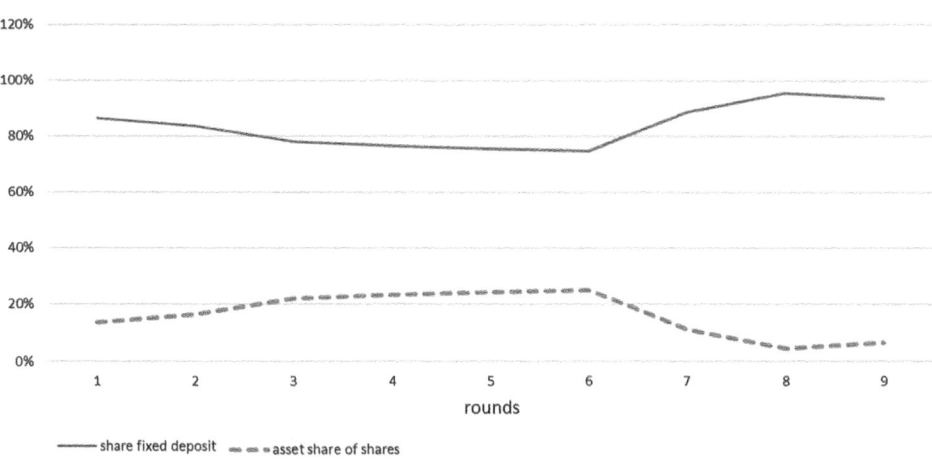

Fig. 7.39 Asset share of shares and fixed deposits

The buying of the shares seemed to be consistent and rational as the dividends and earnings increased. The price to earning ratio shows that the impact of the lower interest rates compensated the higher share prices (see Fig. 7.41) as borrowing cost decreased and thus the earnings increased.

Conclusion Game B

Our hypothesis was not proven false, as the interest rates influenced the capital allocation according to the portfolio-theory. The students invested in the stocks as assets with

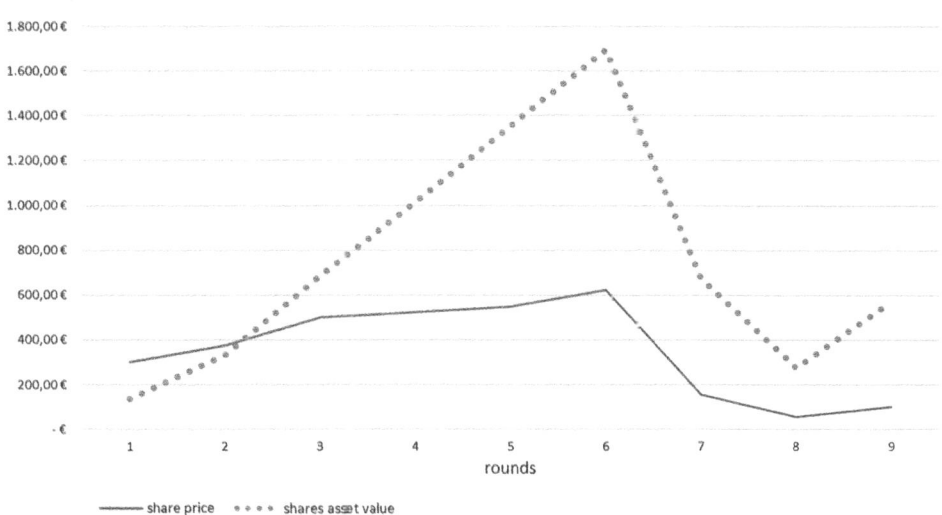

Fig. 7.40 Share prices and the asset value of shares

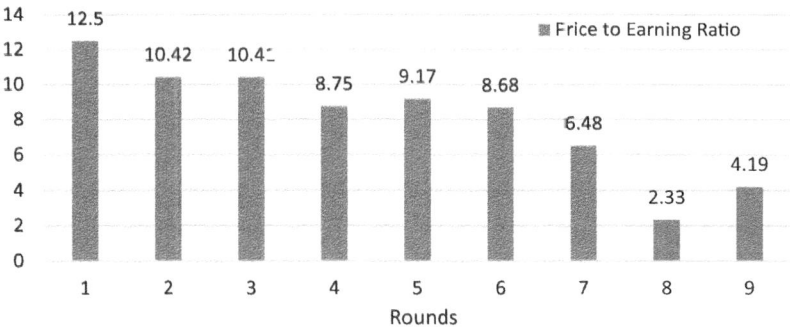

Fig. 7.41 Price to Earning Ratio

higher yields as the interest rate dropped and dividends rose. The higher risk of the shares was not a hindrance. The yield from bonds is the alternative of shares and vice versa. A decrease in interest rate led in the experiment to higher share prices and vice versa. In addition, the interest rates influenced the cost of borrowed capital for the enterprises. Therefore, lower interest rates led to higher profits and dividends.

Share prices were clearly driven by the interest rate reduction, which resulted in higher earnings and dividends. The price to earning ratio is deceptive in that the impact of the lower interest rates compensated the higher share prices even though the profit of the core business activities stayed the same. In our experiments we had an increase in profits of 100% as a reaction to a 66% interest rate reduction, thus an elasticity of 1.5.

Thus price to earning ratios are not an adequate pricing tool and cannot help to detect a stock market bubble. The sharp increase in interest rates in round 7 led to a stock market crash due to quick portfolio adjustments. And the crash resulted in a strong decrease of the share asset value.

Final Conclusion

In our experiments the increase of money supply and the decrease of interest rates had a direct positive impact on share prices. All groups show similar behavior and the games may be repeated and reviewed by other scientists in the future. Moreover, the sharp increase in interest rates and the stoppage of money supply increase led to a stock market crash due to quick portfolio adjustments. The crash resulted in a strong decrease of the asset value of shares. Therefore, the central banks must keep in mind that the interest rates do not just influence the investments in the real economy. Boom and bust cycles are a real danger of an expansive monetary policy with low interest rates. If there has been an expansive monetary policy or strong interest rate cuts followed by increasing stock process, the exit from this policy has to be slow to prevent a subsequent crash (boom and bust cycle). Central banks have a responsibility for the stock market if they increase the money supply disproportionately to the real production and intervene in the money market or even in the capital market by a QE-policy. The question if it is wise to do so at all has to be discussed separately.

In addition, the measurement of inflation has to be discussed. The inflation measures used by central banks mainly include consumer goods prices and producer prices. Price developments in the financial sector and asset prices (asset prices) are thus systematically hidden by the measurement method. So it is possible that excessive money production is reflected not in rising prices for consumer goods, but in asset price volatility. If only consumer goods prices are considered, this can lead to unpredictable inflation (Mezger & Stahl, 2001; Conrad, C. A. & Stahl, M., 2002).

Experiment B showed that decreasing interest rates encourage risk taking. The portfolio theory was true in our experiments. Interest rate cuts led to a shift towards shares as an alternative asset with higher yield. The higher risk of the shares was not a hindrance. The mechanism "search for yield" took place. The students reacted to the lower interest rates by taking on risk.

Share prices were clearly driven by the interest rate reduction, which resulted in higher earnings and dividends. The price to earning ratio is deceptive in that the impact of the lower interest rates compensated the higher share prices even though the profit of the core business activities stayed the same. Thus price to earning ratios are not an adequate pricing tool and cannot help to detect a stock market bubble. The valuation indicators for equities would have to be adjusted for the refinancing costs. Even a smooth price-earnings ratio like that of Shiller (CAPE, Cycle-Adjusted Price Earnings Ratio) could be distorted by a prolonged period of low interest rates.

The results of our experiments show that money supply and interest rates not only influence investments in the real economy, they also have a direct impact on the stock markets and tend to favor speculative bubbles. To avoid a crash the exit from such a policy must be slow. As happened in 1929, crashes can damage the financial system and the real economy. Central banks must take this into account in their monetary policy.

7.9.7 Monetary Policy Conclusion

We can conclude the following recommendations for monetary policy:

1. Potential-oriented, rule-based monetary policy
   Since asset prices are mainly influenced by expectations and at the same time expectations about future monetary policy play a very central role, a monetary policy that is as constant and potential-oriented as possible is to be recommended. It contributes significantly to the stabilization of expectations. With an orientation of the money supply to the development of gross domestic product and production potential, a money supply surplus that supports a stock market bubble is no longer possible.
2. Inclusion of asset prices as additional indicators for monetary policy steering
   Asset prices should be integrated into the models of central banks as an "inflation early indicator" in order to make rule-based counter-steering possible. This includes informing the public about the development of the indicators. The investors would anticipate the counter-steering of the central bank in the event of a deviation of the indicators and would no longer speculate on a rise in prices. This would also counteract a bubble.
3. No bail-outs
   The rule-based monetary policy also includes the consistent implementation of the basic principle of liability and thus also a renunciation of explicit or implicit bail-out promises. If investors can no longer shift the speculation risk to the central bank, this counteracts a self-reinforcing speculation. On the other hand, the rule-based automatisms described above must ensure in advance that there is no asset bubble that would endanger the system and require a bail-out.
4. Flanking of monetary policy by measures of banking and stock market supervision:
   a) By lowering the lending rate for stock loans (i.e. the percentage of stocks used as collateral for lending) the demand for stocks could be reduced in the event of an overheated stock market.
   b) An increase in the amount of collateral required by regulatory authorities, so-called "margins", would reduce the leverage of derivatives on the demand for stocks.

c) The inclusion of previously unregulated market participants, such as hedge funds
   and offshore banks, in financial market supervision and capital requirements would
   prevent the risk of the spread of financial market crises (see also Chap. 8).

With these measures, bubbles can not be prevented, but their development can be coun-
tered earlier.[75]

7.10   Psychological Factors as a Cause of the Business Cycle

7.10.1 Adaptive Expectations in Monetarist Theories

Monetarist theories of the business cycle are, in a narrow sense, not business cycle
theories, because they only explain nominal national product fluctuations, and not real
fluctuations in the utilization of production potential. The two best-known monetarist
approaches are those of FRIEDMAN[76] and LAIDLER[77] FRIEDMAN reinterprets the
quantity theory of money, basing himself on empirical studies which assume that the
interest rate has a negligible effect on money demand. Consequently, nominal income
is proportional to the money supply through the velocity of circulation, and the velocity
of circulation is a stable function of the inflation rate. Economic subjects have a given
portfolio structure of assets with a transaction-related demand for cash which depends on
real income. Equilibrium is disturbed by an increase in the money supply, which is not
immediately noticed by economic subjects, but only later (adaptive expectations). The
increase in the money supply causes an increase in the cash holdings of economic subjects above the desired level. The difference is directly used for consumption demand
or, first, for capital supply and then for investment demand. With a given production,
only nominal income rises as a result of the price level increase. Economic subjects correct their inflation expectations upwards and react with a shorter cash-holding duration
(higher velocity of circulation), which leads to a further increase in nominal income
(overshooting). In the course of time, inflation expectations equal the actual inflation
rate, so that fluctuations in nominal income decrease. Consequently, this is a market-
clearing model or shock reaction model, with which a complete business cycle cannot be

---

[75] See Markus Stahl and Christian A. Conrad 2000, pp. 383–385 and Conrad, Christian, A. and
Stahl, Markus (2002).

[76] See Friedman, M. (1970); Heubes, Jürgen (1991, pp. 84 ff.) as well as Teichmann, Ulrich (1997,
p. 20).

[77] See Laidler, D. (1976a); Laidler, D. (1976b); Heubes, Jürgen (1991, pp. 87 ff.) as well as Teichmann, Ulrich (1997, p. 21).

simulated. FRIEDMAN tries to circumvent this limitation by assuming regular monetary shocks. However, FRIEDMAN does not represent the real effects of the shocks.

LAIDLER fills this gap by connecting the monetary and the real sector via the Phillips curve. Real income results from the utilization of the labor potential. The money supply is exogenously given; the money demand depends positively on real income and price level. As with FRIEDMANN, the Phillips curve is based on the assumption of adaptive inflation expectations and thus a delayed wage reaction. In the long run, changes in money supply have no effect on the real sector. The old equilibrium with a constant natural unemployment rate and inflation rate, which results from the difference between the money supply growth rate and the income growth rate, is always reestablished. Short-term, unexpected increases in money supply lead to an increase in employment levels as a result of the money illusion of workers. As with FRIEDMANN, monetary shocks must occur regularly in order to represent a business cycle. The real sector then reacts to the expansion or contraction depending on the prevailing expectations.

7.10.2 Fluctuations in Demand Due to Incorrect Adjustment Reactions: The Original Approach of New Classical Macroeconomics

New Classical Macroeconomics has been further developed in numerous publications and goes back to LUCAS (1975), MCCALLUM (1980) and BARRO (1981).[78] The approaches are a response to the criticism of the assumption of constant coefficients within structural econometric models expressed by LUCAS (1976). Given the systematic changes of exogenous policy variables actually observed, this is unrealistic (Lucas Criticism).[79] Within New Classical Macroeconomics, therefore, the exogenous change of policy variables is a main determinant of the business cycle. New Classical Macroeconomics can be divided into exogenous and endogenous approaches. Within the exogenous approaches one differentiates again according to the type of external business cycle cause into monetary theories, in which the money supply is the exogenous cause, and Real Business Cycle theories, which see real shocks as the business cycle determining factor. The endogenous theories have an nonlinear internal dynamics (intrinsic dynamics, Chaos Theory) or explain the business cycles by means of a modified theory of rational expectations (Sunspot Theories).[30]

---

[78] For New Classical Macroeconomics see Assenmacher, Walter (1998, pp. 302 ff.); Ramser, H. J. (1988, pp. 96 ff.); Lucas, R.E. (1975); McCallum (1980); Barrc, R.J. (1981); Tichy G. (1995, pp. 185 ff.); Minford, Patrick and Peel, David (1983) as well as Fischer, S. (1980).

[79] See Lucas, R.E. Jr. (1976) as well as McCallum, B.T. (1980).

[80] See Heubes, Jürgen (1991, pp. 83 ff.) as well as Assenmacher, Walter (1998, pp. 301 ff.).

The basic assumptions are the existence of a long-term equilibrium state and rational expectations in the sense of subjective formal rationality. The latter point is where the difference lies from monetarist models, which basically assume adaptive expectations. The economic subjects have a non-contradictory goal system and optimize their decisions on the basis of their subjective image of the economic framework conditions. They use all the information available to them. However, the information is incomplete (asymmetrically distributed), so that a situation of uncertainty prevails. The economic subjects are informed about the basic macroeconomic relationships, i.e. they do not make systematic errors.

Due to the incomplete information about the economic framework conditions, the economic subjects make wrong decisions. Two types of irritations are distinguished here: the permanent-transitory confusion and the absolute-relative confusion. With permanent-transitory confusion, economic subjects cannot tell whether a change in monetary indicators is permanent or only temporary. If, however, economic subjects cannot tell whether relative prices or the overall price level are rising, this is called absolute-relative confusion. The uncertainty is increased by the assumption of an overall and stochastically fluctuating state demand on the part of the state. This implies that only unexpected changes in the money supply can influence real variables. Economic subjects are fully informed about money supply changes initiated by politics. They are therefore anticipated and have no effect (policy ineffectiveness hypothesis). Only unsystematic changes in the money supply can lead to misjudgments and thus to real adjustments.

Further, it is assumed that a market equilibrium always automatically adjusts in the long term. Consequently, business cycle fluctuations can only be caused by exogenous factors. Exogenous, time-delayed, unexpected monetary shocks (e.g., money supply mismanagement, imported inflation at fixed exchange rates, short-term monetary pressures due to international agreements, such as the G8) lead to changes in monetary indicators (prices, interest rates). The data changes are misinterpreted by economic actors. The real adjustment reactions of economic actors triggered thereby differ depending on the underlying type of confusion. For example, an absolute-relative confusion leads the economic actors to expand production $[Y = Y (p)]$, whereas a permanent-transitory confusion can cause an expansion in investment due to the lower interest rate. There is a self-reinforcing (cumulative) upward process. After some time, the economic actors recognize in the absolute-relative confusion that all prices—including those of their own intermediate products—are rising, not just those of their own final products. They then revise their expansive production decision. In the case of the permanent-transitory confusion, a correction of the data changes made by the political decision-makers takes place in the medium term. The money supply expansion or interest rate cut is reversed, whereupon the economic actors also correct their decisions. The correction of the decisions triggers contractionary effects, which initiate a cumulative process downwards.

New Classical Macroeconomics thus provides a transmission mechanism between the monetary and real sector and thus also an explanation for the empirically observed positive correlation between money supply and real national product. However, the general assumption of the New Classical Macroeconomics of a complete market clearing is critically to be questioned. The wage and price mechanism always works. There is therefore no involuntary unemployment. This hypothesis is in contrast to the empirically observed short-term wage and price rigidities. Furthermore, in the New Classical Macroeconomics, irritations can immediately result in an increase in production. This means that there must always be underutilization or a time lag of zero assumed, which is both unrealistic. Also, the assumption of isolated market behavior in the absolute-relative confusion appears to be unrealistic in today's generally accessible information, especially since economic agents usually act on several markets at the same time.[81] In general, all procyclical "stylized facts" can be explained with the New Classical Macroeconomics. They occur as a result of the confusion in the cumulative upward process. However, the New Classical Macroeconomics cannot explain business cycles, but only short-term deviations from equilibrium, which are corrected again (persistence problem). The business cycle fluctuations as a result of the adjustment reactions lead back to the Pareto-optimal equilibrium. Another, neglected by the New Classical Macroeconomics, but necessarily to be answered question is whether the behavior of economic subjects will not change once they have been subject to confusion and thus suffered monetary losses. It is to be assumed that they either do not react anymore or that their assets will be invested in investments that are not affected by monetary shocks, such as physical assets. Overall, however, it can be said that the difficulty of the economic theory to show whether and to what extent monetary shocks are transmitted to the real sector at all, supports the hypothesis that monetary causes generally have less cyclical effects than real ones.[82]

Independently of this, there are three further directions, which can be classified as neo-classical, Walrasian, the Real Business Cycles models, the Sunspot theories and the non-linear models of Chaos theory. First, the Real Business Cycles approaches are to be analyzed, which emerged as a result of the criticism of the transmission mechanism from

---

[81] See Assenmacher Walter (1998, p. 309).

[82] In addition, the assessment of New Classical Macroeconomics of credit-financed fiscal policy should be mentioned here. According to the Ricardian equivalence theorem, economic subjects anticipate the future tax increases required for debt service when taking out loans, which is why they do not feel more prosperous when the state issues bonds and therefore do not consume more. Only the demand effect of government spending remains, which is offset by the future reduction in consumption due to the tax increase. Since economic subjects also anticipate this and increase their savings rate preventively, this effect also disappears. See Felderer, Bernhard and Homburg, Stefan (1989, pp. 275 et seq.). This view is critically questioned. Above all, it is argued that economic subjects will distinguish between the taxes levied during their lifetime and the taxes that the following generation will have to pay. For a discussion of the financing effects of government demand increases, see Musgrave R. A. et al. (1987, pp. 120 et seq.)

the monetary to the real sector. They reverse the causality and see the money supply in dependence on real exogenous shocks.[83]

7.10.3 Disturbance of the Market Equilibrium By Real Exogenous Shocks: The Real Business Cycles Theories

According to the Real Business Cycles approach, real positive shocks, such as technological progress, longer working hours and foreign direct investment, but also government demand, are responsible for the fluctuations in the utilization of production potential. The fluctuations arise from the adjustment reactions of economic subjects to external shocks. The money supply adjustment to the new real national product is carried out by the institutions that determine the money supply, such as the central bank and the banking system: The real shocks act, whereas the money supply only reacts. On behalf of the Real Business Cycles approach, the business-relevant parts of the model by KYDLAND and PRESCOTT[84] should be presented here.

A stochastic progress function is the central component of the model. Technical progress is, next to work and capital, a factor of a neoclassical production function with constant scale returns. At profit maximization, the demand for capital and labor is dependent on their marginal productivity, to which the technical progress acts equally. For technical progress (λ_{t+1}) it applies: $\lambda_{t+1} = p\lambda_{t} + E_{t}$; with $0 \leq p \leq 1$ as a coefficient for the effect on the national product. E_{t}, the technology shock variable, is stochastic and auto-correlated according to a first-order Markov process. E_{t} is exclusively random, independent and identically distributed. If $p = 1$, the shocks are transmitted unweakened over time to the national product, if $p = 0$, the shock only affects the national product in the period of its occurrence. The investment function is positively dependent on technical progress and a stochastic difference equation of first order, which is why, due to the autocorrelation of technical progress, cyclical oscillations can arise, which are amplified by the investments due to the assumed time lag (as maturation time).

With the Real Business Cycles Theory, a new empirical methodology was introduced into macroeconomics. Since these models are not suitable as a business cycle forecasting model due to the exogeneity of their business cycle causes (persistence problem), one investigates whether, using realistic input variables, observable business cycle developments can be simulated in reality. This succeeds in surprisingly many cases.[85] However,

---

[83] See Kydland, F. E. and Prescott, E. C. (1982); Long, John B. and Plosser, Charles I. (1983); Azariadis, C. and Guesnerie, R. (1986); Ramser, H. J. (1988); Tichy, G. (1995, pp. 191 et seq.); Stadler, George W. (1994) as well as Komphardt, Jürgen (1989, p. 213).

[84] See Kydland, Finn E. and Prescott, Edward C. (1982) as well as Assenmacher Walter (1998, pp. 310).

[85] See Kugler, Peter (1998, p. 33).

the empirical check carried out by KYDLAND and PRESCOTT itself is criticized in that the stochastic modeling was adapted to the real national product curves until the desired agreement was reached. Whether the real shocks occurring in reality, with the exception of exceptions, are strong enough to generate business cycle fluctuations therefore remains open. In the Real Business Cycles approaches, probability distributions, here the innovations (i.e. technical progress), explain the business cycle. There is again the persistence problem: Only by means of the assumption of repeated, independent, strong exogenous technology shocks can cyclical fluctuations in employment and demand be represented. Without a sound empirical check, however, the Real Business Cycles theories unfortunately remain abstract mathematical models.

7.10.4   Sunspot Variables as Psychological Influences On Business Cycle Development

In addition, psychological variables have been included as random variables in New Classical Macroeconomics in numerous approaches[86]. So-called "sunspot variables" are psychological factors that influence expectations of model-immanent variables, but without affecting preferences, technologies or initial endowments. It does not matter whether these factors have a real impact on economic development. What matters is that economic actors assume this and carry out real transactions. In this way, even "sunspots" (sunspots) can cause business cycle fluctuations.

Interim Conclusion
In the approaches of New Classical Macroeconomics and Real Business Cycles as well as in psychological approaches, it is shown by means of mathematical modeling how short-term negative real-economic effects of misjudgments, expectations and psychological factors arise. They cause fluctuations in supply and demand, i.e. instability. The monetarist approaches thus show, like those of New Classical Macroeconomics, that discretionary monetary policy has no long-term effect on employment, on the contrary. Consequently, it can be concluded for economic policy that the institutional framework (such as that of financial markets) is to be designed in such a way that as few irritations and misjudgments of private economic subjects are generated as possible.[87] A rule-based monetary policy must ensure a constant relationship between the quantity of goods and the quantity of money. EUCKEN's demand for the constancy of economic policy[88] is given special importance by these approaches, since the state can also act as a disturbing factor through discretionary interventions. New Classical Macroeconomics suggests

---

[86] For example, Azariadis, C. and Guesnerie, R. (1986).
[87] See Ramser, H. J. (1988, pp. 98).
[88] On the necessity of the constancy of economic policy. See Eucken, Walter (1952, pp. 285).

stabilization of the development of money supply and interest rates. On the other hand, the state can use errors of economic subjects, such as permanent-transitory confusion, deliberately and counteract in shock situations where overreactions of economic subjects are to be expected. An example of such a reaction can be the expansive monetary policy which was carried out in many states as a reaction to the stock market crisis of 1987. The lower interest rates caused a positive, expansive confusion which could later be corrected. New Classical Macroeconomics emphasizes the importance of "moral suasion": politicians and other people with public influence must be aware of the economic policy effects of their statements. If they spread rumors that lead to a false assessment of economic policy indicators, this will lead to economic fluctuations. However, if they explain their policy and pursue it consistently, they can prevent economic fluctuations.

7.10.5 Speculative Bubbles as Triggers of Economic Fluctuations

Speculative bubbles can trigger economic fluctuations through asset effects and increased profits.[89] The equity interests of companies are valued at fair value under IFRS or US GAAP, which increases profits. The equity assets of private households also increase, encouraging households to increase their consumption spending (asset effect). The banks tend to lend more due to the high asset values. This can lead to credit bubbles through credit-financed securities purchases, as in the 1929 global economic crisis, or credit-financed real estate purchases, as in the 2007 US subprime financial crisis. If this development is accompanied by lax monetary policy, stock price and real estate price bubbles usually occur in parallel (as in the Japan bubble in the late 1980s). The downturn is triggered by the write-down of loans in the banking system, where a lack of liquidity alone is no longer sufficient to drive price increases.[90]

Speculative bubbles (engl. speculative bubbles) is a word from everyday language and is usually used to characterize a strong overvaluation in prices. "A price bubble is a deviation in the price of an asset (gold, foreign currency, stock) from the price consistent with the fundamentals."[91] In the literature, depending on the assumed cause, different titles for speculative bubbles can be found, such as rational and irrational bubbles as well as agency-oriented bubbles, intrinsic bubbles and stochastic bubbles.[92] The distinction between rational and irrational bubbles is artificial, since a deviation of the courses (prices) from the fundamental data is always irrational. However, according to a broad definition of "rationality", all decisions are considered rational if they are confirmed over

---

[89] See also Minsky's theory. See Minsky, H. P. (1986).

[90] Stahl, Markus and Conrad, Christian, A. (2000, pp. 415–422).

[91] See Santoni, Gary J. and Dwyer, Gerald P. Jr. (1990, p. 190) and Diba, Behzad T. and Grossman, Herschel I. (1988, p. 520).

[92] See Bruns, Christoph (1994, pp. 23).

time. However, in the case of a dynamically growing bubble, the return expectations are always confirmed by rising prices, so that every bubble can be referred to as rational. Conversely, every—according to the broad definition rational—bubble after its bursting becomes an irrational bubble.

Intrinsic Bubble is when a change in the fundamental market variables is overvalued only once and, for this reason, there is no growth (swelling) of the bubble.[93] Agency-oriented bubbles arise as a result of distorted information processing by investors.[94] This approach to explanation is currently being given new impetus by the New Behavioral Finance, which will be addressed later. Finally, one speaks of stochastic bubbles when there is an auto-accelerating, that is, self-reinforcing, psychological overvaluation development. The original course (price) increase can be fundamentally justified here. However, the past price increases are predicted by the investors as an expectation for the future and overestimated, whereby psychological backgrounds dominate the investment decision (social dynamics). However, these exaggerated expectations are confirmed again and again by the prices that have risen as a result of the purchases (self-fulfilling prophecies or self-fulfilling expectations), until the bubble bursts.[95]

The German analogy for "bubble" is "blister". This word expresses the assessment that the overvaluation will not be of long duration—the soap bubble bursts. In a narrower sense, there can be no overvaluation of a good, since the market price is determined by supply and demand and is always an equilibrium price. The overvaluation must therefore relate to the durability of the market price.

A dynamic, growing bubble can only arise if the current market price is positively dependent on its expected increase.[96] The goods must not be subject to a temporal depreciation which is greater than the possible increase. They must, for example, not spoil or cause high storage costs. Shares as company shares are therefore particularly susceptible to the formation of speculative bubbles, since their storage costs are low and the possible future increases in profits are very high.[97]

7.10.5.1   The Efficient Market Hypothesis

Until the mid-1980s, the Efficient Market Hypothesis held an undisputed monopoly in financial market theory. The Efficient Market Hypothesis was significantly shaped by Milton Friedman from the University of Chicago. This hypothesis assumes that all price-relevant information from the past, present and future is contained. If there were a fundamental price imbalance, arbitrageurs would immediately use this source of revenue and restore the fundamental price through offsetting transactions. So-called "smart

---

[93] See Aschinger, Gerhard (1991, p. 271).

[94] See Menkhoff, Lukas and Röckmann, Christian (1994, p. 280).

[95] See Bruns, Christoph (1994, p. 25) and Aschinger, Gerhard (1991, pp. 270 ff.).

[96] See Flood, Robert P. and Garber, Peter M. (1980, p. 746).

[97] See Ito, Takatoshi and Iwaisako, Tokuo (1995, p. 1).

money" from funds and in the hands of professional arbitrageurs, supported by researchers who investigate 24 hours a day in which direction the fundamental market trend is
moving, guarantee the efficiency of the market. Since basically rational investor behavior is assumed, irrational investor behavior or wrong decisions are not price-influencing.
Non-fundamentally justified investment decisions are immediately punished by the market. Investors who behave irrationally lose money and have to withdraw from the market.
Stock prices therefore reflect the latest and best information. Price changes can only be
caused by new information. Therefore, purchases and sales may not have any effect on
prices, since the smart money is always ready to form the opposite side, i.e. to buy or sell
at the fundamental price. According to the Efficient Market Hypothesis, investors cannot
outperform the market by increasing their individual level of information.[98]

For a long time, an explanation approach predominated in science that assumed
rational behavior on the part of market participants when explaining stock market bubbles. Representatives of this theory are, for example, Flood, Garber, Blanchard and Watson.[99] According to this explanation approach, investors are well aware that the rates
are speculatively overpriced and thus unrealistic. Although the probability of a crash
is greater than the probability of further growth in the bubble, the expected price gains
compensate for the probability of a crash, so that the expected value of further price
increases is higher than the probability of a crash. Every investor assumes that he can
get out in time, that is, before the others. This can be true for the individual, but not for
the totality of investors. One could speak of rational errors here. The bubble bursts when
the price increases necessary to compensate for the probability of a crash are no longer
expected for some reason. However, do these explanation approaches correspond to the
course patterns of stock market bubbles that can be observed in practice?

7.10.5.2 Testing the Efficient Market Hypothesis

The known crashes in 1929 and 1987 can be observed with parallels in the course development. First, there is a steep upward process, whose growth rate then decreases a few
weeks before the crash. In this short phase before the crash, relatively strong course
breaks and strongly growing sales can be observed in relation to the upswing phase.[100]
The stock market upswing phase lasts for several years. The decline or course break usu-

---

[98] See Sloan, A. and Stern, R. L. (1988, pp. 55–59); Shleifer, Andrei (2000a, pp. 1 ff.) as well as
Menkhoff, Likas and Röckemann, Christian (1994, p. 278).

[99] See Flood, Robert P. and Garber, Peter M. (1980, pp. 746 ff.) as well as Blanchard O. J. and Watson, M. W. (1982), and Jüttner, Johannes (1989, p. 474).

[100] See Rasch, Steffen (1993, p. 300).

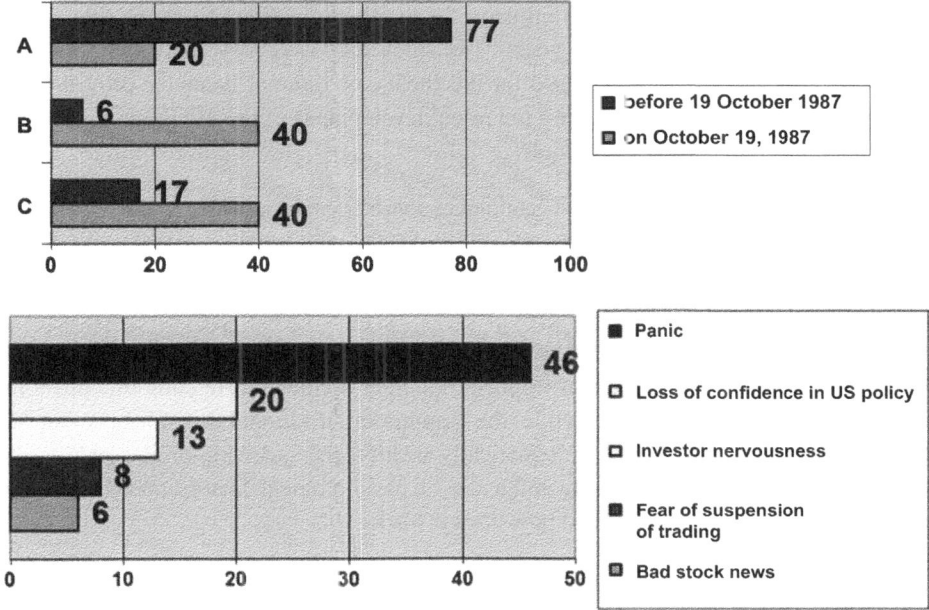

Fig. 7.42 The most important reasons for the stock market crash in the US in 1987. (A total of 470 [upper graph] and 231 market participants [lower graph] were surveyed). (Source: The Presidental Task Force, 1988 as well as Jüttner, Johannes, 1989, p. 475)

ally takes place within a few days.[101] The sales and the subsequent falling prices induce new sales and price declines:[102]

> As the 19th wore on, investors witnessed symptoms of market failure and were frightened by rumors that the NYSE would close. They also worried that other investors had come to believe the market was overvalued. Fear fed upon fear as investors en masse rushed to sell their stocks.[103]

This is where psychology comes in as one of the most important influencing factors of stock market development. After the 1987 crash, opinion polls were conducted to find the crash's causes. The most significant one was conducted by the Brady group and yielded the following results (see Fig. 7.42):

---

[101] The course display had a several-hour delay in 1987, which is why the NYSE expanded the computer-based automatic trading systems to a volume of 1 billion shares per session. See Rasch, Steffen (1993, pp. 282–283.

[102] See The Presidental Task Force (1988, p. V).

[103] Leland, Hayne und Rubinstein, Mark (1988, p. 46).

Figure 7.42 shows the increased influence of psychological factors at the time of the crash. An old stock market saying goes: "The stock market is 50% facts and 50% psychology." However, the models based on the theory of rational behavior proved to be unsuitable for explaining or depicting the price development of the 1987 crash, which is why economists demanded new models:

> We need to build models of financial equilibrium which are more sensitive to real life trading mechanism, which account more realistically for the information of expectations, and which recognize that, at any one time, there is a limited pool of investors available with the ability to evaluate stocks and take appropriate action in the market.[104]

Shiller, for example, showed that the historical development of stock prices cannot be explained solely by expectations of future profits and dividends. He calls this phenomenon "Excess Volatility".[105] Meanwhile, the assumption of rational investor behavior has been falsified. Investors behave systematically irrationally and with similar patterns of behavior.[106] Where does the strong influence of psychological factors on the development of stock prices come from and how does it work?

7.10.5.3 Noise Trading Approaches

As a countermovement to the Efficient Market Hypothesis, a number of psychologically oriented explanatory approaches emerged, which are referred to as Noise Trading approaches, with "Noise" standing for a disturbance (-noise) that causes the deviation of prices from the fundamental data. Some Noise Trading approaches work explicitly with investor groups in their models that make their decisions on the basis of distorted probability distributions, that is, they behave unconsciously irrational.[107] Shiller, for example, models an emotionally charged cyclical stock demand, with speculation bubbles forming.[108] Bubbles can also be triggered by positive market participant moods (boom), which are amplified by feedback (positive feedback) and can lead to mass behavior in the same direction (so-called. Herding).[109] An example of Shiller's "information cascade" illustrates the herding behavior.[110]

---

[104] Leland, Hayne und Rubinstein, Mark (1988, p. 50).

[105] See Shiller, Robert J. (2000, pp. 180 ff.).

[106] See Shleifer, Andrei (2000a, pp. 10 ff.).

[107] See Blume, L. and Easley, D. (1992, pp. 9–40).

[108] See Shiller, R.J. (1984, pp. 457–498).

[109] See Froot, Kenneth A. et al. (Froot et al., 1992, pp. 1461 ff.).

[110] See Shiller, Robert J. (2000, p. 152).

Example

Two restaurants, A and B, are, visible through a shop window, from the outside one hundred percent identical. At first they are empty. Then a hungry guest comes and has to decide for one of the two restaurants. A second hungry person comes. He has no additional information about the quality of the restaurants, but only sees that in one restaurant nobody is eating and in the other restaurant A at least the first guest. Probably he will trust the choice of the first guest and also decide for restaurant A. The decision situation can be continued with further hungry guests until restaurant A is overcrowded as the most popular restaurant, and that, although it is one hundred percent identical with B and thus of equal value. Although this behavior leads to a grotesque result, it is individually seen from the perspective of the guests, rational and could, if the assumption that the already eating people have a higher level of information, had been correct, quite successful. ◄

In general, human behavior is oriented towards learning by imitation. The human being first learns from his parents and also trusts them blindly and also in his further development he gets his information from other people. Because of their complexity and the limited decision time, these information often cannot be checked at all. The human being has to help himself with simplifying behavior patterns. If people flee, he joins them, even though he does not know what everyone is fleeing from. In the Stone Age this behavior apparently secured the survival, because the people who first waited for the pursuing predator were killed. It has also been offered to copy others who have survived the berries when eating them.

The herding expresses the sociological group orientation of man. In the stock market typical uncertainty situation, the investor orients himself to the other market participants, which also honors the stock market—at least in the short term—by rising prices. In the approach of Shefrin and Statman, bubbles are built up which burst when the irrational noise traders adjust their distorted expectations again to those of the rational market participants.[111] The expectations of market participants influence each other. For example, empirical studies show that the assessment of market development by analysts and investors is influenced by previous evaluations of other analysts.[112] Also extrapolative expectation formation and strategies of technical analysis lead to stock purchases at rising prices. The herding behavior is thereby reinforced by the mostly short-term oriented speculation horizon. A crash then seems less likely. This is especially true for professional investment managers who are subject to a one-year performance evaluation.[113]

---

[111] Quoted from Menkhoff, Lukas and Röckmann, Christian (1994, pp. 284 ff.).

[112] See De Bondt, Werner F. M. and Forbes, William P. (1999).

[113] See Shleifer, Andrei and Vishny, Robert W. (1990, pp. 148–153).

Individual market participants cannot oppose a Herding development, even if they notice the deviation from the fundamental price factors. If they speculate against such a strong market trend, they lose, as long as the bubble does not burst. On the contrary, in the process of appreciation there are self-reinforcing distribution effects which support the emergence of a bubble[114]. Let us assume, for example, that in a given uncertainty situation at the stock exchange there are investors with two risk settings, and that they have the same purchasing power. The risk-loving optimists (bulls) expect higher price or company profit increases than the risk-averse pessimists (bears) at the same level of information. If now new positive information arrives which leads to a price increase, the potential buyers (long position) have more purchasing power due to the previous price gains than the potential sellers, who did not invest in shares but held liquidity or a selling position (short position), which has losses.[115] The unequal purchasing power causes a demand surplus and thus favours the process of appreciation. Since the bulls can bring about their own success in the form of rising prices through the purchase surplus, the process of appreciation is self-reinforcing. The mirror image of this development occurs when the new information is negative.

The same applies to cyclical upward movements: procyclical investing is rewarded and strengthens the risk-loving companies, while the waiting companies lose market share.

In addition, there is a psychological effect that amplifies the stock market upwards. The investor feels richer due to his increased stock portfolio, which will reinforce his buying attitude (wealth effect). Man adapts his behavior to his environment, more precisely to his experiences. If new price increases occur over a longer period of time, he will adjust his risk assessment. His own price gains encourage him and make it appear rational to invest in stocks again. As a rule, the second investment will be larger because the investor assumes that his successful first investment will be repeated.

7.10.5.4 The New Behavioral Finance

More recent studies by the behavior-oriented research direction of New Behavioral Finance confirm the psychologically oriented, non-deterministic explanatory approaches. It turned out that investors perceive and evaluate the information available to them very subjectively and do not always maximize the expected utility in their decisions—contrary to the neoclassical world of models. The investor gets angry about losses more than he enjoys gains and behaves more risk-loving in the loss area than in the profit area, which is why he tends to get rid of the stocks in the profit area rather than in the loss area (disposition effect). He gets angry about his "wrong decision" and hopes to be right after all—a phenomenon that one can usually observe in oneself. Investment decisions

---

[114] See Treynor, Jack (1998, pp. 69–74).

[115] A potential seller (bear) does not have to act passively at the market by holding liquidity, but he can also acquire selling positions (long-short futures or long put options).

are also influenced by the presentation of information (framing effect). If the historical return of a security is shown, this leads to an underestimation of the future Volatility of the course. The so-called splitting effect, on the other hand, causes securities to be preferred when they offer more investment variants (for example, German and foreign shares) than the equally weighted alternative (for example, bonds). Furthermore, it can be observed that investors tend to overestimate their level of information and their abilities. This is called "overconfidence". Overconfidence causes an overestimation of the probability of success of one's own decisions. Behavioral finance researchers, for example, attribute the frequent, yield-reducing purchase and sale of shares to overconfidence, which would be comparable to the constant change of lanes in a traffic jam. Investors tend to overweight the information that they receive first compared to the later ones. Conversely, older information recedes in perception compared to newly added information. The same can be observed with regard to the complexity of the information. Investors pay more attention to reports of takeovers, sales declines and stock market flotations than to information that they cannot classify or have to process, such as the publication of balance sheet figures. New information is processed and implemented with a delay. This causes an overreaction on the stock markets in both directions (overreaction). There are price bubbles and price depressions because the information that contradicts the trend is considered too late in the decision-making process. Last but not least, the value of the information source is not properly assessed. From the investor's point of view, it is hardly taken into account whether the information comes, for example, from an investment advisor or a recognized expert, but rather how determined and resolute it is presented.

Since psychologically oriented approaches are not deterministic, their disadvantage is the lack of a unified, generally applicable model concept and the possibility of a situation-independent, exact verifiability (verification). In view of the weaknesses of the classical theory, which is based solely on rational behavior, they have, however, significantly enriched the financial market theory. The psychologically oriented approaches lead the over-interpretation of the rational behavior assumption as always valid in reality back to the original abstracting model approach of neoclassicism, which only assumed the rational Homo oeconomicus for the simplification of the complexity of human behavior.[116] If human behavior is not determinable and predictable because it is not rational, however, the applicability of exact mathematical models is also limited and the generality of economic findings in general.

External shocks cannot be predicted. The psychological influences then destabilize the system. This is also best shown by the failure of the hedge fund LTCM, founded by Nobel laureates Robert Merton and Myron Scholes. Merton and Scholes had received the Nobel Prize for the discovery of a calculation method for the price of options. Based on this calculation approach, the LTCM fund mainly operated in market-neutral bond arbi-

---

[116] See *Behavioral Finance Group* (2000) as well as Conrad, Christian A. (2016).

trage. However, the calculation method is based primarily on historical volatilities and does not take into account irrational human behavior, such as panic, as was observed, for example, as a result of the Russia crisis. In the autumn of 1998, the LTCM fund finally stood on the brink of insolvency. Its open positions and credit commitments threatened the international financial system to such an extent that Alan Greenspan felt obliged to organize a rescue operation.

The approach of herding can be transferred to the theory of the business cycle. Even irrational, aligned human behavior can amplify business cycles. Fear and panic intensify a downturn, while greed and overconfidence cause an exaggeration, an overshooting in the boom. If all market participants behave similarly with their investment and purchase decisions, demand cycles arise that determine economic development. Bonus systems can amplify this by supporting aligned risk-taking behavior.[117] If the actors are only involved in the opportunities and not in the risks, that is, if they are not liable for losses but participate in the profits, this destabilizes the system. Risk-taking over-investment drives the upswing, while the following write-downs in the financial system cause the crash and downturn.

7.10.5.5 The Liquidity and Speculation Cycle

We want to develop a plausible dynamic explanation approach that combines the psychological and deterministic bubble-causing factors that have been identified.[118] We assume that, due to technical progress or other macroeconomic influencing factors, such as corporate tax cuts, the expected profits of companies increase or interest rates are lowered, both of which lead to an increase in stock prices. An increase in stock prices signals missed profits: If the investor had entered, he could have realized the price difference as a profit. The missed profits trigger a self-reinforcing process (the bull market feeds the bull market). The more shareholders enter, the higher the price increase and the missed profit for those who have not yet entered. The upward movement of prices creates a positive market mood. In stock market jargon, it is said that the market is "bullish". More and more population groups are added until finally even the small investor invests, who has never dealt with stocks before. He buys at the most expensive price.[119] There is an overvaluation of the prices, a speculative bubble (explosion of the price volume). However, the upward trend cannot continue indefinitely. More and more liquidity is needed to drive prices up with a constant supply of securities. Additional buyers are required who, despite the already very high prices, expect further price increases. The prices absolutely

---

[117] See Conrad, Christian A. (2015).

[118] In doing so, the author draws on, among other things, suggestions he gained from a lecture by André Kostolany in Duisburg on December 2, 1988 and from attending the seminar "Stock Market and Other Financial Markets" at Georgetown University, Washington, USA.

[119] This is also reinforced by the small investor's distance from the market. The small investor therefore learns price-relevant information last.

have to rise more and more strongly in order for a constant percentage return to be given. The course of this process can be compared to the course of epidemics. The infection rate (contagion) increases exponentially as long as an "infected" person only comes into contact with "uninfected" people. The more investors are already invested in the stock market, the flatter the growth rate will be.

The crash is inevitable when all potential stock buyers have entered the market. A stock market crash can be caused by minimal changes in overall economic indicators or simply by expressions of opinion. If there is a tendency to doubt a further increase in prices, a minimal interest rate increase or the expression of an expert who predicts a stock market crash is enough to make the fear of value losses exceed the hope of profits (panic reactions). Small investors have a higher marginal utility of money due to their lower assets and therefore value a price loss higher than large investors, professionals or fund managers (Bernoulli principle). If prices fall below their entry prices, they tend to panic and sell their holdings, thus promoting the downward trend. On the other hand, funds are drivers of upward trends. Due to the intense competition (performance pressure), they are forced to be engaged as long as the stock market is rising. If prices fall, it is much easier for them to justify the losses to their customers, as other funds also incur losses.

In the event of a stock market crash, there is a sudden revaluation of the shares. The economic subjects are no longer willing to pay the historical values. The prices break. There is a speculative overreaction, an implosion of the price volume. The stock market signals price losses. The investors who have purchased the shares at a low price sell to realize the remaining price gains. The investors who have entered late and would therefore already realize losses at the existing selling prices have to sell if they do not have any liquidity reserves. This is especially the case if the stock purchases are financed by credit and the investors do not have any further securities. They threaten to become illiquid or bankrupt. There is again a self-reinforcing process. The decline feeds the decline. Also, automatic stop-loss orders depress the prices.[120] If the devaluation process continues, the investor loses faith in the value of his shares. As a group phenomenon, fear is contagious; there are panic sales.

7.10.5.6 Indicators of Asset Bubbles

Stock market fluctuations can be transmitted to the development of the economy via wealth effects. Households feel richer because their stock portfolios have gained in value, they consume more. Companies have greater refinancing options because their equity has gained in value. The value of company shares increases under US GAAP and IFRS and increases profits. The mood rises and companies invest more.

---

[120] From the experiences of the past, it has been learned. At the New York Stock Exchange, trading is interrupted for one hour when the price losses exceed a certain value.

For the evaluation of the shares of publicly traded companies, numerous key figures are used. The best known are the price-earnings ratio (P/E ratio) and the dividend yield. The latter has lost importance in recent years as more and more companies are moving towards hoarding their profits and only allowing investors to participate in the value appreciation of their company stake, in the form of shares. The P/E ratio is the ratio between the share price and the company's profit. For example, with a share price of 100 € and a profit of 5 €, the P/E ratio would be 20. A P/E ratio of 20 means that the company will need 20 years to generate the invested capital if profits remain constant. This corresponds to the interest rate of a bond over the same term of 5%. Since profits can fluctuate greatly, Yale professor Shiller developed a P/E ratio based on the average of the last ten years.

The P/E ratio is indeed a suitable value indicator, but its statement content has to be strongly related. The reported profit can be manipulated by creative bookkeeping, such as provisioning and resolution. The price-earnings (earnings before interest and taxes)— as well as the price-cash flow ratio would be more suitable. After all, if they were consistently applied, it would not have led to the—ex post—massive overvaluation of many start-ups on the New Market, which only showed losses or negative cash flows. On the other hand, in their evaluation, the high initial losses, negative EBITs and cash flows were seen as a sign of a consistent expansion and growth strategy against the background of the predicted enormous value creation opportunities of the New Economy. This is an argumentation that is still valid in principle. The prerequisite is that profit growth occurs and thus the crossing of the break-even point is realizable. Revenue growth thus replaces the P/E ratio as a value approach here. The danger of this approach is obvious: growth without economic efficiency, as was the case on the New Market and on the Nasdaq. But even the earnings-oriented key figures and past-oriented risk key figures such as volatility in percent fail when valuing in a "new era" in which not only the historical profit increases and price trends are extrapolated into the future and then discounted, but also their growth is extrapolated into the future and then discounted or the calculations are based solely on forecasts. In such an euphoric environment on the basis of uncertain and unverifiable expectations, there is only one thing for the investor, common sense. This at least questions such euphoric forecasts against the background of previous historical innovation booms. Nevertheless, there are relations that reflect the setback potential and thus the price risk in the event that the positive forecasts do not materialize or are no longer believed to materialize. These include, for example, the current P/Es and other ratios such as market capitalization to current sales and also to equity as an indicator of a book value.

The dangerous thing about the New Market was the same as with the New Era, the adjective "new". Stock exchanges with history can be measured against past periods, stock exchanges with economic representativeness can even be measured against gross national product. The starting point here is the question of whether a stock exchange rep-

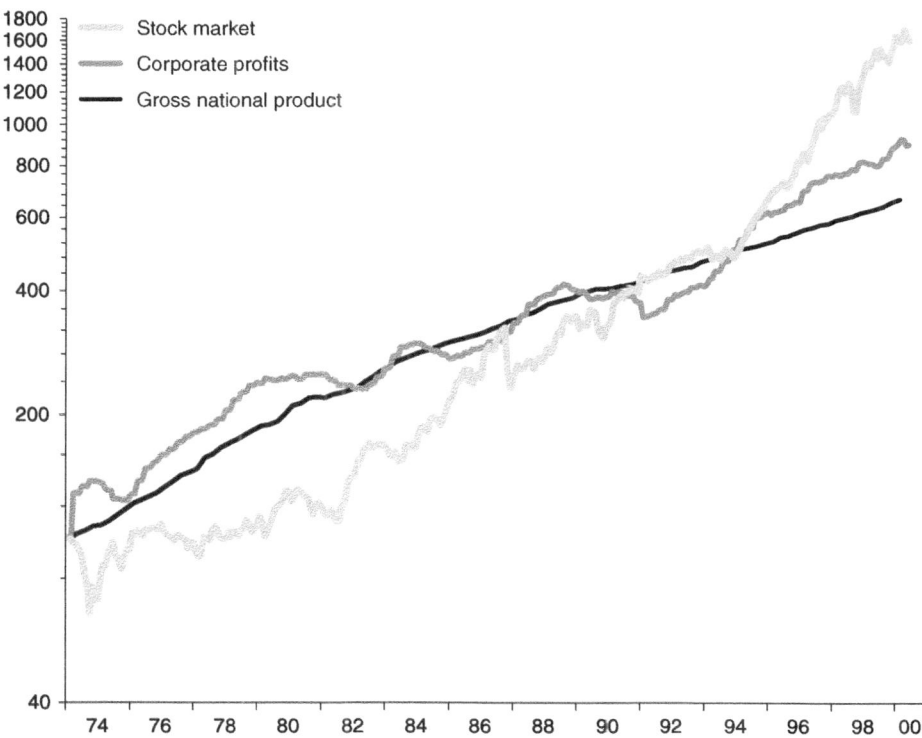

Fig. 7.43 Indexed development of the stock market, corporate profits and gross national product in the USA (compare Kydland, Finn, E. and Prescott, Edward C. [1977] as well as Lucas, R.E. Jr. [1976])

resentative of an economy as a whole can grow stronger over a longer period of time than the economy as a whole. Figure 7.43 shows such a comparison for the USA.

Conclusion and Summary of Psychological Factors

Stock market fluctuations can be transmitted to economic fluctuations. However, psychological factors can also directly affect corporate decision-making and thus trigger or intensify cycles. How do psychological factors affect economic fluctuations?

New Behavioral Finance Theory

1. It can thus be observed that investors tend to overestimate their level of information and their abilities. This is called **Overconfidence**. Overconfidence causes an overestimation of the probability of success of one's own decisions. People tend to overestimate their own abilities after a series of successes and then take on excessive risks.

This human weakness is the basis of the business approach of the shell game. The inexperienced player is initially skeptical, so the game leader first lets the player win to lull him into a false sense of security. Then, when the player thinks he has mastered the game and the success, the game leader tricks him, plays faster than before and thus takes away the player's money. This human weakness also affects the upswing, when, due to high demand, almost all corporate decisions and investments are successful. The managers then tend to overestimate themselves and invest too much. The boom is thus further increased and the resulting excess supply is all the greater when the investments have been realized and the supply comes onto the market.

2. New information is processed and implemented with a delay. This causes an overreaction in the boom and in the recession, that is, in both directions **(Overreaction).** There are exaggerations and underestimations in investments because the information contrary to the trend is not taken into account early enough in the decision-making of corporate managers. In the boom, the managers do not realize early enough that, in the meantime, the costs of the raw materials and the wages have risen and also other companies have invested or the demand has already weakened. They invest too long in the expansion of their capacities. Conversely, in the recession, they do not realize early enough that, in the meantime, the costs have fallen again, the demand has stopped falling or suppliers have left the market. They invest too late. As a result, the recession lasts too long.

Noise Trading Approaches

3. For example, Shiller modeled an emotionally driven cyclical stock demand, where speculation bubbles form. Let's say that entrepreneurs are also plagued by envy, greed and fear. In the upswing, the entrepreneurs have done well, now they want more and more and expand too much. The boom is amplified and the subsequent downturn as well. Envy of the success of other entrepreneurs would have the same effect. On the other hand, fear leads to the fact that entrepreneurs do not invest in the recession, although here the highest profits would be possible, because investment costs, wages and pre-product costs are low.

4. Bubbles can also be caused by positive market participant moods (price euphoria) which are amplified by feedback loops (positive feedbacks) and can lead to mass behavior in the same direction (so-called. Herding). The same applies to business cycles. In the upswing and boom, the managers are euphoric. Everything succeeds, they sell and earn more than expected. They hear of start-ups, expansion investments and takeovers. This positive mood is contagious. The upswing and boom are amplified.

7.11   Final Assessment of the Theories of Economic Development

If we try to work out an economic policy trend statement of the presented theories of economic cycles, we can make the following observations:[121]

- The long-term national product development is determined by the growth determinants of capital goods and human resources, including technical progress.
- There is no long-term positive relationship between inflation and employment. On the contrary, the price distortions and the uncertainties of the planning economic subjects lead to a reduction of long-term economic growth.
- For the effect of monetary and fiscal policy, the expectations of economic subjects are decisive.
- Due to the numerous implementation problems (recognition, planning, implementation and effect lag) and the difficulty of clearly identifying the cause responsible for the respective economic development, fiscal policy should be used in the long term and not discretionarily in the short term.
- Monetary policy should serve primarily to ensure price stability and may only help to cushion external shocks in exceptional cases. Growth cannot be artificially generated by an expansive monetary policy.

The economic approaches that were developed after Keynes complement each other to form a much more comprehensive and balanced understanding of the economy. They expand existing models to include new economic determinants or an analysis over multiple periods (dynamization). The most significant theoretical achievement that economic theory after Keynes has produced is the theoretical proof that fluctuations in the utilization of production potential are not necessarily caused by demand-side factors, but that supply-side shocks can also be responsible for this. This is the merit of New Keynesian macroeconomics and New Classical macroeconomics with their further developments. The disadvantage of these approaches is that they fail to explain a complete economic cycle endogenously. They all suffer from the persistence problem and are dependent on exogenous stochastic shocks in order to simulate economic fluctuations. The economic influences, i.e. the trend component of the time series, are not deterministic here and thus explained, but stochastic, which appears less convincing. The explanatory value and thus the value for economic education are lower than for deterministic models. In addition, these models are unsuitable for economic forecasting due to the indeterminacy of the economic situation.

---

[121] This is the basic tenor in almost all overviews of economic cycle theory of the last 50 years. See in particular *Kugler, Peter* (1998, pp. 34 ff.).

All models assume a closed economy. Foreign influences are exogenous factors. Although the Mundell-Flemming model can serve as a supplement to these approaches, the international economic context is often forgotten in economic policy discussions. This is incompatible with today's conditions, as the current globalization discussion shows. With a high proportion of imports to domestic demand, the effects of an increase in government demand are greatly reduced. The interest rate responsiveness of investments is also lower in an open economy, as investments are made where the highest profitability expectations exist when capital and goods are freely traded internationally.[122]

The development of Keynesian economics has shown above all the limits of economic theory. While the German Stability and Growth Act of 1967 still showed faith in the controllability of the economy, this view is hardly held today. This is especially true for discretionary fiscal policy. If we want to explain this change of heart, we have to look for the causes of the target-actual deviation of the applied economic theory. What the economists have available as economic indicators are the statistically aggregated effects of billions of individual decisions of economic subjects, which were coordinated over many different markets. From this sentence four insoluble problems of the applied economic theory can be derived:

1. The multi-causality due to the billions of individual decisions. Only through a high abstraction can dominant determinants be filtered out.
2. In aggregation, the structural problems of industries or anomalies of individual markets, for example due to distortions of competition, are lost.
3. The superimposition and lag problem: The effects of the many different economic determinants occur superimposed and delayed.
4. The non-determinable behavior of human decision-makers. This is especially true if one assumes irrational behavior. However, Kydland and Prescott showed that even with rational behavior, optimal economic policy is impossible due to the unforeseeable reactions of economic subjects as a result of adaptive expectations, which they have formed on the basis of previous economic policies.[123]

The newer approaches are mostly based on the "policy inefficiency hypothesis". Consequently, the influence of policy on the economy is to be kept as low as possible. The future environmental conditions are unknown. The market participants therefore make decisions under uncertainty. The state must not increase this uncertainty by a "non-constancy" of economic policy. Rather, what is required is a rule-binding in the form of clear, long-term policy programs based on a comprehensible, order-compliant concept, that is, order-based rather than process-based policy. Kydland and Prescott therefore recommend—as does Lucas—the institutional involvement of politicians in fixed behavioral

---

[122] See Jaeger, Klaus (1999, p. 31) and Hesse, Helmut (1999, p. 39).

[123] See Kydland, Finn, E. and Prescott, Edward C. (1977).

rules that have been selected in advance by economic theory as relatively best.[124] Politicians are then obliged within this institutional involvement to explain their goals and instruments to the economic subjects and to implement them consistently. Discretionary intervention is only defensible in cases where irritations already exist and policy can prevent possible over- or malfunction. Moral Suasion is in this context a suitable instrument. However, in order not to impair the credibility and thus the effectiveness of this instrument, it is to be used sparingly. The political influence on the economic process is to be limited to the unavoidable minimum (minimal policy). This gain in knowledge is a not to be underestimated contribution of the newer theories of economic cycle to economic cycle policy.

The newer approaches to business cycle theory contribute significantly to a better understanding of business cycle developments.[125] They extend the existing models by adding new business cycle determinants or by considering multiple periods (dynamization). It turns out that the causes of business cycle fluctuations are much more complex than what many Keynesian-influenced economists assumed back in the 1970s. While HICKs and New Keynesian Macroeconomics are able to provide a new theoretical justification for the need for government countercyclical demand management, these models require a government that is even more omniscient than the "simple" Keynesian demand management. The new Keynesian-oriented models take into account more influencing factors and development interdependencies over a longer period of time. Therefore, the state must follow more influencing factors by using suitable indicators and identify deviations from the norm even faster in order to prevent negative demand processes that can initiate a business cycle downturn. The problems of recognition and implementation were, however, already unsolvable on the basis of the "old" Keynesian theory in practical economic policy.[126] The structure of government demand never corresponds to the structure of private sector demand, which severely limits the effect of government demand increases and, in addition, causes a displacement of private demand, which in turn partially causes price increases. The probability of making errors in economic policy thus appears to be even greater than under the "old" theoretical framework.[127]

Overall, the newer approaches represent the course of the economy as a dynamic process influenced by many factors. The factors taken up by the theories, with their multitude and diversity, show the complexity of the business cycle and thus also the risks of discretionary government demand management. Business cycles are therefore no longer controllable, but at best influenced.

---

[124] See Kydland, Finn, E. and Prescott, Edward C. (1977) as well as Lucas, R.E. Jr. (1976).

[125] See also Conrad, Christian, A. (1999).

[126] See Berg, Hartmut; Cassel Dieter (1992, pp. 163–238).

[127] ISSING summarizes this as follows: "... the development was most stable where – as in the Federal Republic of Germany – Demand Management was not even tried at first" Issing, Otmar (1982).

For practical economic policy, the value of the new business cycle theories therefore lies above all in pointing out the risks of discretionary state demand management. The theoretical finding is that economic developments, due to the unforeseeable multi-causality and the unquantifiable time interdependencies, are not controllable. What is needed are automatisms that weaken individual pro-cyclical determinants, such as progressive taxation. For economic policy, this means that the state must design the economic framework in such a way that as few misjudgments by economic subjects are caused by lack of transparency as possible. In addition, the state must refrain from discretionary interventions in order to not increase the irritation. This has been shown above all by the New Political Economy and NORDHAUS. The New Classical Macroeconomics also starts from a "policy inefficiency hypothesis". Consistently, the influence of politics on the economy is to be kept as low as possible. The actions of market participants, above all investors, are future-oriented. The future environmental conditions are unknown. The market participants therefore make decisions under uncertainty. The state must not increase this uncertainty by "non-constancy" of economic policy. Rather, what is needed is a rule-binding in the form of clear, long-term policy programs, based on a comprehensible, order-compliant concept. Politicians are obliged to explain their goals and instruments to the economic subjects and then implement them consistently. Discretionary intervention is only justifiable in cases where irritations already exist and the policy can prevent possible over- or malfunction. Moral suasion is a suitable instrument in this context. However, in order not to jeopardize the credibility and thus the effectiveness of this instrument, it is to be used sparingly.

The financing effects of the government's demand increase have not been integrated into the new business cycle models. All models assume a closed economy. Foreign influences are exogenous factors. This is incompatible with today's framework conditions, as the current globalization discussion shows. With a high proportion of imports in domestic demand, the effects of a government demand increase are greatly reduced. The interest rate responsiveness of investments is also lower in an open economy, as investments are made where the highest profitability expectations exist when capital and goods traffic are internationally free. Overall, it can be said that all models show the dangers of political economic influence directly or indirectly. Political influence on the economic process is to be limited to the unavoidable minimum (minimal politics). This is the contribution of the new business cycle theories to economic policy. Business cycles are part of economic development.

Summary: Determinants of the Business Cycle

1. Market clearing, marginal suppliers leave, profit margin also rises through restructuring, initiating upturn
2. Procyclical banks (lending only with positive company numbers), amplifying upturn and downturn. The credit policy of banks is procyclical. Companies only

Fig. 7.44 Fluctuations in
economic activity around
potential output

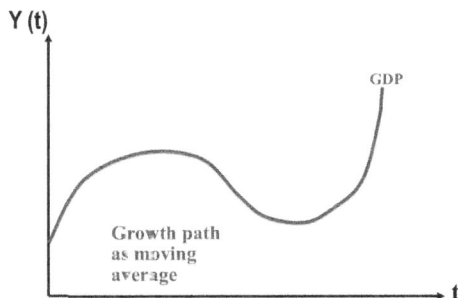

get loans with the presentation of good balance sheet figures and good economic
conditions.[128]

3. Psychology (good and bad mood due to expectations about future economic development is self-reinforcing, overconfidence)
4. Interdependencies (multipliers and accelerators), amplifying upturn and downturn.
   Keynes: demand leads to more demand
5. If demand is greater than supply, this causes investments, which increases the
   excess demand. Since companies cannot assess the demand and the capacity
   expansions of their competitors, there can be too much investment. The opposite process takes place during a recession, when demand is smaller than supply.
   YD>YS ->I>S as well as YD<YS ->I<S
6. Maturity of investments, initiating recession (Schumpeter, overinvestment theory).
7. Procyclical profit margin, amplifying boom and recession. Goodwin model →
   high profits lead to high investments, little profit leads to little investment
8. Evaluations of assets and company shares, (wealth effect: not only more consumption with more income, but also more wealth → if economic subjects feel richer,
   they also spend more), amplifying boom and recession. Approaches to valuation
   based on market value such as IFRS and US-GAAP also amplify cycles through
   valuation fluctuations (mark-to-market or fair value valuation).
9. Backward-looking wage, cost and price adjustments, initiating turning point (Fig.
   7.44) ◄

Exercise Questions

1. What phases of the business cycle are there?
2. What types of business cycles are there, differentiated by length?
3. Name one leading and one lagging economic indicator.
4. What are three essential reasons for economic fluctuations?
5. To what extent can economic fluctuations be caused by monetary policy?

---

[128] See also Rottmann, Horst and Wollmershäuser, Timo (2010) on the credit behavior of banks.

6. Describe the phases of the Schumpeterian business cycle.
7. To what extent does psychology play a role in business cycles? Which theories can be used for this purpose?

References

Aghion, P., & Saint-Paul, G. (1993). *Uncovering some causal relationship between productivity, growth and the structure of economic fluctuations: A tentative survey* (Working Paper No. 4603). Cambridge: National Bureau of Economic Research.

Albers, W., et al. (Hrsg.). (1976). *Handwörterbuch der Wirtschaftswissenschaften* (Bd. 4). Vandenhoeck und Ruprecht.

Andel, N. (1990). *Finanzwissenschaft* (3. Aufl.). Tübingen: Mohr Siebeck.

Arteta, C., Kose, M. A., Stocker, M., & Taskin, T. (2016). Negative interest rate policies sources and implications. *Worldbank Policy Research Working Papers, 7791,* August 2016. http://econ.worldbank.org.

Aschinger, G. (1991). *Theorie der spekulativen Blasen. Wirtschaftsstudium, 20*(6), 270–274.

Assenmacher, W. (1998). *Konjunkturtheorie* (8. Aufl.). Oldenbourg.

Assenmacher K., & Krogstrup, S. (2018). Monetary policy with negative interest rates: Decoupling cash from electronic money (*IMF Working Paper*, 18/191). https://www.imf.org/en/Publications/WP/Issues/2018/08/27/Monetary-Policy-with-Negative-Interest-Rates-Decoupling-Cash-from-Electronic-Money-46076.

Azariadis, C., & Guesnerie, R. (1986). Sunsports and cycles. *Review of Economic Studies, 53,* 725–738.

Baks, K., & Kramer, C. (1999). *Global liquidity and asset prices: Measurements, implications and spillovers.* (IMF Working Paper No. 99/168). Washigton: International Monetary Fund.

Ball, L., & Mankiw, N. G. (1994). Asymetric price adjustment and economic fluctuations. *The Economic Journal, 30,* 247–261.

Barro, R. J. (1971). A general disequilibrium model of income and employment. *American Economic Review, 61,* 82–93.

Barro, R. J. (1981). *Money, expectations and business cycles.* Academic.

Barro, R. J., & Grossmann, H. I. (1976). *Employment, and inflation.* Harvard University Press.

Behavioral Finance Group. (2000). Behavioral Finance – Idee und Überblick. *Finanz Betrieb, 5,* 311–318.

Berg, H., & Cassel, D. (1992). Theorie der Wirtschaftspolitik. *Vahlens Kompendium der Wirtschaftstheorie und Wirtschaftspolitik* (5. Aufl., Bd. 2, S. 163–238). Vahlen.

Bergstrom, A. (1962). A model of technical progress, the production function and cyclical growth. *Economica, 29*(116), 357–370.

Black, F. (1987). *Business cycles and equilibrium.* Basil Blackwell.

Blanchard, O. J., & Watson, M. W. (1982). Bubbles, rational expectations, and financial markets. In P. Wachtel (Hrsg.), *Crises in the economic and financial structure.* Lexington.

Blume, L., & Easley, D. (1992). Evolution and market behavior. *Journal of Economic Theory, 58,* 9–40.

Borio, C., & Zhu, H. (2008). Capital regulation, risk-taking and monetary policy: A missing link in the transmission mechanism? (*BIS Working paper*, 268).

Borio, C., Gombacorta, L., & Hofmann, B. (2015). *The influence of monetary policy on bank profitability.* Bank for International Settlements. (Working Paper, 514).

Braley, R. (1983). *An introduction to risk and return* (2. edn.). Oxford University Press.

Bruns, C. (1994). *Bubbles und Excess Volatility auf dem deutschen Aktienmarkt*. Betriebswirtschaftlicher Verlag Dr. Th. Gabler GmbH.

Campbell, J. Y., & Ammer, J. (1993). What moves the stock and bond markets? A variance decomposition for long-term asset returns. *The Journal of Finance, 48*(1), 3–37.

Caruana, J. (2013). *Hitting the limits of "outside the box" thinking? Monetary policy in the crisis and beyond*, Official Monetary and Financial Institutions Forum lecture (Golden Series Lecture), London: https://www.bis.org/speeches/sp130516.htm.

Chancellor, E. (1999). *Devil take the hindmost. A history of financial speculation*. Plume.

Chenery, H. B. (1952). Overcapacity and the acceleration principle. *Econometrica, 20,* 1–28.

Claessens, S., & Kose, M. A. (2013). Financial crises: Explanations, types, and implications. (*IMF Working Paper*, 13/28). https://www.imf.org/external/pubs/ft/wp/2013/wp1328.pdf.

Claessens, S., Kose, M. A., & Terrones, M. E. (2012). How do business and financial cycles interact? *Journal of International Economics, 87*(1), 178–190.

Claessens, S., Coleman, N., & Donnelly, M. (2016). Low-for-long interest rates and net interest margins of banks in advanced foreign economies. *Federal Reserve Board, IFDP Notes,* April 11.

Clarke, S. (1967). *Central Bank Cooperation: 1924–1931*. Federal Reserve Bank of New York.

Clower, R. W. (1965). The Keynesian counter-revolution: A theoretical appraisal. In F. H. Hahn & F. Brechling (Hrsg.), *The theory of interest rates* (pp. 103–125). Macmillan.

Conrad, C. (1999). Entwicklungen der Konjunkturtheorie seit Keynes und ihr Beitrag zur Konjunkturpolitik – Eine vergleichende kritische Bewertung. *Konjunkturpolitik, 45*(3), 188–220.

Conrad, C. A. (2000). Theorie und Praxis der Speculative Bubbles, In C. A. Conrad & M. Stahl (Eds.), *Risikomanagement an den internationalen Finanzmärkten*. Schaeffer Poeschel.

Conrad, C. A. (2015). Incentives, risk and compensation schemes: Experimental evidence on the importance of risk adequate compensation. *Applied Economics and Finance, 2*(2), 50–55. https://doi.org/10.11114/aef.v2i2.1053.

Conrad, C. A. (2016). The image of man in the economic sciences in light of the financial crisis and recent research results. *Applied Economics and Finance, 3*(1), 95–103.

Conrad, C. A. (2019). The effects on investment behavior of zero interest rate policy, evidence from a roulette experiment. *Applied Economics and Finance, 6*(4), 18–27. https://doi.org/10.11114/aef.v6i4.4272.

Conrad, C. A. (2020). *Political economy*. Springer-Gabler. https://doi.org/10.1007/978-3-658-30884-1.

Conrad, C. A. (February 2021). The effects of money supply and interest rates on stock prices, Evidence from two behavioral experiments. *Applied Economics and Finance, 8*(2), 33–41. https://doi.org/10.11114/aef.v8i2.5173.

Conrad, C. A. (2022). The effects of demand and interest rates on investments, Evidence of overinvestment from two behavioral experiments. *Applied Economics and Finance, 9*(1), 19–28. https://doi.org/10.11114/aef.v9i1.5452.

Conrad, C. A., & Schoett, H. (2000). Das Börsenjahr 1998 – Nur knapp vorbei am Crash? In C. A. Conrad & M. Stahl (Hrsg.), *Risikomanagement an den internationalen Finanzmärkten* (S. 151–159). Schäffer-Poeschel.

Conrad, C. A., & Stahl, M. (2000a). Wirtschaft, Börsenfieber und Geldpolitik in den USA. *Orientierungen zur Wirtschafts- und Gesellschaftspolitik der Ludwig-Erhard-Stiftung, 85,* 24–32.

Conrad, C., & Stahl, M. (2000b). Ein Alan Greenspan macht keine neue Ära. *Handelsblatt, 1*(146), 49–50.

Conrad, C. A., & Stahl, M. (2002) Asset-Preise als geldpolitische Zielgröße – Das Beispiel der USA. *Wirtschaftsdienst, 82*(8), 486–493.

Conrad, C. A., & Stahl, M. (2003). Geldpolitik und Spekulationsblasen – Das Beispiel der USA. *Österreichisches Bankarchiv, Zeitschrift für das gesamte Bank- und Börsenwesen,51,* 685–693.

Cúrdia, V. (2019). How much could negative rates have helped the recovery? *FRBSF Economic Letter,* 2019–04, February 4, Research from the Federal Reserve Bank of San Francisco. https://www.frbsf.org/economic-research/publications/economic-letter/2019/february/how-much-could-negative-rates-have-helped-recovery/.

Daxhammer, R., & Schmied-Wörle, T. (2000). Japan seit 1990: Das schmerzhaft lange Platzen einer Bubble. In C. Conrad & M. Stahl (Hrsg.), *Risikomanagement an den internationalen Finanzmärkten* (S. 45–58). Schäffer-Poeschel.

De Bondt, W. F. M., & Forbes, W. P. (1999). Herding in analyst earnings forecasts: Evidence from the United Kingdom. *European Financial Management,5*(2), 143–163.

Dell'Ariccia, G., Laeven, L., & Marquez, R. (2010). Monetary policy, leverage, and bank risk-taking. (*IMF Working Papers,* 10/276), International Monetary Fund. https://www.imf.org/external/pubs/ft/wp/2010/wp10276.pdf.

Dell'Ariccia, G., Igan, D., Laeven, L., & Tong, H. (2013). Policies for macrofinancial stability: Dealing with credit booms and busts. In S. Claessens, M. A. Kose, L. Laeven, & F. Valencia (Hrsg.), *Financial crises, consequences, and policy responses.* IMF. https://www.elibrary.imf.org/view/IMF071/20264-9781475543407/20264-9781475543407/20264-9781475543407.xml?redirect=true.

De Long, B. D., & Summers, L. (1988). How does macroeconomic policy affect output? *Brookings Paper on Economic Activity,2,* 433–480.

De Nicolò, G., Dell'Ariccia, G., Laeven, L., & Valencia, F. (2010). Monetary policy and bank risk-taking. *IMF Staff Position Note,* SDN/10/09. https://www.imf.org/external/pubs/ft/spn/2010/spn1009.pdf.

Diba, B. T., & Grossman, H. I. (1988). Explosive rational bubbles in stock prices? *The American Economic Review,78*(3), 520–530.

Downs, A. (1968). *Ökonomische Theorie der Demokratie.* Mohr.

Drozd, L. (2018). *The policy perils of low interest rates,* Federal Reserve Bank of Philadelphia, Discussion Paper, Q1. https://philadelphiafed.org/-/media/research-and-data/publications/economic-insights/2018/q1/eiq118-policy_perils.pdf?la=en.

Eucken, W. (1952). *Grundsätze der Wirtschaftspolitik* (4. unveränderte Aufl.). Mohr.

Ezekiel, M. (1938). The Cobweb Theorem. *The Quarterly Journal of Economics, 52*(2), 255–280. https://doi.org/10.2307/1881734.

Fama, E. (1970). Efficient capital markets: A review of theory and empirical work. *Journal of Finance, 25*(2), 383–417. https://doi.org/10.2307/2325486

Felderer, B., & Homburg, S. (1989). *Makroökonomik und neue Makroökonomik.* Springer.

Feldstein, M. (2013). *The taper chase.* Project Syndicate, September 30. https://www.project-syndicate.org/commentary/why-the-fed-postponed-the-qe-taper-by-martin-feldstein?barrier=accesspaylog.

Fischer, S. (1980). *Expectations and economic policy.* University of Chicago Press.

Flannery, M. J., & Protopapadakis, A. A. (2002). Macroeconomic factors do influence aggregate stock returns. *Review of Financial Studies, 15*(3), 751–782.

Flood, R. P., & Garber, P. M. (1980). Market fundamentals versus price-level bubbles: The first tests. *Journal of Political Economy,88,* 745–770.

Franke, S. F. (1996). *(Ir) rationale Politik?* Metropolis.

Franz, W. (Hrsg.). (1999). *Trend und Zyklus, Wirtschaftswissenschaftliches Seminar Ottobeuren* (Bd. 28). Mohr.

Frenk, D. (2011). Review of Irwin and Sanders 2010, OECD Report. In Institute for Agriculture and Trade Policy (Ed.). *Excessive Speculation in Agriculture Commodities, Selected writings from 2008–2012,* 43–49. http://www.iadb.org/intal/intalcdi/PE/2011/08247.pdf.

Frey, B. S. (1981). *Theorie demokratischer Wirtschaftspolitik*. Vahlen.

Frey, B. S., & Lau, L. J. (1968). Towards a mathematical model of government behaviour. *Zeitschrift für Nationalökonomie, 28*, 355–380.

Friedman, M., & Schwartz, A. J. (1965). *The great contraction 1929–1933*. Princeton University Press.

Friedman, M., & Schwartz, A. (1969). *A monetary history of the United States*. Princeton University Press.

Froot, K. A., Scharfstein, D. S., & Stein, J. C. (1992). Herd on the street: Informational inefficiencies in a market with short-term speculation. *The Journal of Finance, XLVII*((4), 1461–1484.

Gagnon, J. E. (2016). Quantitative Easing: An underappreciated success, Peterson Institute for International Economics. *Policy Brief*, PB16-4, APRIL. https://piie.com/system/files/documents/pb16-4.pdf.

Gerfin, H., & Möller, J. (1980a). Neue Makroökonomie. *Wirtschaftswissenschaftliches Studium, 9*, 201–206.

Gerfin, H., & Möller, J. (1980b). Neue Makroökonomische Theorie. *Wirtschaftswissenschaftliches Studium, 4*, 153–160.

Glöser-Chowhound, S., Hartwig, J., Wheat, I. D., & Faulstich, M. (2017). The cobweb theorem and delays in adjusting supply in metals' markets. *System Dynamics Review, 32*(4), 279–308. https://doi.org/10.1002/sdr.1565.

Goodwin, R. M. (1951). The nonlinear accelerator and the persistence of business cycles. *Econometrica, 19*, 1–17.

Goodwin, R. M. (1967). A growth cycle. In C. H. Feldstein (Hrsg.), *Socialism, capitalism and economic growth, essays presented to maurice dobb* (S. 54–58). Cambridge University Press.

Grosskettler, H. (1989). Johan Gustav Knut Wicksell. In J. Starbatty (Ed.), *Klassiker des ökonomischen Denkens II* (pp. 191–210). Beck.

Guerrieri, P., & Padoan, P. C. C. (1989). *The political economy of european integration*. Harvester & Wheatsheaf.

Hannoun, H. (2015). *Ultra-Low or negative interest rates: What they mean for financial stability and growth*. Speech at the Eurofi High-Level Seminar, Riga, April 22. https://www.bis.org/speeches/sp150424.pdf.

Hayek, F. A. (1976). *Geldtheorie und Konjunkturtheorie*. Reprinting of the original from 1929. Wolfgang Neugebauer.

Hesse, H. (1999). Korreferat zum Referat K Jaeger, Der Beitrag der traditionellen Theorie zur Erklärung von Trend und Zyklus. In W. Franz, et al. (Hrsg.), *Trend und Zyklus, Wirtschaftswissenschaftliches Seminar Ottobeuren* (Ed. 28, S. 1–34). Mohr.

Heubes, J. (1986). *Grundzüge der Konjunkturtheorie*. Vahlen.

Heubes, J. (1991). *Konjunktur und Wachstum*. Vahlen.

Hicks, J. R. (1950). *A contribution to the theorie of the trade cycle*. Clarendon.

Hirata, H., Kose, M. A., Otrok, C., & Terrones, M. E. (2012). Global house price fluctuations: Synchronization and Determinants. NBER International Seminar on Macroeconomics 2012, National Bureau of Economic Research. (Working Paper No. 18362). https://www.nber.org/papers/w18362.

Homa, K. E., & Jaffee, D. M. (1971). The supply of money and common stock prices. *The Journal of Finance, 26*(5), 1045–1066.

Homburg, S. (1996). Makroökonomik. In A. Börsch-Supan, J. von Hagen, & P. J. J. Welfens (Hrsg.), *Springers Handbuch der Volkswirtschaftslehre*. Springer.

Humphreys D. (2012). Mining investment trends and implications for minerals availability. *Polinares Working Paper, 15*. Brussels.

International Monetary Fund. (2000). *World economic outlook*. Asset Prices and the Business Cycle.

Irwin, S. H., & Sanders, D. R. (2012). Testing the masters hypothesis in commodity futures markets. *Energy Economics, 34,* 256–269.

Issing, O. (1982). Hat der Keynesianismus noch eine Zukunft? In O. Vogel (Hrsg.), *Wirtschaftspolitik der 80er Jahre: Leitbilder und Strategien.* Deutscher Instituts-Verlag.

Ito, T., & Iwaisako, T. (1995). *Explaining asset bubbles in Japan*, National Bureau of Economic Research, Working Paper 5358.

Jaeger, K. (1999). Der Beitrag der traditionellen Theorie zur Erklärung von Trend und Zyklus. In W. Franz, et al. (Hrsg.), *Trend und Zyklus, Wirtschaftswissenschaftliches Seminar Ottobeuren* (Bd. 28, S. 1–34). Mohr.

Jüttner, J. (1989). Fundamentals, bubbles, trading strategies: Are they the causes of black monday? *Kredit und Kapital, 22*(4), 470–486.

Kampmann C. E. (1992). *Feedback complexity and market adjustment: An experimental approach.* PhD thesis, MIT Sloan School of Management.

Kampmann, C., & Stermann, J. D. (1996). *Feedback complexity, bounded rationality, and market dynamics.* Mimeo. Retrieved from http://web.mit.edu/jsterman/www/SDG/feed.pdf.

Kganyago, T., & Gumbo, V. (2015). An empirical study of the relationship between money market interest rates and stock market performance: Evidence from Zimbabwe (2009–2013). *International Journal of Economics and Financial Issues, 5*(3), 638–646.

Kiehling, H. (2000). *Kursstürze am Aktienmarkt* (2. Aufl.). Dtv Deutscher Taschenbuch.

Komphardt, J. (1989). Konjunkturtheorie heute: Ein Überblick. *Zeitschrift für Wirtschafts- und Sozialwissenschaften, 109,* 173–231.

Krisch, G. (1993). *Neue Politische Ökonomie* (3. Aufl.). Werner.

Kugler, P. (1998). Neuere Entwicklungen in der Konjunkturtheorie. *Allgemeines Statistisches Archiv, 82,* 25–36.

Kurz, R. (1986). Zyklische Wachstum und Verteilung: Das Goodwin-Modell. *WiSu, 86*(6), 305–310.

Kydland, F. E., & Prescott, E. C. (1977). Rules rather than discretion: The inconsistency of optimal plans. *Journal of Political Economy, 85*(3), 473–491.

Kydland, F. E., & Prescott, E. C. (1982). Time to build and aggregate fluctuations. *Econometrica, 50,* 1345–1370.

Laidler, D. (1976a). Inflation in Britain—A monetarist perspective. *American Economic Review, 66,* 467–484.

Laidler, D. (1976b). Inflation—Alternative explanations and policies: Tests on data drawn from six countries. *Journal of Monetary Economics, 4,* 251–306.

Lansing, K. J. (2008). *Speculative growth and overreaction to technology shocks.* (Working Paper Series, 2008–08), Federal Reserve Bank of San Francisco.

Lastrapes, W. D. (1998). International evidence on equity prices, interest rates and money. *Journal of International Money and Finance, 17*(3), 377–406.

Leland, H., & Rubinstein, M. (1988). Comments on the market crash: Six months after. *Journal of Economic Perspectives, 2*(3), 45–50.

Leontief, W. (1966). *Essays in economics. Theories and theorizing.* Oxford University Press.

Lindblom, C. E. (1965). *The intelligence of democracy.* Free Press.

Long, J. B., & Plosser, C. I. (1983). Real business cycles. *Journal of Political Economy, 91*(1), 29–69.

Lucas, R. E. (1975). An equilibrium model of the business cycle. *Journal of Political Economy, 83*(1975), 1113–1144.

Lucas, R. E. (1976). Econometric policy evaluation: A critique. *Carnegie Rochester Conference Series on Public Policy, 1*(1), 19–46.

Maddaloni, A., & Peydró. J.-L. (2010). *Bank risk-taking, securitization, supervision and low interest rates: Evidence from the Euro area and the U.S. lending standards.* (Working Paper Series, 1248), European Central Bank. https://www.ecb.europa.eu/pub/pdf/scpwps/ecbwp1248.pdf.

Maddaloni, A., Peydró-Alcalde, J. L., & Scope, S. (2009). *Does monetary policy affect bank credit standards? Evidence from the Euro area bank lending survey.*https://www.researchgate.net/publication/256000197_Does_Monetary_Policy_Affect_Bank_Credit_Standards_Evidence_from_the_Euro_Area_Bank_Lending_Survey.

Malinvaud, E. (1977). *The theory of unemployment reconsidered.* Basil Blackwell.

Mankiw, G. N. (1985). Small menu costs and large business cycles. *Quarterly Journal of Economics,100,* 529–539.

Mankiw, G. N. (1998). *Makroökonomik* (3. Aufl.). Schäffer-Poeschel.

Marx, K. (1864). *Das Kapital: Kritik der politischen Ökonomie Der Gesamtprozeß der kapitalistischen Produktion* (Bd. 3, 33 Aufl., Kap. 1–3). Dietz.

McCallum, B. T. (1980). Rational expectations and macroeconomic stabilization policy. *Journal of Money, Credit and Banking,18,* 716–746.

Menil, G., & Enzler, J. J. (1972). *Wages and prices in the FRB-MIT-Penn Econometric Model. Econometrics of price determination.* Federal Reserve Board.

Menkhoff, L., & Röckemann, C. (1994). Noise Trading auf Aktienmärkten. *Zeitschrift Für Betriebswirtschaftslehre, 64*(3), 277–295.

Meyer-Krahmer, F. (1979). *Politische Entscheidungsprozesse und Ökonomische Theorie der Politik.* Campus.

Mezger, M., & Stahl, M. (2001a). Gold – Stabilitätspfeiler in Krisenzeiten. *Die Bank,5,* 372–378.

Mezger, M., & Stahl, M. (2001b). Neue Erkenntnisse über Inflation und Finanzkrisen. *Orientierungen Zur Wirtschafts- Und Gesellschaftspolitik Der Ludwig-Erhard-Stiftung, 87,* 15–22.

Mian, A. R., Sufi, A., & Verner, E. (2015). Household Debt and Business Cycles Worldwide. (*NBER Working Paper,* 21581). https://www.nber.org/papers/w21581.pdf.

Minford, P., & Peel, D. (1983). *Rational expectations and the new macroeconomics.* Martin Robertson.

Minsky, H. P. (1986). *Stabilizing an unstable economy—A Twentieth Century fund report.* Yale University Press.

Morishima, M. (1996). *Dynamic economic theory.* Cambridge University Press. https://doi.org/10.1017/CBO9780511628474.

Musgrave, R. A., Musgrave, P. B., & Kullmer, L. (1987). *Die öffentlichen Finanzen in Theorie und Praxis* (Bd. 3). UTB.

Nishad Nishad, P. (2018). Effectiveness of Japan's zero and negative interest rate policy. (*MPRA Paper,* No. 89442). https://mpra.ub.uni-muenchen.de/89442/ MPRA Paper No. 89442.

Nordhaus, W. D. (1975). The political business cycle. *Review of Economic Studies,42,* 169–190.

Ongena, S., Vasso, I., & Peydró, J. L. (2009). *Monetary policy, risk-taking and pricing: Evidence from a quasi-natural experiment.* (Discussion Paper 2009-31). Tilburg University, Center for Economic Research.

Ott, A. (1963). *Einführung in die dynamische Wirtschaftstheorie.* Vandenhoeck & Ruprecht.

Phillips, A. W. H. (1961). A simple model of employment, money and prices in a growing economy. *Economica,28*(112), 360–370.

Phillips, P., & Loretan, M. (1990). *Testing covariance stationarity under moment condition failure with an application to common stock returns,* Cowles Foundation for Economic Research at Yale University New Haven Conneticut Discussion Paper, 947.

Pícha, V. (2017). Effect of money supply on the stock market. *Acta Universitatis Agriculturae Et Silviculturae Mendelianae Brunensis, 65*(2), 465–472.

Pohjola, M. T. (1981). Stable cyclic and chaotic growth: The dynamics of a discrete-time version of Goodwin's growth cycle model. *Zeitschrift für Nationalökonomie,41*(1–2), 27–38.

Popper, K. (1958). *The logic of scientific discovery.* Harper Torchbooks.

Rajan, R. G. (2005). *Has Financial Development Made the World Riskier?* NBER Working Paper No. 11728. https://www.nber.org/papers/w11728.

Ramey, G., & Ramey, V. A. (1991). Technology Commitment and the Cost of Economic Fluctuations. (Working Paper No. 3755). National Bureau of Economic Research.

Ramey, G., & Ramey, V. A. (1995). Cross-country evidence on the link between volatility and growth. *The American Economic Review,85*(5), 1138–1151.

Ramser, H. J. (1988). Neuere Beiträge zur Konjunkturpolitik: Ein Überblick. *IFO-Studien,34,* 95–115.

Ramser, H. J. (1997). Konjunktur und Wachstum: Der Beitrag der Neuen Wachstumstheorie. *Ifo-Studien,43*(2), 211–223.

Rasch, S. (1993). Crashs-Naturkatastrophen an den Finanzmärkten? *ZEW-Wirtschaftsanalysen,1*(3), 269–305.

Rigobon, R., & Sack, B. (2004). The impact of monetary policy on asset prices. *Journal of Monetary Economics, 51*(8), 1553–1575.

Rothschild, K. W. (1981). *Einführung in die Ungleichgewichtstheorie.* Springer.

Rottmann, H., & Wollmershäuser, T. (2010). A micro data approach to the identification of credit crunches. (Working Paper No. 3159: Monetary Policy and International Finance). CESifo.

Rozeff, M. S. (1974). Money and stock prices: Market efficiency and the lag in effect of monetary policy. *Journal of Financial Economics, 1*(3), 245–302.

Rubio, V. J., Hernández, J. M., Zaldvíar, F., Márquez, O., & Santacreu, J. (2010). Can we predict risk-taking behavior? Two behavioral tests for predicting guessing tendencies in a multiple-choice test. *European Journal of Psychological Assessment, 26*(2), 87–94. http://www.uam.es/proyectosinv/psimasd/risktaking.pdf.

Safar, L., & Siničáková, M. (2017). Money supply influence on gross domestic product throughout stock markets in United States and European Union. *Journal of Applied Economic Sciences, 12*(6), 1578–1584.

Samuelson, P. A. (1939). Interactions between the multiplier analysis and the principle of acceleration. *Review of Economics and Statistics,21,* 235–241.

Santoni, G. J., & Dwyer, G. P., Jr. (1990). Bubbles or fundamentals: New evidence from the great bull markets. In E. N. White (Hrsg.), *Crashes and panics: The lessons from history.* Wiley.

Schebeck, F., & Tichy, G. (1984). Die „Stylized Facts" in der modernen Konjunkturdiskussion. In G. Bombach, B. Gahlen, & A. E. Ott (Hrsg.), *Perspektiven der Konjunkturforschung* (S. 207–224). Mohr.

Schlecker, M. (2014). *Kointegrationsanalyse, Stationarität und Augmented-dickey-fuller-Test.* http://www.matthias-schlecker.de/kointegrationsanalyse-stationaritaet-und-augmented-dickey-fuller-test.

Schumpeter, P. (1939). *Business cycles.* McGraw-Hill.

Schumpeter, J. A. (1993). *Theorie der wirtschaftlichen Entwicklung* (8, Erstauflage 1911 Aufl.). Duncker und Humblot.

Shachat, J., & Zhang, Z. (21. June 2012). The Hayek hypothesis and long run competitive equilibrium: an experimental investigation. *Xiamen University Discussion Paper.* https://doi.org/10.2139/ssrn.2089077.

Shiller, R. J. (1984). Stock prices and social dynamics. *Brookings Papers on Economic Activity,2,* 457–498.

Shiller, R. J. (2000). *Irrational exuberance.* Princeton University Press.

Shleifer, A. (1986). Implementation cycles. *Journal of Political Economy,94,* 1169–1190.

Shleifer, A. (2000a). *Inefficient markets, an introduction to behavioral finance*. Oxford University Press. https://doi.org/10.1093/0198292279.001.0001.

Shleifer, A. (2000b). Stock prices and social dynamics. *Brookings Papers on Economic Activity,2,* 457–498.

Shleifer, A., & Vishny, R. W. (1990). Equilibrium short horizons of investors and firms. *American Economic Review,80*(2), 148–153.

Simon, H. A. (1959). Theories of decision-making in economics and behavioral science. *The American Economics Review, 49*(3).

Single, G., & Stahl, M. (2000). Gefahrenherd Hedge-Fonds: der Fall LTCM. *Bank Archiv der Österreichischen Bankwissenschaftlichen Gesellschaft,48*(12), 1060–1066.

Sloan, A., & Stern, R. L. (1988). How $V_o = V_g N(d_1) - E/e^r N(d_2)$ led to black monday. *Forbes,25*(1), 55–59.

Stadler, G. W. (1994). Real business cycles. *Journal of Economic Literature,32,* 1750–1783.

Stahl, M. (2000). Die Lektionen des Jahres 1929. In C. Christian & M. Stahl (Hrsg.), *Risikomanagement an internationalen Finanzmärkten* (S. 3–20). Schäffer-Poeschel.

Stahl, M., & Mezger, M. (2000). Der Schatten des Jahres 1929. *Die Bank,5,* 300–307.

Stavenhagen, G. (1969). *Geschichte der Wirtschaftstheorie*. Vandenhoeck.

Stiglitz, S. E. (1994). Endogenous growth and cycles. In Y. Shiroya & M. Perlmon (Hrsg.), *Innovation in technology, industries and institutions, studies in schumpeterian perspective* (S. 121–156). The University of Michigan Press.

Stiglitz, J. (2016). *What's Wrong with Negative Rates?*, Project Syndicate, April 13. https://www.project-syndicate.org/commentary/negative-rates-flawed-economic-model-by-joseph-e--stiglitz-2016-04?barrier=accesspaylog.

Stiglitz, J., & Weiss, A. (1981). Credit rationing in markets with imperfect information. *American Economic Review,71*(3), 393–410.

Stiglitz, S. E., & Weiss, A. (1992). Asymmetric information in credit markets and its implications for macroeconomics. *Oxford Economic Papers,44*(4), 694–724.

Teichmann, U. (1997). *Grundriss der Konjunkturpolitik* (5. Aufl.). Vahlen.

Temin, P. (1976). *Did monetary forces cause the great depression?* Norton.

Thaler, R. (1989). The psychology of choice and the assumptions of economics. In A. E. Roth (Ed.), *Laboratory experimentation in economics. Six points of view* (pp. 99–130). Cambridge University Press. https://doi.org/10.1017/CBO9780511528316.004.

The Presidental Task Force. (1988). *Report of the presidental task force on market mechanisms, (Brady-Report)*. US Government Printing Office.

Thorbecke, W. (1997). On stock market returns and monetary policy. *The Journal of Finance, 52*(2), 635–654.

Tichy, G. (1995). *Konjunkturpolitik* (3. Aufl.). Springer.

Treynor, J. (1998). Bulls, beers and market bubbles. *Financial Analysts Journal,54*(2), 69–74.

von Hayek, F. A. (1929). *Geldtheorie und Konjunkturtheorie* (Nachdruck der ersten Auflage von 1929 Aufl., S. 81 ff.). Wolfgang Neugebauer.

von Hayek, F. A. (1935). Prices and production (2nd Aufl.). Clifton: Kelley (reprint In The Ludwig von Mises Institute (Eds.), *Prices & production and other works. F. A. Hayek on money, the business cycle, and the gold standard.* Auburn 2008. https://mises.org/library/prices-and-production.

von Hayek, F. A. (Hrsg.). (1969). *Der Wettbewerb als Entdeckungsverfahren*. Freiburger Studien.

Wagner, A. (1990). *Makroökonomik* (2. Aufl.). UTB.

Waugh, F. V. (1964). Cobweb models. *American Journal of Agricultural Economics, 46,* 732–750. https://doi.org/10.2307/1236509.

Wicksell, K. (1898). *Geldzins und Güterpreise. Eine Studie über den Tauschwert des Geldes bestimmenden Ursachen.* Scienta. (Berichtigter Neudruck der Ausgabe Jena 1898).

Wicksell, K. (1922). *Vorlesungen über Nationalökonomie auf Grundlage des Marginalprinzipes: Bd. 2. Geld und Kredit.* 1969. Scienta (first published Stockholm 1906).

Wicksell, K. (1928). *Vorlesungen über Nationalökonomie, Theoretischer Teil, zweiter Band.* Gustav Fischer.

Wicksell, K. (1968). *Geldzins und Güterpreise. Eine Studie über den Tauschwert des Geldes bestimmenden Ursachen.* Scienta (first published Jena 1898).

Wolfstetter, E. (1982). Fiscal policy and the classical growth cycle. *Zeitschrift für Nationalökonomie,42,* 375–393.

Zarnowitz, V. (1997). Business cycles observed and assessed: Why and how they matter (Working Paper No. 6230). National Bureau of Economic Research.

Zame W. (2008). General equilibrium (new developments). In S. N. Durlauf & L. E. Blume (Eds), *The New Palgrave Dictionary of Economics* (2nd ed.). Palgrave Macmillan. https://doi.org/10.1057/978-1-349-95121-5_2354-1.

Further Reading

Conrad, C. A., & Stahl, M. (Eds.). (2000). *Risikomanagement an den internationalen Finanzmärkten.* Schäffer-Poeschel.

Rubio, V. J., Hernández, J. M., & Santacreu, J. *The objective assessment of risk tendency as a personality dimension.* University Autónoma of Madrid. www.uam.es/proyectosinv/psimasd/assessrisk.pdf.

Single, G., & Stahl, M. (2000). Risikopotential Hedge-Fonds – Der Fall LTCM. In C. A. Conrad & M. Stahl (Hrsg.), *Risikomanagement an den internationalen Finanzmärkten.* Schäffer-Poeschel.

Stahl, M. (6. Juni 2000). Die Goldenen Zwanziger im Lichte der Internet Revolution, Chancen und Risiken der Neuen Ökonomie, Die Wirtschafts- und Börsenentwicklung in den USA heute weist große Ähnlichkeit auf mit der Lage vor dem Schwarzen Freitag 1929. Süddeutsche Zeitung (S. 129).

International Financial Markets after the Financial Crisis

8

8.1 The Financial Crisis and the Reforms to Stabilize the Financial Markets

What Follows Why?

The financial crisis led to the worst depression since 1929. Only by massive economic programs could worse be prevented. Here Keynesian theory came into play. Only through globally agreed massive credit-financed government spending increases could depression be prevented. The banks had to be saved with tax money, as many banks had invested in the government bonds of weak European countries whose solvency was called into question. The sovereign debt crisis has emerged from the financial crisis. Against this background, the question arises of state regulations that limit the risk of banks. Politicians and economists have urged such regulation of the financial markets since the onset of the 2007 financial crisis. What has happened in the meantime? Were the right reforms implemented or could there be another financial crisis? After analyzing the causes of the crisis, the main reforms are examined below.

Learning Goals

You should be able to explain the reasons for the financial crisis and the attempts to counteract it.

8.1.1 The Subprime Crisis, the Biggest Financial Crisis After 1929

In 2003, Warren Buffet said of the credit derivatives market that they were "financial weapons of mass destruction, carrying dangers that, while now latent are potentially

C. Conrad, *Applied Macroeconomics*, https://doi.org/10.1007/978-3-658-39315-1_8

lethal." Others also warned that credit based derivatives coupled with a lack of transparency were leading to a significant concentration of risk. Unfortunately, they were right.

Derivative products such as CDOs (Collateralized Debt Obligations) can be directly traced as being one of the major factors leading to the subprime crisis and the greatest financial crisis since the Wall Street crash of 1929. CDOs are structured financial products comprised of a variety of loans, bonds, mortgages and credit derivatives such as Credit Default Swaps or CDSs. For the most part the major Wall Street investment banks put together CDOs using home mortgages, which were then resold as investment products. These CDOs were structured to meet the requirements of the major US rating agencies, which based their risk calculations on complicated economic models and statistical analysis. Two apparently ingenious combinations of factors made it possible to create an innovative financial product with a combined calculated risk in the portfolio lesser than the sum of the individual risk associated with each element in the portfolio.

The basis for the evaluation of risk associated with these financial products as calculated by the rating agencies was based upon the historical default rate of US mortgages. As this data was not always available, it was necessary to draw upon estimates that fit within established portfolio theories and expectations and which would produce the desired reduction of risk between two comparative portfolios. Part of this process was to investigate the relationships and correlations between the individual elements of these portfolios to determine the probability that both or more elements could be eliminated from risk calculations. The complex statistical financial models used by the rating agencies were not always understood or even available to those in the market place as investors. This situation was not considered to be an issue at the time, as the capital markets had a great deal of trust and confidence in the ratings provided by the rating agencies. For decades, the ratings provided by the rating agencies concerning potential risk had been used to determine the terms for credit and loans to borrowers in the capital markets. As a consequence of the subprime crisis, the objectivity of these ratings agencies has now been called into question, most notably due to their previous relationships with the investment banks for which they provided the CDO ratings.

The second situation by which a portfolio rating could be improved was through the use and subordination of various "risk tranches". In the event of a default or failure of one of the elements or "tranches" in the portfolio, the most subordinated tranche (junior note) would be affected. This process would continue on up the scale to the tranches with AA to BB ratings, (mezzanine notes) and in the extreme case on up to the most senior tranches with AAA ratings.

For decades, the value of American real estate has steadily increased. After all, the USA has been a country of considerable growth both in terms of population and economic expansion. This growth has also been the basis for a historically low level of home mortgage defaults. For the most part, home values have been sufficient to cover outstanding mortgage balances in the event of a default. As a consequence, lenders were encouraged to offer ever-increasing mortgage loans based on the projected future value of homes in an ever-expanding market. As home values rose, lenders would offer homeowners access to their equity through refinancing or home equity lines of credit, which would support even further consumption. Much of the mortgage financing made available to borrowers by Freddie Mac and Fannie Mae was also supported by political incentives to encourage home ownership among socially and economically disadvantaged minority groups. This initiative originated in the mid-1990s with the Clinton administration as lending criteria were relaxed[1] and continued under the Bush administration. In 2003, Congressman Ron Paul warned that this relaxed lending policy would eventually lead to individuals borrowing to buy homes that they could ill-afford and eventually require financial intervention on the part of government. In 1994, the market for subprime mortgages made up only 5% of the total mortgage market and amounted to $35 billion dollars, and by 2006 it had increased to become 20% of the mortgage market for a total of approximately $600 billion dollars. This increase in lending volume was only made possible by ever more relaxed lending standards. Borrowers were able to obtain mortgage loans without showing any proof of income or employment or assets, the so-called "ninja loans" meaning "No Income, No Job, and No Assets". This situation was further encouraged by ever-falling interest rates as initiated by the Federal Reserve under the leadership of Alan Greenspan, with short-term rates reaching a low of 1% in 2004. Subprime borrowers were also offered ARMs, or Adjustable Rate Mortgages with low, interest-only payments required, as well as "teaser loans" with initial interest rates well below market rates that would dramatically increase or reset at a later date. Also available were payment option loans which made it possible for borrowers to set their own repayment schedule and thereby postpone repayment for as long as possible. Altogether, US mortgage borrowing rose from $680 billion in 1974 to $14 trillion in 2001. From a total of 8.8 million homeowners with mortgages, about 10.8% had no actual equity in their property or, in fact, owed more than their home was worth.

Average home values in the USA increased 126% from 1997 to 2006, while the relationship between home values and annual income changed from a ratio of 2.9 in 2001 to 4.6 in 2006. This dramatic change in home values, as compared with annual income, was not considered a problem as long as borrowers were able to service their debt and main-

---

[1] "... the Fannie Mae Corporation is easing the credit requirements on loans ... The action ... will encourage those banks to extend home mortgages to individuals whose credit is generally not good enough... Fannie Mae... has been under increasing pressure from the Clinton Administration to expand mortgage loans among low and moderate income people and felt pressure from stock holders to maintain its phenomenal growth in profits. In addition, banks, thrift institutions and mortgage companies have been pressing Fannie Mae to help them make more loans to so-called subprime borrowers whose incomes, credit ratings and savings are not good enough for conventional loans... Fannie Mae is taking on significantly more risk... the government subsidized corporation may run into trouble... prompting a government rescue... the move is intended in part to increase the number of... home owners who tend to have worse credit ratings..." September 30, 1999 New York Times.

tain their mortgage payments. The crisis only came about as a consequence of changing interest rates and the payment structures built into these loans.

Banks can, but in a limited manner, restructure loan intervals as needed to meet business requirements but if they require refinancing at a later date, then it will be necessary for them to draw upon their own liquidity. Therefore every banking student is taught the golden rule of lending, which is to restructure loans through refinancing at appropriate coverage intervals.

When restructuring loans, the risks associated with changing interest rates and refinancing are to be carried and collateralized by the banks themselves. These fundamental rules of finance were unfortunately ignored when it came to the issuance of CDOs by investment banks, which finally amounted to a market value of over $2 trillion dollars. Long-term mortgages were repackaged and sold by the investment banks as special purpose vehicles (conduits) and collateralized at fairly low capital ratios through the use of short-term commercial paper (CPs). In this way, the CDOs could be refinanced at lower interest rates, which created more profitable margins for the banks. The CDOs in these "special purpose entities" did not surface on the bank's balance sheet. As was the case with Enron, these obligations were not listed as consolidated third party liabilities and therefore not readily apparent at first glance. On bank balance sheets these obligations were simply listed as possible liabilities in the comments section and often escaped notice. In the unlikely event that banks were unable to sell these securities on the market, they would be required to provide adequate liquidity to cover these obligations. High leveraging of stock purchases was also a reason for the financial crisis in 1929.

Deregulation further encouraged the direct and indirect use of leverage by investment banks. For example, in 2004 the SEC allowed investment banks to expand their use of leverage by lowering their capital margin requirement from 8 to 6%. By 2007, the five largest US investment banks had increased their borrowing for investment purposes to $4.1 trillion dollars, which equaled approximately 30% of the US gross domestic product. What motivated the investment banks to take on this level of risk? This was the era of the "shareholder value concept", of short-term gain and exceptional bonuses. The simplest way to increase shareholder value and therefore also stock value was to use leverage to boost returns on investment. Finally, in order for a bank to receive a rating of "excellent" from the rating agencies, they were required to show a 25% return on investment of capital and therefore a favorable rating for future refinancing. An attractive aspect of CDOs was that it was not required that they be rated as loans, but could be rated as a security product. This classification allowed the investment banks to realize additional profits by selling them on to other investors and not hold bank funds in reserve as collateral.

Using CDOs, investment banks were therefore able to boost their profitability on invested capital as well as their internal rate of return. Loans would be classified as CDO securities and therefore positively influence the banks balance sheet. As securities, these CDOs would appear to be without risk. In addition, the rating agencies would assign them AAA status, indicating that these "securities" were without risk. As securities, the

CDOs were not subject to the strict federal regulations required for debt products nor would they have to be evaluated as debt obligations on the books of the already highly leveraged banks. Free from complying with external financial requirements and internal lending limits, investment bankers were able to secure profitable sources of revenue and therefore substantial bonuses as well. By repackaging US mortgages as investment products, bankers were able to realize approximately $23.9 billion dollars in bonus payments in 2006. In 2007, Swiss bank UBS paid out $10 billion Swiss Francs in bonus payments alone. The availability and easy access to credit for home mortgages encouraged not only dealers but also lenders who provided loans to ever less qualified borrowers. In the end, these lenders were selling these loans on to other investors and therefore did not have to contend with the risk. The relationship between the lenders issuance of credit and mortgages and the associated risk of default were distinctly separated from one another, which lead to a fundamental violation of the market (order) principles of accountability and transparency. The exceptionally complex structure of the CDOs also contributed to this lack of transparency. It only became clear later that it was all but impossible to separate the various problem loans within the CDOs from the total in the portfolio, and impossible to trace them back to the original borrowers. Also, the system of bonus payments made to bankers selling the CDOs appears to be in contradiction to principles of accountability, as their bonuses were based on short-term profitability while the potential long-term negative consequences of their actions were ignored.

The bubble in the US housing market burst in 2006. A contributing factor was the dramatic rise in short-term interest rates, which made it impossible for many mortgage borrowers to maintain their payments. This rise in interest rates lead to ever-greater defaults and bank repossessions and home prices fell. The consequences for the financial sector first became apparent in February 2007 as HSBC was compelled to write off loans repackaged as CDOs valued $10.5 billion dollars. While serious, the crisis seemed to be limited to the banking sector and did not pose a threat to the real economy. In November 2007, the volume of subprime mortgages was valued at $148 billion dollars. At this point, the extreme difficulty in placing an accurate value on the CDOs became all too apparent. The lack of transparency associated with the CDOs and the high level of risk they carried due to the subprime mortgages they contained made them all but impossible to sell or accurately value. The market for CDOs collapsed entirely, leading to a crisis of capital liquidity for those banks carrying them on their books. This issue leads to an unexpected reduction of liquidity at the banks. In December, the amount of subprime debt was corrected from $200 billion to $300 billion, and then finally in March 2008 from $350 billion to $600 billion dollars.

A rating of AAA was now considered worthless and all trust in the rating agencies had been lost. Without accurate and reliable ratings from the agencies, the capital markets were crippled. It soon became obvious that the crisis was not limited to just the US. As CDOs had been sold on the international market, the risk that they carried was now also an international problem. Swiss banks such as UBS, and German banks IKB and Sachsen Landes Bank had built up considerable portfolios filled with CDOs and as a consequence experienced severe liquidity problems. In addition, these banks required ever increasing amounts of fresh capital to cover the write-offs associated with CDOs and to support lines of liquidity. The banks that had invested too much of their client's capital were in danger of going bankrupt. US investment banks and larger banks such as UBS were able to raise additional capital on their own, while banks such as Germany's IKB and Sachsen Landes Bank had to be rescued by the German federal government. British mortgage lender Northern Rock experienced a run on the bank and had to be nationalized.

The crisis continued to expand. Two basic issues became apparent: increasing suspicion and mistrust between banks and ever further write-offs due to CDOs, which served to accelerate the crisis of liquidity and available capital. Banks felt that they could no longer trust one another and therefore stopped lending to each other. Without transparency and trust between banks, no one could be sure which banks were solvent and how much remaining debt had to be written off. Ratings given to the banks by the ratings agencies could no longer be relied upon. The inter-banking market collapsed. Banks without branch offices, and therefore without access to investors, found themselves short of liquidity. Central banks were compelled to provide infusions of capital into the marketplace and to lower interest rates. The quarterly reports by banks concerning their ever-increasing CDO related write-offs only served to further depress the already discouraged mood in the marketplace. As European banks primarily followed US-GAAP for accounting purposes as well as the internationally accepted IFRS standards, this lead to an even greater difficulty in accurately assigning a value to the CDOs. Following US accounting standards which tend to favor shareholder interests, securities and other financial products such as the CDOs must be "mark to market" to assign a current market value. In contrast to European accounting standards, the costs of acquisition are not included if a reduction in value is only temporary. Although home mortgages continued to operate for the most part unchanged, the market for CDOs had collapsed and banks were compelled to write down the market value of their CDOs by as much as 70%. This development culminated in the partial illiquidity of US investment bank Bear Stearns in March of 2008. The head of Germany's Deutsche Bank Josef Ackermann was quoted at this time as saying that "he no longer believed in the ability of the markets to self-correct and heal themselves".

Bankers called on the government to help them out of the situation. JP Morgan purchased Bear Stearns for $1.2 billion dollars after receiving a bailout loan of $29 billion from the US Federal Reserve. After this action by the Federal Reserve the financial markets seemed to settle down. The danger of collapse of further large financial institutions seemed to be over. At the beginning of 2007, market participants started to believe that perhaps the worst of the subprime crisis was over, only to have the crisis flare up again. But the worst of the crisis was yet to come. The crisis would continue as the banks CDOs increasingly lost value and were written down to comply with accounting regulations. Prices for homes on the US real estate market and the almost non-existent CDO market continued to fall ever further. A shortage of liquidity compelled the banks to sell additional securities, which lead to a vicious cycle of price declines. The mistrust of ratings assigned by the ratings agencies and the general uncertainty in the market lead to investors selling all forms of securities and to seek refuge in government bonds and treasuries.

In September 2008 the entire financial system came close to collapse. Only through a massive intervention by national governments up to and including the nationalization of many banks could the financial crisis be contained. Many newspapers compared the current financial crisis to that of the Wall Street crash of 1929. The US mortgage lender Silver State bank and many other smaller real estate lenders had to be closed and both major mortgage lenders Fannie Mae and Freddie Mac were nationalized. The growing crisis lead to the bankruptcy of Lehman Brothers, the 4th largest investment bank in the US. The CEO of a major German bank was quoted as saying "Lehman was the downfall that lead the financial crisis to a mass panic."

US Treasury secretary Paulson wanted to make an example of Lehman Brothers. Wall Street needed to realize that things could not continue as before, with the government prepared to bail out every bank facing insolvency… as if in keeping with the motto "Privatization of profit and nationalization of loss." This concerned the concept of "moral hazard" as versus the adage "too big to fail". The majority of Americans were against the idea of using taxpayer money to bail out bankers on Wall Street. Paulson had drastically miscalculated the situation. Mohamed El-Erian, co-manager of the market's largest bond fund PIMCO made the case that, after the fall of Lehman Brothers all sense of trust and confidence was lost in the ability of financial institutions to be extricated from the crisis in an orderly fashion. In actuality, the collapse of Wall Street's 4th largest investment bank was an event beyond comprehension. All the major players in the financial markets had expected that the adage "too big to fail" certainly applied to Lehman Brothers, and that after the rescue of Bear Stearns by the federal government that Lehman Brothers could expect the same treatment.

That Paulson allowed the collapse of Lehman Brothers shook the financial world to its core. Nothing more seemed to be certain, and there was no longer any relying on a bail out. The danger for the financial system was that Lehman Brothers was one of the largest traders of derivatives and so its collapse would have profound consequences. The sword of Damocles, as wielded by George Soros in the form of billions of dollars of derivatives contracts, fell. After the bursting of the Internet bubble banks discovered derivatives as the next major source of almost unlimited revenue potential. Derivatives are a form of obligation with their value tied to the occurrence of specific events in the financial markets. Options, for example, give the investor or speculator the right to buy or sell a specific security at specific price during a pre-determined period of time. Options, however, do not belong to the classic form of derivative. A derivative is normally used to cover an exposure to risk as a hedge. For example, the owner of a share of stock would use a sell option (Put-option) to sell his shares at a pre-determined price, or for speculation. The attraction of options derivatives is that with relatively little money an investor can speculate on the movement of a stock price with greater leverage, and also greater risk, than if he had to actually buy and own the underlying stock. Especially risky were a fairly new form of financial innovation known as Credit Default Swaps or CDSs. They also were developed in the US at the start of the 1990s as a form of hedge against loan risk. If a bank, for example, desires to reduce the risk of default for a loan that it has with a borrower, it can hedge the risk of default by buying a CDS from a third party. With a CDS it was possible for banks to increase their rates of return on capital while avoiding the use of their own capital to cover loans. In contrast, those providing the risk coverage were not bound by any specific regulations. They were not required to put up any capital of their own, so the actual risk of default was not covered. Investment banks and highly leveraged hedge funds[2] were also partly involved in these transactions as contrarian speculators. In 2001, the nominal value of outstanding CDS contracts reached approximately $1 trillion dollars, and in 2005 it amounted to $10 trillion dollars. For the most part, this increase in CDS volume was due to speculation on the part of contrarian investors and not from actual transactions to hedge loan risk. The bankruptcy of auto parts supplier Delphi stands as a good case in point, whereby $5.2 billion dollars in loans and bonds were hedged by $28 billion dollars in CDS contracts. In 2008, the total value of all outstanding CDS contracts was approximately $62 trillion dollars. The degree of counter-party risk had become impossible to ignore.

After the collapse of Lehman Brothers complete panic broke out. The domino effect was enormous. It was not only that the banks no longer trusted each other or their level of solvency, but rather the entire financial system was called into question leading to worst-case scenario. The capital markets collapsed. The banks could no longer refinance or restructure the portfolios effectively. In addition, subprime securities such as corporate bonds were no longer marketable, or could only be sold at greatly reduced value. The consequences for the real economy were immediately apparent.

Lehman Brothers certificates had been sold to investors around the world. Now they were worthless. The media took advantage of the negative publicity by running dramatic headlines leading to widespread fear and uncertainty. In this way they helped to spread the panic. Everyone became convinced of a pending catastrophe and recession, and so reduced their investment and consumption. This became a self-fulfilling prophecy. People became fearful of potentially losing their jobs and stopped spending. As a consequence of reduced liquidity and a shortage of available capital, banks stopped making loans. The "credit crunch" had arrived. The greater economy became fearful of declining sales and liquidity problems and stopped investing. Due to the negative sentiments it came to the classical Keynesian case of underinvestment together with the liquidity-trap. Savers lost faith in banks and withdrew their deposits, which further exacerbated liquidity problems at the banks. In order to generate liquidity, the banks sold shares. Falling

---

[2] In 2000, warnings were issued as to the threat posed to the financial system due to the lack of regulation on Hedge Funds as counter-parties to derivative transactions. See Conrad, Christian and Stahl, Markus (2000).

market prices lead to even further price declines as risk limits triggered computerized trading and stock sales at many hedge funds. Investment bank Merrill Lynch was taken over by the Bank of America. The US government set up a special fund of $700 billion dollars to buy up the bank's portfolios of non-performing loans. In a form of reverse auction process, banks were permitted to sell their portfolios of non-performing securities to federal funds offering the highest percentage of face value for the securities. The two remaining US investment banks, Goldman Sachs and Morgan Stanley had to give up their previous business model so as to be considered as universal banks and gain access to refinancing funds from the US Federal Reserve. Further access to capital was given to suffering banks by the federal authorities. The world's largest insurer AIG was partially nationalized through this process. AIG had been speculating as a counter-party to billions of dollars in obligations using CDSs and CDOs following a trading strategy based on the mathematical-statistical model of Yale Professor Gary Gordon. The probability of default as calculated by Gordon proved to be mistaken, however. Further banks were forced into bankruptcy or taken over. Hypo Real Estate in Germany was saved by a combination of private banks and the German federal government. Banks in England and elsewhere had to be nationalized to prevent the collapse of the financial system. Governments came to the rescue of banks through the use of bailout funds from taxpayers. By this time the world's stock markets had fallen from a peak in August 2007 by more than 50% and set the world on the path to recession. Between March 1st and June 18th 2008, the FBI arrested 406 individuals for loan and mortgage fraud, ranging from small mortgage brokers to bank presidents who were later charged with having deceived investors as to the risks of the subprime market.[3]

As with Enron, Merrill Lynch was insolvent. With approximately $9 billion dollars in losses, Merrill's CEO O'Neal was responsible for the worst financial results at the bank in its 93-year history. And in 2008, there were an additional $15 billion dollars in write-offs. Similar to Skillings at Enron, O'Neal was also possessed of an unusually overbearing management style and obsession with profit results. The consequences would soon become all too apparent. By taking on more risk, O'Neal could produce better profit results while the top management at Merrill cashed in on huge bonuses. At Citigroup, CEO Prince was also facing more than $20 billion dollars in write-offs. Here as well, in 2008 it was necessary to write off huge sums. Both Prince and O'Neal were not only responsible for billions in write-offs, but as senior management received exceptionally handsome compensation packages (Prince received $26 million dollars and O'Neal $48 million dollars in 2006), and a severance package in the $100 million range. O'Neal received about $160 million in cash and stock options while Prince received approxi-

---

[3] See Mayr, Brigitte (2007); Handelsblatt 23.10.2008 and 10.01.2008, p. 30; Süddeutsche Zeitung 17.11.2008, p. 22, Neue Zuricher Zeitung 7.02.08; Zeit Online, 26/2008, p. 24, Der Spiegel, No. 47 (2008, p. 46–79) and Conrad, Christian A. (2010, p. 21).

mately \$100 million.[4] Others would assume the losses, namely the shareholders who lost a portion of their investment in the banks while many employees lost their jobs. In other words, not only did the agents of disaster gamble away their investor's money but they were also well rewarded for it. With this disconnect between risk and compensation it's easy to understand why so many bankers took on such huge risks, which lead us to today's subprime crisis.[5]

With the crises described above, the general question arises as to what went wrong? What economic dysfunctions are responsible for this huge resource destruction?

8.1.2   Some Causes of the Financial Crisis in the Light of Behavioral Theory

8.1.2.1 Belief in the Self-correcting Power of the Market

The first serious debate as to the infallibility of the capitalistic economic system arose in 2000 within the framework of the Enron crisis. By 2007, it was obvious that the world economy was in a fundamental crisis with the emergence of the subprime crisis. The subprime crisis was seen as the epitome of the ethical failure of our modern economy. Everything came together and many saw in the crisis the final act of "turbo capitalism",[6] the limitless enrichment of the few at the expense of society, which almost lead to a total collapse of the financial system. The lack of regulation and belief in the self-correcting power of the market was used by a few to take advantage of the situation. Considered historically, financial crises have increased significantly in recent years. This is not the result of simple coincidence, but rather much more an indication of a massive weakness in the present economic system. The market economy has always placed the individual at the forefront for the economic creation of value, which provided him with an ever-growing range of opportunity. Through the pursuit of individual interests, it was believed that this motivation would also create the most beneficial results for society and the greater good. This appears to not be the case. Individuals exploited the absence of rules and the belief in the self-healing forces of the markets to their advantage.

Could the worst financial crisis since 1929 have been prevented? Naturally, in hindsight it would be easy to answer the question with a "yes", given what we know now about the causes and course of the crisis. Above all, the crisis can be traced back to a violation of market order principles through political intervention. Let's start with the

---

[4] This income was exceeded by Goldman Sachs CEO Henry Paulson, who earned a bonus of \$18.7 million along with realizing proceeds from the sale of \$480 million in stock by exercising options issued prior to his becoming US secretary of the treasury. See Der Spiegel No. 8 (2009), p. 62.

[5] See also Shiller, Robert (2007); Gold, Gerry and Feldmann, Paul (2007); Muolo, Paul and Padilla, Matthew (2008) and Woods, Thomas E. (2009).

[6] See Dahrendorf, Ralf, (2009).

inappropriate involvement of the US government in the financial markets. The crisis started in the early 1990's as a consequence of a misguided social program on the part of politicians. In 1995, Fannie Mae and Freddie Mack received a mandate from the office of Housing and Urban Development (HUD) to lend to subprime borrowers using funds to be provided by HUD at below market interest rates. These funds were to provide mortgages to subprime borrowers in what were considered to be economically disadvantaged social groups, so that they could buy homes that they normally could not afford. The volume of loans and the regulations concerning the classification of subprime loans were increasingly expanded. These cheap loans made it possible for both Fannie Mae and Freddie Mac to boost their profit margins. Executives at Freddie Mac reciprocated with illegal campaign contributions while mortgage lender Connie Wide offered low-interest loans to influential politicians in Washington. One could say the basis for the subprime bubble can be traced back to the US government. It's also worth mentioning that the low interest rate policies of Alan Greenspan played an important role. By making cheap money readily available and supporting deregulation, the Fed created fertile ground for the bubble to grow.[7] One can also blame the US government for an exceptional lack of financial oversight. US financial regulators were aware of the growing problem but chose not to act, so as not to influence competition in the markets.

Rather than acting to regulate and control the mortgage markets, they put their faith in the ability of the market to correct itself and deregulated. Without regulators, it was possible for companies to hide the risk inherent in these loans from appearing on their balance sheets. Greenspan refused to act to control these new and innovative financial products. Despite the LTCM crisis,[8] Greenspan and the US government remained unconvinced that unregulated speculation by the hedge funds posed as serious threat to the financial system. Many governments, including the German government had been pushing for more regulation. Belief in the markets and the influence of financial lobbyists was more powerful, however. At no point during this phase of the crisis did financial regulators seem to be aware of the combined risk posed by CDOs and how it was spread among the banks.[9] With their complex mathematical models and AAA ratings,

---

[7] See the film "Inside Job" of 2010 by Charles Ferguson (Sony Pictures) and Conrad, Christian, A. and Stahl, Markus (2002).

[8] In 1998 this hedge fund named Long Term Capital Management (LTCM) then lost the investors around 90% of the $4 billion invested, which threatened to trigger a chain reaction on the international finance markets. The issue here is not just the credit taken by LTCM, but also the derivative positions of LTCM as contracting party, with which other finance market actors had protected themselves. Only when the then US central bank president Alan Greenspan intervened personally and pulled together an emergency package of billions from several large banks could the capital market crisis be averted. See Conrad, Christian A. (2005).

[9] "What we have found over the years in the marketplace is that derivatives have been an extraordinarily useful vehicle to transfer risk from those who shouldn't be taking it to those who are willing to and are capable of doing so." "We think that it would be a mistake" to more regulate the contracts. Greenspan in front of the Banking Committee in 2003. New York Times, 20.10.2008.

these deceptively secure financial innovations and the risk that they posed were able to escape the attention of over-worked federal regulators. National regulators, in the case of those in the US were divided and under-manned. At the federal level in the USA there were four uncoordinated regulating authorities and at the state level additional independent authorities. The most powerful authority, the SEC was considerably weakened and unable to deal with the problem due to massive reductions in personnel in their department for risk control and regulation.[10] These cuts in personnel occurred during a time in which a former head of Goldman Sachs acted as the head of the Office for Management and Budget, and while Henry Paulson, the future head of the Treasury department was CEO at Goldman Sachs. Later, for instance the head of the German banking regulatory authority admitted that his office was unable to come to terms with and regulate the rapid developments of these new financial products. Although they were aware of the problems posed by these unregulated financial products, they chose to not intervene. The banks had complete independence of action. Motivated by short-term profits and handsome bonuses, banking managers took on ever-greater levels of risk using ever-greater amounts of leverage. Many wanted to just get rich quick and gave little thought to the consequences of their actions. This actions lead as well to criminal activity. The most dangerous risk was kept off the balance sheets or allocated to unregulated, hidden offshore accounts. Also, the level of risk to counter-parties through the use of these innovative financial products seemed to be unknown to the regulating authorities. Due to the excessive use of leverage, many of the hedge funds had also taken on considerable risk. Nonetheless, the hedge funds remained unsupervised.

Paulson seemed to be unaware that the collapse of Lehman Brothers would lead to an unstoppable chain reaction. With the bankruptcy of Lehman, US policy regarding the issue became unpredictable. For the financial markets, it seemed that the Fed was willing to allow for the collapse of some banks, and that an intervention to save those in crisis should not be expected. Market participants completely lost their trust and confidence. Permitting the collapse of Lehman was one of two major mistakes made by Paulson. The other was the failure to change financial accounting requirements for the balance sheet in a timely manner. The mark-to-market regulations concerning CDOs as securities was the main reason for the ongoing write-offs, along with continuous reductions in the value of CDOs due to an almost non-existent market for them. On-going earnings warnings and loss reports strained not only the existing capital of the bank, but also awakened in the mind of the public the perception that a huge, uncontrollable and uncontainable financial catastrophe was occurring. Unfortunately, we will never know how many mortgage loans could have been saved from default by quick government intervention, as the opportunity was missed to act quickly to prevent the financial crisis from spreading to the real

---

[10]The chief controller of the SEC later spoke at a conference when questioned about "the systematic elimination of personnel from the regulatory office,... so that became impossible for the office to perform any regulation whatsoever." Der Spiegel, No. 47 (2008, p. 78).

economy. At least it's certain that if the banks had been permitted to balance the value of their CDO portfolios, taking into account the portion of the securities not affected by bad mortgage loans, the write offs could have been greatly reduced. In consideration of this remaining base value, the banks could apply to the Fed as a "lender of last resort" for refinancing with the CDOs acting as collateral. This funding conversion and extension of debt servicing could have been implemented at the beginning of the crisis, already in the middle of 2007 and not at the end of 2008. The banks and the US administration must have had great interest in keeping mortgage borrowers facing foreclosure in their homes. This could have kept the pressure off of the housing market and home prices. As this did not happen, many borrowers lost their homes and some even ended up living on the streets as the homeless, which raises the question of moral and economic responsibility. Many vacant houses were neglected and others were vandalized.

The banks' trading departments responsible for internal and external credit supervision withdrew their risky long-term loans and refinanced them as short-term securities. Any bank would realize that this was a violation of the golden rule of lending and would have significant consequences. This lack of control, the failure to implement responsible business practices and immoral behavior deserves critical review. It is beyond comprehension how bankers could be so misled by their statistical and mathematical models, as well as how many could have such unlimited trust in the rating agencies and their recommendations. Despite the ratings assigned by the rating agencies, we can expect senior management planning an investment of billions of dollars to perform at least some degree of due diligence to gain an understanding of the rating agency's procedures. To rely so completely on the judgment of what may be a biased third party is completely irresponsible. In the USA, the dramatic increase in home prices had become impossible to ignore and the easy access to subprime loans was often criticized. Warnings were sounded as to the impending bursting of the real estate and derivatives bubble.

The central problem of derivatives is that the leverage of the invested capital distorts the risk distribution between the speculator and the financial system. If the speculator is wrong he will lose only a portion of what is at stake for the system. The loan derivatives CDS did not have to be funded with equity, so banks earned much more than was appropriate on a risk adjusted basis in the good years. When the bad years came there was no capital to cover the losses so society had to bail out the speculators because they were too big to fail. Bonus payments had been made in the good years and there were no repayments in the bad years, when the bill was presented.

Speculators normally do not speculate against each other, but with each other. There is a familiar saying that "the trend is your friend". Only a stable trend facilitates speculation with nearly no risk. The biggest danger of derivatives is the leverage. If futures are used for speculative purposes for instance, the leverage multiplies artificially the effects of the derivatives on prices (via arbitrage and expectations)[11] and does not reflect an underlying real demand or supply. Therefore derivatives can distort the fundamental market functions. As a consequence, the price develops differently as it would normally to cover the needs of demand and supply. The price signals become distorted, which leads to wrong resource allocation. For instance, if prices of commodities like oil become too high because from derivative speculation, it increases the costs for the producing economy and for the consumers. Because of the high commodity prices the commodity sector invests to increase its capacities. The missing demand causes the speculation bubble to burst sooner or later. The new capacities are overcapacities and the commodity sector is in trouble.[12]

The economy worked well without derivatives. Either the risks of derivatives can be controlled or the use of derivatives should be restricted to a mere hedge against risks, their original purpose. An underlying transaction should be compulsory. At least the leverage of the derivatives should be reduced significantly and credit derivatives should be treated like credits so they have to be funded with equity. Otherwise the next financial crisis might be too big for the governments to bail out. The argument that regulations on financial markets cannot be implemented because the world is too divided might be true. Also, the incentive not to regulate is strong, since the free rider position is the most profitable.[13] But also the losses of a possible crisis are too big for each single state. An unregulated financial market is a risk for all other countries. This loss risk has to be paid for to avoid distortion. A tax on financial deals of individual states with unregulated institutions would be the right solution to avoid a free-rider behavior and it could be implemented by each state individually.

At least the current reforms on banking regulation go in the wrong direction as they increase the equity requirements to cover the systemic risk instead of decreasing the risks of derivatives. We will discuss that below.[14]

Can the financial crisis be explained by behavioral science? Heuristics are simplified rules of behavior that people use to respond quickly and easily. They are mainly

---

[11] Empirical studies show that the spot prices follow the future prices. See Deutsche Bundesbank (2006, p. 59).

[12] For the discussion of the effects of food and commodity speculation see *Conrad, Christian A.* (2014).

[13] Governments find themselves internationally in a dilemma, since the best outcome for a single state is if all other sates regulate their financial market and it is therefore with its unregulated market the most attractive location for financial institutions (Free-rider position). The worst result for the individual state is if it regulates its financial market while the others do not. Since everyone is subject to this situation of insecurity, everyone decides to behave uncooperatively, which provides the worst results for everyone, national and international not regulated financial markets. Such a dilemma is called in the Public Choice Theory "prisoner's dilemma". For the expression "prisoner's dilemma" see *Brennan, G. and Buchanan, James* (1985, p. 3).

[14] See *Conrad, Christian A.* (2014).

based on experience. One coulc speak of prejudice, for example. People are more likely to recognize events when they can remember or see things more often, which is called availability heuristics. Also, the effort to get to the infcrmation affects the assessment. For example, Schwartz and Vaughn et al. found that respondents rated themselves as less assertive when they had to write down 12 situations in which they succeeded instead of just 6. They then felt the situations they were able to remember were too few.[15] In response to this observation, the concept of bounded rationality was developed, implying limited information processing capacities as opposed to complete rationality. A decision is then rationally limited if, taking account of information access and processing effort, the decision that maximizes utility is chosen.[16]

Group adaptation behavior can become market-relevant if market participants have social contact and identify themselves as a group. This is possible in financial centers or online chat platforms, where market participants can exchange their opinions and adapt them to each other. Here too, in the sense of groupthink, false dominant market opinions can arise. This is what New Behavioral Finance calls herding behavior.[17] We can call this collective erring. In the case of the financial crisis this was the common belief in the self-correcting power of the market and the ongoing prosperity and housing price increases.

8.1.2.2 Exaggerated Belief in Figures

During her visit of the London School of Economics in November 2008 the British Queen asked: "Why did no one see it coming?".[18]

Krugman responded: "As I see it, the economics profession went astray because economists, as a group, mistook beauty, clad in impressive-looking mathematics, for truth."[19]

Several studies analyzed the risks management practices and came to the conclusion that there was an over-reliance on quantitative analysis (studies by the Financial Stability Forum, the Working Group on Risk Assessment and Capital, the Senior Supervisors Group, the Basel Committee on Bank Supervisions, the International Institute of Finance and the International Monetary Financial Committee) (Voinea & Anton, 2009).

As the Classic-Neoclassic theory after the Great Depression of 1929, today's economic theory has explanation and justification problems. Neither of the statistical models foresaw the crisis nor are they now able to explain it. Moreover, the econometric models

---

[15] See Schwarz, Norbert; Vaughn, Leigh Ann (2002) and Schwarz, Norbert/Bless, Herbert/Starck, Fritz/Klumpp, Gisela/Rittenauer-Schatka, Helga/Simons, Annette (1991).

[16] See Simon, Herbert A. (1959), Theories of Decision-Making in Economics and Behavioral Science. In: The American Economics Review. Band 49, Nr. 3, 1. Januar 1959, pp. 262 f.

[17] See De Bondt, W. F. M., & Forbes, W. P. (1999). Herding in analyst earnings forecasts: Evidence from the United Kingdom. European Financial Management, 5(2), 143–163.

[18] See The Financial Times,November 25th 2008. https://www.ft.com/content/50007754-ca35-11dd-93e5-000077b07658.

[19] Krugman, Paul (2009).

based on historical figures pretended there was a safety where there wasn't one, which was itself one reason for the crisis. Nassim Nicholas Taleb wrote about the delusions of control and reliability held by Wall Street and many other businesses. He pointed at the dangers of trusting the "bell-curve" models used by many financial institutions to mitigate risks. He questions the reliance on past historical information and brings the example of the black swan, that nobody expected until its discovery in Australia, or the example of the turkey who spends a thousand days being well-fed before being killed on the thousand-and-first day.[20] Justin Fox also criticizes the belief in models and especially the belief in efficient markets—a belief that was qualified by Robert Shiller as the "most remarkable error in the history of economic theory."[21]

Derivative products such as Collateralized Debt Obligations (CDOs) can be directly traced as being one of the major factors leading to today's subprime crisis and the greatest financial crisis since the Wall Street crash of 1929. The calculation of risk and value or price for derivatives on the basis of historical time periods was celebrated as a major breakthrough. This advance in financial mathematics was only made possible through the use of the ever more powerful calculating capacity of computers. This made it possible to create many new financial products. It later became apparent that these calculations were in error, and that it was only due to the confidence people had in the ability to calculate them that made these products possible. For example, it was determined that the risk and therefore the price for credit derivatives (Credit Default Swaps) as calculated by Yale Professor Gary Gorton was inaccurate. The confidence and faith in his calculations almost cost AIG its existence and the US government several billion dollars, as it was bailed out to save the financial system in October 2008 and partially nationalized. Gordon blamed the problem on the use of non-conforming data from the current marketplace and unprecedented developments, which deviated from his forecasts based on historical data. But the future is never like the past.

It is difficult to understand why such an over-confidence in these calculations endured for so long, finally resulting in the subprime crisis, although the LTCM crisis had already illustrated the dangers and weaknesses of these financial calculations. In 2005 there were already warnings against using models for financial calculations based on historical figures.[22] The formulas for option prices (Black & Schools-Formel), which were responsible for the LTCM-crisis, are the best example for the incalculability of the economy. Robert Merton, Myron Scholes and Fischer Black received the Nobel Prize in 1997 for groundbreaking work in Option Pricing Theory. Based on the volatilities of the past, the formulas were developed to calculate prices for rights to sell or buy assets in the future (options). This is apparently an instrument to calculate the future. A hedge fund named

---

[20] See Taleb, Nassim Nicholas (2007) and Taleb, Nassim Nicholas (2001).

[21] See Fox, Justin (2009) und Conrad, Christian A. (2010, p. 56).

[22] "The method of calculation is based upon historic volatility and does not take into account irrational human behaviour, such as panic,...." Christian A. (2005, p. 398).

Long Term Capital Management (LTCM) wanted to use for speculation, and he hired Robert Merton as a consultant. In 1998 LTCM then lost the investors around 90% of the $4 billion invested, which threatened to trigger a chain reaction on the international finance markets. The issue here is not just the credit taken by LTCM, but also the derivative positions of LTCM as contracting party, with which other finance market actors had protected themselves. Only when the then US central bank president Alan Greenspan intervened personally and pulled together an emergency package of billions from several large banks could the capital market crisis be averted. The second of the hedge funds Merton consulted, named IFC Continuum, closed in 2006. The future was in fact not predictable.[23]

The flaw in the option price theory or risk values such as "value of risk" which were determined on the basis of historical volatility was that future relationships between demand and supply could not fundamentally be accurately depicted. This is how in 2008 Porsche could raise its stake in VW to 74% through the purchase of VW call options, at a much reduced price than if it had bought the shares on the open market. The option price for VW shares did not reflect the actual shortage of shares, which had been calculated on the basis of past price volatility. This miscalculation lead to the share prices being set much too low. The excessive demand for VW shares eventually lead to a short squeeze.

The use of the same seemingly correct risk models led also to a similar investing behavior of the market participants. If the models were wrong all investors came to the same wrong risk assessment, which worsened the subprime crisis. Also the rating agencies used the wrong models to calculate their CDO-ratings. Based on these wrong ratings the investors underestimated the risks substantially and decided all to invest. Therefore the risk models increased the systemic risk and did not decrease it.

Abstract and isolated models of thought are fine in principle. They make it possible to take the complex economy apart into separate connections and thus to allow discoveries about economic processes. Econometrics is thus a valuable ancillary science for economics. There is also nothing to be said against using mathematics, as long as the effort remains proportional to the usefulness of knowledge gained. The models have unfortunately become so complex however, that they are no longer useful for teaching purposes. The effort required to learn them is greater than the knowledge gained. It is problematic when econometrics, thus the statistics applied to the economy with economic mathematics, is taught as exclusive representation of the only true economics. Without order theory and order politics of order there can be no understanding of the state and economics.

Derivatives as the so-called Collateral Debt Obligations were the trigger and the main reason for the subprime crisis. They are based on complex economic modeling and statistics. Basically we can say that the image of the economy is distorted when only determinist models are applied. More thinking and less calculating would have been much

---

[23] See Conrad, Christian (2005) and Welt-Kompakt dated 08/22/2006, p. 15.

more appropriate. So can the subprime crisis can also be traced back to developments in the economic sciences.

Be that as it may, econometrics, statistics and mathematics have contributed significantly to the continued development of economic science. They deserve recognition, no doubt, but this is no reason for economic science to consist solely of these subjects. At the end of the scientific chain there must be somebody to explain the science of practice and weigh the various theories and approaches against one another on the basis of practical considerations in order to make statements relevant to practices in a comprehensive economic overview. To make statements relevant for practical application the theories and models must be related to the respective practical situation. Only then is it possible to decide what parts of the respective models of thought can be applied. In this highest of disciplines, the relation exists both in theory and in practice, at least within economic science. This requires an analytic, combining intelligence. The considerations must be logically deductive and verbal, since there is no calculability of the economy as a whole. In economic science as a social science mathematic abilities are less important, and the creative approaches to explanation gain importance.

Kahnemann and Tversky found, that the presentation and formulation of questions affects the decision of subjects.[24] In the financial crisis the investment decisions were influenced by the by the wrong ratings and the securitization. The behavior of the lenders was changed. The investors did not question the creditworthiness of the debtors, which would normally be requirement for lending.

Framing can be used to manipulate decisions to the benefit or disadvantage of the decider. For example, you may be more likely to encourage people to take a health check-up by telling them the risks of illness if they fail to get a check-up than by emphasizing the opportunities for early discovery and recovery.[25]

The ratings of the subprime CDOs were based on old data from the US real estate market. Tversky and Kahneman call a behavior focused on old data anchoring. People are biased because they depend too heavily on the first set of data they receive. This data is the "anchor" that distorts the decision.[26] Tversky and Kahneman found also insensitivity to sample size, which is a bias to see patterns in small numbers of results even though more results are needed to regress significant correlations.[27]

The belief in experts was finally criticized after the financial crisis. The complexity of derivatives like the CDO was so high that nobody but the experts of the rating agencies

---

[24] See Kahneman, Daniel; Tversky, Amos (1981); Kahneman, Daniel; Tversky, Amos (1982); Kahneman, Daniel; Tversky, Amos (1984). Kahneman, Daniel; Tversky, Amos (1986). Kahneman et al. (1991, pp. 193–206).

[25] See Meyerowitz, Beth E.; Chaiken, Shelly (1987) and Beck, H. (2014, p. 154).

[26] See Tversky, A., and D. Kahneman (1974).

[27] See Tversky, A., and D. Kahneman (1974, pp. 1, 125).

was able to understand their structure and value. Some authors called for the "de-expertizing" of experts.[28]

The wrong ratings of the CDOs were a sign of overconfidence as a subjective favorable judgment of one's self. Subjects regularly overestimate their own knowledge, their control options, their abilities as well as their achievements.[29] Lichtenstein and Fischhoff found that the harder the tasks, the greater the overconfidence. Rating the CDOs was a very complex hard task that only experts were able to perform and understand.[30]

Weinstein tested students and found that they overestimate their positive outcomes and underestimate their negative outcomes. They estimated the likelihood of earning more than $10,000 as their starting salary, 41.5% higher than their fellow students, and the likelihood of a heart attack before the age of 40, 38.4% lower than their peers.[31] **Overconfidence** increases with the difficulty level of the tasks. It is also subject to experts who feel that they are better informed.[32] This is also a problem in economic consulting, which Hayek called the presumption of knowledge. Confirmation bias reinforces the problem.

The confirmation bias describes how people process facts in a way that confirms their own opinions. Contradictory facts are not taken into account or are subordinate.[33] These include:

- Pseudo-diagnostics: Humans tend to favor their own hypotheses rather than weighing them objectively critically against others. Doctors should not commit themselves so early to their diagnosis, for example.[34] The belief perseverance bias goes in the same direction: In order not to have to change their opinion, hypotheses are maintained even when they have already been refuted.[35]

Added to this is the illusion of control as an overestimation of one's own influence on processes, such as throwing dice to influence the outcome or selecting a winning ticket. Experiments showed that test takers overestimate their dice skills if they were lucky in the beginning[36] and that test takers are willing to buy the more expensive tickets if they can choose the numbers themselves.[37] Thus, there is a tendency to rate more expensive

---

[28] See Khan, Ashraf (2018, p. 25).

[29] See Metcalfe, Janet (1998).

[30] See Lichtenstein et al. (1982).

[31] See Weinstein, Neil D. (1980).

[32] See Angner, E. (2006) and Russo, J. Edward and Schoemaker, Paul J. H. (1992).

[33] See Wason, Peter C. (1960, pp. 129–140); Nickerson, Raymond S. (1998, pp. 175–220) and Beck, H. (2014).

[34] See Doherty et al. (1979).

[35] See Ross et al. (1975).

[36] See Langer, Ellen J. and Roth, Jane (1975).

[37] See Langer, Ellen J. (1975).

products as higher quality, although the correlation is very weak. And the willingness to pay a higher price for a product increases when it externally resembles a quality product.

People shy away from change when they cannot assess how they are affected. The status quo is preferred over another alternative (status quo bias). Samuelson and Zeckhauser found that the majority of test subjects do not change their investment portfolio in the case of inheritance. The subjects retained the shares they had inherited or did not buy any shares in cash.[38] In principle, sticking to the status quo can be a rational and efficient approach. Boxall, Adamowicz and Moon found that the status quo bias increases the more complex and time-consuming the decision-making process is.[39] Another explanatory approach is the regret aversion. To revise a decision that has already been made means, on the one hand, that one has to admit to having made a mistake. This generates regret and negative emotions.[40]

This would explain why nobody of the experts corrected or questioned the wrong ratings. The biases show that ratings are not precise or might even be wrong because people make them.

8.1.2.3 Missing Moral Values

The enrichment of managers at the expense of their company and the society was criticized long before the subprime crisis. A scandal is really nothing more than immoral conduct in the eyes of society. Whether we look at top managers just trying to get the most out of the company they have been entrusted with, or manipulating the balance sheets to get rich with stock options or bonus payments at the expense of clueless stockholders, or employees lower down in the hierarchy who try to cheat their colleagues or the market, we are looking at proof that across the globe the economy has to wrest with massive ethical problems. It is worth noting that even model companies, such as Enron, are affected by moral lapses. There are many US companies, as well as internationally known investment banks such as Merrill Lynch, Morgan Stanley and Credit Swiss First Boston in the USA and Goldman Sachs, Morgan Stanley and Deutsche Bank in Germany, who have all been accused of stock analyses advocating sales.[41]

The largest bank in the world and the American branch leader Citigroup seems to have had ethical problems as well. The Citygroup head Charles Price addressed his employees with these words: "No one may damage our long-term interests for short-term advantages." He said he would check into "unnecessary risks and unethical behavior" personally if necessary.[42] He prescribed ethics seminars for his employees and had

---

[38] See Samuelson, William et al. (1988, p. 12) and Kahneman, Daniel et al. (1991, pp. 193–206). Beck, H. (2014, p. 164).

[39] See Boxall, Peter et al. (2009) and Beck, H. (2014, p. 167).

[40] See Bell, David E. (1982) and Loomes, Graham and Sudgen, Robert (1982, pp. 805–824).

[41] See Chediak, Felipe and Escudero, Silvio (2004, p. 79) and Ogger, Günther (2001, p. 103).

[42] Quoted from Capital, 18/2005, p. 54.

a behavioral code drawn up, and established a department where the employees could anonymously inform the company of unethical behavior. What happened? His predecessor Sandy Weill had set the employees a growth rate target of 15% and seems to have implemented it absolutely. The pressure was apparently so great that the employees, voluntarily or involuntarily, turned to illegal methods to reach the targets. The bank was then only able to avoid lawsuits and the subsequent damage to its image by agreeing to pay out settlements, connected with damage compensation. In 2002 it paid $400 million because Citi analysts portrayed stocks too positively, which Citi investment banking wanted to sell. In 2004 the Citigroup paid $2.65 billion for Worldcom and $70 million to the US Federal Reserve after being accused of lending usury credit and giving credit only in connection with the sale of superfluous insurance. Another accusation was that the bank did not pass on rebates to the customers of their investment funds. In 2004 Citygroup lost their license for private banking in Japan because of abuses of the law against money laundering and market manipulation. In 2005 the US bank supervision forbid Citigroup from any new takeovers until internal rules of ethics had been implemented. In 2005 there were also settlements paid for involvement in the bankruptcies of Global Crossing ($75 million) and Enron ($2 billion). There was also a 4 million British Pound settlement and returned profits of 9.96 million British Pounds for manipulated prices on the London bond market. These are of course just the ethical missteps that were brought to light.[43]

It seems conspicuous that the firms that had seemed to be among the most financially stable for years would wind up in a state of collapse. This is valid for Enron and other firms as well as for Citigroup and the investment banks involved in the subprime crisis. But with an unethical business policy they were only successful in the short term. Long term these firms had financial problems.

The subprime crisis can be considered the epitome of the ethical failure of our modern economy. Everything came together, and many saw in the crisis the final act of our "turbo capitalism", the limitless enrichment of the few at the expense of society, which almost lead to a total collapse of the financial system.[44] The lack of regulation and belief in the self-correcting power of the market was used by a few to take advantage of the situation. The victims were, above all, the socially and economically disadvantaged who were convinced by predatory lenders to buy homes that they could ill-afford and which would lead them to personal bankruptcy, or at worst, homelessness and a life on the streets. This was truly the creation of social misery. Mortgage lenders had to be aware of this, as they were directly involved in working with the subprime borrowers most at risk of default, which should be considered the height of moral irresponsibility. These lenders only gave thought to their personal profit without any consideration for the fate of

---

[43] See Wirtschaftswoche dated September, 01, 2005, pp. 52–58 and Capital, No. 18, 2005, pp. 54–56.

[44] See Dahrendorf, Ralf, (2009).

borrowers. In the end, they were rewarded on the basis of their success in issuing loans. The difficulties that these borrowers would have in repaying these loans were of no consequence to them. For the most part, these borrowers did not have the education or the capacity to understand the nuances of how their mortgages were structured, and lacked the protection of appropriate consumer agencies or law enforcement. All those who knowingly took part in this deception and intentionally inflicted this suffering on unsuspecting borrowers are morally culpable. The Clinton and Bush administrations encouraged lending to subprime borrowers through Fannie Mae and Freddie Mac as part of an ill-conceived social program are also in-part responsible. Also culpable are those who knowingly encouraged this process and profited from the housing and mortgage bubble while helping to finance the ensuing social misery. Noteworthy here are also those bank managers who knowingly gambled with the long-term viability of their banks and the financial system so that they could maximize their profits and bonuses over the short-term. The moral responsibility lies with the financial regulating authorities that tolerated the creation and growth of the real estate bubble and the spread of subprime mortgage products that made it possible. They permitted the creation of a new, unregulated credit market without intervening. In the USA, there were widespread and timely warnings concerning the dangers of a bubble in the real estate, the subprime mortgages and financial innovations that made it all possible.

It is no wonder that societal recognition for managers has dropped to the current low, which the manager's guild should be taking to heart. In a Wall Street Journal survey in 2003, 64% of those questioned said that they do not trust managers. Only one other profession trumped this result. Only 16% of those questioned trusted politicians, and 84% expressed distrust.[45] Other studies determined that managers in the USA and Germany to have a very utilitarian attitude on ethical and moral questions, in particularly among young managers and American economic students. Typical statements included "One has to look after one's own interests," "Morality is just a matter of feelings," or "Sometimes small injustices are necessary in order to reach greater goals."[46] According to a survey among Swiss managers, 75% assume that the market forces automatically provide for an ethically and morally justifiable behavior.[47] It is interesting to note that many managers do not seem to feel comfortable with immoral, unethical conditions. Studies have shown that meanwhile the majority of managers go to work with more or less consciously felt fear.[48]

Studies had already established a very egoistic attitude among American business students in the late 1980s. The behavior is purposeful and opportunistic. Moral reflexivity is severely restricted. Success and continuity are unconditionally the first priority. Typical

---

[45] See Ergenzinger, Rudolf and Krulis-Randa, Jan S. (2004, p. 4).

[46] See Noll, Bernd (2002, p. 168).

[47] See Ulrich, Peter (1993, pp. 1172, 1173).

[48] See Noll, Bernd (2002, p. 168).

words are "winning is everything".[49] But this is a global problem. According to a survey among Swiss executives, 75% of managers assume that the market forces automatically provide ethically and morally justified behavior. Another survey among German executives comes to a similar conclusion, inasmuch as 50% assume that their company automatically contributes to the common good through its activities.[50]

According to a survey by GFK market research from 2008, 61% of Germans asked were of the opinion—that sincerity and honesty does not pay—the world is dishonest and people expect to be lied to. And 38% consider it appropriate to lie if it will advance their career.[51]

Ethical problems are increasingly making things more difficult for companies as an internal problem of loyalty. In a study conducted by the German personnel consultation firm Kienbaum, Human Resources managers complain about a generation of applicants with little inclination to fully engage themselves. Nearly every other Head of Human Resources bemoans a lack of social competence. Young people increasingly act to maximize their own benefits. This means, for example, that when they have a question to answer, they consider what answer will be the most advantageous. This generation of streamlined opportunists does not please personnel, because they neither provide the necessary creative input, nor can their supervisors trust them. "The question of what one actually wants to do in five years can hardly be answered. Personnel employees know that employees and companies no longer enter a bond for life. But enthusiasm for a task and the desire of the applicant to do something special is still important to the companies."[52] According to Walter Jachmann, Manager of Human Resources consulting at German Kienbaum, applicants lack backbone and personality:

> "Exactly at the time of crisis the company leaders do not get the information they need. No one discusses or contradicts, because everyone just nods and follows the managers"[53]

The internal and external selection processes are also criticized, however. Assessment centers make Human Resources' job easier when evaluating a large number of applicants according to objective criteria in a relatively short amount of time. The tests can be prepared for in advance though, and in order to be successful the candidates must optimize their answers according to predetermined criteria. In these mass tests there is no

[49] See Löhr, A. (1997, p. 198).

[50] See Ulrich, Peter (1993, p. 1172).

[51] See Rheinische Post, 04/18/08 and http://de.statista.com/statistik/daten/studie/292/umfrage.

[52] Walter Jachmann, Manager of Personnel Consultants Kienbaum, quoted from Handelsblatt dated October 20/21/2022 2006, p. 1.

[53] Stefan Tilk, Member of Management at the Bertelsmann subsidiary Arvato Direct Services, quoted from Handelsblatt dated October 20/21/2022 2006, p. 1, translated into English.

room for the rough edges of a creative personality. The internal selection processes often reward conformity, making contradiction an unattractive option.[54]

In the meantime, the notion that honesty is stupidity has apparently prevailed not only in the economy, but also across society. It is often said that "one must be able to afford morality". Everyone is his own best friend. Communion and sacrifice are replaced by ruthless utility maximization. According to a survey of CSF market research conducted in 2008, 61% of the Germans surveyed felt that sincerity did not pay off—the world was finally lied to. And 38% thought it would be justifiable to lie if it served their own career.[55]

It is interesting that many managers in immoral unethical conditions do not seem to be able to lie. Studies show that the majority of executives now have more or less consciously felt anxiety at work. The fear of job loss, the fear of making mistakes and the fear of misinformation are dominant here.[56] Fear at the workplace, exaggerated performance pressure and interpersonal competition pressure play an important role in mental illness.[57]

The behavior of bankers did not change significantly after the financial crisis. In 2013, only 36% of Wall Street employees surveyed believed their industry had changed for the better. On the other hand, 52% were convinced that the competition was involved in "illegal or unethical" actions. This information was answered by nearly a quarter of respondents in the "own house experienced" or "first hand" experienced. However, 29% considered unethical or illegal tricks "to be successful," an increase of 17% over 2012 when the study was first conducted. Particularly in the case of younger employees, an ethical attitude seems to be lacking. 36% of young bankers with less than ten years of experience advocated windy tricks, versus 18% of Wall Street veterans with more than 20 professional years. A quarter would be ready for insider trading "if they could earn at least ten million dollars." In the case of the younger colleague, this share even rises to 38%. 17% are convinced "that their bosses look away if they suspect a top performer of insider trading." This is justified by the fact that the income is too low: 26% think that the remuneration plans or bonus structures of their companies are an incentive to betray ethical norms or break the law. This is the case for the younger 31% and the older 21%.[58]

The managers are thus not fulfilling their role model function. The internal company contract for the distribution of work, stress and income is turned upside down, which is rightly felt to be unfair, thus has negative effects on the other employees.

---

[54] See Handelsblatt dated October 20/21/2022 2006, p. 1.

[55] See Rheinische Post, 04/18/2008 and http://de.statista.com/statistik/daten/studie/292/umfrage (01/22/2010).

[56] See Volk, Hartmut (2000, p. 57).

[57] See Volk, Hartmut (2000).

[58] See Sucharow, Labaton (2013).

It is difficult to change the business culture in the financial organizations. However, people stick to their ethical internal standards even if this means efforts or sacrificing financial gains.[59] If people are remembered of their honesty-standards, they behave more ethically.[60]

Research shows that a code of ethics only influences manager behavior ethically when the code includes a certification choice. The reason is that the signing of the code increases the moral reasoning in the manager.[61] Thus, employees should sign ethical standards and should be remembered of them during their work. A similar approach is an oath.

In some countries there were attempt so increase the ethical commitment of the employees like the Dutch banking oath initiated by the Dutch Banking Association. As of 2015, all 80,000 bankers and banking staff in the Netherlands had to swear that they will endeavor to maintain and promote confidence in the financial sector, that they will put clients' interests first and take care of shareholders. A breach of the oath can lead to fines, suspension, or even blacklisting.[62]

8.1.2.4 The Importance of Risk Adequate Compensation

Since the Enron, Worldcom and the financial crisis, compensation for bank managers and managers in other public companies have come under intense scrutiny. Compensation has been held responsible for encouraging excess risk-taking, particularly within the financial system. It has been asserted that bonus compensation schemes have caused asymmetries in the treatment of gains and losses, which can lead to excessively risky behavior. The purpose of this chapter is to test this hypothesis.[63] Do unilaterally constructed incentive schemes encourage undue risk-taking? This question is examined with a behavioral experiment using the game roulette. It is used to analyze how unilateral compensation affects risk behavior.

Related Literature

According to principal agent theory (Ross, 1973; Jensen & Meckling, 1976; Novak 1997) correlating a manager's compensation with either their performance or that of the firm promotes better incentive alignment and leads to higher motivation and thus stronger company values. However, there is an asymmetric imbalance between the term, magnitude and probability of gains and losses in common compensation schemes. Short-term results are rewarded even when these results are later reversed. This encourages risk

---

[59] See Aronson, Elliot and Carlsmith, J. Merrill (1962, pp. 178–182) and Harris, Sandra L. et al. (1976, pp. 123–135).

[60] See Mazar, Nina et al. (2008, pp. 633–644).

[61] See Ariely, D. (2010, p. 28).

[62] See Khan, Ashraf (2018, p. 10).

[63] See Conrad, Christian A. (2015, pp. 50–55).

taking by the employees—agents—at the cost of the company—the principal. The agents undertake actions that generate a high probability of gains in the short-term, while the risk of a larger loss in the longer-term is not taken into consideration, causing the principle to bear all of the long-term risk. A substantial body of literature has emerged to test the relationship between manager compensation and manager behavior and performance.

Figures of the Office of the New York State Comptroller show that bonuses in Wall Street financial institutions continued to register large positive numbers in 2007 and 2008, even while the banks suffered large losses (Sharma, 2012). Surveys by the Financial Stability Forum (2009) showed that over 80% of financial market participants and experts believe that compensation practices played a role in promoting the accumulation of risks that led to the financial crisis. Cuomo (2009) shows that bonuses and overall compensation did not vary significantly even though profits diminished during the financial crisis. Cai, Cherny and Milbourn (2010) studied the pay structures of banking executives before the financial crisis. They found some problematic practices (such as too much bonus and stock-related compensation). These practices might have encouraged "short-termism" and excessive risk-taking.

Agarwal and Ben-David (2011) results show that the explosion in mortgage volume during the crisis and the deterioration of underwriting standards can be partly attributed to the incentives of loan officers. They studied a controlled experiment conducted by a large bank. The compensation scheme of loan officers was changed from fixed salary to commission-based compensation. Loan officers were 19% more likely to accept loan applications, approved loan amounts larger by 23%, and the loans were 28% more likely to default. The increase in default occurred primarily within the population of loans that would not have been accepted in the absence of commission-based compensation.

However, Gregg et al. (2012) found that the cash-plus-bonus pay-performance sensitivity of financial firms is not significantly higher than in other sectors and concluded that it is unlikely that incentive structures could be held responsible for inducing bank executives to focus on short-term profits. This would mean that we are facing a general compensation problem.

Cooper et al. (2014) found evidence that industry and size-adjusted CEO pay is negatively related to future shareholder wealth changes for periods up to five years after payment. Sun reviewed the early executive compensation studies, bonus plan maximization hypotheses and equity-based compensation. Opportunistic management incentives encourage creative earnings management, which may have negative consequences for the company and shareholders. He shows that firms pay a price and its negative impact on shareholders is economically significant (Sun, 2012).

Schotter and Weigelt (1992) use four different compensation schemes to demonstrate that a compensation scheme that induces behavior consistent with lower discount rates is a necessary condition for reconciling divergent time preferences between principals and agents, and that subjects become more myopic in their investment decisions if compensation contracts are incorrectly structured.

Colesa et al. (2006) found that higher sensitivity of CEO wealth to stock volatility encourages riskier policy choices, including relatively more investment in R&D, less investment in PPE, more focus, and higher leverage. They also provide empirical evidence of a strong causal relation between managerial compensation and investment policy, debt policy, and firm risk. Cheating is also influenced by compensation schemes. Gilla et al. (2013) show that exposing workers to a compensation scheme based on random bonuses makes them cheat more but has no effect on their productivity.

Andersson et al. (2013) studied risk-taking on behalf of others in an experiment. The decision makers were facing high-powered incentives to increase the risk on behalf of others through hedged compensation contracts or with tournament incentives. The decision-makers responded strongly to incentives that result in an increased risk-exposure for others. There have also been experimental studies concerning the binary choice task and the study concerning the binary double gamble to explore the predictive validity of dispositional traits and affective states in decision making under risk and uncertainty (Papaeconomou, 2012).

This chapter provides a simple incentive-based experiment regarding unilateral bonus compensation schemes based on the game roulette, which can be easily repeated with the students. There have been several experiments with roulette but with the objective to scrutinize the gambling behavior (Rubio; Hernández & Santacreu) and guessing tendencies (Rubio et al., 2010). The following experiment simulates most common short-term bonus compensation schemes without accountability. They were also the dominating compensation schemes before and during the financial crisis.

Experimental Design Roulette

The purpose of this chapter is to test the hypothesis that unilaterally constructed incentive schemes encourage excess risk-taking. The methodology is to simulate decision-making under asymmetric incentive structures. Therefore an experimental environment similar to the compensation schemes had to be constructed. Roulette has the advantage of clearly demonstrating the probabilities for gains and losses. In the game Roulette the probability of losses is compensated with higher payouts (apart from zero). A higher risk has an equivalent higher payout. In order to simulate behavior with different incentive and risk structures, decision-makers have to be exposed to different remuneration schemes, which is why there were game rounds with different considerations of gains and losses.

Game 5: Roulette

The experiment is started with symmetrical incentive structures. Round A and B have identical incentive structures. Round A serves as a control round for B. Finally in round C a unilateral consideration of the profits takes place and the changes in the betting behavior are recorded. An indicator for higher risk-taking would be a higher capital set even though the winning probability stayed the same.

In round A, the students are able to play Roulette with an initial play capital of €1000. Losses and gains are credited with 100%. The students are asked to check each other's calculations after each game.

In the round B the gambling losses and gains are counted each with 50% and are added to the initial capital of €1000. Thus there were still no conflicting interests and no asymmetries in the treatment of gains and losses. Round B therefore has identical incentive structures as round A. So A is able to serve as a control group for B.

In round C a unilateral consideration of the profits takes place. The set capital is not deducted, if the roulette bet is wrong. Conversely, the payout is credited with 50%, and added to the €1000 of initial capital. The results of the rounds B and C are added, starting from an initial capital of €1000 each and the player with the highest result is rewarded with €10 real money. For this game we chose real money to have a stronger link to compensation in real life. The rules are explained to the students before starting the experiment.

Round C thus corresponds to the unilateral performance-based remuneration of the common bonus-based compensation schemes. Loss and profit incentives are not equally distributed. Losses are borne by the companies and profits are rewarded with bonuses. This simple experiment shows clear results.

Results

The experiment was conducted with 69 students from different Business Bachelor and Master courses at the University of Applied Science HTW at Saarbrücken.[64] The students played 3 rounds Roulette (A, B and C), each with three games. They could bet on red or black, on one of the three thirds of the 36 numbers or on one number. The roulette wheel determined the winning number and color. If it was zero, the game was repeated and not registered. The payouts were distributed according to the probability of winning ($\times 2, \times 3, \times 36$) and accumulated in each round.

In round C, the sum of the average capital set rose from €1361.88 in round B to € 3,899.28, by 186%. The highest possible profit (calculated as the product of the set capital and the possible payout) in all three games rose to €30,000.72 (see Figs. 8.2 and 8.3). If you set the maximal possible gain in relation to set capital as a risk measurement indicator, the willingness to take risks increased from 5.05 to 7.69 (see Fig. 8.1). The significantly higher standard deviation in round C shows that some players were more willing to take risks than the average (see Figs. 8.4 and 8.5).

Conclusion

It has been demonstrated that unilaterally constructed incentive schemes encourage excess risk-taking. This would indicate that common bonus-based compensation

---

[64] See Conrad, Christian A. (2015).

	Round A	Round B	Round C
Average set capital	€1,252.63	€1,361.88	€3,899.28
Average maximal possible gain	€5,946.83	€6,874.49	€30,000.72
Risk as max. possible gain/set capital	4.75	5.05	7.69
Standard deviation average set capital	€779.65	€650.32	€2,408.89
Standard deviation maximal possible gain	€634.21	€9,687.06	€31,585.46

Fig. 8.1 Statistical data

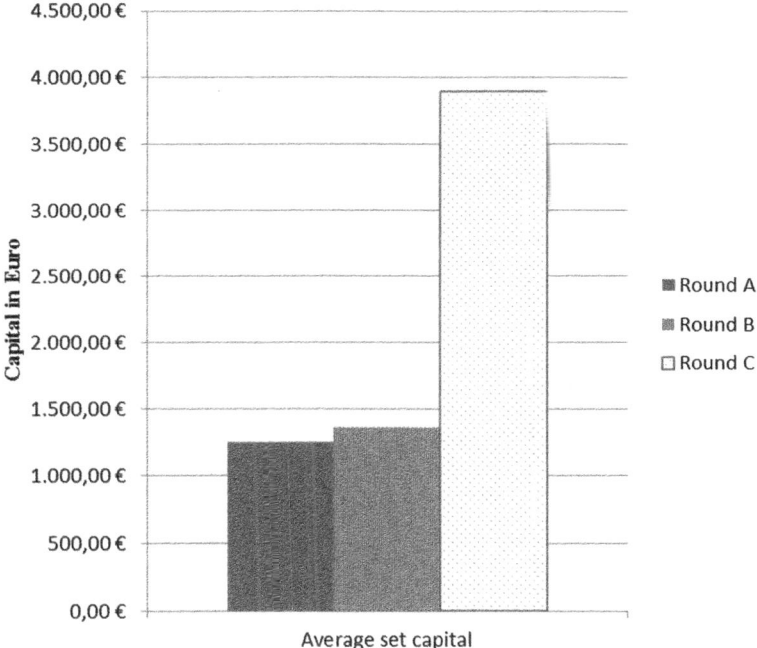

Fig. 8.2 Set capital

schemes enhance risk because of the asymmetries in the treatment of gains and losses. Unilaterally constructed compensation schemes were one reason for the financial crisis.

The experiment showed that unilaterally constructed incentive schemes encourage excess risk-taking. This would indicate that common bonus-based compensation schemes are not a good idea and in face enhance risk because of the asymmetries in the treatment of gains and losses. In most cases compensation can only decrease down to the base salary while gains from bonuses can be limitless. Short-term results are rewarded even when these results are subsequently reversed. This encourages risk-taking by the

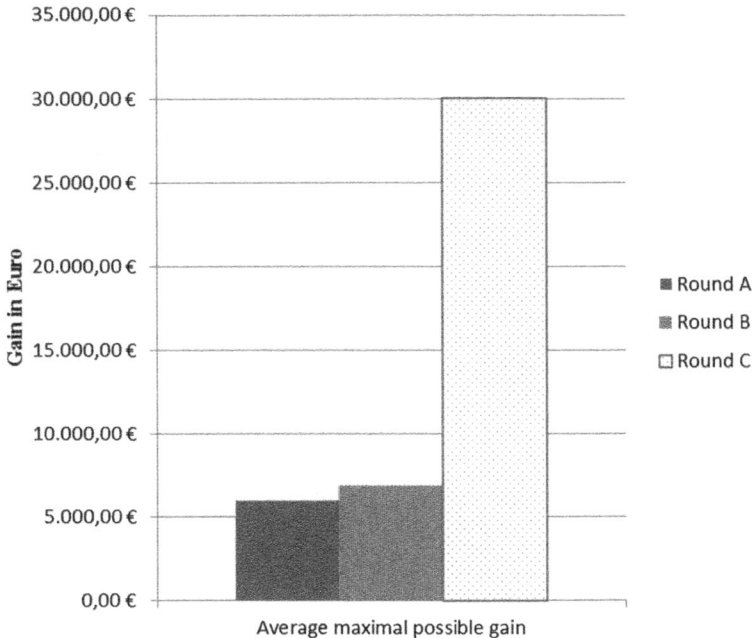

Fig. 8.3   Maximum possible gain

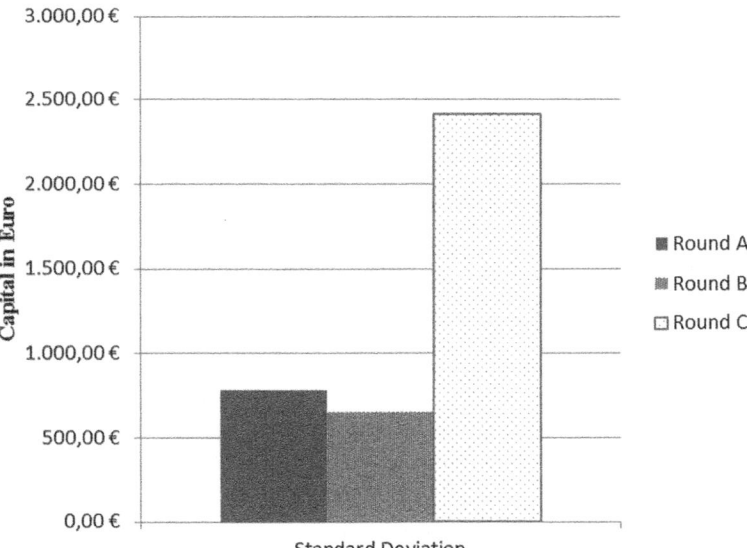

Fig. 8.4   Standard deviation set capital

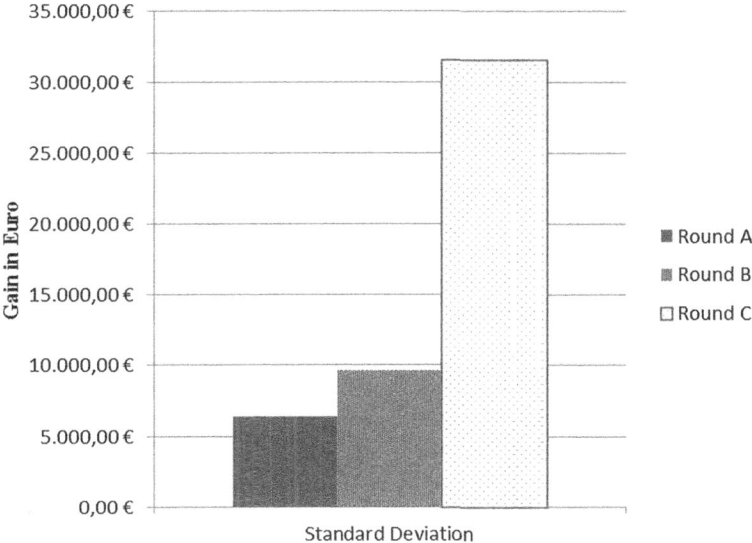

Fig. 8.5 Standard deviation maximum possible gain

employees (agents) at the cost of the company (the principal). They undertake actions that generate a high probability of gains in the short-term while the risk of a larger loss in the longer-term is not taken into consideration, thus becoming a liability to the principal. This does not align with the basic idea of principal-agent theory. Of course a connection between a manager's compensation and a firm or manager's performance will promote better incentive alignment and lead to higher motivation, which increases firm value, but only if losses and profits are remunerated symmetrically.

The existing asymmetries of bonus compensation schemes have led to a divergence of interests between employees on the one hand and the health of financial institutions and other companies at large on the other hand. Compensation packages for CEO's and other managers have gotten out of control. Remuneration and bonuses depend on short-term profitability, which increases share prices in the short-term, but not the long-term health of the company. In the financial system, investment managers increased the risks for their employer by buying highly profitable but risky assets and were rewarded with high bonuses, which led to the financial crisis in the long term. In addition, the review of research literature showed that cheating is promoted by high and unilateral variable compensations. CEOs have incentives to manipulate earnings if executive compensation is strongly linked to performance. Opportunistic earnings management behavior has been detected.

Risk adequate compensation is therefore an important prerequisite for good performance in all risk-handling professions. Without accountability variable compensation schemes become unilateral bonus maximization schemes with negative effects for the company and the principal. It means risking other people's money which will generally be abused (moral hazards) (Andersson et al., 2013).

It is difficult to change the business culture in the financial organizations if the compensation schemes contradict the ethical guidelines. The employees react in the way the company sets the guidelines. If the earning goals cannot be reached with ethical work, unethical methods are applied as the example of Sears has shown. Cheating is also influenced by compensation schemes. Gilla, Prowseb and Vlassopoulosc show that exposing workers to a compensation scheme based on random bonuses makes them cheat more but has no effect on their productivity.[65]

Conclusion

Group adaptation behavior can become market-relevant if market participants have social contact and identify themselves as a group. In the case of the financial crisis there was the common belief in the self-correcting power of the market and the ongoing prosperity and housing price increases. We can call this collective erring.

Kahnemann and Tversky found, that the presentation and formulation of questions affects the decision of subjects. In the financial crisis the investment decisions were influenced by the by the wrong ratings and the securitization. This kind of framing changed the behavior of the lenders. The investors did not question the creditworthiness of the debtors, which would normally be requirement for lending.

The ratings of the subprime CDOs were based on old data from the US real estate market. Tversky and Kahneman call a behavior focused on old data anchoring. People are biased because they depend too heavily on the first set of data they receive. This data is the "anchor" which distorts the decision.[66] Tversky and Kahneman also found insensitivity to sample size, which is a bias to see patterns in small numbers of results even though more results are needed to regress significant correlations.[67]

After the financial crisis the belief in experts was criticized. The complexity of derivatives like the CDO was so high that nobody but than the experts of the rating agencies were able to understand their structure and value.

The wrong ratings of the CDOs were a sign of overconfidence as a subjective favorable judgment of one's self. There was also confirmation bias and regret aversion. Investors processed the facts in a way that confirm their own opinions. This would explain why nobody of the experts corrected or questioned the wrong ratings. The biases show that ratings are not precise or might even be wrong because people make them.

As we have seen unmoral aspiration for enrichment of managers was common in the financial crisis. The bank managers were not fulfilling their role model function. People

---

[65] See Colesa, J. et al. (2006, pp. 431–468) and Gilla, D. et al. (2013, pp. 120–134).

[66] See Tversky, A., and D. Kahneman (1974).

[67] See Tversky, A., and D. Kahneman (1974, p. 1, 125).

are influenced in their behavior by their view of the world. Ideas and attitudes, or moral values, must be shown by example and included in education.

Bad examples can ruin common decency as much as it can be dangerous to continually preach thinking in models and maximizing benefit as the only reasonable, rational behavior. The consequence will be that people orient themselves on these behavioral maxims and repress their positive human characteristics such as sympathy, helpfulness, general willingness to sacrifice and selflessness. Management education in particular must ask itself if it did not indirectly create monster managers; business ethics receives too little attention.

It is difficult to change the business culture in the financial organizations. However, if people are remembered of their honesty-standards, they behave more ethically. Employees should sign ethical standards and should be remembered of them during their work. Finally, it has been demonstrated that unilaterally constructed incentive schemes encourage excess risk-taking. Unilaterally constructed compensation schemes were one reason for the financial crisis.

Comprehension Questions
1. Name some causes of the financial crisis.
2. What are the common moral causes of economic crisis?
3. Can you imagine some reasons for the unethical attitude of the managers?
4. What reforms would you suggest to improve the financial system?

8.1.3   The Reforms of the International Financial Market Order

What Follows Why?
After the financial crisis several studies analyzed the risks management practices and came to the conclusion that the investors have underestimated the risks due to products complexity and over-reliance on quantitative analysis (studies by the Financial Stability Forum, the Working Group on Risk Assessment and Capital, the Senior Supervisors Group, the Basel Committee on Bank Supervisions, the International Institute of Finance and the International Monetary Financial Committee) (Voinea & Anton, 2009).

New financial instruments such as derivatives showed their risk potential in the financial crisis. There were also new market participants, whose market influence has grown. By using a qualitative research approach we examine in this chapter the extent to which these two developments affect the economic processes of the market and put financial markets at risk. We also analyze the extent to which the new financial market regulations Basel III and the American Dodd Frank Act are sufficient to limit the systemic risk they cause.

Learning Goals

You should be able to explain what weaknesses of the financial order lead to the financial crisis and what reforms were implemented.

8.1.3.1 Risk and Non-transparency in Derivatives

The bilateral over-the-counter derivatives (OTCs), which are not traded on the stock exchange and therefore not registered, were a central problem in the financial crisis. The supervisory authorities still do not know the exact amount and distribution of the derivatives, which means they cannot know the systemic risk (e.g. the CDS to Greece in the European debt crisis) and cannot intervene. In the financial crisis, the counterparty risks were not properly priced, for example through a reasonable capital securitization. The default of a counterparty or credit could lead to a system risk as a result of contagion, as in the case of Lehman.

Basel III and the Dodd Frank Act provide a framework for trading via central clearinghouses (stock exchanges) as well as standards for a collateral deposit of the CDS seller and a capital backing which the CDS buyer must take to hedge the counterparty risk. The equity requirements of derivatives is determined by comprehensive models; the rating-related bond equivalence approach and the internal Advanced CVA (Credit Value Adjustment) approach, which is based on market data, specifically spreads, have been developed for this purpose (Hofman, 2011; *Deutsche* Bundesbank, 2011; Peirce & Soliman, 2016; Giancarlo, 2016). For the remaining OTC derivatives, higher equity requirements apply to counterparty risk, which makes them unattractive to banks. The volume of OTC derivatives is already decreasing (Conrad, 2013a; Gaumert et al., 2011). However, the collateral and the equity capital for the counterparty risk are insufficient to cover the systemic risk of derivatives. The financial crisis has shown very clearly how fast market data can change. If the spreads of the CVA and ratings of the bond equivalence approach change, banks must collateralize the difference.[68]

8.1.3.2 Weaknesses of Risk Indicators and Pricing Methods

Ratings

Uniform ratings are dangerous because all market players are subject to this assessment. If securities such as AAA-rated CDOs prove to be worthless in the financial crisis, asset bubbles can occur, followed by asset crashes. The financial innovations created a false sense of security with their complex mathematical models and AAA ratings. One of the main causes of the subprime crisis was that investors relied on the credit judgments of the rating agencies. The ratings were too good, which meant that the credits were understated with insufficient capital and that during the crisis the valuation adjustments put the creditors at risk.

---

[68] See Conrad, Christian A. (2018, pp. 32–40).

The Dodd Frank Act decouples the acceptable amount of capital securitization from external ratings. In general, the regulatory and supervisory authorities should remove all references to external ratings and rating agencies from the regulations (Dullien, 2012). In addition, the Dodd Frank Act subordinates the rating agencies to the SEC. The SEC will regularly monitor the ratings and methods of the agencies and impose fines in the event of infringements, which may include the revocation of licenses. In the financial crisis, rating agencies were not responsible for their valuations. According to the Dodd Frank Act, the rating agencies can be sued for damages by the investors in case of grossly negligent rating errors (*US-Senate*).

The German Council of Experts still sees a risk in wrong or matching external ratings. In the Liquidity Coverage Ratio (LCR) of Basel III, government bonds are equated with cash and in principle the government bonds are weighted lower in the net-stable funding ratio (NSFR). All OECD government bonds and loans are weighted at zero capital, which is what the EU Commission has assumed for the EU member states (*European Commission*, 2012). As a result, government bonds are preferred by the supervisory regulations, which is why it is assumed that the banks will continue to invest disproportionately in government bonds.

While this preference is desirable for governments, it raises the systemic risk substantially, which does not make sense in view of the present state debt crisis. This preference for government bonds is currently being discussed and has also prompted the Advisory Council to point to the risk of lump risks associated with government bonds. He also proposed foregoing a risk weighting of the claims and advocated large credit limits on government bonds (especially those of one's own state) (Sachverständigenrat, 2011). In the case of bonuses based on equity returns, the zero risk weighting causes moral hazards and discriminates against other loans, such as companies (Schäfer, 2011). In general, risk weighting is an incentive to manipulate ratings.

Value at risk and option pricing models

The problem with a distorting basis of past values is that it results in other capital market approaches, such as the value at risk (VaR) (Taleb, 2001, 2007), a risk indicator for securities, mainly derivatives, which is based on the historical value changes (volatilities) or assumed distributions of future influencing factors (Conrad, 2010). VaR failed as risk indicator in the financial crisis (Stulz, 2009). VaR models assume that prices correspond to a normal distribution. The occurrence of the financial crisis was incompatible with the assumption of a normal distribution. Such a "fat tail" phenomenon occurs every five to ten years (Crotty, 2009). Actually, the term "value at risk" promises too much and encourages a false sense of security, because the risk is the maximum possible loss and this is usually the capital employed. In order to circumvent the historical limitations of environmental conditions, Basel III prescribes fictitious stress scenarios for the VAR models (*Deutsche* Bundesbank, 2011). This is a significant improvement, but it should be a general understanding that the future remains unpredictable, and the rating is a very imprecise estimate (Stahl & Conrad, 2000).

The best example of the non-calculability of the economy is the option price formulas (Black & Schools formula). Robert Merton, Myron Scholes and Fischer Black received the Nobel Prize for Breaking Breakthroughs in War Warfare. Building on the volatilities of the past, they developed formulas for the price of buying or selling rights to values that can be exercised in the future (options). It is therefore apparently an instrument with which one can calculate the future, which is why they are also suitable for speculation. A hedge fund hired Robert Merton as a consultant. In 1998, this hedge fund, with the name Long Term Capital Management (LTCM), lost 90% of the $ 4 billion invested and threatened to trigger a chain reaction on the international financial markets.

This was not only about the loans taken by the LTCM, but also by the derivative positions drawn up by the LTCM as a counterparty, which had secured other financial market participants. It was not until the then Federal Reserve president Alan Greenspan personally intervened and created a several billion dollar rescue package, that the capital market crisis could be averted (Single & Stahl, 2000). In 2006, the second Merton advisory hedge fund with the lofty name IFC Continuum closed. So the future could not be calculated.

The weakness of the option price theories or risk indices such as value at risk, which are based on historical volatilities, is that they do not represent the future supply and demand ratios. For example, Porsche was able to buy the majority of VW stock by buying call options more favorably than on the stock market and increased its VW share secretly to 74%. The option prices did not reflect the scarcity of VW shares, as they had been calculated on the basis of past price fluctuations. They were much too low. The demand overhang then led to a short squeeze.

Is risk calculable?

Just like the Classic-Neoclassic theory after the Great Depression in 1929, today's economic theory has explanation and justification problems. The statistical models neither foresaw the crisis nor are they now able to explain it. Moreover, the econometric models based on historical figures presumed a safety where there was none, which was in itself one reason for the crisis (Stulz, 2009).

Ratings are estimates of future developments based on past figures. Strictly speaking, the risk of default cannot be calculated because the possible environmental conditions and the probability of their occurrence are not known. Unlike the static experiment of throwing a coin, the basic conditions of random events change constantly. The financial crisis has once again shown how quickly ratings can turn out to be wrong or fall behind events. The risk models thus led to an increase in the systemic risk rather than to a reduction. Nassim Nicholas Taleb wrote about the delusions of control and reliability under which much of Wall Street and many other businesses function. He pointed at the dangers of trusting the "bell-curve" models used by many financial institutions to mitigate risks. He questions the reliance on past historical information and uses the example of the black swan, which nobody expected until its discovery in Australia or the example of the turkey who spends a thousand days being well fed before being killed on the thousand-and-first day (Taleb, 2001, 2007). Justin Fox also criticizes the belief in models and especially the belief in efficient markets—a belief that was qualified by Robert Shiller as the "most remarkable error in the history of economic theory." (Fox, 2009; Malkiel, 2014).

We acknowledge that due to the countless and constantly changing environmental influences and the unpredictable factor of man, only trend forecasts for economic development can be made. Hayek already recognized this. There can be only so-called "pattern predictions" (*Hayek*, 2014).

Even after the financial crisis, the principle still applies that the worse the rating the more equity capital needs to be put aside in order to cover the default risk. Oddly, Basel III and the Dodd Frank Act massively increased the capital requirements for banks (Kern, 2010). The proposals of the Basel Committee on Banking Supervision (BCBS), as well as those of the Swiss and British expert groups, called for even higher capital requirements on investors (Sachverständigenrat, 2011). On the other hand, no one can predict how the ratings will change in a crisis and thus also how high the capital requirements will be in order to prevent the insolvency of a system-relevant institution. For example, according to the Basel II criteria, the Swiss UBS had a constant risk-weighted equity ratio of 10%, while the unweighted equity ratio had already fallen to 2% (Sachverständigenrat, 2011).

Basel III tries to solve this problem by a 2.5% additional anticyclical capital buffer (Gaumert et al., 2011). This is a good approach but arbitrary and inconsistent. No one can guarantee that this buffer is sufficient. If credit or default risks are still weighted with ratings, any accuracy that does not correspond to reality is just made up. The financial crisis has shown that ratings are too uncertain as a future prognosis in order to build up the stability of the financial system. The apparent predictability under Basel II led to a dangerous feeling of security. It would therefore be more consistent and risk-averse to forego a risk weighting (Miller, 2016). As in Basel I, the rating should not be decisive for capital adequacy, but all loans should be subject to a flat rate of 8%. Different creditworthiness could then be reflected, as in the periods of Basel I, in the banks' internal risk assessments, and thus in the loan interest rates. A global deterioration of the creditworthiness or an increase in the risks would not, as in the financial crisis, force a higher capital requirement in the short term, which would intensify the crisis. Then, government bonds should also be subject to equity, which seems urgent in view of the current international debt crisis.

8.1.3.3 Introduction of a Separation System

Debt write-offs for banks came mainly from investment banking, both in the financial crises and in the latest state debt crisis. There were also huge bonuses, which were paid out after short-term targets were reached. There should not be long-term credit risks here, which is why this bank is not subject to the credit rules. Bank-internal risk control and monitoring is much lower than in the credit sector. If, therefore, business with credit derivatives and bonds is to be continued in proprietary trading, the credit and default risks from investment banking should be subject to the same internal and external supervision and control. In particular, the rules on equity capital and the treatment of cluster risks must also apply to trading positions. Basel III stipulates that, the banks carry out their own model-based internal risk assessment in the purchase of bonds (securitization positions) and base the price risk in the account books on the basis of the investment portfolio with more equity. However, equity underwriting in the account books is still lower than in the investment portfolios, despite the fact that in the classic corporate and real estate lending businesses there were relatively minor failures in the financial crisis. In addition, the short-term trading positions, unlike corporate loans, are not included in the liquidity indices, which means they do not have to be refinanced. This is difficult to understand in light of the experience gained during the financial crisis when the markets for many trading positions disappeared. After the bankruptcy of Lehman many derivatives could no longer be sold. The failure of Lehman as a major derivative counterparty triggered the system crash. Lehman was too big to fail (*Deutsche* Bundesbank, 2011; Götzl, 2012).

After the financial crisis fewer and bigger thus even more systemic relevant banks were left in de market (Miller, 2016). The designation of "too big to fail" was introduced in 1998 with the rescue of LTCM by the US Federal Reserve president Greenspan and has been considered irrefutable since then. Here, too, there is a breach of the market-based principle of private liability. This led to negative incentives, so-called moral hazard problems (Conrad & Stahl, 2002, 2003). The profits from high-risk investments in the financial markets are only limited by a corresponding loss potential. For this, there is only one solution approach: system-relevant banks must be dismantled. Banks must also be able to go bankrupt in order for market incentives to work. Otherwise, a system change takes place moving toward a central administration economy, that is, to socialism. A break-up of the large corporations would also strengthen competition between the banks again.

An alternative approach would be the reintroduction of the separate banking system, i.e. the separation of investment and lending business. This would take account of the different business concepts of investment banking and commercial banking, and would give the financial institutions a non-contradictory objective function. An important argument for a separate bank system is greater risk transparency because processes and risks are handled through markets and are not visible only internally in a universal bank. The supporters of the universal system are opposed to the advantages of combining, scaling and information. However, the extremely high systemic costs of the financial crisis, which had to be borne mainly by taxpayers, are opposed to this (Blum, 2012).

US President Clinton and his Finance Minister Rubin abolished the Glass Steagall Act, and thus the separation system, in 1999. It was originally introduced as a result of the financial crisis in 1929, which was mainly caused by a credit-financed stock bubble.

Against the background of the experience in the financial crisis, the reintroduction in the USA or the international introduction of the separation banking system would only be consistent to prevent the transfer of risks from investment banking to credit banks and thus a systemic domino effect of outstanding claims and the transfer to the real economy. Investment banks would no longer be too big to fail and would no longer have to be saved by the state. According to the English Vickers report, the risky investment businesses are no longer allowed for retail banks internally shielded and demarcated within the framework of a ring-fence approach. By 2019, Britain's banks must have ring-fenced their retail banking operations from their parent companies (Jenkins, 2017; Sachverständigenrat, 2011). Like the corresponding American Volcker rule in the Dodd Frank Act, these approaches are not as broad as the Glass Steagall Act (Conrad, 2013a; Krahnen et al., 2017).

The introduction of a separation system would only prevent the risks of investment banking from bleeding into to the retail area of banks, while the debtor and counterparty risk of the investment banking and the accompanying systemic risk would continue. A ban on retail banks financing hedge funds by offering credit—as the Vickers report demands—is a complementary condition sine qua non. A possible total write-off must be considered when banks invest in investment houses, which is why we need a ban on the participation of retail banks in financial institutions with investment risks or at least giving up the value of these holdings. In the Dodd Frank Act the upper limit for investments in investment institutions was set at 3%. These American and English approaches are structurally complementary to Basel III and should therefore be adopted by European governments. The Volcker rule served as a model for the German Separation Act, which came into force on 14 January 2014 (Conrad, 2013; Kern, 2010; Sachverständigenrat, 2011).

If the pure investment banks only had receivables and liabilities in a separate banking system, all the institutions could theoretically fail without the deposits and loans of the commercial bank system being affected. However, it is precisely the CDS that creates a risk division between all market players, which also entails a risk transfer from the investment banks to the commercial banks. In order to ensure the functioning of a separation system, it would therefore be important to exclude trade of CDSs between these two types of institutes.

8.1.3.4   The Trade-off Between Yield and Risk and Unilaterally Constructed Incentive Schemes

The high credit risks associated with too little reserve equity also explain the relatively high returns in the financial sector. Between 2002 and 2005, the profits of the financial sector accounted for 40% of domestic corporate profits, and between 2009 and 2011 still 25% (Dullien, 2012). The credit risk of the CDS was not covered by equity as it is with comparable loans, which is why the banks have shown much higher profits in recent years than would have been permissible. When then the bad years came in the form of the subprime crisis, no capital was available to bear the losses. Many speculators had to be bailed out because their failure threatened the financial system. On the other hand, the bonuses were paid in the good years and did not have to be repaid as it turned out that the reported earnings were not sustainable. The financial crisis thus also revealed weaknesses in corporate governance. The bonuses of the companies violated the principle of liability, because only the short-term goal was rewarded. Long-term negative developments were not considered.

The experiment in chapter 8.1.2.4 showed that unilaterally constructed incentive schemes encourage excess risk-taking. This would indicate that common bonus-based compensation schemes are not a good idea and in fact enhance risk because of the asymmetries in the treatment of gains and losses (Conrad, 2015). In most cases compensation can only decrease down to the base salary while gains from bonuses can be limitless. Short-term results are rewarded even when these results are subsequently reversed. This encourages risk-taking by the employees (agents) at the cost of the company (the principal). They undertake actions that generate a high probability of gains in the short-term while the risk of a larger loss in the longer-term is not taken into consideration, thus becoming a liability to the principal. This does not align with the basic idea of principal-agent theory. Of course a connection between a manager's compensation and a firm or manager's performance will promote better incentive alignment and lead to higher motivation, which increases firm value, but only if losses and profits are remunerated symmetrically.

The existing asymmetries of bonus compensation schemes have led to a divergence of interests between employees on the one hand and the health of financial institutions and other companies at large on the other hand. Compensation packages for CEOs and other managers have gotten out of control. Remuneration and bonuses depend on short-term profitability, which increases share prices in the short-term, but not the long-term health of the company. In the financial system, investment managers increased the risks for their employer by buying highly profitable but risky assets and were rewarded with high bonuses, which led to the financial crisis in the long term. In addition, the review of research literature showed that cheating is promoted by high and unilateral variable compensations. CEOs have incentives to manipulate earnings if executive compensation is strongly linked to performance. Opportunistic earnings management behavior has been detected.

Risk adequate compensation is therefore an important prerequisite for good performance in all risk-handling professions. Without accountability, variable compensation schemes become unilateral bonus maximation schemes with negative effects for the company and the principal. It means risking other people's money which will generally be abused (moral hazards) (Andersson et al., 2013).

In view of the principal agent problem and the resulting lack of shareholder control, a state intervention seems unavoidable to prevent moral hazard. The Dodd Frank Act offers at least a legal basis to demand that overly generous bonuses be repaid, in the event of a balance sheet correction (Kern, 2010). In addition, many bank managers seem to lack the professional qualification to correctly assess the risks from subprime loans. This also reveals weaknesses in corporate governance, particularly in the case of staff recruitments. Here, the national financial supervisory authorities are called upon to review in particular the experience of the board members in the lending business.

8.1.3.5 Fair Value Loan Valuation

Bank loans are not impaired until they are no longer serviced or permanent deteriorations in the creditworthiness of the borrower exist, which jeopardize the repayment of the loan. One problem, however, is the balance sheet valuation of tradable loans, so-called securitizations, at fair value, i.e. at market value. This was reflected in the financial crisis when the markets for the CDOs had fallen away and the values plummeted. In other words, the fair values were meaningless because of exaggerated values, and they devolved into understated values because of lack of demand and transparency.

The fair value problem reappeared again during the European debt crisis. As the prices of government bonds declined, many European banks needed fresh equity because the price losses resulted in write-offs. US-GAAP and IFRS are aligned to the shareholder's informational needs, which reflect the level of the fair value. A long-term evaluation based on creditor protection and caution would be more appropriate, as it avoids excessive volatility in both revaluations and devaluations (Ballwieser et al., 2009). Market values are determined by supply and demand. This can lead to imbalances that have nothing to do with creditworthiness, or to exaggeration and understatement through herding, that is, irrational human mass behavior (). Here, there should be a balance sheet option to suspend the market value on the basis of current internal ratings that can be verified by the bank supervisor, for trading positions such as loans. The IFRSs are to be geared more strongly to long-term values (Ballwieser et al., 2009).

8.1.3.6 Conclusion

The biggest shortcoming of the recent reforms to the stabilization of the financial system, such as Basel III and the American Dodd Frank Act, is that they increase the capital requirements rather than decreasing the risk from the new financial products like derivatives. They do this in order to absorb the increased risk of speculation following the financial market deregulation and the spreading of derivatives, yet this also greatly increases the costs of borrowed capital. This means that growth losses are accepted and the costs of the financial crisis are once again forced upon the general public.

An alternative option to limit systemic risk would be the internalization of systemic risk into market prices. High capital requirements could be renounced if the systemic risks arising from non-regulated financial contractors are correctly priced or reported. It would be feasible to levy a risk tax on transactions with offshore institutions and other counterparties from unregulated financial markets that create a systemic risk but are not subject to the new regulatory requirements. This could be in the form of a flat-rate penalty tax or on the basis of an analysis of the respective systemic risk. In addition, a valuation discount for the claims against these institutions would be required under accounting law.

This would also reduce the problem of the prisoner's dilemma. The cost of the risk posed by these institutions would be internalized and free-rider benefits reduced. This tax could be collected individually by each state, thus without international financial market regulation. This would be in line with the Basel III regulation described above, which provides additional capital requirements for the risk of default for derivatives that are not settled via central counterparties. However, the problem of market influence by speculation with derivatives remains.

It would generally be better to forbid risky and complex financial products than to further increase regulation complexity and the capital requirements as in Basel III and the American Dodd Frank Act. Real-world problems can arise from the investor behavior whenever there are raw materials that fulfill important economic functions, such as foodstuffs. In the case of commodity trading, the position limits should therefore be reintroduced and the leverage of the derivatives restricted. As with medicines, derivatives should be reviewed by their national regulatory authorities for their systemic risk and transparency before they enter the market. Consumer protection should also be considered. No non-transparent derivatives with unlimited risk such as credit-ladder swaps should be permitted.

Comprehension Questions
1. Name the reasons for the financial crisis.
2. What countermeasures have been implemented since then?
3. Do you think that the measures are sufficient to prevent a new financial crisis?

8.2   Speculation in the International Financial Markets

What Follows Why?
One reason for the financial crisis is called speculation with credit derivatives. To what extent is speculation a part of the financial markets? Is it a normal market economy and what are the economic effects? These questions will be answered below.

For some time now, there has been an intensive discussion about the effects of speculation especially with commodities and agricultural product. In the following we examine the effects of speculation based on the most recent research. The following questions will be addressed: Will futures prices and price volatility be influenced by speculation? Would that create false price signals, and if yes, what effects will that have? In specific will there be demand effects for the spot market prices, which would increase the living costs thus could be seen as unethical?

Learning Objectives
You should be able to explain the economic effects of speculation.

8.2.1   What Empirical Evidence do we Have About Speculation Influencing Markets?

Many empirical studies show a relationship between speculation on futures markets and the price development of goods affected on the cash markets, as well as the volatility of prices for goods. Christopher Gilbert shows, for example, the relationship between index-based investments and the prices for foods, and uses it to explain the exorbitant price increases from 2007 to 2008. This connection, and the peak in food prices from 2010 to 2011, was shown by Mario Lagi in a comprehensive model that included surveys for merchants and producers. These papers show that in their respective time frames, speculation caused prices to be about 50% above the level that would have been appropriate for the physical demand and supply. Other researchers from Harvard University and the Federal Reserve Bank of Boston have checked their results. Many other studies arrive at the same conclusions (Deutsche Bundesbank, 2006, Gilbert, 2010, Singleton, 2011, Lagi et al., 2011, Chilto, 2012). Mayer (2009) points out the influence from various types of speculation on commodity prices.

Pies offers a contradictory argument, namely that the prices for commodities also rose within the same time periods, yet they were not the object of index-fund speculation or even traded on futures markets.[69] It cannot be concluded from this however, that there was no effect from index speculation until long-term correlations between these commodities have been examined, eliminating phenomena such as a price transfer substituting non-indexed commodities for indexed commodities (cross-price elasticity). There are also investors who speculate on increasing commodity prices outside of index funds, thus buying non-indexed commodities forward or investing in long futures.

In a study from 2009 the United States Permanent Subcommittee on Investigations concluded that from 2006 to 2008 investments in index funds inflated grain futures prices in relation to the spot prices on the Chicago stock market.[70] This study was contested[71] by another research team (Stoll and Whaley), which was funded by Gresham Investment Management LLC.[72] Stoll and Whaley test index fund inflows for any

---

[69] See Pies, Ingo (2012a, p. 3).

[70] "This Report finds that there is significant and persuasive evidence to conclude that these commodity index traders, in the aggregate, were one of the major causes of "unwarranted changes"— here, increases—in the price of wheat futures contracts relative to the price of wheat in the cash market. The resulting unusual, persistent, and large disparities between wheat futures and cash prices impaired the ability of participants in the grain market to use the futures market to price their crops and hedge their price risks over time, and therefore constituted an undue burden on interstate commerce." Levin, Carl and Coburn, Tom (2009, p. 2).

[71] See Stoll, Hans R. and Whaley, Robert E. (2009, p 65).

[72] The objectivity of this study must be questioned, since financial positions in commodities are key business of Gresham: "Gresham offers several commodity investment programs. Our goal is to provide a responsible way to invest (as opposed to speculate) in the asset class, and to offer

influence on futures prices. In contrast to other studies, they do not find any significant connection between index fund investments and commodity price increases, however, they only take the large positions reported in the COT Report and only the positions of index funds into account.[73] Neither did Scott Irwin and Dwight Sanders determine increased prices or increased volatility on futures markets for commodities as a result of investments in indexed commodity funds. In fact, according to their empirical research, the index investments caused decreased price volatility.[74]

Stoll and Whaley also analyzed the development of commodity prices both in and out of the index, finding a weak correlation of between 0.13 and 0.20 in both cases. They found a similarly weak correlation to index commodities for commodity prices outside of the indexes. From these findings they conclude that the index investments had no effect on the prices.[75] Tang und Xiong calculated however, that there was no correlation (less than 0.1) between indexed commodities in the 1990s and early 2000s. The same was true among non-indexed commodities. In 2009 however, the correlation among indexed commodities increased to over 0.5, while the correlation for non-indexed commodities only increased to 0.2.[76] This result can be traced back to the influence of index investments. The prices for indexed and non-indexed commodities developed differently between 2004 and 2008. The indexed commodities increased evenly in that period then fell, which did not reflect fundamental changes in supply and demand, rather in the flows of investment capital. The other commodities developed very differently.[77] The same increase in demand for various products can have differing effects on prices if the supply elasticity differs. The market power on the supply side would also need to be considered, such as the OPEC cartel on the oil market.

Stoll and Whaley also offer the argument that the shifts in futures positions before the phase-out would have led to significant jumps in prices if the index investors had influence over pricing, which was not the case.[78] We can counter however, that the opposing positions must phase-out and be extended as long as we are not talking about a physical delivery that has been agreed upon. Bass points out that the investors keep their demand constant by rolling over their contracts.[79]

---

our clients the benefits of systematic exposure to a wide range of commodities and commodity groups through the use of commodity futures in Diversified Commodity Portfolios (DCP)." http://greshamllc.com/en/pages.php?s=2 (02/10/2014).

[73] See Stoll, Hans R. and Whaley, Robert E. (2009, p. 66).

[74] See Irwin, Scott H. and Sanders, Dwight R. (2010).

[75] See Stoll, Hans R. and Whaley, Robert E. (2009, pp. 29 and 65).

[76] See Tang, Ke and Xiong, Wei (2012, p. 65).

[77] See Tang, Ke/Xiong, Wei (2012, pp. 55+and 64+).

[78] See Stoll, Hans R. and Whaley, Robert E. (2009, p. 66).

[79] See Bass, Hans-Heinrich (2011, p. 45+).

At bottom Stoll und Whaley contradict the Subcommittee and do not consider the functionality of futures markets to have been restricted by index investments because only 3% of the contracts from 2005 to 2009 were physically fulfilled, and thus could not have influenced the spot market. This also means that the differences from spot prices are not due to index investments.[80] However this does not mean that the futures prices were not positively influenced, however. 97% non-physically fulfilled contracts indicate a large influence of non-commercial goods.

Supporters of speculation offer other causes for the increase in food prices from 2007 to 2008. Irwin and Sanders argue that the greatly increased demand for commodities from China, India and other emerging markets, interruptions in oil production, less demand elasticity in consumers and US monetary policy were all causes of the price increases. Given the negative correlation between the real interest rate and commodity prices, Inamura concludes that too light of a US monetary policy supported the boom in commodity prices.[81] The increased cost of biofuels and weather were given as causes for the increased grain prices.[82] Frenk counters that although the Chinese demand for oil rose by 12% in 2008, Europe and the US entered a recession that brought the international demand for oil down. In fact oil supply increased in the first 6 months of 2008, which makes an increase in oil prices of 50% within the same time period inexplicable.[83] Baffes and Haniotis, like Lagi et al., come to the conclusion from their study that neither the demand from emerging economies nor from biofuel production contributed significantly to the price boom in foods, rather that it was the demand from finance investors.[84] Inamura also considers weather, tensions in the Middle East, and in particular the economic boom in emerging economies (output gap) insufficient to explain the large increase.[85]

In the end the slump in commodity prices after 2008 can only be explained by the lapse in speculation demand resulting from the financial crisis, since all other factors remained constant. The hedge fund manager Masters points out that neither the absolute increases of 2007 and 2010, nor the slump that followed, had been seen before. Such volatility can only be explained by the parallel financial flows, since there were no substantial changes in commodity supply in these time periods.[86]

---

[80] See Stoll, Hans R. and Whaley, Robert E. (2009, p. 67).

[81] See Inamura, Yasunari et al. (2011, p. 5).

[82] See Irwin, Scott H. and Sanders, Dwight R. (2010, p. 4+).

[83] See Frenk, David et al. (2011, p. 45).

[84] See Baffes, John and Haniotis, Tassos (2010). "The demand for grains and oilseeds as biofuel feedstocks has been cited as the main cause of the price rise, but there is little direct evidence for this contention. Instead, index-based investment in agricultural futures markets is seen as the major channel through which macroeconomic and monetary factors generated the 2007–2008 food price rises." Lagi, M. et al. (2011).

[85] See Inamura, Yasunari et al. (2011, p. 3+).

[86] See Masters, Michael W. (2009, p. 4).

Inamura found an increasing correlation between commodities and other forms of investment since 2005, and considers it to be an expression of the increased financialization of commodity markets by finance investors. The commodity markets reflect the same liquidity flows in this period as the stock markets.[87] This is indeed an important observation, as the negative correlation is a main reason investors in commodities would diversify and thus reduce the risk of the portfolio as a whole.[88] High futures prices would indicate replenishing stocks and increasing storage capacity. Without high futures prices there would be no sure basis for the calculation of profit from commodity stocks, making it purely speculative.[89] The higher future prices are, the higher the assured profits will be. Krugman therefore sees an influence of futures prices on spot prices only via arbitrage, thus a scarcity in spot offers due to stock holding with a view to selling at higher future prices. He only sees this effect with copper and cotton however, not for agrarian products whose stock holding did not increase.[90] For agrarian markets Pies used wheat to determine a decline in stock keeping until 2008. He admits that the data are incomplete however, since private stocks were not registered. Nonetheless, if storage capacities did not increase there is not necessarily anything we can conclude. If the investment costs for new storage capacity are high, futures prices must exceed spot prices for a longer time in order to make the investment worthwhile.

8.2.2   Critique of Methodology

Within the discussion both sides criticize one another's methodological weaknesses in econometric studies based primarily on Granger. Irwin and Sanders' results are criticized based on the fact that the Granger test is not an appropriate method with highly volatile variables, thus distorting results.[91] The problem is of a more fundamental nature, however. If causal variables are not eliminated, false correlations can show up in Granger tests (spurious regression). The same is true for purely coincidental correlations, which can show up particularly in short time periods of observation.

As we have already shown, many speculation proponents argue that the greatly increased demand for commodities from China, India and other emerging economies, interruptions in oil production, less consumer demand elasticity and US monetary policy

---

[87] See Inamura, Yasunari et al. (2011, p. 7).

[88] Portfolio theory from Markowitz. See Markowitz, Harry (1952).

[89] See Peck, Anne (1985, pp. 44–45).

[90] "If high futures prices induce increased storage, this reduces the quantity available to consumers, and it can raise the price. And you can, in fact, argue that something like this has been happening for cotton and copper, where there are apparently large and growing inventories. But for food, it's just not happening: stocks are low and falling." Krugman, Paul (2011b).

[91] For a critique of Irwin and Sanders see Frenk, David et al. (2011).

were all responsible for the price increases. Increased biofuel production and weather were considered to have caused the price increases.[92] If so many factors were truly affecting prices the Granger test would not have been applicable due to multi-causality. The same is true for the effects of weather, since the required stationarity of variables would not be given.[93] Highly volatile variables such as stock prices or commodities were also determined to have insufficient covariant stationarity, thus the requirement for the regression of time series is not met.[94]

Irwin and Sander have been criticized for using lags of one week and not limiting price influences to one week,[95] as well as for using non-representational data. The same is true for the Stoll and Whaley study. The positions of the index funds are not transparent because the DCOT Swap Dealer Data also contains positions from other market participants. The Commodities Futures Trading Commission (CFTC) estimates in fact that only 41% of the positions for crude oil futures belong to the index funds.[96] This represents a general problem. The quality of the data is also questionable, since it is generally based on questionnaires or is incomplete.[97] OTC derivatives were not even required to be posted in the time periods examined. Only after the financial crisis was it decreed that derivatives had to be registered or dealt via clearing houses.[98]

According to the scientists of the Raiffeisen Association the majority of empirical studies show no verifiable connection between stock volumes and the price increase.[99]

---

[92] See Irwin, Scott H. and Sanders, Dwight R. (2010, p. 4).

[93] See Schulze, Peter M. (2004, p. 17.+ and Hassler, Uwe (2003, p. 813).

[94] See Pagan, A. and Schwert, C. (1990); Phillips, P. and Loretan, M. (1990); Frenk, David et al. (2011). p 45 and http://www.matthias-schlecker.de/kointegrationsanalyse-stationaritaet-und-augmented-dickey-fuller-test (04/04/2014).

[95] See Frenk, David et al. (2011, p. 47).

[96] See Frenk, David et al. (2011, p. 47) and Masters, M.W. and White, A.K. (2008, p. 33).

[97] "There have been ongoing complaints that the legacy COT trader designations may be inaccurate … As one example, speculators may have an incentive to self-classify their activity as commercial hedging to circumvent speculative position limits in some markets. But, the CFTC implements a fairly rigorous process—including statements of cash positions in the underlying commodity—to ensure that commercial traders have an underlying risk associated with futures positions. However, in recent years industry participants began to suspect that these data were contaminated because the underlying risk for many reporting commercials was not a position in the physical commodity… Rather, the reporting commercials were banks and other swap dealers hedging risk associated with over-the-counter (OTC) derivative positions." Irwin, Scott H. and Sanders, Dwight R. (2012, p. 258). See also Frenk's critique of the Irwin and Sanders study from 2010. See Frenk, David et al. (2011, p 48).

[98] See Conrad, Christian A. (2013b).

[99] "Ganz im Gegenteil kommt die weit überwiegende Mehrzahl der bis dato zu diesem Thema verfassten empirischen Arbeiten – allerdings ebenfalls auf dem Boden der suboptimalen Terminmarktdatensätze – zu dem Ergebnis, dass kein nachweisbarer Kausalzusammenhang zwischen Anlagevolumina und Preisanstieger besteht." Translation: "Quite the opposite, the large majority

The NGO WEED disagrees and lists over 100 empirical studies that are critical of speculation.[100] The economic ethicist Pies examined 35 studies and concluded that no negative effect from commodity speculation could be proven.[101] WEED accuses Pies of not examining important studies critiquing speculation and having biased criticism against the methodology used in studies critical of speculation.[102] Irwin reviews the evidence from recent studies and argues that "the growing body of literature fails to find compelling evidence that buying pressure from commodity index investment in recent years caused a massive bubble in agricultural future prices."[103] Both positions are in fact supportable using the empirical studies that have been conducted. One part of the studies shows that speculation has influenced commodity prices and the other part proves the opposite. Again we see here the dilemma and weakness of econometric research. There is no proof of causality, as there can be many factors behind a correlation.

The scientific content of the predominantly Granger-based econometric studies must be questioned. There are fundamental method problems here. Because of the risk of false results, the Granger test is not recommended if the variables under study are extremely volatile, which is the case for commodity prices.[104] For highly volatile variables such as stock prices or commodities, a lack of covariance stationarity was found, which does not provide a condition for regressing time series.[105] Due to innumerable influencing factors on supply and demand, we have a strong multi-causality here in which the individual influencing factors cannot be filtered out precisely. If causal variables have not been extracted, Granger tests can show correlations that are not present (spurious regression). The same applies to purely random correlations, which may arise in particular in the case of short observation periods or incorrect time intervals.[106] Also, weather effects such as those that occur in agricultural products are problematic, because then the necessary stationarity of the variables is missing.[107]

---

of papers written on this topic to date – though also based on suboptimal futures market data sets – come to the conclusion that there no causal connection exists between stock volumes and price increases." Petersen, Volker J et al. (2012, p. 14).

[100] See http://www2.weed-online.org/uploads/evidence_on_impact_of_commodity_speculation.pdf (Stand 26. November 2013, 04/01/2014).

[101] See Will, Matthias Georg et al. (2012).

[102] See Henn, Markus (2013).

[103] See Irwin, Scott (2010) H., p. 1.

[104] See Irwin, Scott H. and Sanders, Dwight R. (2012, p. 258).

[105] See Pagan, A. and Schwert, C. (1990, pp. 165–170); Phillips, P. and Loretan, M. (1990); Frenk, David et al. (2011, p. 45) and http://www.matthias-schlecker.de/kointegrationsanalyse-stationaritaet-und-augmented-dickey-fuller-test (04.04.2014).

[106] See Frenk, David et al. (2011, p. 47).

[107] See Schulze, Peter M. (2004, p. 17) and Hassler, Uwe (2003, p. 813).

Also, the positions of the index funds are not transparent because the DCOT swap dealer data also contains many positions from other market participants. The Commodities Futures Trading Commission (CFTC) estimates that, for example, crude oil futures accounted for only 41% of positions in index funds.[108] So we also have a general problem here. Likewise, the quality of the data is called into question because they are usually based on interviews or not complete.[109] OTC derivatives did not have to be reported during the investigated periods. Only after the financial crisis was it decreed that they be registered or traded through clearing houses.[110]

Precisely because of such a background, it does not seem to me scientifically founded to derive extreme positions from the existing econometric studies. But this happens again and again, and without logically questioning the results. The absence of a logic-based discussion is a major drawback to current econometric research.

After innumerable studies examining the same thing and coming to different conclusions, it is time to make a change. It is clear that using econometrics proves neither the influence of speculation nor its absence. Additional studies will not change that fact. The two camps of advocates and critics of speculation are still at a draw. Logic should therefore be used as an alternative economic method to analyze the effects of commodity speculation based on known and widely accepted facts.

8.2.3   The Logic of Speculation

Stoll and Whaley argue that investment in commodities is no different than invest in stocks, for example. They fail to note however, that the money flowing into commodities is not productive. No production sites are financed, as may be the case with stocks. Commodity investments do not increase the growth of a national economy. There is also no direct offset for scarcities, such as arbitrage and thus making the most of spatial price differences. An investment in commodities is always in the expectation of future price increases and is therefore speculation. Even if the motivation is to diversify a portfolio,

---

[108] See Frenk, David et al. (2011), a. a O., p. 47 and Masters, M.W. and White, A.K. (2008).

[109] "There have been ongoing complaints that the legacy COT trader designations may be inaccurate …. As one example, speculators may have an incentive to self-classify their activity as commercial hedging to circumvent speculative position limits in some markets. But, the CFTC implements a fairly rigorous process—including statements of cash positions in the underlying commodity—to ensure that commercial traders have an underlying risk associated with futures positions. However, in recent years industry participants began to suspect that these data were contaminated because the underlying risk for many reporting commercials was not a position in the physical commodity…. Rather, the reporting commercials were banks and other swap dealers hedging risk associated with over-the-counter (OTC) derivative positions." Irwin, Scott H. and Sanders, Dwight R. (2012, p. 258). See also Frenk, David et al. (2011, p. 48).

[110] See Conrad, Christian A. (2013b, pp. 233–241).

the investor still expects increasing commodity prices. Prices may increase due to scarcity, but there are other causes such as cost increases and inflation. As the utilization of spatial price differences, speculation can balance out future imbalances between supply and demand if the speculation demand leads to a price increase that signals producers to increase their supply. Such a chain of events is not necessarily the case however, since the future scarcity of goods, thus prices different from current prices, is not assured. In order to divert production in the right direction, the speculators must be better informed than the market, which is not generally to be assumed. The opposite is also a possibility, namely that speculation creates a false signal for production.

Speculating at one's own risk is a fundamental part of a market-based system. New market participants entering both sides of the market through speculation by buying or selling has a stabilizing effect on prices because of the increased liquidity. Gary Cohn, Co-President, Managing Director and CEO of Goldman Sachs New York, argues in favor of allowing non-commercials because where once there were only producers that wanted to sell on futures markets to secure their interests against price fluctuations, now liquidity is available from the other side thanks to non-commercials.[111] With this argument Cohn is forgetting to mention the downstream users of commodities, who are the traditional buyers of commodities and agrarian products on the futures market. In addition, index investors sell differently than speculators because they buy to diversify their portfolios or they want to keep long positions in commodities and risk diversification at a certain proportion to their other stocks. Their profit orientation is also contrary to the downstream users, who want to buy at low prices. Increasing prices attract more investors.[112]

Cheng, Kirilenko and Xiong also show the flip side of liquidity flow. Liquidity flowing in from non-commercials makes the goods dealt on the market fungible, but the 2008 reduction in liquidity put the market under pressure. Emerging markets experienced a similar phenomenon during the Asian crisis of 1997.[113]

Krugman considers speculation to be a zero sum game. Every futures long contract is accompanied by a short contract, which is why he does not see any influence on prices. "Buying a futures contract for oil *does not* reduce the quantity of oil available for consumption; there's no such thing as "virtual hoarding"".[114] One must point out however, that the supply and demand on the spot market may not be influenced, but they are on the futures market. Of course a futures contract can only be concluded on the futures

---

[111] See Cohn, Gary, Co-President, Managing Director and COO of Goldman Sachs, New York, NY, in: U.p. Government Printing Office (2008), Senate Hearing 110–654, SUMMIT ON ENERGY.

[112] "Traditional Speculators provide liquidity by both buying and selling futures. Index Speculators buy futures and then roll their positions by buying calendar spreads. They never sell. Therefore, they consume liquidity and provide zero benefit to the futures markets." Masters, Michael W. (2009, p. 4).

[113] See Cheng, Ing-Haw et al. (2012).

[114] See Krugman, Paul (2008).

market if there is a short position corresponding to the long position, but excess demand will only increase prices until a market participant considers the offset lucrative. In short, if everything else says the same, an additional demand for commodities increases prices on futures markets. Even if futures prices do not influence spot prices with a supply scarcity resulting from increased stock holding, it is still possible for expectations to have an influence. Lagi and others have shown this as "… we interviewed participants in the spot market who state unequivocally that they base current prices on the futures market. The use of futures prices as a reference enables speculative bubbles on the futures market to influence actual food prices."[115]

Krugman is correct in that speculation is in principle a zero sum game. What one actor wins, another must lose. In the case of commodity speculation, the speculators can fulfill an important function by buying forward the commodities from downstream users and thus reducing the risk of price changes. In such a case they fill the purpose of insurance, which also a central argument of those in favor of unimpeded speculation.[116] With such an argument however, we must remember that a producer can meanwhile be facing up to 4 speculators and thus speculation goes far beyond simple insurance. The speculators may buy and sell amongst one another,[117] which can lead to an increase of futures prices with excess demand. The index funds invested almost exclusively long until the peak of 2008, which created a great deal of excess demand.[18]

8.2.4   Price Distortions and Price Manipulation

Markets can be influenced in many ways by speculation.

An artificial price influence occurs, for example, through short selling on the supply side. When something is sold that either does not exist or is only lent or bought for which there is no real economic use, supply and demand are artificially altered. The price develops differently than it would to influence supply and demand to the desired extent.[119]

As early as 2010, the share of high-speed trading in US equities trading was approx. 60%. Errors in the computer-aided model algorithms can trigger crashes, such as in 2003 for the shares of the US company Corinthian Colleges. Highly fluctuating prices are an

---

[115] Lagi, M. et al. (2011, p. 5).

[116] See Pies, Ingo and Will, Matthias Georg Will (2013, p. 5+).

[117] There are empirical studies for this as well, which prove a high degree of trade among finance investors. See Domanski, Dietrich/Heath, Alexandra (2007, p. 65). https://www.bis.org/publ/qtrpdf/r_qt0703g.pdf.

[118] See Stoll, Hans R. and Whaley, Robert E. (2009, p. 21).

[119] See Masters, Michael W. (2009, p. 17).

expression of a higher risk, which can deter security-oriented market participants. Short-term mathematical algorithms supersede fundamental long-term value strategies. Such a connection would be conceivable on the stock market. Apart from higher market liquidity, no economic advantage is obvious. On the contrary, a ban on high-frequency trading would stabilize the markets.

The impacts of credit default swaps are still contentious. There are the so-called Naked CDS as derivative loan loss insurance without underlying loans. There are those who see a positive effect even in speculative credit default swaps because of the higher liquidity in the market. There are also market participants who believe that the interest rates of the Greek government bonds would be higher if the investors could not insure themselves against a CDS default. However, the Greek Government complained that the betting of hedge funds on Greek bankruptcy over the purchase of CDS would have led to higher margins in Greek government bonds in the European debt crisis. Who is right?

If many hedge funds are speculating against European government bonds, for example, they buy the corresponding CDS as a credit default insurance. This leads to an increase in the CDS spreads, which is not only seen as a reflection of the bond yields but is also seen as a risk indicator by the market participants, thus directly and indirectly driving up the price of the bonds. George Soros also sees the CDS 'very critically'. In his opinion, there is the risk of a "bear raid", i.e. a profitable price influence, at CDS due to the asymmetric risk distribution between the buyer (limited risk of loss, value or premiums of the CDS) and the seller (high risk of loss in the event of bankruptcy). A purchase of CDS' increases the borrowing costs of the borrower and thereby improves its credit rating, which in turn increases the value of the CDS'. According to George Soros, this connection together with the short selling of the shares caused the collapse of Lehman, AIG and Bear Stearns (Soros, 2009).

The risk of a "bear raid" originates from derivatives because their value is determined by real prices. Due to the theoretically unlimited leverage of derivatives, in small-volume markets it may be worthwhile to influence or manipulate the real price on the market in order to be successful with the derivatives position. This was the basis for the arrangements for Libor and gold fixing between major international banks. Even a collectively coordinated behavior for the manipulation of the courses cannot be ruled out in smaller markets.

Derivatives such as call options affect the cash price if the option holder can insist on physical delivery. Thus in 2008 Porsche was able to purchase VW with call options cheaper than on the stock market and then increase the VW share secretly to 74%. The option prices did not reflect the scarcity of the VW share, since they had been calculated on the basis of past price fluctuations. They were therefore much too low. The demand surplus then led to a short squeeze and a huge increase of the VW price. Option writers must therefore make sure they are at least partially physically secure and inquire about the commodity.

Short selling should generally be banned because someone is selling something they do not own. There is a lot of room for speculative influence. The damage is suffered by the owners who lent the shares.

In a market economy short selling undermines the system because the owners are liable and not the seller. Funds (including ETF funds) should therefore be banned from lending stocks.

8.2.5   Irrationality and Bubble Creation?

As already stated, according to Eugene Fama's fundamentalist efficiency market hypothesis, speculation-induced deviation of futures prices from fundamental data would not be possible because prices always reflect all information rationally. Rising futures prices would therefore only indicate scarcity in the future.[120] However, speculation would not be worthwhile, because the price difference would only reflect the cost of storage. It is often argued that when bubbles form, other than the fundamentals, other market participants form counterparts. This contradicts—as was shown above—the New Behavioral Finance. The empirical investigations of this behavior-oriented research direction confirm the psychologically oriented, non-deterministic explanatory approaches. It turned out that investors perceive and evaluate the information available to them in a very subjective way, and that they do not always maximize the expected benefits in their decisions—contrary to the neoclassical model world.[121] For example, so-called herding can occur, whereby the sociological group orientation of humans dominates. In an uncertain stock-market situation, the investor orients via the other market participants, which the stock market also—at least in the short term—rewarded with rising prices.

Speculation, while exploiting temporal price differentials, can offset future imbalances in supply and demand, for example, where speculative demand leads to a rise in prices that signals producers to increase supply, but this need not be the case as future shortages other than the current prices at arbitrage are uncertain. The speculators must be better informed than the market, but this cannot be assumed. Speculation can therefore also be a non-rational behavior that does not differ from betting and gambling. So the reverse is also conceivable that speculation for the production produces false signals and thus causes bubbles and crashes.

---

[120] See Gilbert, Christopher L. (2010, p. 10).
[121] See Conrad, Christian (2005).

8.2.6   Conclusion

Does speculation have an effect on spot prices that could increase the living costs with unethical effects especially for poor countries? The fact is that financialization has caused new market participants to join commodities and agricultural markets with distinct economic motivations. Because the investors were interested in diversifying their portfolios, massive long positions were built up until the financial crisis. Many billions of dollars thus came into the markets as additional demand. Since the investors did not want the commodities delivered, the additional demand ad a direct influence only on futures markets, not on spot markets. This caused an increase in the secure stock profits that, as long as they were greater than the cost of storage, would lead sooner or later to a scarcity in supply and thus to increased spot market prices. We can therefore assume an influence of futures prices on spot prices if the excess demand on the futures market is high and stays high over a longer time period. If commodity and agriculture producers think futures prices are at a historic high they will sell their production forward, which removes the supply from the future spot market. Increasing prices for end and intermediate goods involving commodities and agriculture product are also possible if the downstream producers secure their positions on futures markets. So we come to the conclusion that speculation influence spot prices of commodities and food prices if it creates a significant excess demand over a significant time period. In this case speculation might be seen as unethical, why regulation is needed.

Many scientists see a distorting market interaction in the restriction of speculation. They see themselves as advocates of liberalized markets, or market-based basic functions. However, the so-called liberalization of the markets around the year 2000 allowed derivatives instruments, which were not market-compliant because they relate to goods or values but do not have to correspond to any real demand or supply. In addition, non-commercial actors were admitted to the market with non-economic but speculative objectives. This has dramatically increased systemic risk.

Only as insurance do derivatives have economic advantages. Derivatives should therefore be permitted only to hedge risks, just before deregulation as a financial instrument, i.e. only in connection with a basic transaction. A corresponding regulation would be an important contribution to the reduction of market influence and systemic risk caused by derivatives. For example, a physical settlement could be prescribed for all derivatives, such as the transfer of the reference security or the corresponding goods. This speculative instrument would be omitted for hedge funds. Speculation would then have to be carried out as before with equity or borrowed capital, thus without the derivatives *leverage*, which would significantly reduce systemic risk.

Behavioral science shows the limits of financial regulation with the help of human beings. The biases show that ratings are not precise or might even be wrong as people make them. The right incentives, thus risk adequate compensation, are more important to induce correct behavior.

In the financial system, investment managers increased the risks for their employer by buying highly profitable but risky assets and were rewarded with high bonuses, which led to the financial crisis in the long term.

Comprehension Questions
1. Explain the economic effects of speculation
2. Is it a normal market economy phenomenon?
3. In your opinion, should speculation with derivatives be limited? How could this be done and what would be the pros and cons?

8.3 Conclusion International Financial Markets After the Financial Crisis

The subprime crisis can be considered the epitome of the ethical failure of our modern economy. The limitless enrichment of the few at the expense of society, which almost lead to a total collapse of the financial system, was heavily criticized. The victims were, above all, the socially and economically disadvantaged who predatory lenders had convinced to buy homes that they could ill-afford and which would lead them to personal bankruptcy, or even homelessness. There were fines for several banks but not for the managers. They got away with high compensation bonuses and were not held personally responsible. Unilaterally constructed incentive schemes encourage excess risk-taking and they were a cause of the financial crisis. The compensation schemes are still unilateral.

Unfortunately, the moral attitude and behavior of bankers did not change significantly after the financial crisis. It is obvious that the business culture in financial organizations must change. Employees should be required to sign ethical standards or vow an oath and should be reminded of them regularly. A breach of such an oath should lead to fines, suspension, or even blacklisting. It is admittedly difficult to change the business culture in financial organizations if the compensation schemes contradict the ethical guidelines, however.

Investors perceive and evaluate the information available to them in a very subjective way.

We can differentiate between short-term and long-term decisions. Short-term decision-making behavior is about speed. Heuristics and emotions are dominant. Only when individuals consciously think about problems does rational thinking dominate.

New Behavioral Finance Theory shows that investors tend to overestimate their level of in-formation and skills. This is called overconfidence. Overconfidence causes an overestimation of the likelihood that one's decisions will lead to success. In addition, new information is processed and implemented with a delay. This causes an overreaction on the stock exchanges in both directions (overreaction). Price exaggeration and price underestimation occur because the information that contradicts the trend is taken into account too late in the decision-making process. This means that systemic crises like the financial crisis can be explained by human error. Group orientation and adaption (herding) increase the likelihood that all market participants will make the same mistake and therefore cause systemic risk. In the case of the financial crisis, the collective mistake was the common belief in the self-correcting power of the market and the ongoing prosperity and housing price increases. The incorrect ratings of the CDOs were a sign of overconfidence and insensitivity to sample size. Neither was the belief in experts rational. The ratings of the subprime CDOs were based on old data from the US real estate market, a bias that is called anchoring. Status quo bias and regret aversion would explain why none of the experts corrected or questioned the incorrect ratings.

Behavioral science shows the limits of financial regulation due to the actions of human beings. The biases show that ratings are not precise or might even be wrong because people make them.

Speculating at one's own risk is a fundamental part of a market-based system. The biases and the group orientation of investors can lead to collective mistakes in the form of speculation bubbles on the stock market or real estate market.

The Efficient Market Hypothesis has been falsified because the market players are human. Since the psychologically oriented approaches are not deterministic, their drawback is the lack of a uniform universal model conception and the possibility of verification independent of the situation. However, in view of the weaknesses of the classical theory based exclusively on rational behavior, they have considerably enriched financial market theory.

Behavioral science shows that systemic crises such as the financial crisis can be explained by human error. Group orientation and adaption (herding) increase the likelihood that all market participants make the same mistake and therefore create systemic risk. In addition, the financial crisis showed that credit based derivatives coupled with a lack of transparency were leading to a significant concentration of risk. The biggest danger of derivatives is the leverage. If futures are used for speculative purposes for instance, the leverage multiplies artificially the effects of the derivatives on prices (via arbitrage and expectations) and does not reflect an underlying real demand or supply.

We also detected an influence of futures prices on spot prices if the excess demand on the futures market is high and stays high over a longer time period.

Future trading and derivatives should therefore be permitted only to hedge risks, just before deregulation as a financial instrument, i.e. only in connection with a basic transaction. Speculation would then have to be carried out as before with equity or borrowed capital, thus without the derivatives leverage, which would significantly reduce systemic risk.

Thus the biggest shortcoming of the recent reforms to the stabilization of the financial system, such as Basel III and the American Dodd Frank Act, is that they increase the capital requirements rather than decreasing the risk from the new financial products like derivatives. They do this in order to absorb the increased risk of speculation following the financial market deregulation and the spreading of derivatives, yet this also greatly increases the costs of borrowed capital. This means that growth losses are accepted and the costs of the financial crisis are once again forced upon the general public. Unilaterally constructed compensation schemes lead to moral hazard. They encourage excess risk-taking and were one reason for the financial crisis. So compensation schemes should be regulated. Compensation must be limited and balanced.

Comprehension questions
1. What are the main reasons for the financial crisis?
2. Discuss does speculation belong to the human nature? What are the pros and cons?
3. Do you think that derivatives and manager compensation should be regulated or is this a limitation of positive market forces? Explain your position.

References

Agarwal, S., & Ben-David, I. (2011), The effects of loan officers' Compensation on loan approval and performance: Direct evidence from a corporate experiment. http://citeseerx.ist.psu.edu/viewdoc/summary?doi=10.1.1.365.7234

Angner, E. (2006). Economists as experts: Overconfidence in theory and practice. *Journal of Economic Methodology*, 13, 1–24.

Agranov, M., & Tergiman, C. (2013). Incentives and compensation schemes: An experimental study. *International Journal of Industrial Organization, 31,* 238–247.

Andersson, O., Holm, H. J., Tyran, J., & Wengström, E. (2013). *Risking other people's money: Experimental evidence on bonus schemes, competition, and altruism.* IFN Working Paper No. 989. www.ifn.se/wfiles/wp/wp989.pdf.

Ariely, D. (2010). *Predictably irrational: The hidden forces that shape our decisions.* Harper.

Aronson, E., & Carlsmith, J. M. (1962). Performance expectancy as a determinant of actual performance. *Journal of Abnormal and Social Psychology, 65*(3), 178–182.

Baffes, J., & Haniotis, T. (2010). Placing the 2006/08 Commodity Price Boom into Perspective, Policy Research Working Paper No. 5371, The World Bank, July 2010. http://www-wds.worldbank.org/external/default/WDSContentServer/IW3P/IB/2010/07/21/000158349_20100721110120/Rendered/PDF/WPS5371.pdf.

Ballwieser, W., Küting, K., & Schildbach, T. (4. December 2009). Fair Value in der Krise. *Der Betrieb, 49.*

Bass, H.-H. (2011). Finanzmärkte als Hungerverursacher? *Studie für die Deutsche Welthungerhilfe e.V.* Bonn. http://www.welthungerhilfe.de/fileadmin/user_upload/Mediathek/Studie_Nahrungsmittelspekulation_Bass.pdf

Blum, U. (2012). Pro Trennbankensystem: Transparente Systematik. *Wirtschaftsdienst, 92*(1).

Beck, H. (2014). *Behavioral Economics: Eine Einführung* (1st ed.). Springer.

Behavioral Finance Group. (2000). Behavioral finance – Idee und Überblick. *Finanz Betrieb, 5*(2000), 311–318.

Brennan, G., & Buchanan, J. (1985). *The reason of rules.*

Brown, M. E., & Treviño, L. K. (2006). Ethical leadership: A review and future directions. *The Leadership Quarterly, No., 17*(2006), 595–616.

Bundesbank, D. (2006). Finanzderivate und ihre Rückwirkung auf die Kassamärkte. Monatsbericht Juli 2006, 55–68.

Burghof, H.-P. (2012). Contra Trennbankensystem: Kreative Vielfalt zulassen! *Wirtschaftsdienst,* *92*(1). http://www.wirtschaftsdienst.eu/archiv/jahr/2012/1/2692/?PHPSESSID=5cc1139f6b6f0 4a31cb201174a4cfd95.

Cai, J., Cherny, K., & Milbourn, T. (2010). Compensation and risk incentives in banking. Compensation and risk incentives in banking and finance (Research of the Federal Reserve Bank of Cleveland, September 24, 2010). https://www.clevelandfed.org:443/Newsroom and Events/ Publications/Economic Commentary/2010/ec 201013 compensation and risk incentives in banking and finance apps.olin.wustl.edu/.../BankExecuPayCommentary.p.

Chediak, F., & Escudero, S. (2004). Ethics ratings: The case of five leading U.S. Investment Banks. In R. Berndt, et al. (Ed.), *Competitiveness und Ethik, Herausforderungen an das Management, Schriftenreihe der Graduate School of Business Administration* (Bd. 11, pp. 77–87).

Cheng, I.-H., Kirilenko, A., & Xiong, W. (2012). *Convective risk flows in commodity futures markets* (Working Paper). Department of Economics, Princeton University. http://www.princeton. edu/~wxiong/papers/RiskConvection.pdf. Accessed: 10. Jan. 2014.

Cohn, G. (2008). Co-President, Managing Director and COO of Goldman Sachs, New York, U.S. Government Printing Office (2008), Senate Hearing 110–654, *SUMMIT ON ENERGY.*http:// www.gpo.gov/fdsys/pkg/CHRG-110shrg45837/html/CHRG-110shrg45837.htm.

Colesa, J. L., Danielb, N. D., & Naveenb, L. (2006). Managerial incentives and risk-taking. *Journal of Financial Economics, 79*(2), 431–468.

Committee on the Global Financial System. (2011). The macrofinancial implications of alternative configurations for access to central counterparties in OTC derivatives markets. CGFS Papers No. 46, November 2011. http://www.bis.org/publ/cgfs46.htm. Accessed: 10. Sept. 2012.

Collin, D. (2006). *Behaving badly.* Dog Ear.

Conrad, C. A. (2005). Kapitalallokation in der Irrational Exuberance – Erkenntnisse aus Theorie und Praxis. In R. Eller et al. (Eds.), *Handbuch Asset Management* (pp. 387–406.). Schäffer-Poeschel.

Conrad, C. A. (2010). *Morality and economic crisis—Enron, Subprime & Co..* Disserta.

Conrad, C. A. (2012). Risiken im Finanzsystem – Der Status quo der Finanzreformen. *Wirtschaftsdienst,92*(7), 439–444.

Conrad, C. A. (2013a). Auf dem Weg zu einer besseren Finanzmarktordnung. *Bankarchiv (Journal of Banking and Finance), 61*(4), 233–241.

Conrad, C. A. (2013b). Reformen zur Stabilisierung der Finanzmärkte. *Orientierungen zur Wirtschafts- und Gesellschaftspolitik,136,* 52–58.

Conrad, C. A. (2014). Commodity and food speculation, Is there a need for regulation? A discussion of the international research. *Applied Economics and Finance, 1*(2), 58–64.

Conrad, C. A. (2015). Incentives, risk and compensation schemes: Experimental evidence on the importance of risk adequate compensation. *Applied Economics and Finance, 2*(2), 50–55.

Conrad, C. A., & Stahl, M. (2002). Parallels with the 1920s stock market boom and the monetary policy. *Kredit Und Kapital, 35*(4), 533–549.

Conrad, C. A., & Stahl, M. (2003). Geldpolitik und Spekulationsblasen – Das Beispiel der USA. *Österreichisches Bankarchiv, Zeitschrift Für Das Gesamte Bank- Und Börsenwesen, 51*(2003), 685–693.

Conrad, C. A., & Stahl, M., (Eds.). (2000). *Risikomanagement an den internationalen Finanzmärkten.* Schäffer-Poeschel.

Conrad, C. A., & Stahl, M. (2002). Parallels with the 1920s stock market boom and the monetary policy. *Kredit und Kapital,35*(4), 533–549.

Cooper, M. J., Gulen, H., & Rau, P. R. (1. October 2014). Performance for pay? The relation between CEO incentive compensation and future stock price performance. http://ssrn.com/ abstract=1572085 or https://doi.org/10.2139/ssrn.1572085.

Crotty, J. (2009). Structural causes of the global financial crisis: A critical assessment of the 'new financial architecture.' *Cambridge Journal of Economics, 33*(2009), 563–580. https://doi.org/10.1093/cje/bep023.

Cuomo, A. (2009). *No rhyme or reason: The 'Heads I Win, Tails You Lose' bank bonus culture.* http://www.workplacebullying.org/multi/pdf/Cuomo.pdf.

Dahrendorf, R. (2009). Die verlorene Ehre des Kaufmanns. *Tagesspiegel,* 12.07.2009. http://www.tagesspiegel.de/wirtschaft/dahrendorf-essay-die-verlorene-ehre-des-kaufmanns/1555814.html.

Deutsche Bundesbank. (2011). *Leitfaden zu den neuen Eigenkapital- und Liquiditätsregeln für Banken.* Frankfurt. https://www.bundesbank.de/Redaktion/DE/Downloads/Veroeffentlichungen/Bundesbank/basel3_leitfaden.pdf?__blob=publicationFile.

Doherty, M. E., Mynatt, C. R., Tweney, R. D., & Schiavo, M. D. (1979). Pseudodiagnosticitiy. *Acta Psychologica,* 1979, 111–121.

Domanski, D., & Heath, A. (March 2007). Financial investors and commodity markets. *BIS Quarterly Review* (2007), 53–67. https://www.bis.org/publ/qtrpdf/r_qt0703g.pdf. Acessed: 12 Febr. 2014.

Donohue, J. J., & Levitt, S. D. (May 2001). The impact of legalized abortion on crime. *The Quarterly Journal of Economics, CXVI*(2), 379–420.

Dullien, S. (2012). Bankenregulierung: Schwindende Statik. *Wirtschaftsdienst, 92*(7), 431–434.

Ergenzinger, R., & Krulis-Randa, J. S. (2004). Anforderungen an das Management unter dem Aspekt von Competitiveness und Ethics in der Gegenwart. In R. Berndt et al. (Hrsg.), *Competitiveness und Ethik, Herausforderungen an das Management, Schriftenreihe der Graduate School of Business Administration* (Bd. 11, S. 3–16).

Commission, E. (2011). *Proposal for a regulation of the European Parliament and of the council on prudential requirements for credit institutions and investment Firms.* (p. 452). COM.

Fedako, J. (18. February 2007). Correlating nonsense. http://antipositivist.blogspot.com.

Feldstein, M. (1974). Social security, induced retirement an aggregate capital accumulation. *The Journal of Political Economy, 82*(8–9), 905–926.

Financial Crisis Inquiry Commission. (2010). *The financial crisis inquiry report: Final report of the national commission on the causes of the financial and economic crisis in the United States,* Washington.

Financial Stability Forum. (2. April 2009). FSF principles for sound compensation practices. www.financialstabilityboard.org/wp.../r_0904b.pdf?...

Financial Stability Board (FSB). (2010). Progress since the St Andrews meeting in implementing the G20 recommendations for strengthening financial stability. Report of the Financial Stability Board to G20 Finance Ministers and Governors, 19 April 2010. http://www.financialstabilityboard.org/publications/r_100419.pdf. Accessed: 13. Febr. 2012.

Financial Stability Board/Basel Committee on Banking Supervision. (BCBS). (2011). Assessment of the macroeconomic impact of higher loss absorbency for global systemically important banks, 10.10.2011. http://www.bis.org/publ/bcbs202.htm. Zugegriffen: 10. Sept. 2012.

Frenk, David et al. (2011), Review of Irwin and Sanders 2010 OECD Report, In: Institute for Agriculture and Trade Policy (Ed.), *Excessive Speculation in Agriculture Commodities,* Selected writings from 2008–2012

Fox, J. (2009). *The Myth of the Rational Market, A History of Risk, Reward, and Delusion on Wall Street.* HarperBusiness.

Fox, L. (2006). *Enron: The rise and fall.* Wiley.

Gaumert, U., Götz. S., & Ortgies, J. (2011). Basel III – Eine kritische Würdigung. *Die bank – Zeitschrift für Bankpolitik und Praxis, 2011*(5). http://www.die-bank.de/betriebswirtschaft/basel-iii-2013-eine-kritische-wurdigung.

Giancarlo, H. J. C. (2016). Reconsidering the Dodd- Frank swaps trading regulatory framework. In H. Peirce & B. Klutsey (Eds.), *Reframing financial regulation – Enhancing stability and protecting consumers* (pp. 155–179). Mercatus Center, George Mason University.

Gilbert, C. L. (2010). How to understand high food prices. *Journal of Agricultural Economics, 61*(2). http://econpapers.repec.org/article/blajageco/v_3a61_3ay_3a2010_3ai_3a2_3ap_3a398-425.

Gilla, D., Prowseb, V., & Vlassopoulosc, M. (December 2013). Cheating in the workplace: An experimental study of the impact of bonuses and productivity. *Journal of Economic Behavior & Organization, 96,* 120–134.

Gold, G., & Feldmann, P. (2007). *A house of cards – From fantasy finance to global crash.*

Götzl, S. (2012). *...fokussiert: Baseler Paradoxien.* http://www.gv-bayern.de/Admin/GVB_Module/Druckversion/Druckversion?artikel=73627.

Gregg, P., Jewell, S., & Tonks, I. (2012). Executive pay and performance: Did bankers' bonuses cause the crisis? *International Review of Finance, Special Issue: Governance, Policy and the Crisis: Part I, 12*(1), 89–122.

Harris, S. L., Mussen, P. H., & Rutherford, E. (1976). Some cognitive, behavioral, and personality correlates of maturity of moral judgment. *Journal of Genetic Psychology,* 128(1), 123–135.

Hassler, U. (2003). *Zeitabhängige Volatilität und instationäre Zeitreihen* (Wirtschaftsdienst Nr. 12, pp. 811–816

von Hayek, F. A. (11. December 1974). The pretence of knowledge, Lecture to the memory of Alfred Nobel. https://www.nobelprize.org/nobel_prizes/economic-sciences/laureates/1974/hayek-lecture.html. Accessed: 12 Dec. 2017.

Henn, M. (2013). Kommentar zum Literaturüberblick zur Spekulation mit Agrarrohstoffen von Will et al., WEED, 14. Mai 2013. http://www2.weed-online.org/uploads/kommentar_literatuerueberblick_agrarspekulation.pdf. Zugegriffen: 2. Apr. 2014.

Hermalin, B. E., & Weisbach, M. S. (2007). Transparency and corporate governance. http://ssm.com/abstract=958628, pp. 1–26.

Hofmann, C. (2011). *Basel III – Kontrahentenrisiko.* http://www.1plusi.de/dokumente/1_plus_i_fachbeitrag_basel_3_Kontrahenten.pdf. Zugegriffen: 27. Dez. 2011.

Irwin, Scott H. & Sanders, Dwight R. (2010). The Impact of Index and Swap Funds on Commodity Future Markets, OECD Food, *Agriculture and Fisheries Working Papers,* No. 27, Paris 2010.

Irwin, S. H., & Sanders, D. R. (2012). Testing the masters hypothesis in commodity futures markets. *Energy Economics, 2012*(34), 256–269. http://ideas.repec.org/a/eee/eneeco/v34y2012i1p256-269.html.

Jenkins P. (18 December 2017). Why UK bank ringfences don't make everyone safer. *Financial Times.* https://www.ft.com/content/1d529c3c-e1a6-11e7-a8a4-0a1e63a52f9c.

Jensen, M., & Meckling, W. (1976). Theory of the firm. Managerial behavior, agency costs, and ownership structure. *Journal of Financial Economics, 3*(4), 305–360.

Kahneman, D., Knetsch, J., & Thaler, R. (1991). Anomalies: The endowment effect, loss aversion and status quo bias. *The Journal of Economic Perspectives, 5*(1), 193–206.

Kahneman, D., & Tversky, A. (1981), The Framing of Decisions and the Psychology of Choice, in: SCIENCE, VOL. 211, 30 JANUARY 1981, pp. 453–457

Kahneman, D., & Tversky, A. (1982). The psychology of preferences. *Scientific American, 146,* 160–173.

Kahneman, D., & Tversky, A. (1984). Choices. *Values and Frames, American Pschologist, 39*(4), 342–350.

Kahneman, D., & Tversky, A. (1986). Rational Choice and the framing of decisions. *Journal of Business, 59*(4), 5251–5278.

Kern, S. (2010). *US-Finanzmarktreform, Deutsche Bank Research*, Finanzmarkt Spezial, EU-Monitor 77, http://www.db.com/mittelstand/downloads/US_Finanzmarktreform_12_2010.pdf.

Khan, A. (2018). *A behavioral approach to financial supervision, regulation, and central banking* (IMF working paper, No. WP/18/178).

Kling, A. (2016). Risk- based capital rules. In H In H. Peirce & B. Klutsey (Eds.), *Reframing financial regulation – Enhancing stability and protecting consumers* (pp. 13–34). Mercatus Center, George Mason University.

Krahnen, J. N., & Schüwer, U. (2017). Structural reforms in banking: The role of trading. *Journal of Financial Regulation, 3*(1), 66–88. https://doi.org/10.1093/jfr/fjw018.

Krugman, P. (21 June 2008). Calvo on commodities, *New York Times*. http://krugman.blogs.nytimes.com/2008/06/21/calvo-on-commodities/?_php=true&_type=blogs&_r=0.

Krugman, P. (2. September 2009). How did economists get it so wrong? *New York Times*. https://www.nytimes.com/2009/09/06/magazine/06Economic-t.html.

Lagi, M., Bar-Yam, Y., Bertrand, K. Z., & Bar-Yarn, Y. (2011). *The food crises, A quantitative model of food prices including speculators and ethanol conversion*. New England Complex Systems Institute. http://necsi.edu/research/social/food_prices.pdf.

Langer, E. J. (1975). The illusion of control, In: *Journal of Personality and Social Psychology, 32*(2), 311–328.

Langer, E. J., & Roth, J. (1975). Heads I win, Tails it's chance: The illusion of control as a function of the sequence of outcomes in a purely chance task. *Journal of Personality and Social Psychology, 32*(6), 951–955.

Ledgerwood, S., & Taylor, G. (14. January 2016). Enron's California schemes haunt regulators 15 years later. In Risk.net. https://www.risk.net/commodities/energy/2441392/enrons-california-schemes-haunt-regulators-15-years-later. Accessed: 29 Dec. 2017.

Lichtenstein, S., Fischhoff, B., & Phillips, L. D. (1982). Calibration of probabilities: The state of art to 1980. In: D. Kahneman, P. Slovic, & A. Tversky (Eds), *Judgment under uncertainty: Heuristics and biases* (pp. 306–334). Cambridge University Press. file:///C:/Eigene%20Dateien2016/Political%20Economy/Material/callibration_probabilities_lichtenstein_fischoff_philips.pdf

Löhr, A. (1997). Die moralische Urteilskraft von Wirtschaftsstudenten: Bemerkungen zum empirischen Forschungsstand. In G. Blickle (Ed.), *Ethik in Organisationen: Konzepte, Befunde, Praxisbeispiele* (pp. 185–208). Angewandte Psychologie . ISBN 3801710556.

Malkiel, B. (2014). *What does the efficient market hypothesis have to say about asset bubbles?* https://www.forbes.com/sites/quora/2014/06/13/what-does-the-efficient-market-hypothesis-have-to-say-about-asset-bubbles/amp/.

Markham, J. W. (2006). *A financial history of modern U.S. corporate scandals from Enron to reform*. Sharpe.

Markowitz, H. (1952). Portfolio selection, in: Journal of Finance 12, 1952, pp. 77–91. https://www.math.ust.hk/~maykwok/courses/ma362/07F/markowitz_JF.pdf

Mazar, N., Amir, O., & Ariely, D. (2008), The dishonesty of honest people: A theory of selfconcept maintenance. Journal of Marketing Research, 45(6), 633–644. Available at SSRN: https://ssrn.com/abstract=979648

Masters, M.W.; White, A.K. (2008), The Accidental Hunt Brothers: How Institutional Investors are driving up Food and Energy Prices, 2008, http://www.loe.org/images/content/080919/Act1.pdf

Masters, M. W. (2009). Testimony of Michael W. masters managing member//portfolio manager masters capital management LLC before the Commodity Future Trading Commission. http://www.cftc.gov/ucm/groups/public/@newsroom/documents/file/hearing080509_masters.pdf. Accessed: 12. Febr. 2014.

Mclean, B. (24. December 2001). Why Enron went bust. *Fortune*, 53–58.

Metcalfe, J. (1998). Cognitive Optimism: Self-Deception or memory-based processing heuristic? *Personality and Social Psychology Review, 2*(2), 100–110.

Meyerowitz, B. E., & Chaiken, S. (1987). The effect on message framing on breast-self-examination attitudes, intentions and behavior. *Journal of Personality and Social Psychology, 52*(1987), 500–510.

Miller, S. M. (2016). On simpler, Higher capital requirements. In H. Peirce & B. Klutsey (Eds.), *Reframing financial regulation – Enhancing stability and protecting consumers* (pp. 35–59). Mercatus Center, George Mason University.

Mocan, Naci /Tekin, Erdal (2006), Ugly Criminals, NBER Working Paper No. 12019, Issued in February 2006. http://www.nber.org/papers/w12019.

Muolo, P., & Padilla, M. (2008). *Chain of blame: How wall street caused the mortgage and credit crisis.*

Nickerson, R. S. (1998). Confirmation bias: An ubiq-uitous phenomen in many guises. *Review of General Psychology, 2*(2). 175–220.

Noll, B. (2002). *Wirtschafts- und Unternehmensethik in der Marktwirtschaft.*

Nowak, E. (1997). *On investment performance and corporate governance.*

Ogger, G. (2001). *Der Börsenschwindel.* Bertelsmann.

Pagan, A./Schwert, C. (1990), Testing for covariance stationarity in stock market data. Economics Letters, 33(2), S. 165–170. http://schwerts.com/el90_ps.pdf, https://doi.org/10.1016/0165-1765(90)90163-U

Papaeconomou, P. (2012). Individual differences & instance based decision making: putting "bounded rationality" to the test. https://www.era.lib.ed.ac.uk/handle/1842/9942.

Peirce, H., & Soliman, V. (2016). Rethinking the swaps clearing mandate. In H. Peirce & B. Klutsey (Eds.), *Reframing financial regulation – Enhancing stability and protecting consumers* (pp. 180–224). Mercatus Center, George Mason University.

Petersen, V. J./ Herlinghaus, A./Menrad, M. (2012). *Risikomanagement auf globalen Agrarmärkten,* Deutscher Raiffeisenverband e.V., DZ Bank 2012. http://www.raiffeisen.de/wp-content/uploads/downloads/2012/11/DRV-Brosch-Risiko_10_02.pdf.

Pies, I. (2012a). Wirtschaftsethik konkret: Wie (un)moralisch ist die Spekulation mit Agrarrohstoffen?, Martin-Luther-Universität Halle-Wittenberg: Diskussionspapier No. 2012- 15, Halle 2012. http://wcms.uzi.uni-halle.de/download.php?down=25900&elem=2602684

Pies, I., & Will, M. G. (2013). *Finanzmarktspekulation mit Agrarrohstoffen, Analyse und Bewertung aus wirtschaftsethischer Sicht.* Diskussionspapier 2013–24 des Lehrstuhls für Wirtschaftsethik an der Martin-Luther-Universität Halle-Wittenberg, Halle.

Pies, I., Prehn, S., Glauben, T., & Will, M. G. (2013). *Kurzdarstellung Agrarspekulation,* Diskussionspapier, 2013-2, Halle: Martin-Luther-Universität Halle-Wittenberg. http://wcms.uzi.uni-halle.de/download.php?down=27545&elem=2636563.

Phillips, P. and Loretan, M. (1990), Testing Covariance Stationarity Under Moment Condition Failure with an Application to Common Stock Returns, Discussion Paper No. 947, *Cowles Foundation for Economic Research at Yale University New Haven Conneticut* 1990. p 45.

Ross, S. A. (1973). The economic theory of agency: The principal's problem. *American Economic Review, 1973, 63*(2), 134–139.

Ross, L., Lepper, M. R., & Hubbard, M. (1975). Perseverance in self perception and social perception: Biased attributional processes in the debriefing paradigm. *Journal of Personality and Social Psychology,* 1975, 880–892.

Rubio, V. J., Hernández, J. M., & Santacreu, J. (2014). The objective assessment of risk tendency as a personality dimension. University Autónoma of Madrid. file:///C:/Eigene%20Dateien2016/Political%20Economy/Material/THE_OBJECTIVE_ASSESSMENT_OF_RISK_TENDENCY_AS_A_PER.pdf.

Rubio, V. J., Hernández, J. M., Zaldívar, F., Márquez, O., & Sartacreu, J. (2010). Can we predict risk-taking behavior? Two behavioral tests for predicting guessing tendencies in a multiple-choice test. *European Journal of Psychological Assessment, 26*(2), 87–94.

Russo, J. E., & Schoemaker, P. J. H. (1992). Managing overconfidence. *Sloan Management Review, 33*, 7–17.

Sachverständigenrat. (2011). *Verantwortung für Europa wahrnehmen*. https://www.sachverstaendi-genrat-wirtschaft.de/fileadmin/dateiablage/download/gutachter/ga11_ges.pdf.

Schäfer, D. (2011). Banken: Leverage Ratio ist das bessere Risikomaß. *DIW Wochenbericht, 46*. http://www.diw.de/documents/publikationen/73/diw_01.c.388897.de/11-46-3.pdf.

Schulze, P. M. (2004, August). Granger-Kausalitätsprüfung – Eine Anwendungsorientierte Darstellung. Institut für Statistik und Ökonometrie, Johannes Gutenberg-Universität Mainz, Arbeitspapier No. 28. http://www.statoek.vwl.uni-mainz.de/Arbeitspapier_Nr_28_Granger-Kausalitaetspruefung.pdf

Schotter, A., & Weigelt, K. (September 1992). Behavioral consequenses of corporate incentives and long-term bonuses: An experimental study. *Managemet Sience, 38*(9), 1280–1298.

Schwarz, G. C., & Holland, B. (13. September 2002). Enron, WorldCom ... und die Corporate-Governance-Diskussion. *Zeitschrift für Wirtschaftsrecht, 23*(37) 1661–1672.

Schwarz, N., & Vaughn, L. A. (2002). The availability heuristic revisited: Ease of recall and content of recall as distinct sources of information. In D. W. Griffin & D. Kahneman (Eds.), *Thomas Gilovich* (pp. 103–119). The Psychology of Intuitive Judgment; Cambridge University Press.

Schwarz, N., Bless, H., Starck, F., Klumpp, G., Rittenauer-Schatka, H., & Simons, A. (1991), Ease of Retrieval as Information: Another Look at the Availability Heuristic, Journal of Personality and Social Psychology, 1991, Vol. 61, No. 2, 195–202.

Sharma, K. (April 2012). Financial sector compensation and excess risk-taking—a consideration of the issues and policy lessons, DESA Working Paper No. 115 ST/ESA/2012/DWP/115. www.un.org/esa/desa/papers/.../wp115_2012.pdf.

Shiller, R. (2007). *The subprime solution: How today's global financial crisis happened, and what to do about it.*

Shleifer, A. (2000). *Inefficient markets, an introduction to behavioral finance.*

Single, G., & Stahl, M. (2000), Risikopotential Hedge-Fonds – Der Fall LTCM. In C. A. Conrad & M. Stahl (Eds.), *Risikomanagement an den internationalen Finanzmärkten* (pp. 379–391). Schäffer-Poeschel.

Singleton, K. J. (2011). *Investors flows and the 2008 boom/bust in oil prices.* Stanford University of Business School. http://www.stanford.edu/~kenneths/OilPub.pdf.

Soros, G. (24 March 2009). One way to stop bear raids. Credit default swaps need much stricter regulation. *The Wall Street Journal.* https://www.wsj.com/articles/SB123785310594719693.

Stahl, M., & Conrad, C. A. (2000). Strategien zur Risikovermeidung an internationalen Finanzmärkten. In C. A. Conrad & M. Stahl (Eds.), *Risikomanagement an den internationalen Finanzmärkten* (pp. 207–221). Schäffer-Poeschel.

Steinberg, P., & Somnitz, C. (2012). Wege zu einer stärkeren Trennung von Investment- und Geschäftsbanking. *Wirtschaftsdienst, 92*(6), 385–391.

Stoll, H. R., & Whaley, R. E. (September 2009). *Commodity index investing and commodity future prices*, Owen Graduate School of Management. http://www.cftc.gov/ucm/groups/public/@swaps/documents/file/plstudy_45_hsrw.pdf.

Stulz, R. (March 2009). Six ways companies mismanage risk. *Harvard Business Review, 86*–94.

Stulz, R. M. (2010). Credit default swaps and the credit crisis. *Journal of Economic Perspectives, 24*(1), 73–92.

Sucharow, L. (July 2013). Wall street in crisis: A perfect storm looming, Labaton Sucharow's, U.S. Financial services industry survey. http://www.secwhistlebloweradvocate.com. Accessed: 28. Oct. 2013.

Sun, L. (2012). Executive compensation and contract-driven earnings management. *Asian Academy of Management Journal of Accounting and Finance, 8*(2), 111–127.

Taleb, N. N. (2001). *Fooled by randomness.* Penguin.

Taleb, N. N. (2007). *The black swan; The impact of the highly improbable.* Penguin.

Tang, K., & Xiong, W. (2010). *Index Investment and Financialization of Commodities. NBER* (Working Paper No. 16385). Cambridge.

Tang, K., & Xiong, W. (2012). Index investment and the financialization of commodities. *Financial Analyst Journal, 68*(6), 54–74. https://www.princeton.edu/~wxiong/papers/commodity.pdf

Tversky, A., & Kahneman, D. (1974). Judgment under Uncertainty: Heuristics and Biases. *Science, 185,* 1124–1131.

Ulrich, P. (1993). Unternehmerethos. In Enderle et al. (Ed.), *Lexikon der Wirtschaftsethik* (pp. 1165–1175).

UNCTAD. (2012). Don't blame the physical markets: Financialization is the root cause of oil and commodity price volatility. Policy Brief No. 25, September 2012. http://unctad.org/en/pages/publications/UNCTAD-Policy-Brief.aspx.

US-Senate. *Brief Summary Of The Dodd-Frank Wall Street Reform And Consumer Protection Act.* http://banking.senate.gov/public/_files/070110_Dodd_Frank_Wall_Street_Reform_comprehensive_summary_Final.pdf, https://www.dpc.senate.gov/pdf/wall_street_reform_summary.pdf.

Voinea, G., & Anton, S. (2009), Lessons from the current financial crisis. A risk management approach. *Review of Economic and Business Studies, 3,* 139–147.

Volk, H. (18. September 2000). Verunsicherte Mitarbeiter werden schneller krank. *Frankfurter Allgemeine Zeitung, 27,* 37.

W.A. (4. Februar 1999). Der wahre Experte weiß nicht nur viel, er weiß auch, was er nicht weiß. *Handelsblatt,* 29.

Wason, P. C. (1960). On the failure to eliminate hypothesis in a conceptual task. *Quarterly Journal of Experimental Psychology,* 129–140.

Weinstein, N. D. (1980). Unrealistic optimism about future life events. *Journal of Personality and Social Psychology, 39,* 806–457.

Williamson, O. E. (1979). The economic institution of capitalism, 1985.

Will, M. G., Prehn, S., Pies, I., & Glauben, T. (2012). Is financial speculation with agricultural commodities harmful or helpful? – A literature review of current empirical research. Discussion Paper No. 2012–27, of the Chair in Economic Ethics, Martin-Luther-University Halle-Wittenberg, edited by Ingo Pies, Halle 2012. http://wcms.uzi.uni-halle.de/download.php?down=27388&elem=2633683.

Woods, T. E. (2009). *Meltdown: A free-market look at why the stock market collapsed, the economy tanked, and government bailouts will make things worse.* Regnery.

Zorita, E. (2006). Interactive comment on "On the verification of climate reconstructions". In G. Bürger & U. Cubach (Eds.). https://www.clim-past-discuss.net/2/S153/2006/cpd-2-S153-2006.pdf.

Further Reading

Ashcraft, A. B., & Schuermann, T. (2008). Understanding the securitization of subprime mortgage credit, Federal Reserve Bank of New York, Staff Report no. 318, March 2008. http://www.newyorkfed.org/research/staff_reports/sr318.pdf. Accessed: 17. Dec. 2012.

BCBS. (2010). *Report and recommendations of the cross-border resolution group.* Baseler Aus-
schuss für Bankenaufsicht (BCBS): Bank für Internationalen Zahlungsausgleich.

BIS. (2011). OTC derivatives market activity, first half 2011, Basel 2011. http://www.bis.org/publ/
otc_hy1111.pdf.

Danfelson, J. (2008). Blame the models. *Journal of Financial Stability, 4*(4), 321–328. www.
RiskResearch.org.

Financial Stability Board. (2011a). Shadow banking: Scoping the issue. 12.04.2011. http://www.
financialstabilityboard.org/publications/r_110412a.pdf. Accessed: 10. Sept. 2012.

Financial Stability Board. (2011b). Shadow banking: Strengthening oversight and regulation,
27.11.2011. http://www.financialstabilityboard.org/publications/r_120420c.pdf. Accessed: 10.
Sept. 2012.

Fonteyne, W., et al. (2010). *Crisis management and resolution for a european banking system.*
Internationaler Währungsfonds (IWF Working Paper Nr. 10/70).

Footwatch. (2011). Die Hungermacher – Wie Deutsche Bank, Goldman Sachs & Co. auf Kosten
der Ärmsten mit Lebensmittel spekulieren. http://foodwatch.de/foodwatch/content/e10/e45260/
e45263/e45318/foodwatch-Report_Die_Hungermacher_Okt-2011_ger.pdf. Zugegriffen: 20.
Febr. 2012.

Frank, D., et al. (2010). Better markets, Review of Irwin and Sanders. OECD Reports speculation and financial fund activity and the impact of index and swap funds on commodity future
markets. Washington, 30.06.2011.03.2011. *Institute for Agriculture and Trade Policy (2011):*
Excessive   Speculation   in   Agriculture   Commodities.   http://www.iadb.org/intal/intalcdi/
PE/2011/08247.pdf. Accessed: 26. March 2012.

FSB. (2012). Strengthening the oversight and regulation of shadow banking. http://www.financial-
stabilityboard.org/publications/r_111027a.pdf. Accessed: 16. Apr. 2012.

Goldstein, M., & Veron, N. (2011). *Too big to fail: The transatlantik debate. Peterson Institute for*
International Economics (Working Paper No. 11–2).

Nicholas, C., Mila,G., Shane, M. H., & Andrew W. L. (2005). *Systemic Risk and Hedge Funds,*
NBER. (Working Paper 11200). March 2005. http://www.nber.org/papers/w11200.

Paul, S. (2012). Bankenregulierung: Schwindende Statik. *Wirtschaftsdienst,92*(7), 435–439.

U.PP. Government Printing Office (2008). Senate Hearing 110–654, SUMMIT ON ENERGY
(http://www.gpo.gov/fdsys/pkg/CHRG-110shrg45837/html/CHRG-110shrg45837.htm,
04/03/2014).

von Hayek, F. A. (1976). *Law, legislation and liberty. The mirage of social justice* (Bd. 2). University of Chicago Press.

von Hayek, F. A. (1979). *Law, legislation and liberty. The political order of free people.* Chicago:
University of Chicago Press.

Solutions to Exercise Questions

9

To Chap. 2 National Accounts

To Sects. 2.1 **and** 2.2

Comprehension Questions

1. What is the difference between current and stock variables?
   While current variables are period-related quantities, stock variables are time-related quantities. Example current variable: income; example stock variable: wealth
2. Give examples of transactions that are not captured in the NIPA.
   Not captured are, inter alia, undeclared work, housework, voluntary work, illegal transactions
3. Explain why GDP can be captured from two sides.
   Solution: Each transaction has two sides: one buys and the other sells something. Accordingly, the one also has income and the other expenditure. GDP can therefore also be calculated from two sides: on the one hand by the sum of all economic incomes from factor services (including corporate profits) and on the other hand by expenditure on produced goods.
4. What is meant by a closed circuit?
   A closed circuit exists if for each pole of the circuit it applies that the value of the flows flowing out of it is equal to the value of all flows flowing into it (circuit axiom).
5. In country A, more transactions are carried out via markets than in country B. Where is GDP higher? In country A, because more transactions are captured here.

© The Author(s), under exclusive license to Springer Fachmedien Wiesbaden GmbH, part of Springer Nature 2022
C. Conrad, *Applied Macroeconomics*, https://doi.org/10.1007/978-3-658-39315-1_9

Exercise

Households Income: 100 billion euros in profits and 200 billion euros in wages results in an income of 300 billion euros.
Expenditure: 300 billion euros for consumption goods.
GDP is therefore 300 billion euros on the expenditure and income side.

To Sect. 2.3
Task on the balance of primary income with the rest of the world
Germany has the following net income: rental income: -300 million €, interest income: -100 million € profits: $+500$ million €, resulting in a balance of primary income of 100 million €, so that German gross national product is 100 million € larger than gross domestic product.

Comprehension questions

1. Explain net investment and expansion investment.
   Expansion investments are used to expand the production apparatus without changing the existing factor input ratio.
   Net investment: difference between gross investment and depreciation of a certain period
2. Why can an economy with a high state share have a lower GDP than others?
   Because the state benefits only go into their costs (expenses)
3. How do domestic and national products differ?
   Gross domestic product is based on where the product is produced or the income is generated. Gross national product is based on who produced the product or generated the income. Alternative answer: The difference is called the balance of primary income with the rest of the world.
4. What is the consequence if maintenance investments are less than depreciation or net investment is negative?
   The capital stock shrinks.

Exercise tasks

1. Task
   a)

$$\text{GDP(nom2010)} = \text{P(caravan2010)} \times \text{amount(caravan2010)} + \text{P(mobile phone2010)}$$
$$\times \text{amount(mobile phone 2010)}$$
$$= 60{,}000\,€ \times 1100 + 10\,€ \times 900{,}000$$
$$= 75{,}000{,}000\,€$$

$$GDP(nom2020) = P \, (\text{caravan2020}) \times \text{amount (caravan2020)} + P(\text{mobile phone2020})$$
$$\times \text{amount(mobile phone2010)}$$
$$= 70{,}000 \, \text{€} \times 1200 + 15 \, \text{€} \times 300{,}000$$
$$= 88{,}500{,}000 \, \text{€}$$

The real GDP for 2020 must be calculated with the prices from 2010

$$GDP(real2020) = P(\text{caravan2010}) \times \text{amount(caravan2020)} + P(\text{mobile phone2010})$$
$$\times \text{amount(mobile phone2020)}$$
$$= 60{,}000 \, \text{€} \times 1200 + 10 \, \text{€} \times 300{,}000$$
$$= 75{,}000{,}000 \, \text{€}$$

The real growth was therefore zero.

b)
$$\text{Deflator} = Y_{\text{nom.}} / Y_{\text{real}}$$
$$= 88{,}500{,}000 / 75{,}000{,}000$$
$$= 1.18$$

So I have to divide the values from 2020 by 1.18 to get the real values, so I deflate.

2. HTW: state investments
   Daimler AG: private investments
   H. Müller private consumption
   ALSTOM: export
   Siemens AG: private inventory investment
   Renault: import

3.

	Gross domestic product (domestic concept)	3364.2 €
±	Balance of primary incomes with the rest of the world	+51.4 €
=	Gross national income or product at market prices (inlander concept)	3415.6 €
−	Depreciation	−431.6 €
=	Net national income (–product) at market prices	2984 €
−	Production and import taxes to the state (−v. a. Goods taxes) + Subsidies	−411.2 €
=	National income	2572.8 €

Net national income (-product) at factor costs

To Sect. 2.4

Example

Added value: $\Delta 1.50\,€ + \Delta 2\,€$

Farmer → **1.50 € for grapes** → **winery** → **wine for 3.50 €** → **supermarket chain**
→

$+ \Delta 3.50\,€ = 7\,€$ value added

Wine for 7 €→ architect

Or all prices $12\,€ -$ inputs $(1.50\,€ + 3.50\,€) = 7\,€$

Comprehension questions

1. The calculation of GDP at market prices takes place on the supply side here and is differentiated by economic sectors in order to be able to map economic structural change over time. The central variable of the production account is the gross value added, that is, the added value created in the production process. The gross value of production is calculated from the production value of a company minus the inputs. GDP is then calculated by summing up the gross value added of all domestic economic sectors. Since GDP is usually given at market prices, the sum of the gross value added must finally be extended by the balance of taxes and subsidies on goods.

2. Under-the-table work, neighborhood help

3. Since the wage and profit share only says something about the income source, but not about the income recipients.

Exercise questions

1. a)   Daimler's value creation: $90{,}000\,€ - 40{,}000\,€ - 15{,}000\,€ - 15{,}000\,€ - 5000$
         $€ = 15{,}000\,€$

   b)   Company A: $40{,}000\,€ - 10{,}000\,€ = 30{,}000\,€$,
         Company B: $15{,}000\,€ - 10{,}000\,€ = 5000\,€$,
         Company C: $15{,}000\,€ - 8000\,€ = 7000\,€$

2. Gross domestic product 2008 in bn. €

	Private consumption	2138.4 €
+	State consumption	536.1 €
+	Gross fixed capital formation	601.3 €
±	Changes in inventories	−2.7 €
+	Exports	1948.5 €
−	Imports	1547.8 €
		3673.8 €

3.

	Gross national income	1880.2 €
Net national income (-product) at factor costs		
+	Production and import duties to the state	+285.7 €
	(+ e.g. goods taxes) - subsidies	
=	Net national income (-product) at market prices	2165.9 €
+	Depreciation	+363.9 €
=	Gross national income or -product at market prices (domestic concept)	2529.8 €
±	Balance of primary incomes with the rest of the world	−40.4 €
=	Gross domestic product	2489.4 €

4. a)

Gross national product at factor costs	1004
− National income (net national product at factor costs)	935
= Depreciation	69
Gross national product at factor costs	1004
− Commodity subsidies	15
+ Commodity taxes	199
Gross national product at market prices	1188
− Depreciation	69
= Net national product at market prices	1119
Or	
National income (net national product at factor costs)	935
− Subsidies for goods	15
+ Goods taxes	199
= Net national product at market prices	1119
+ Depreciation	69
= Gross national product at market prices	1188

5. a) $GDP = C + I + G + Ex − Im = 5.0 + (2.9 − 0.3) + 1.9 + 4.1 − 3.2 = 10.4$

Gross national product (at market prices) = gross national income (at market prices) = GNP + balance of primary incomes with the rest of the world = 10.4 + 0.5 = 10.9

b) Net national income (at market prices) = gross national income (at market prices) − depreciation = 10.9 − 3 = 7.9

National income = net national income (at factor costs) = wages + enterprise and property incomes = 4.2 + 2.1 = 6.3

c) Net national income (at market prices) − commodity taxes + commodity subsidies = national income (net national income at factor costs)

=> commodity taxes = net national income (at market prices) + commodity subsidies − national income (net national income at factor costs) = 7.9 + 0.6 − 6.3 = 2.2

Profit ratio = (enterprise and property incomes)/(national income) = 2.1/6.3 = 0.3333 = 33.33%

6.

Wages	1600.3
+ Business and property income	737.7
= National income (net national product at factor costs)	2338.0
+ Production and import duties (incl. goods taxes)	334.7 €
− Commodity subsidies	27.8 €
= Net national product at market prices	2644.9
+ Depreciation	552.3 €
= Gross national income	3197.2
− Balance of primary incomes with the rest of the world	53.1
= Gross domestic product	3144.1

7.

Gross domestic product (domestic concept)	3144.1 €
± Balance of primary incomes with the rest of the world	+53.1 €
= Gross national income (inhabitants' concept)	3197.2 €
− Depreciation -	−552.3 €
= Net national income at market prices	2644.9 €
− Production and import duties (incl. goods taxes)	−306.9 €
334.7 €+Goods subsidies	27.8 €
= Net national income at factor costs National income	2338.0 €
− Business and property incomes	737.7
= Wages and salaries	1600.3
− Employers' social security contributions	288.9
= Gross wages and salaries	1311.4
− Deductions from employees	444.2

= Net wages and salaries	867.3
+ Monetary social benefits	943.9
= Available income of employees	1811.1

8.

Agriculture and forestry	17.4	
+ Manufacturing without construction	728.6	
+ Construction	134.9	
+ Service sectors		1951.0
= Total gross value added	2831.9	
+ Goods taxes	319.3	
− Goods subsidies	7.2	
Gross domestic product	3144.1	

To Chap. 3 Neoclassical Overall System
To Sect. 3.5

Exercise problems
First, the profit function is to be set up (note that 10% is equal to 0.1!) and derived with respect to the variables N and K. By setting the derivatives to zero, the values for labor and capital input are obtained:

$$\pi = 8 \cdot \left(N^{3/4} + K^{1/2}\right) - 2N - 8 \cdot 0.1K$$

$$d\pi/dN = 6 \text{ x } N^{-1/4} - 2 = 0 \text{ necessary condition profit max!}$$

$$\Leftrightarrow 6N^{-1/4} = 2$$

$$\Leftrightarrow N^{-1/4} = \frac{1}{3}$$

$$\Leftrightarrow 1/\sqrt[4]{N} = 1/3$$

$$\Leftrightarrow \sqrt[4]{N} = 3$$

$$\Leftrightarrow N = 3^4$$

$$\Leftrightarrow N = 81$$

$$d\pi/dK = 4 \text{ } K^{-1/2} - 0.8 = 0 \text{ necessary condition for Gmax!}$$

$$\Leftrightarrow 4K^{-1/2} = 0.8$$

$$\Leftrightarrow 1/\sqrt{K} = 0.8/4$$

$$\Leftrightarrow \sqrt{K} = 4/0.8$$

$$\Leftrightarrow K = 5^2$$

$$\Leftrightarrow K = 25$$

The supply of goods is obtained by substituting the found value of N and the initial capital stock into the production function (the final capital stock must not be taken, because the capacity effect is not noticeable in the following period according to the assumption). The investment demand is the difference between the final and the initial capital stock:

$$Y^S = 81^{3/4} + 9^{1/2}$$

$$\Leftrightarrow Y^S = \left(\sqrt[4]{81}\right)^3 + \sqrt{9} = 3^3 + 3 = 27 + 3$$

$$\Leftrightarrow Y^S = 30$$

$$I = K - K_0 = 25 - 9$$

$$\Leftrightarrow I = 16$$

To Sect. 3.8

1. a) N increases, which is why dY/dN decreases and thus also the real wage. If N is increased, dY/dK will increase, which will cause the real interest rate to rise.

   b) N decreases, which is why dY/dN increases and thus also the real wage. If N is reduced, dY/dK will decrease, which will cause the real interest rate to fall.

2. A war destroys part of the capital stock. The marginal product of capital increases (dY/dK) ↑, which is why companies will demand more capital for investments, the interest rate will rise until i $=$ dY/dK. Due to the lower capital investment after the earthquake, the marginal product of labor and thus the real wage (dY/dN $=$ w/p) and the demand for labor will decrease.

3. The velocity of money circulation increases.

   4. a) Only the value preservation function

   b) Only the value preservation function

   c) Exchange function and value preservation function

Exercise problems

1. a) See drawing in lecture notes

   b) In neoclassical economics, markets are always in equilibrium (price mechanism), then all plans succeed and the planned supply meets the planned demand. The labor market determines production, and because I (i*) $=$ S (i*), investment demand exactly replaces the demand shortfall from savings:

$$Y^S(N*) = I(i*) + C(i*) = Y^D$$

2. The nominal interest rate is given at 13%. We can write the quantity equation as growth rates: m% + v% = y% + p%. For the inflation rate (rate of price increase) we have: p = m + v − y, so p = 15% + 0 − 7% = 8%. For the real interest rate we then have: Real interest rate = 13% − 8% = 5%.

To Sect. 3.9

1. see book
   2. a) The state increases taxes by 1 billion € and spends the money. What are the consequences in the neoclassical model?
   None, employment depends given the capital stock only on labor productivity and the real wage.
   b) Why is national product independent of the money supply in neoclassicism?
   It is Y = Y (N, K), that is, national product depends solely on the productivity of labor and capital as well as the real wage and interest rates, that is, real variables.
   c) Would you recommend a minimum wage as a neoclassicist?
   No, because there is a risk that if the minimum wage is higher than the equilibrium real wage, it will lead to unemployment.
   d) What would you think of the stimulus programs that were adopted as a result of the financial crisis by the German government?
   It is a waste of money because we do not have a demand problem in neoclassicism. The government's debt on the capital market only leads to a displacement of private investment and thus less growth in the long term.
3. In a neoclassical model, the following applies:

1.	Production function:	$Y = 2 N^{3/2}$
2.	Labor supply function:	$N^S = 2/3$ w/p
3.	Investment function:	$I = 20 - 200i$
4.	Savings function:	$S = 200i$
5.	Money supply:	$M = 200$
6.	Cash holding coefficient:	$k = 1/4$

Calculate the equilibrium values for the equilibrium interest rate, the real wage, the equilibrium employment level on the labor market, national income as real output, the price level, the nominal wage and consumption.
   Approach: Which equations are given by the model?

1. Equilibrium condition for the capital market: $I = S$
2. Profit maximization condition of the companies for the labor market: $dY/dN = w/p$!!!
3. Cambridge equation: $L = k \cdot p \cdot Y = M$ (equilibrium condition for the money market)
1. **Capital market**
   i can be calculated immediately:

$$I = S \text{(equilibrium condition)}$$
$$10 - 100i = 100i$$
$$\Leftrightarrow 200i = 10$$
$$\Leftrightarrow i = 5\%$$

The *equilibrium interest rate* is 5%.

2. **Labor market**

Given	Supply of labor $N^S = 2w/p$
Wanted	Demand for labor

For this, there is the profit maximization condition of the companies $dY/dN = w/p$. To get dY/dN, we have to derive the production function $Y = 8\,N^{1/2}$ after N:

$$dY/dN = 4N^{-1/2} = w/p \quad \text{profit maximum condition!!!}$$
$$\Leftrightarrow 1/\sqrt{N} = 1/4\,w/p$$
$$\Leftrightarrow \sqrt{N} = 4/(w/p)$$
$$\Leftrightarrow N^D = 16/(w/p)^2$$

$N^D = N^S$ Gleichgewichtsbed.Arbeitsmarkt

$$\Leftrightarrow 16/(w/p)^2 = 2w/p$$
$$\Leftrightarrow 8 = (w/p)^3$$
$$\Leftrightarrow w/p = 2$$

The *equilibrium real wage* is 2.
This makes the *equilibrium employment level (demand for labor)* $N^D = \frac{16}{(2)^2}$ or *(supply of labor)* $N^S = 2 \bullet 2$, so 4.

3. **Supply of goods**
   Looking for Y^S, it applies: $Y^S = 8N^{\frac{D1}{2}}$
   $N^D = \frac{16}{(w/p)^2}$, w/p has already been calculated and can be used with 2. This results in ND = 4 as the amount of work used.
   For production as *national income* this results in 16:

   $$Y^S = 84^{1/2} = 16$$

4. **Money market**
   What is being sought is the price level. Since M and k were mentioned and Y was calculated, the price level can now be calculated using the Cambridge equation.

   $$M = k \bullet p \bullet Y \text{(profit maximum condition for the money market)}$$
   $$100 = 1/8 \bullet 16 \bullet p$$
   $$\Leftrightarrow p = 50$$

The *price level* is therefore 50.
This results in the *nominal wage*:
$$w = w/p \bullet p$$
$$\Leftrightarrow w = 2 \bullet 50 = 100,$$

$S = 100i$, $i = 0.05$ and $Y = 16$ have already been calculated.

Consumption results from the difference between income and savings:

Budget equation for income expenditure: $C = Y - S$

$$C = Y - S$$
$$C = 16 - 100 \cdot 0.05$$
$$= 11$$

The *consumption* is therefore 11.

7. Case Study Population Change: Try something new in the neoclassical model. Show graphically in the neoclassical overall model the effects of a population increase and explain them briefly.

Population change: The population can increase or decrease depending on the birth rate. In addition, there is immigration and emigration (Fig. 9.1).

The labor supply increases as an exogenous variable, so the supply curve must shift to the right and production and income must increase absolutely. The real wage (nominal wage and price level) adjusts to the marginal product, which has fallen as a result of the higher labor supply, since companies no longer pay to stay in the profit maximum.

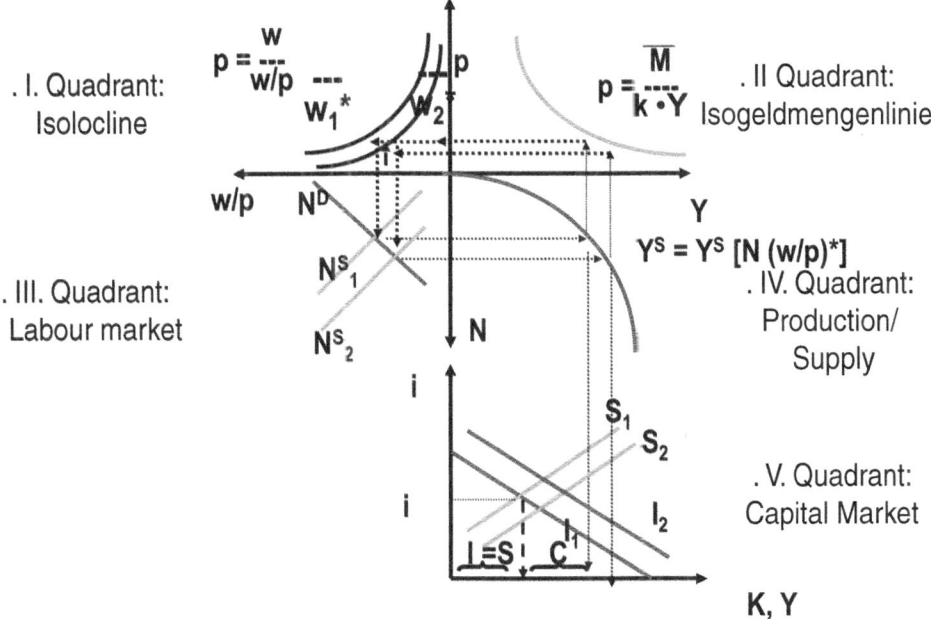

Fig. 9.1 Population increase

Increasing the use of the factor labor increases the marginal product of capital. Therefore, investments rise. The I-curve moves to the right. If income absolutely rises because more labor is used, more will be saved at the same interest rate. Also, the S-curve moves to the right.

Real wages fall and profits rise. Overall, due to the decreased real wage, even the total wage sum can decrease (see Figs. 3.15 and 3.16). The distribution gap further widens. Overall, GDP and tax revenue rise.

For a decrease in population due to emigration or demographic change, the opposite applies.

To Chap. 4. Inflation
Comprehension Questions
For solutions, see the corresponding explanations in the book.

Exercises

1. The price index for 2020 is calculated by setting the prices to the quantities and prices of the base year in relation:

$$\text{Price index (2020)}$$
$$= \frac{P(\text{caravan2020}) \times \text{amount (caravan2010)} + P(\text{mobile2020}) \times \text{amount(mobile2010)}}{P(\text{caravan2010}) \times \text{amount(caravan2010)} + P(\text{mobile2010}) \times \text{amount(mobile2010)}}$$
$$= \frac{70.000 \,\text{€} \times 1100 + 15\,\text{€} \times 900.000}{60.000 \,\text{€} \times 1100 + 10\,\text{€} \times 900.000}$$
$$= 1,21$$

The price index is therefore 1.21, with the price increase rate between 2010 and 2020 being 21%.

To Chap. 5. The Monetary Policy of the European Central Bank
Comprehension Questions

1. Explain the function of interest and quantity tenders.
   See explanation in the book
2. Describe the money creation process.
   By always only retaining a part of the deposited money as a liquidity reserve and lending the rest again, new sight deposits are created, which are also deposited and then lent again in proportion.
3. Why is the independence of the ECB so important for the ECB's price stability target?
   If the regular means of financing expenditure are exhausted, governments tend to finance their own expenditure by printing money. If the central bank is independent of the government, it cannot access the central bank's money.

4. Why are rising stock prices often followed by ECB interest rate cuts?
   The ECB's key interest rates determine the credit interest rates and the investment interest rates. When the ECB cuts interest rates, the credit costs for companies decrease, which increases their profit. The return on investment at the bank or
   in money market funds decreases, so that investors increasingly switch to stocks as
   an alternative investment. no longer worth it. In addition, the costs of credit-financed
   stock purchases decrease. The demand for stocks increases.

Exercise

1. The ECB wants to achieve an inflation rate of 1.8%. GDP growth is expected to be
   2% next year. The velocity of circulation remains constant. By how much does she
   have to increase the money supply M3?

In growth rates, quantity equation:

$$Y + P = M + V$$
$$M = Y + P - V$$
$$M = 2\% + 1.8\% - (0) = 3.8\%$$

Bank	Interest rate Interest period	Amount of money	Quantity tendered	Amount of money x Repartition rate: 0.5
A	3.07	10 (10)	3.06	15 (25%; 7.5)
B	3.06	10 (10)	3.06	5 (8.3%; 2.5)
C	3.05	10 (2.5)	3.06	10 (16.7%; 5)
D	3.05	10 (2.5)	3.06	15 (25%; 7.5)
E	3.03	5 (0)	3.06	15 (25%; 7.5)
				60 (30)

Der marginale Zuteilungssatz beträgt 3.05%

Weighted average interest rate:
$(3.07\% \times 10 + 3.06\% \times 10 + 3.05\% \times 5) : 25 = 3.062\%$

To Chap. 6 The Keynesian Theory
To Sect. 6.7

1. Explain in your own words the difference between Keynes and neoclassicism.
   In neoclassicism, saving and investment are dependent on interest rates. Supply and demand are always in balance because $I = S$ always holds true. The market

mechanism always causes a balancing of saving and investment through interest rates. With Keynes, consumption and saving depend on income. If total supply and total demand differ, the adjustment to the new equilibrium takes place through the adjustment of production and, as a result, income (unemployment, etc.). With a lower supply, saving also decreases, as does income. $I < S$ ($Y\downarrow$) until $I = S$

2. How does the expenditure multiplier work?

   A sustained increase in demand causes increased production and, as a result, increased income in the next period (year). However, the higher income also causes a proportional increase in consumption, which in turn leads to increased demand and, as a result, increased production and a corresponding increase in income and consumption in the following period. This process continues.

3. Is the Say's theorem wrong?

   It depends on the economic situation. In normal cases, the Say's theorem applies and every supply creates its own demand. However, if the economy is in a depression with a sustained underdemand, a Keynesian demand policy is necessary because the supply cannot create its own demand.

1. a) Effective demand:

$$Y^D = C + I + G$$
$$= 300 + 0.60(Y - 100) + 200 + 100$$
$$= 540 + 0.60Y$$

b) The equilibrium income is obtained by setting the effective demand and production, GDP, as the supply.

$$Y = Y^D$$
$$\Leftrightarrow Y = 540 + 0.60Y$$
$$\Leftrightarrow (1 - 0.60)Y = 5400$$
$$\Leftrightarrow Y_0 = 1350$$

c) After the increase in government spending from 100 to 150, the effective demand $Y^D = 590 + 0.60Y$

$$Y = Y^D$$
$$\Leftrightarrow Y = 590 + 0.60Y$$
$$\Leftrightarrow (1 - 0.60)Y = 590$$
$$\Leftrightarrow Y_0 = 1475$$

Also calculable via the government spending multiplier:

$$\Delta Y = \frac{1}{1 - c'}\Delta G, \text{ also } \Delta Y \frac{1}{(1 - 0.6)} 50 = 125$$

If the old equilibrium income was 1350, the new one is 1475.

d) We set the given equilibrium income 2350 in our equation to calculate the equilibrium income and solve for G.

$$Y_0 = 300 + 0.60(Y - 100) + 200 + G$$
$$\Leftrightarrow 2350 = 300 + 0.60(2350 - 100) + 200 + G$$
$$\Leftrightarrow G = 500$$

So government spending would have to rise to 500 to generate an equilibrium income of 2350.

2. a) You get the equilibrium income by setting the effective demand and production, the GDP, as the supply.

$$Y = 30 + 0.6Y + 20$$
$$\Leftrightarrow 0.4Y = 30 + 20$$
$$\Leftrightarrow Y_0 = 125$$

So the equilibrium income is 125.

$$Y = 20 + 0.6Y + 20$$
$$\Leftrightarrow 0.4Y = 20 + 20$$
$$\Leftrightarrow Y_0 = 100$$

If, due to saving, autonomous consumption decreases by 10 (to 20), the equilibrium income decreases to 100.

So the equilibrium income is 125.

$S = -Ca + s' \bullet Y$ Saving function ($Y = C + S$ i.e. $S = Y - C$, $s' = 1 - c'$)

$$S = -20 + 0.4 \bullet Y \text{ savings function}$$

$$S = -20 + 0.4 \bullet 100 = 20$$

(for the numerical example: $Ca = 20$, $s' = 0,4$)

Compared to equilibrium income 125 at $Ca = 30$

$$S = -30 + 0.4 \cdot 125 = 20$$

The equilibrium saving remains the same.

b) In this case, the paradox of saving means that households can no longer save, even though they wanted to save more, because the demand for saving has decreased the overall economic supply and, with it, their income.

To Sect. 6.12

Comprehension questions

1. Explain the adjustment process to the equilibrium interest rate and income combination when the interest rate is to the right or below the LM curve.
   See explanations in the book
2. Explain the adjustment process to the equilibrium interest rate and income combination when the interest rate is to the left or below the IS curve.
   See explanations in the book
3. Why is there a range of the LM curve that is infinitely interest-elastic? How do investors behave here?
   At a certain minimum interest rate, the demand for money for speculative purposes is
   completely interest-elastic, i.e. all money goes into the cash to stay liquid (liquidity
   preference function). Investors fear price losses.

Exercise

1. Task for the LM money market
   Equilibrium condition
   $M = L_T + L_S$
   $L_T = k\,Y = 0.2\,Y$
   $L_S = 180/i$
   $460 = 0.2\,Y + 180/i$
   $\Leftrightarrow 0.2\,Y = 460 - 180/i$
   $\Leftrightarrow Y = 2400 - 900/i$
   Thus, the equilibrium incomes in dependence of i are:
   $Y\,(i = 1) = 1500$
   $Y\,(i = 1.5) = 1800$
   $Y\,(i = 2) = 1950$
   $Y\,(i = 3) = 2100$
2. For the goods market equilibrium and thus also the IS curve, it is true that the supply
   of goods must correspond to the demand for goods:
   $Y = C\,(Y - T) + I\,(i) + G$. We insert the consumption function, the investment function and the government spending:

$$Y = 300 + 0.60(Y - 100) + 300 - 50i + 100$$
$$\Leftrightarrow 0.4Y = 640 - 50i$$
$$\Leftrightarrow Y = 1600 - 125i$$

For the LM curve, i.e. the money market equilibrium, it applies:
$M / P = L\,(Y, i)$, we insert:

$2000/4 = Y - 200i$

$\Leftrightarrow Y = 500 + 200i$

In equilibrium, both incomes (intersection of the IS and LM curve) must match, so we can set equal to calculate the equilibrium interest rate i:

$1600 - 125i = 500 + 200i$

$\Leftrightarrow 1100 = 325i$

$\Leftrightarrow i = 3.4$

To determine the equilibrium income Y, we insert the equilibrium interest rate in one of the two equations:

$Y = 1600 - 125 \bullet 3.4 = 1175$

The equilibrium interest rate is thus 6.3 and the equilibrium income 812.5.

3. a) For the goods market equilibrium and thus also the IS curve, it is true that the supply of goods must correspond to the demand for goods:

$Y = C (Y) + I (i) + G$. We insert the consumption function and the investment function:

IS curve:

$$Y = 60 + 0.5Y + 50 - 500i + 40$$
$$Y = 150 + 0.5Y - 500i$$
$$\Rightarrow 0.5Y = 150 - 500i$$
$$\Rightarrow Y = 300 - 1000i$$

For the LM curve, i.e. the money market equilibrium applies:

$$LM - curve : M/p = L(Y, i)$$
$$\Rightarrow 800/4 = Y - 4000i$$
$$\Rightarrow Y = 200 + 4000i$$

b) In equilibrium, both incomes (the intersection of the IS and LM curves) must match, which is why we can set them equal to calculate the equilibrium interest rate i:

Intersection of IS and LM curve:

$$300 - 1000i = 200 + 4000i$$
$$100 = 5000i$$
$$i* = 100/5000 = 0.02 = 2\%$$

1. To determine the equilibrium income, we can use both equations:
   $Y* = 200 + 4000 \bullet 0.02 = 300 - 1000 \bullet 0.02 = 280$

2. The equilibrium interest rate is therefore 2% and the equilibrium income 280.

c) For consumption and investment:

$$C = 60 + 0.5 * 280 = 200$$
$$I = 50 - 500 * 0.02 = 40$$

d) The equilibrium income is at 280 and the equilibrium interest rate is at 2%.
   Therefore, an income of 350 at an interest rate of 2% must be to the right of the inter-
   section of both curves, that is, below the LM curve and above the IS curve.
   There is a shortage of money below the LM curve
   => M/p < L(Y,i) => The investors have less money than they want and buy fewer
   securities, which is why the price falls and the interest rate rises.
   Above the IS curve we have a deficiency, => Y > C(Y) + I(i) + G which is why pro-
   duction and income decrease.

To Sect. 6.13
Exercise problems

a) We can set I and S equal to each other to get the IS function:

$$I = S$$
$$\Leftrightarrow 6 - 60i = 0.6Y$$
$$\Leftrightarrow i = 0.1 - 0.01Y$$

The LM curve is obtained by setting the money demand equal to the money supply:

$$L = M$$
$$\Leftrightarrow 3Y - 200i = 5$$
$$\Leftrightarrow i = 0.015Y - 0.025$$

In equilibrium, the LM and IS curves intersect at the same interest rate, so we can set
both equations equal to each other and calculate the equilibrium income:

$$IS = LM$$
$$\Leftrightarrow 0.1 - 0.01Y = 0.015Y - 0.025$$
$$\Leftrightarrow 0.125 = 0.025Y$$
$$\Leftrightarrow Y = 5$$

We set $Y = 5$ in the IS or LM function and get for i:
$i = 0.015 \cdot 5 - 0.025$
$\Leftrightarrow i = 0.05$
So $i = 5\%$

b) We want to find out how the equilibrium income changes as the intersection of the
   IS and LM curves when the price level changes, with a money supply of 30.

We set the IS and LM curves equal to each other again, but this time we enter 30 for M in the LM curve:

$$0.015Y - 0.15/p = 0.1 - 0.01Y$$
$$\Leftrightarrow 0.025Y = 0.15/p + 0.1$$
$$\Leftrightarrow Y^D = 4 + 6/p$$

$$M/p = LT + LS$$
$$\Leftrightarrow \frac{30}{p} = 3Y - 200i$$
$$i = 0.015Y - 0.15/p$$

That is, if p increases, the aggregate demand Y^D decreases and vice versa.

We can check our calculation by setting $p = 6$, then at $M = 30$ we get the cash reserve of 5 that was given in (a), and an associated Y^D of 5, as we calculated above.

To Sect. 6.18
Comprehension questions

1. Explain why monetary policy is ineffective in the investment trap. Why does the overall necessary demand not occur by itself?
   See the explanations in the book
2. Explain why monetary policy is ineffective in the liquidity trap. Why does the overall necessary demand not occur by itself?
   See the explanations in the book
3. Explain how the recent financial crisis is comparable to the situations described by Keynes.
4. There was both an investment trap and a liquidity trap. Investments broke away and became interest inelastic due to negative expectations. Neither banks nor companies could refinance because investors only wanted to keep cash. There were even bank runs because investors wanted to withdraw their money as cash. The consequence was a depression that would have continued without the state-financed credit-financed stimulus programs.

Exercise

1. We cannot set I=S because we lack Y and p. So we first have to calculate Y over the labor market:
a) Labor market
   1. The labor supply function is given, so we are looking for the labor demand function. We know that the company reaches its maximum profit when the marginal

productivity of labor is equal to the real wage. We therefore derive the production function after N and set the result equal to the real wage:

$$dY/dN = 2N^{-1/2} = w/p \text{ profit maximum condition!}$$
$$\Leftrightarrow N^{-1/2} = 1/2w/p$$
$$\Leftrightarrow 1/\sqrt[2]{N} = 1/2w/p$$
$$\Leftrightarrow \sqrt[2]{N} = 2/(w/p)$$
$$\Leftrightarrow N^D = 4/(w/p)^2$$

Now we can calculate the equilibrium on the labor market $N^D = N^4$:

$$\Leftrightarrow 4/(w/p)^2 = 1/2w/p$$
$$\Leftrightarrow 8 = (w/p)^3$$
$$\Leftrightarrow w/p = 2$$

We can now set $w/p = 2$ in $N^D = N^4$ to determine the equilibrium employment:

$$N* = N^4 = 1/2 \bullet 2 = 1$$

So employment is 1.

b) Supply of goods

We can now set $N = 1$ in the given production function $Y = 4 \ N^{1/2}$ and get the equilibrium income:

$$Y = 4 \cdot 1^{1/2} = 4$$

c) Capital market

If you set this value in the savings function and set it equal to the investment function (IS curve), you get the equilibrium interest rate on the capital market:

$S = 0.2\,Y$

$S = 0.4 = I = 2 - 20i$

$\Leftrightarrow -1.8 = -20i$

$\Leftrightarrow I = 0.06$, so $i = 6\%$

d) Money market

We can now calculate the equilibrium price level with the money demand function $L = 6Y - 30i$ by setting it equal to the real cash M/p with $M = 28.8$ (LM curve).

$M/p = L$

$M/p = 6Y - 30i$

$28.8/p = 6 * 4 - 30 * 0.06$

$22.2 = 28.8/p$

$\Leftrightarrow p = 1.3$

We had already calculated 2 for w/p, so that we get 2.6 for the nominal wage w $=$ w/p
* p $=$ 2 * 1.3.

2. Draw the effect of an expansionary fiscal policy in the Keynesian aggregate model in the investment trap.

   See the explanations in the book

3. Draw the effect of an expansionary fiscal policy in the Keynesian aggregate model in the liquidity trap.

   See the explanations in the book

The explanations for the remaining comprehension questions can also be found on the corresponding pages in the book.

Appendix

Figure Correlations of important economic variables in the U.S.A.

Correlation by color:
- Strongly positive
- Weakly positive
- Weakly negative
- Strongly negative

No colored background:
- very weak or none Correlation

	Unemployment rate (in % of labor force)	Consumption (Household spending Total, Million US dollars, 1970–2014)	Saving rate (in Million US Dollar)	Investment (Gross capital formation) (in Million US dollars)	Short-term interest rate (in % per annum)	Long-term interest rate (in % per annum)	Broad money (M3) (Total, 2010=100, 1959–2014)	Narrow money (M1) (Total, 2010=100, 1955–2014)	Consumer Price Index CPI	GDP (in Million US dollars)	Credit volume (Household debt Total, % of net disposable income, 1995–2014)	Stock index (Share prices Total, 2010=100, 1957–2014)	Real Estate Index (-preise) (Housing Real house prices, 2010=100, 1960–2015)
Unemployment rate (in % of labor force)		0.34	0.71	0.08	-0.68	-0.42	0.46	0.46	-0.35	0.33	0.26	0.00	-0.11
Consumption (Household spending Total, Million US dollars, 1970 – 2014)	0.34		-0.19	0.96	-0.74	-0.94	0.97	0.86	-0.44	1.00	0.66	0.92	0.71
Saving rate (in Million US Dollar)	0.71	-0.19		-0.10	0.39	0.20	-0.21	-0.06	0.18	-0.18	-0.55	0.12	-0.12
Investment (Gross capital formation) (in Million US dollars)	0.08	0.96	-0.10		-0.60	-0.88	0.89	0.74	-0.45	0.96	0.76	0.97	0.84
Short-term interest rate (in % per annum)	-0.68	-0.74	0.39	-0.60		0.87	-0.79	-0.77	0.61	-0.74	-0.35	-0.52	-0.36
Long-term interest rate (in % per annum)	-0.42	-0.94	0.20	-0.88	0.87		-0.93	-0.85	0.58	-0.94	-0.50	-0.83	-0.60
Broad money (M3) (Total, 2010=100, 1959 – 2014)	0.46	0.97	-0.21	0.89	-0.79	-0.93		0.94	-0.45	0.97	0.50	0.86	0.58
Narrow money (M1) (Total, 2010=100, 1955 – 2014)	0.46	0.86	-0.06	0.74	-0.77	-0.85	0.94		-0.47	0.86	0.21	0.75	0.35
Consumer Price Index CPI	-0.35	-0.44	0.18	-0.45	0.61	0.58	-0.45	-0.47		-0.44	0.06	-0.36	-0.21
GDP (in Million US dollars)	0.33	1.00	-0.18	0.96	-0.74	-0.94	0.97	0.86	-0.44		0.66	0.93	0.72
Credit volume (Household debt Total, % of net disposable income, 1995 – 2014)	0.26	0.66	-0.55	0.76	-0.35	-0.50	0.50	0.21	0.06	0.66		0.57	0.92
Stock index (Share prices Total, 2010=100, 1957 – 2014)	0.00	0.92	0.12	0.97	-0.52	-0.83	0.86	0.75	-0.36	0.93	0.57		0.75
Real Estate Index (-preise) (Housing Real house prices, 2010=100, 1960 – 2015)	-0.11	0.71	-0.12	0.84	-0.36	-0.60	0.58	0.35	-0.21	0.72	0.92	0.75	

Interpretation

The interpretation of the correlations presented above must be done with caution. The number series were only roughly calculated without time lags and a correlation can have many reasons up to chance. A causality does not have to be given (see also Sect. 8.2.2). In general, the following comprehensible relationships can be seen.

Gross domestic product, real estate prices and stock prices develop parallel. The money supply is weakly correlated with real estate prices and stock prices. However, this can also be due to the monetary policy oriented towards gross domestic product.

Credit volume and real estate prices develop strongly parallel, while the connection to stock prices is weaker. Interest rates are negatively correlated with stocks and real estate.

Interest rates and savings are positively correlated. Prices and unemployment are slightly negatively correlated.

Investments are positively correlated with gross domestic product, consumption and money supply and negatively with interest rates.

Sources

Consume (Household spending Total, Million US dollars, 1970 – 2014)	https://www.chapman.edu/ESI/wp/Recessions_1929_2007.pdf
Consume (Household spending Total, % of GDP, 1970 – 2014)	https://www.chapman.edu/ESI/wp/Recessions_1929_2007.pdf
Saving rate (in % of GDP)	
Investment (Gross capital formation) (annual growth rate in %)	-
Investment (Gross capital formation) (in Million US dollars)	-
Short-term interest rate (in % per annum)	https://www.federalreserve.gov/PUBS/FEDS/2000/200051/200051pap.pdf
Long-term interest rate (in % per annum)	https://www.federalreserve.gov/PUBS/FEDS/2000/200051/200051pap.pdf
Broad money (M3) (Total, 2010=100, 1959 – 2014)	-
Narrow money (M1) (Total, 2010=100, 1955 – 2014)	-
Consumer Prices (Index 2010=100)	http://libraryguides.missouri.edu/c.php?g=28284&p=174166
Consumer Price Index CPI (Consumer Price index for the ten years from 1920 through 1929 based upon a 1982-84 base of 100)	https://inflationdata.com/articles/inflation-consumer-price-index-decade-commentary/inflation-cpi-consumer-price-index-1920-1929/
GDP (in Million US dollars)	https://bea.gov/iTable/iTable.cfm?reqid=19&step=2#reqid=19&step=3&isuri=1&1910=x&0=-9&1921=survey&1903=5&1904=1929&1905=2017&1906=a&1911=0
real GNP	http://piketty.pse.ens.fr/files/BalkeGordon1989.pdf
Credit granting (Net lending/borrowing by sector % of GDP)	http://www.nber.org/chapters/c7530.pdf
Credit granting (Household debt Total, % of net disposable income, 1995 – 2014)	-
Share index (Share prices Total, 2010=100, 1957 – 2014)	-
Real Estate Inde (-preise) (Housing Real house prices, 2010=100, 1960 – 2015)	https://www.fhfa.gov/DataTools/Downloads/Pages/House-Price-Index.aspx
People's Assets (National wealth)	-

The manufacturer's authorised representative in the EU is Springer
Nature Customer Service Centre GmbH, Europaplatz 3, 69115 Heidelberg,
Germany. If you have any concerns regarding our products, please
contact ProductSafety@springernature.com

Printed and bound by CPI Group (UK) Ltd, Croydon, CR0 4YY
24/04/2026
02096346-0010